BIG APPLE BASEBALL WARS

About the Author

Ammie Nurse grew up in Brooklyn and remembers hearing radio broadcasts of the Dodgers through apartment windows. Her passion for the Dodgers abated some when they moved to Los Angeles, but baseball pulled her back when the Mets hired her favorite "Bum," Gil Hodges, to be manager.

Ammie's love of baseball and for reading about and researching the game has been a passion her whole adult life. From the days of numerous New York daily papers, to the era of the MacMillan Baseball Encyclopedias, to the internet age, she has been collecting and organizing information, stats, and stories.

In 2001, Ammie obtained a patent for a baseball trivia game; in 2009, her first book was published, *The All-Star Reference Guide*, the story of and behind every All-Star Game ever played. But it was two books by other authors about the World Series that triggered the development of Ammie's most significant baseball creation, a detailed and robust database of all things World Series, from the first in 1903, to today. It is this amazing database that made possible the incredible detail and historical perspective contained in *Big Apple Baseball Wars*.

BIG APPLE BASEBALL WARS

New York's 14 Subway Series

Ammie Nurse

With Contributions from Summer Game Books

SUMMER
GAME
BOOKS

ISBN: 978-1-938545-75-7 (print)
ISBN: 978-1-938545-76-4 (eBook)

For information about permission, bulk purchases, or additional distribution, write to

Summer Game Books

P. O. Box 818

South Orange, NJ 07079

or contact the publisher at www.summergamebooks.com

Pictured front cover: Clockwise from top - Mike Piazza and Roger Clemens in Game 2 2000 World Series (AP Photo/Ron Frehm); Billy Martin tagged out by Roy Campanella, Game 4 1953 World Series (National Baseball Hall of Fame and Museum); Casey Stengel slides home on his ninth inning inside-the-park home run in Game 1 of the 1923 World Series (National Baseball Hall of Fame and Museum).

Dedication

To Marie Walker and Brenda Jenkins

Acknowledgments

While the vast majority of information in the book is drawn from the author's extensive World Series database, the publisher and author are indebted to baseball-reference. com for the use of their statistical information for the "Top Batters" and "Top Pitchers" tables, as well as the team composite stats tables appearing at the end of each section. Baseball-reference.com was also used for fact-checking purposes. Some of the play-by-play details were drawn from *The World Series: Complete Play-by-Play of Every Game 1903-1989*, by David S. Neft and Richard S. Cohen.

Contents

Introduction:
Geographic Rivalries in the World Series

The Big Apple Baseball Wars were not the only same-city World Series, or even the first between opponents from the same state. But even when including match-ups in the same state, let alone the same city, no other pairing comes anywhere close to the number or intensity of New York City's 14 Subway Series.

Consider Pennsylvania, long-time host to three major league teams—two in Philadelphia and one in Pittsburgh. For a time the Athletics and Phillies even shared the same ball yard, Shibe Park. But although the Pirates (1903) and Athletics (1905) were among the first league champions during the World Series Era, they never met in the Fall Classic.

The Pirates were strong in the Honus Wagner era, but after the Flying Dutchman, post-season action for the Bucs was rare until the 1970s, long after their American League neighbor the Athletics had vacated for Kansas City. The Phillies, meanwhile, did not win a pennant until 1915, nor a World Series until 1980, providing very few opportunities for an all-Pennsylvania Fall Classic.

Boston had its chances until the Braves left for Milwaukee in 1953, but for the most part, over the years both were cellar dwellers, rarely coming close to making it to the Series. The Red Sox were strong until they invoked the Curse of the Bambino, while the Braves have won exactly one World Series in each of their three locations—Boston (1914), Milwaukee (1957), and Atlanta (1995). 1914 was their big chance. It was the year the Miracle Braves stormed from last to first and won the pennant, but it was also a year before Babe Ruth came to the Red Sox, and they won 90 games, 9 fewer than the Athletics.

What about Ohio? Two long-time franchises, the Cincinnati Reds and Cleveland Indians, call that state home. They have been in only 15 World Series between them, but in many years had below-average teams, so the odds have not been in favor of a Fall Classic match-up there. Despite some success in recent years, Cleveland has been the weaker of the two, now having gone more than 70 years without a championship. And other than a few division crowns and a Lou Piniella-led 1990 juggernaut, the Reds have not been a strong franchise since the 1970s, and before then they weren't too hot either.

Chicago holds the distinction of being the first same city or state to host a World Series. The Northsiders and the Southsiders clashed in 1906, with the "Hitless Wonders" White Sox shocking the 116-36 Cubs in six games. Since that early battle, trips to the World Series have been legendarily rare for the Cubs, while the White Sox have not been much better—winning zero pennants between 1906 and 1959, and winning only their third World Series in well over 100 years in 2005. It's not really surprising then that there have been no "Windy City Series" between since that one 114 years ago in 1906.

Another city that hosted two teams in baseball's early years was, of course, St. Louis, home of the oft-powerful Cardinals and almost entirely inept Browns. The Browns did manage one pennant in their half-century in St. Louis, in 1944, no doubt helped by the depleted talent levels in the game due to World War II. And 1944 became the second non-New York intercity World Series as the Browns matched up with their crosstown rival Cardinals, who took the series in six games.

Not very many years later the Browns relocated to Baltimore, but into Missouri came the Philadelphia Athletics for a time, and when they left for Oakland, the void was filled by the expansion Kansas City Royals. The Royals and Cardinals met in one World Series, in 1985, with the American Leaguers taking the "Sho-Me Series" in seven games.

Major League baseball has been played in California for "only" about 60 years, but with five teams now, they have had ample opportunities for same-state Fall Classic clashes. And in fact, only the Padres of the five teams has not met a California team in the Series. San Francisco clashed with bay rival Oakland in 1989, with the A's taking the series, and the Giants played the Anaheim Angels in 2002, and lost that time too. The Dodgers and A's have met twice, in 1974 and 1988, with Oakland winning their third consecutive title in 1974 and the Dodgers stunning the heavily favored A's in 1988.

All of this makes it that much more incredible that with all the teams playing in the same city and even the same state for well over 100 years, there have been only a handful of local Fall Classic clashes. Yet no fewer than 14 times New York teams have appeared against each other in the World Series, including seven times in a ten-year stretch from 1947-1956.

The recurrent theme of the Subway Series is, of course, the Yankees, perhaps the greatest franchise all time of any American professional sport. When you're in 40 World Series and there are two National League teams for many of those seasons, you're bound to be in a lot of Subway Series. That has been the case, and the Yankees have not been satisfied with being AL champs. They have also won 11 of the 14 clashes with their fellow New York teams.

But it also is the case that the New York Giants, led by John McGraw, was the strongest team overall of the first several decades of the World Series Era. In fact, the Giants were the Yankees' opponent in the first five Subway Series—1921-1923, 1936, and 1937. After decades of poor play, Brooklyn became a National League powerhouse, and they were in six of the next seven Subway Series, with only Bobby Thomson's "Shot Heard Round the World" in 1951 interrupting the streak.

Of course, in the 1950s, both of New York's NL teams escaped to California, where their own rivalry intensified, and 44 years passed between the last Dodgers-Yankees battle and the Mets clawing to the World Series in 2000. The Yankees' 5-game defeat of the Mets belies how tight a Series it was, with every game being decided by one or two runs.

But the beauty of the 14 Subway Series is the beauty of baseball itself—great achievement mixed with heart-breaking failure, shining stars and surprise heroes, the convergence of the past with the present. The focus of *Big Apple Baseball Wars* is, of course, New York, but more than that it is a celebration of the long and colorful history of baseball at its best.

List of Features

In addition to team backgrounds, game accounts and box scores, highlights, trivia, and stats, *Big Apple Baseball Wars* tells the story of the players and managers of New York's 14 Subway Series through numerous photos, sidebars, and tables. A list of these special feature is provided here.

"Photo" indicates a photograph; "sidebar" indicates text call-outs; "pho/side" indicates a photograph accompanied by narrative text; and "table" indicates a statistical table.

Page	Year	Feature	Description	Team(s)
5	1921	pho/side	WS Program (McGraw & Huggins)	NYY, NYG
5	1921	table	McGraw & Huggins managerial record	NYY, NYG
7	1921	pho/side	Art Nehf	NYG
13	1921	pho/side	Bob and Irish Meusel	NYY, NYG
17	1921	pho/side	Carl Mays	NYY
19	1921	pho/side	Roger Peckinpaugh	NYY
20	1921	pho/side	Babe Ruth	NYY
27	1922	pho/side	Bullet Joe Bush	NYY
29	1922	photo	Giants/Yankees WS patch	NYY, NYG
29	1922	photo	Action scene · 1922 WS	NYY, NYG
31	1922	sidebar	Jack Scott	NYY
31	1922	pho/side	Ross Youngs	NYG
33	1922	pho/side	Aaron Ward	NYY
36	1922	pho/side	Polo Grounds	NYY, NYG
36	1922	pho/side	Babe Ruth	NYY
36	1922	pho/side	Casey Stengel	NYG
43	1923	photo	Dave Bancroft	NYG
46	1923	sidebar	Casey Stengel	NYG
47	1923	photo	NY Giants team picture	NYG
49	1922	sidebar	Frankie Frisch	NYG
51	1923	photo	Frankie Frisch	NYG
54	1923	table	Keeping it in the family	ALL
61	1936	photo	1936 World Series program	NYY, NYG
61	1936	pho/side	Red Ruffing	NYY
72	1936	pho/side	Freddie Fitzsimmons	NYG
72	1936	table	HOF members in 1936 WS	NYY, NYG
79	1937	pho/side	Lefty Gomez	NYY
81	1937	pho/side	Mel Ott	NYG
83	1937	pho/side	Lou Gehrig	NYY
87	1937	pho/side	Frank "Home Run" Baker	NYY
87	1937	table	Players with 9 hits in 5 games	ALL
88	1937	table	Pitching Triple Crowns in WS	ALL
88	1937	table	Batting Triple Crowns in WS	ALL
97	1941	sidebar	Spud Chandler	NYY
97	1941	photo	Spud Chandler	NYY
99	1941	pho/side	Mario Russo	NYY
101	1941	pho/side	Pete Reiser	BRK

BIG APPLE BASEBALL WARS

1921

GIANTS

NEW YORK GIANTS   VS.   NEW YORK YANKEES

FUNGOES

- 1921 is the Subway Series debut for both teams.
- It is the second same state/city contest (Chicago, 1906) and the fourth best of nine contests.
- Tickets sold for $5.50.
- Irish and Bob Meusel are the second set of brothers to play against each other (Bob as a Yankee RF and Irish as a Giant LF).
- Babe Ruth led MLB and George "High Pockets" Kelly led the National League in home runs.
- Pittsburgh's KDKA is the first radio station to do a live broadcast, WBZ in Massachusetts did a re-broadcast and Newark's WJZ did a relay.
- Umpire George Moriarty played 3B on various teams, including both Chicago clubs, from 1903-1916; Moriarty also managed the Detroit Tigers (1927/28).

SERIES SUMMARY

1921 marked the beginning of an intercity rivalry that spanned the 1920s through the 1950s, went missing for 43 years, and then resurfaced at the start of the new century. The first World Series in New York came in 1905, in which John McGraw's Giants defeated the Philadelphia Athletics in five games. The season before, New York missed out on its first Series when McGraw refused to let his team participate, not wanting to give legitimacy to the upstart American League.

Different managerial styles were on display in John McGraw, who believed in the inside game, versus Miller Huggins who relied on the power game. The enthusiasm of this contest spread across the United States, overflowing into Mexico and Cuba. So, the stage was set for a second World Series championship in New York.

Games 1 and 2 featured back-to-back shutouts by Yankee aces Carl Mays and Waite Hoyt on identical scores of 3-0. Handcuffed over the first 18 frames, the Giants could only muster eight base hits, one for extra bases.

The Giants bats broke out in Game 3 with a 13-hit attack that did not include a home run. Neither starter pitched past the third inning. At the start of the seventh inning, tied at four each, 12 Giants stepped into the batter's box and produced eights in hits and runs off of three Pinstripe pitchers. All but one National League New Yorker scored, all but one got a hit and all but three drove in a teammate.

Mound opponents Carl Mays and Phil Douglas again pitched complete games in Game 4, but with a reversal of fortunes this time around. The scoring didn't start until the fifth inning but that Yankees one-run lead evaporated after the Giants took the lead in the eighth inning, expanding that lead by one in the ninth. The Yankees did score in the bottom of the ninth on Babe Ruth's first World Series home run, which was also the first ever by the Yankees in the Series.

After four games, the New York pennant winners were even. The Yankees tied Game 5 in the third inning, took the lead in the fourth to gain the lead in the Series by one.

Game 6 was disastrous for both starters. Both Fred Toney and Harry Harper were around long enough to see their ERAs balloon well into double-figures. Ultimately, the Giants prevailed, so after six games, the scheduled nine-game series was a best of three.

Game 7 featured the third match-up between Phil Douglas and Carl Mays. Both starters gave up one earned run but it was an unearned run, charged to Mays that put the Giants up by one, after their second 2-game streak of the Series.

The eighth and final game was a low-scoring thriller, in which the game's only run came on an error by one of the Yankees' most reliable fielders. The narrow 1-0 victory gave the Giants their second world championship, and for the time being kept their crosstown rivals in their place.

THE TEAMS

NEW YORK GIANTS
94 – 59 .614 +4.0 G

The Team
- Subway Series debut; 6th overall World Series appearance.
- Facing fourth different American League pennant winner.

The Players
- George Burns is the only returning player from the 1913/17 pennant-winning clubs.
- Jesse Barnes, Phil Douglas, Art Nehf, and Fred Toney, dubbed the "Fearsome Foursome," anchored the staff.
- George "High Pockets" Kelly clouted 23 home runs, while Frankie Frisch stole 49 bags to lead the National League.
- Frisch's 311 total bases led the league.
- Irish Meusel, who hit .343 on the season, was acquired in a mid-season trade with the Philadelphia Phillies, along with Johnny Rawlings.

The Manager
- John McGraw, in his sixth World Series appearance overall, is the first to manage in three decades.

Top Batters

Pos	Name	AB	R	H	HR	RBI	BA	OPS
1B	High Pockets Kelly	587	95	181	23	122	.308	.884
SS	Dave Bancroft	606	121	193	6	67	.318	.830
3B	Frankie Frisch	618	121	211	8	100	.341	.870
OF	Ross Youngs	504	90	165	3	102	.327	.868

Top Pitchers

Pos	Name	W	L	ERA	G	SV	IP	SO
St	Art Nehf	20	10	3.63	41	1	260.2	67
St	Jesse Barnes	15	9	3.10	42	6	258.2	56
St	Fred Toney	18	11	3.61	42	3	249.1	63
St	Phil Douglas	15	10	4.22	40	2	221.2	55

NEW YORK YANKEES
98 – 55 .641 +4.5 G

The Team
- Subway Series debut, as well as the 13th team overall to appear in the Fall Classic.
- Six Yankees have prior World Series experience.

The Players
- Frank "Home Run" Baker played on the 1910/11/13/14 pennant-winning Philadelphia Athletics.
- Wally Schang played on three pennant-winning franchises (1913/14 Philadelphia Athletics/1918 Boston Red Sox), winning two titles (1913/18).
- Babe Ruth pitched on the 1915/16/18 title winning Boston Red Sox.
- Carl Mays pitched on the 1916/18 title-winning Boston Red Sox.
- Bob Shawkey and Mike McNally appeared once previously.
- Carl Mays led the league in wins, going 27 – 9.
- Babe Ruth led the majors in runs scored (177) and RBI (168) for the third time.
- Ruth's fourth home run title (59); first appearance of a 50 home run hitter.

The Manager
- Miller Huggins is the 18th manager to debut.
- Huggins played 2B for the Cincinnati Reds and the St. Louis Cardinals.

Top Batters

Pos	Name	AB	R	H	HR	RBI	BA	OPS
1B	Wally Pipp	588	96	174	8	103	.296	.774
SS	Roger Peckinpaugh	577	128	166	8	72	.288	.777
OF	Bob Meusel	598	104	190	24	138	.318	.915
OF	Babe Ruth	540	177	204	59	168	.378	1.359

Top Pitchers

Pos	Name	W	L	ERA	G	SV	IP	SO
St	Carl Mays	27	9	3.05	49	7	336.2	70
St	Waite Hoyt	19	13	3.09	43	3	282.1	102
St	Bob Shawkey	18	12	4.08	38	2	245.0	126
Rel	Rip Collins	11	5	5.44	28	0	137.1	64

Game 1

NEW YORK YANKEES vs. NEW YORK GIANTS

October 5

LINE SCORE	1	2	3	4	5	6	7	8	9	R	H	E
NEW YORK YANKEES	1	0	0	0	1	1	0	0	0	3	7	0
NEW YORK GIANTS	0	0	0	0	0	0	0	0	0	0	5	0

RECAP

The Yankee hitters began building their lead in their very first at-bat, scoring on a Babe Ruth single. Their second run scored on the steal of home plate by 3B Mike McNally. In the sixth inning, Bob Meusel drove home Roger Peckinpaugh with their final run.

On the mound Carl Mays pitched a complete game shutout. He gave up five hits. He held nine of the Giants 11 batters hitless. Mays did not issue a walk nor did his teammates commit an error. The cooperative effort secured the New York Yankees win in their first World Series game.

SCORING SUMMARY

First Inning - New York Yankees
– Douglas starting.
– Miller singled over the second base bag.
– Peckinpaugh sacrificed Miller to second base, Kelly to Douglas.
– Ruth singled up the middle, driving Miller home.
– B. Meusel hit into a double play, Frisch to Rawlings to Kelly.

1 Runs **2** Hits **0** Errors **0** LOB

YANKEES – 1   **GIANTS – 0**

Fifth Inning - New York Yankees
– McNally whacked a double into left field.
– Schang sacrificed McNally to third base, Douglas to Kelly.
– Mays was a strikeout; McNally stole home plate.
– Miller bounced out, Frisch to Kelly.

1 Runs **1** Hits **0** Errors **0** LOB

YANKEES – 2   **GIANTS – 0**

Sixth Inning - New York Yankees
– Peckinpaugh hustled a hit to the shortstop spot; slid into second base on Snyder's passed ball.
– Ruth was a strikeout.
– B. Meusel tripled into deep left field, driving in Peckinpaugh; hit nullified, called out for not touching first base, I. Meusel to Kelly.
– Pipp got to first on a free pass; caught trying to steal second base, Snyder to Rawlings.

1 Runs **1** Hits **0** Errors **0** LOB

YANKEES – 3   **GIANTS – 0**

HIGHLIGHTS

- Babe Ruth's debut as a New York Yankee, playing LF
- CF Elmer Miller stroked the first Yankee hit and scored the first Yankee run
- Miller is only the fourth batter leading off in World Series history to get the first hit of the game
- 3B Mike McNally is the seventh player to swipe home plate, the first in a Game One
- 3B Frankie Frisch had a 4-for-4 day, stroking all but one of the of the Giants' five base hits, but never scoring
- In openers, the Yankees win their first while the Giants go to 2-4

DIAMOND DUST

- Frisch is the first player to stroke hits in first four at-bats
- Carl Mays hurled the third opening game shutout
- Mays is the sixth pitcher to craft a shutout without a walk
- Mays is the first to win a WS game for 2 teams in the same league (Red Sox, 1918)

Game 1 BOX SCORE SUMMARY

NEW YORK YANKEES	AB	R	H	RBI	BB	K	1B	2B	3B	HR	TB	SB
ELMER MILLER, CF	4	1	1	0	0	0	1	0	0	0	1	0
ROGER PECKINPAUGH, SS	3	1	1	0	0	1	1	0	0	0	1	0
BABE RUTH, LF	3	0	1	1	1	1	1	0	0	0	1	0
BOB MEUSEL, RF	4	0	0	1	0	0	0	0	1	0	3	0
MIKE McNALLY, 3B	4	1	2	0	0	1	1	1	0	0	3	1
NEW YORK GIANTS	AB	R	H	RBI	BB	K	1B	2B	3B	HR	TB	SB
FRANKIE FRISCH	3B	4	0	4	0	0	0	3	0	1	0	6

NEW YORK YANKEES	IP	H	R	ER	HR	K	BB	HBP	ERA
CARL MAYS W (1-0)	9	5	0	0	0	1	0	1	0.00
NEW YORK GIANTS	IP	H	R	ER	HR	K	BB	HBP	ERA
PHIL DOUGLAS L (0-1)	8	5	3	3	0	6	4	0	3.38

| Manager | Yrs | Regular Season | | | | World Series | | | | |
		W	L	PCT	Tie	W	L	Gm W	Gm L	WS Pct
John McGraw	33	2763	1948	.586	58	3	7	23	24	.489
Miller Huggins	17	1413	1134	.555	23	3	3	18	15	.545

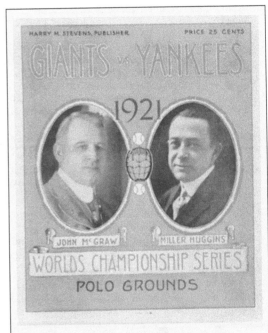

Both Miller Huggins and John McGraw were scrappy infielders in their playing days. Only 11 feet long put end to end, the two were powerhouses as managers, winning 16 pennants between them, making up for their small physiques with fearsome personalities.

GAME TIME:	**1:38**
ATTENDANCE:	**30,203**
BEST OF 8:	**GIANTS - 0 YANKEES - 1**

Game 2

NEW YORK GIANTS vs. NEW YORK YANKEES

October 6

LINE SCORE	1	2	3	4	5	6	7	8	9	R	H	E
NEW YORK GIANTS	0	0	0	0	0	0	0	0	0	0	2	2
NEW YORK YANKEES	0	0	0	1	0	0	0	2	X	3	3	0

RECAP

It was Waite Hoyt's turn to blanket the Giants line-up. Rawlings and Frisch, the same two Giants to hit in the prior game white wash, hit in this game too. Hoyt walked and struck out five but he was never in any real trouble, due in part to the fine fielding of his cohorts.

The Yankees were not knocking the cover off of the ball either. Art Nehf held them to three hits and three runs. The runs scored on a ground out, a single and a steal of home plate. However, the Bombers were the winners and unbeaten in this contest as they switched dugouts.

SCORING SUMMARY

Fourth Inning - New York Yankees
– Nehf starting.
– Pipp flied out to Youngs.
– Ward stroked a single into right field.
– McNally flashed across first as Ward slid into second on Nehf's wild throw.
– Schang stacked the sacks on a walk.
– Hoyt scored Ward on a grounder, Rawlings to Kelly.
– McNally nailed, Kelly to Smith, on an attempted steal of home.

1 Runs **1** Hits **0** Errors **0** LOB

GIANTS – 0   **YANKEES – 1**

Eighth Inning - New York Yankees
– Peckinpaugh reached first base on Frisch's flub.
– Ruth forced Peckinpaugh at second base, Kelly to Bancroft.
– B Meusel singled Ruth to second; both runners advance on throw in.
– Pipp scored Ruth on ground out, Rawlings to Kelly.
– B. Meusel swiped home plate.
– Ward fouled out to Kelly.

2 Runs **1** Hits **1** Errors **0** LOB

GIANTS – 0   **YANKEES – 3**

HIGHLIGHTS

• Babe Ruth, on base via a walk in the fifth inning, swiped second and third but did not score
• The Bombers line-up did not strikeout
• Waite Hoyt hurled the fifth two-hit shutout
• Hoyt and the Giants Art Nehf, pitched a complete game
• Giants' 1B George Kelly is the first player to hit into consecutive game-ending double plays

DIAMOND DUST

- Yankee RF Bob Meusel is the eighth player to steal home
- The Yanks are the first team to steal home in consecutive games
- Sixth time same team back-to-back shutouts were crafted
- Third game in WS history in which a team had 0 strikeouts (the others occurred in 1918)
- Yankees are the third team to win its first two games and the sixth team to hurl two shutouts in a World Series

Game 2 BOX SCORE SUMMARY

NEW YORK YANKEES	AB	R	H	RBI	BB	K	1B	2B	3B	HR	TB	SB
BABE RUTH, LF	1	1	0	0	3	0	0	0	0	0	0	2
BOB MEUSEL, RF	4	1	1	0	0	0	1	0	0	0	1	0
AARON WARD, 2B	4	1	1	1	0	0	1	0	0	0	1	0
WAITE HOYT, P	3	0	1	1	0	0	1	0	0	0	1	0

NEW YORK GIANTS	IP	H	R	ER	HR	K	BB	HBP	ERA
ART NEHF L (0-1)	8	3	3	1	0	0	7	0	1.12

NEW YORK YANKEES	IP	H	R	ER	HR	K	BB	HBP	ERA
WAITE HOYT W (1-0)	9	2	0	0	0	5	5	0	0.00

Babe Ruth took out his frustration at being walked his first three times up by stealing second and third base with 2 outs in the fifth. Meusel, however, stranded him at third. Ruth badly cut his arm during one of his slides, which resulted in significant infection and swelling. The injury became so serious that after Game 5, Ruth sat out the final 3 games of the Series (all Yankees losses), other than a pinch hitting appearance in the 9th inning of the final game.

Art Nehf was a tough-luck loser in Games 2 and 5 of the 1921 World Series, losing 3-0 and 3-1. But Nehf won the finale, hurling a shutout in Game 8. Nehf also won the final game in 1922, making him the first pitcher to win two World Series clinchers.
Nehf started 9 games in the Giants' 4-year World Series run (1921-1924), going just 4-4, but compiling an overall ERA of 1.96 in 10 appearances.
Nehf won 182 games in his career with four different NL teams and was a pretty good hitter. In 1924, he belted 5 home runs in just 57 at-bats, tying him for fifth most on the Giants.

GAME TIME:	**1:55**
ATTENDANCE:	**34,939**
BEST OF 8:	**GIANTS - 0 YANKEES - 2**

Game 3

NEW YORK YANKEES vs. NEW YORK GIANTS

October 7

LINE SCORE	1	2	3	4	5	6	7	8	9	R	H	E
NEW YORK YANKEES	0	0	4	0	0	0	0	1	0	5	8	0
NEW YORK GIANTS	0	0	4	0	0	0	8	1	X	13	20	0

RECAP

After 18 scoreless innings became 20, the Giants mounted a 20 hit, 13 run assault. In the third inning both teams plated four runs on three hits. In the seventh inning the home team struck for crazy eights (hits and runs). Two Yankee pitchers faced 11 Giant hitters. Three players batted twice. Reliever Jack Quinn got no outs, gave up a single, a walk and two doubles for four runs. Reliever Rip Collins got two outs in between allowing four runs on a triple, four singles and two walks.

Great days at the plate as CF George Burns and C Frank Snyder stroked four safeties; RF Ross Youngs drove in four; 3B Frankie Frisch scored three times; LF Irish Meusel and 2B Johnny Rawlings each drove in three. The law of averages dictated that the Giants would eventually win and they did, big time.

SCORING SUMMARY

Third Inning - New York Yankees

- Schang jogged to first base on a walk.
- Shawkey singled Schang to second base.
- Miller singled into right field, driving Schang home.
- Peckinpaugh walked to put runners on each base.
- Ruth singled up the middle, driving in Shawkey and Miller; Peckinpaugh pulled up at third base; Ruth thrown out trying to steal second, Snyder to Rawlings; Peckinpaugh held.
- Barnes relieved Toney.
- B. Meusel got to first on walk.
- Pipp scored Peckinpaugh on a grounder, Rawlings to Kelly.
- Ward was a strikeout.

4 Runs **3** Hits **0** Errors **1** LOB

YANKEES – 4　　　　**GIANTS – 0**

Third Inning - New York Giants

- Barnes whipped a single into left field.
- Burns flied out to Miller.
- Bancroft singled Barnes to second base.
- Frisch walked all bags full.
- Youngs walked; Barnes scored; bases loaded.
- Kelly walked; Bancroft scored; bases loaded.
- Quinn relieved Shawkey.
- I. Meusel scored Frisch on a ground out to Pipp.

- Rawlings hustled an infield hit, driving Youngs home.
- Snyder fouled out to Pipp.

4 Runs **3** Hits **0** Errors **2** LOB

YANKEES – 4　　　　**GIANTS – 4**

Seventh Inning - New York Giants

- Frisch singled through the box.
- Youngs doubled Frisch to third base.
- Kelly stacked the sacks on a free pass.
- I. Meusel doubled into right field, driving in Frisch and Youngs; Kelly made third.
- Collins relieved Quinn.
- Rawlings singled into right field, driving in Kelly and I. Meusel; Rawlings thrown out trying to steal second base, Schang to Peckinpaugh.
- Snyder lobbed a single over the mound.
- Barnes singled Snyder to second base.
- Burns loaded the bases on a center field single.
- Bancroft hoisted a sacrifice fly to Ruth plating Snyder.
- Frisch walked; bases loaded.
- Youngs tripled into dead center field, driving home Barnes, Burns and Frisch.
- Rogers relieved Collins.
- Kelly thrown out on a come-backer, Rogers to Pipp.

8 Runs **8** Hits **0** Errors **1** LOB

YANKEES – 4   **GIANTS – 12**

Eighth Inning - Yankees and Giants

– Ruth walked and Fewster pinch ran for him
– Fewster advanced on a wild pitch and ground out
– Ward singled up the middle to score Fewster

1 Runs **1** Hits **0** Errors **1** LOB

– I. Meusel singled to center and stole second base
– Snyder singled into left field, driving home I. Meusel

1 Runs **2** Hits **0** Errors **2** LOB

YANKEES – 5   **GIANTS – 13**

HIGHLIGHTS

- Bob and Irish Meusel are the first brothers to hit in the same game
- Both mound staffs issued three walks in the third frame, a new record for most combined walks in an inning
- 12 Giants batted in the seventh inning
- Babe Ruth was removed in the eighth inning due to an injured elbow
- George Burns and Frank Snyder, batting first and eighth in the Giants line-up, stroked four hits each
- The Giants eight runs set a record for most runs in one inning
- Giants reliever Jesse Barnes is the fifth pitcher to hit a batter and throw a wild pitch in the same game
- Jack Quinn became the first Yankees pitcher to lose a World Series game
- Barnes hurled seven innings of relief for the win

DIAMOND DUST

- Yankee starter Bob Shawkey, in the third inning, is the first to walk three consecutive batters
- Shawkey is the first pitcher to walk in two runs
- Yankee C Wally Schang is the first player to hit and score for three different teams (Philadelphia A's, Boston Red Sox)
- Youngs is the first player to stroke two hits in the same frame, both for extra bases, setting the record for most total bases in an inning with five;
- Frisch is the first player to score twice in an inning, as well as the first to reach base five times in a game
- Frisch, Youngs and Kelly are the first trio of teammates to bat twice in an inning
- Youngs is the fifth player to drive in four runs in a game

Game 3 BOX SCORE SUMMARY

NEW YORK YANKEES	AB	R	H	RBI	BB	K	1B	2B	3B	HR	TB	SB
ELMER MILLER, CF	5	1	1	1	0	2	1	0	0	0	1	0
ROGER PECKINPAUGH, SS	3	1	0	0	1	0	0	0	0	0	0	0
BABE RUTH, LF	3	0	1	2	1	2	1	0	0	0	1	0
CHICK FEWSTER, PR/LF	0	1	0	0	0	0	0	0	0	0	0	0
WALLY PIPP, 1B	3	0	0	1	0	0	0	0	0	0	0	0
AARON WARD, 2B	4	0	2	1	0	1	2	0	0	0	2	0
WALLY SCHANG, C	2	1	1	0	1	0	1	0	0	0	1	0
BOB SHAWKEY, P	1	1	1	0	0	0	1	0	0	0	1	0
NEW YORK GIANTS	AB	R	H	RBI	BB	K	1B	2B	3B	HR	TB	SB
GEORGE BURNS, CF	6	1	4	0	0	0	2	1	1	0	7	1
DAVE BANCROFT, SS	5	1	1	1	0	1	1	0	0	0	1	0
FRANKIE FRISCH, 3B	2	3	2	0	3	0	2	0	0	0	2	1
ROSS YOUNGS, RF	3	2	2	4	2	0	0	1	1	0	5	0
GEORGE KELLY, 1B	3	1	0	1	2	1	0	0	0	0	0	0
IRISH MEUSEL, LF	5	2	3	3	0	0	2	1	0	0	4	1
JOHNNY RAWLINGS, 2B	5	0	2	3	0	1	2	0	0	0	2	0
FRANK SNYDER, C	5	1	4	1	0	0	4	0	0	0	4	0
JESSE BARNES, P	5	2	2	0	0	0	2	0	0	0	2	0

NEW YORK YANKEES	IP	H	R	ER	HR	K	BB	HBP	ERA
BOB SHAWKEY	2.1	5	4	4	0	0	4	0	15.43
JACK QUINN L (0-1)	3.2	8	4	4	0	2	2	0	9.82
RIP COLLINS	0.2	4	4	4	0	0	1	0	54.00
TOM ROGERS	1.1	3	1	1	0	1	0	0	6.75
NEW YORK GIANTS	IP	H	R	ER	HR	K	BB	HBP	ERA
FRED TONEY	2	4	4	4	0	1	2	0	18.00
JESSE BARNES W (1-0)	7	4	1	1	0	7	2	1	1.13

GAME TIME:	**2:40**	
ATTENDANCE:	**36,509**	
BEST OF 8:	**GIANTS - 1**	**YANKEES - 2**

Game 4

NEW YORK GIANTS vs. NEW YORK YANKEES

October 9

LINE SCORE	1	2	3	4	5	6	7	8	9	R	H	E
NEW YORK GIANTS	0	0	0	0	0	0	0	3	1	4	9	1
NEW YORK YANKEES	0	0	0	0	1	0	0	0	1	2	7	1

RECAP

The scoreless innings piled up again as both starters brought their "A" game to the ballpark. In frame five C Wally Schang tripled home 3B Mike McNally for the first Yankee run. The Giants scored all of the runs they needed in the eighth. One triple, two singles and a double off of the bats of LF Irish Meusel, 2B Johnny Rawlings, C Frank Snyder and CF George Burns built a two run lead. Babe Ruth's first World Series home run was too little, too late. The Series stood tied at two apiece, each team having won two in a row.

SCORING SUMMARY

Fifth Inning - New York Yankees
– Douglas starting.
– Pipp zipped a single into left field.
– Ward sacrificed Pipp to second base, Douglas to Kelly.
– McNally safe at first base on a fielder's choice; Pipp chased out in a run down, Frisch to Rawlings to Frisch.
– Schang tripled into deep left field, driving McNally home.
– B. Meusel tapped out, Rawlings to Kelly.

1 Runs **2** Hits **0** Errors **1** LOB

GIANTS – 0   **YANKEES – 1**

Eighth Inning - New York Giants
– Mays starting.
– I. Meusel torqued a triple into dead center field.
– Rawlings singled into right field, driving I. Meusel home.
– Snyder got to first as Rawlings slid into second on an infield hit.
– Douglas advanced both runners on a sacrifice, Mays to Ward.
– Burns doubled into left field, driving home Rawlings and Snyder.
– Bancroft flied out to Ruth.
– Frisch fouled out to Schang.

3 Runs **4** Hits **0** Errors **1** LOB

GIANTS – 3   **YANKEES – 1**

Ninth Inning - New York Giants
– Youngs thrown out on a come-backer, Mays to Pipp.
– Kelly dumped a double into left field.
– I. Meusel singled into left field, driving in Kelly; caught trying to steal second base, Schang to Peckinpaugh.
– Rawlings stroked a single into right field.
– Snyder popped up to Ward.

1 Runs **3** Hits **0** Errors **1** LOB

GIANTS – 4   **YANKEES – 1**

Ninth Inning - New York Yankees
– Peckinpaugh nubbed out, Rawlings to Kelly.
– Ruth slugged a solo shot into the right field seats.
– B. Meusel fouled out to Snyder.
– Pipp grounded out to Douglas.

1 Runs **1** Hits **0** Errors **0** LOB

GIANTS – 4   **YANKEES – 2**

HIGHLIGHTS

- Yankee starter Carl Mays pitched his second consecutive complete game without issuing a free pass
- Mays's lone strikeout was of leadoff hitter CF George Burns
- Babe Ruth's home run was a personal first, a franchise first, and the first for this Fall Classic
- Phil Douglas and Carl Mays, pitching complete games in their second duel, are 1-1

DIAMOND DUST

- Bomber C Wally Schang is the first player to drive in a run for three different teams (Philadelphia A's, Boston Red Sox)
- Third time neither mound staff issued a walk

Game 4 BOX SCORE SUMMARY

NEW YORK GIANTS	AB	R	H	RBI	BB	K	1B	2B	3B	HR	TB	SB
GEORGE BURNS, CF	4	0	2	2	0	1	1	1	0	0	3	0
GEORGE KELLY, 1B	4	1	1	0	0	0	1	0	0	0	2	0
IRISH MEUSEL, LF	4	1	2	1	0	0	1	0	1	0	4	0
JOHNNY RAWLINGS, 2B	4	1	2	1	0	0	2	0	0	0	2	0
FRANK SNYDER, C	4	1	1	0	0	0	1	0	0	0	1	0
NEW YORK YANKEES	AB	R	H	RBI	BB	K	1B	2B	3B	HR	TB	SB
BABE RUTH, LF	4	1	2	1	0	1	1	0	0	1	5	0
MIKE McNALLY, 3B	3	1	1	0	0	1	1	0	0	0	1	0
WALLY SCHANG, C	3	0	2	1	0	1	1	0	1	0	4	0

- Phil Douglas and Art Nehf each logged 26 innings in the 8 games, helping the Giants require only 4 pitchers for the entire Series! Their third starter, Fred Toney, was of almost no help at all, as he only managed a total of 2.2 IP in his two starts.

NEW YORK GIANTS	IP	H	R	ER	HR	K	BB	HBP	ERA
PHIL DOUGLAS W (1-1)	9	7	2	2	1	8	0	0	2.65
NEW YORK YANKEES	IP	H	R	ER	HR	K	BB	HBP	ERA
CARL MAYS L (1-1)	9	9	4	4	0	1	0	0	2.00

GAME TIME:	**1:38**
ATTENDANCE:	**36,372**
BEST OF 8:	**GIANTS - 2 YANKEES - 2**

Game 5

NEW YORK YANKEES vs. NEW YORK GIANTS

October 10

LINE SCORE	1	2	3	4	5	6	7	8	9	R	H	E
NEW YORK YANKEES	0	0	1	2	0	0	0	0	0	3	6	1
NEW YORK GIANTS	1	0	0	0	0	0	0	0	0	1	10	1

RECAP

A curious game played in less than two hours. A combined 16 base hits netted only four runs. Yankee winner Waite Hoyt gave up 10 base hits but only one run. Giants starter Art Nehf allowed six base hits and three runs. Giants George Kelly singled three times but was never driven home. After starting two games apiece, the records of Hoyt and Nehf were at opposite ends of the wins and losses, 2-0 versus 0-2. It was not lost on anybody that with a 3-2 edge the Yankees were beating the Giants in their own ballpark.

SCORING SUMMARY

First Inning - New York Giants
- Hoyt starting.
- Burns flashed across first base on McNally's fielding error.
- Bancroft forced Burns at second base, Peckinpaugh to Ward.
- Frisch singled Bancroft to second base.
- Youngs stacked the sacks on a walk.
- Kelly singled up the middle, driving in Bancroft; bases loaded.
- I. Meusel was a strikeout.
- Rawlings forced Kelly at second base, Peckinpaugh to Ward.

1 Runs **2** Hits **1** Errors **1** LOB

YANKEES – 0   **GIANTS – 1**

Third Inning - New York Yankees
- Nehf starting.
- McNally sprinted to first base on a free pass.
- Schang doubled McNally to third base.
- Hoyt out on a grounder, Bancroft to Kelly; both runners stayed put.
- Miller lifted a sacrifice fly to I. Meusel plating McNally.
- Peckinpaugh out on a ground ball to Kelly.

1 Runs **1** Hits **0** Errors **0** LOB

YANKEES – 1   **GIANTS – 1**

Fourth Inning - New York Yankees
- Ruth laid down a perfect bunt down the third base line.
- B. Meusel doubled into left field, driving Ruth home.
- Pipp pushed B. Meusel to third base on a grounder, Rawlings to Kelly.
- Ward lofted a sacrifice fly to Burns plating B. Meusel.
- McNally flied out to Burns.

2 Runs **2** Hits **0** Errors **0** LOB

YANKEES – 3   **GIANTS – 1**

HIGHLIGHTS
- Bob and Irish Meusel hit in the same game for the second time
- Waite Hoyt and Art Nehf matched up for the second of three times in the series, with both pitching complete games in all three

---

DIAMOND DUST

• Ten base hits grooved by the Giants, as the starting eight stroked at least one

Game 5 BOX SCORE SUMMARY

NEW YORK YANKEES	AB	R	H	RBI	BB	K	1B	2B	3B	HR	TB	SB
ELMER MILLER, CF	3	0	1	1	0	0	0	1	0	0	2	0
BABE RUTH, LF	4	1	1	0	0	3	1	0	0	0	1	0
BOB MEUSEL, RF	4	1	2	1	0	0	1	1	0	0	3	0
AARON WARD, 2B	3	0	0	1	0	1	0	0	0	0	0	0
MIKE MCNALLY, 3B	2	1	0	0	1	0	0	0	0	0	0	0
NEW YORK GIANTS	AB	R	H	RBI	BB	K	1B	2B	3B	HR	TB	SB
DAVE BANCROFT, SS	4	1	1	0	0	0	1	0	0	0	1	0
GEORGE KELLY, 1B	4	0	3	1	0	1	3	0	0	0	3	0

NEW YORK YANKEES	IP	H	R	ER	HR	K	BB	HBP	ERA
WAITE HOYT W (2-0)	9	10	1	0	0	6	2	0	0.00
NEW YORK GIANTS	IP	H	R	ER	HR	K	BB	HBP	ERA
ART NEHF L (0-2)	9	6	3	3	0	5	1	0	2.12

Bob and Emil "Irish" Meusel are one of 3 sets of brothers to oppose each other in World Series history. The others are Doc Johnston (Cle) and Jimmy Johnston (Bkln) in the 1920 World Series, and Ken (StL) and Clete (NYY) Boyer in 1964. The Boyer brothers both homered in Game 7 of that Fall Classic.

The Meusels were solid major league performers for their respective New York franchises through the 1920s. In the 1921 Series, Irish led all players with 8 RBI; in 1923, Bob took his revenge, driving home 7 in the Series and helping the Yankees capture their first title.

For more about World Series family connections, see page 54.

GAME TIME:	**1:52**
ATTENDANCE:	**35,758**
BEST OF 8:	**GIANTS - 2 YANKEES - 3**

Game 6

NEW YORK GIANTS vs. NEW YORK YANKEES

October 11

LINE SCORE	1	2	3	4	5	6	7	8	9	R	H	E
NEW YORK GIANTS	0	3	0	4	0	1	0	0	0	8	13	0
NEW YORK YANKEES	3	2	0	0	0	0	0	0	0	5	7	2

RECAP

By the end of the second inning, both starters had been knocked out. Giants hurler Fred Toney was gone after the fourth and sixth batters ripped RBI singles giving the Yankees three runs. Yankee pitcher Harry Harper was sent to the showers after allowing two home runs in the second to tie the score.
Relievers Bob Shawkey and Jesse Barnes pitched to diametrically different results. Shawkey, in six plus innings, took the loss and was charged with five Giants runs. Barnes pitched 8.1 innings, allowing two runs on four hits. He struck out 10, some to end a frame, sapping potential Bomber rallies while keeping the Giants' hopes alive.

SCORING SUMMARY

First Inning - New York Yankees
– Toney starting.
– Fewster trotted to first on a free pass.
– Peckinpaugh fouled out to Frisch.
– Miller smacked a hit-and-run single; Fewster ended up at third base.
– B. Meusel singled into left field, driving in Fewster; Miller raced into third.
– Pipp popped up to Rawlings.
– Ward singled into center field, driving home Miller and B. Meusel.
– Barnes relieved Toney.
– McNally flied out to Youngs.

3 Runs **3** Hits **0** Errors **1** LOB

GIANTS – 0   **YANKEES – 3**

Second Inning - New York Giants
– Kelly worked a walk.
– I. Meusel hammered a home run into the lower right-field seats, driving Kelly home.
– Rawlings flied out to Miller.
– Snyder slugged a solo shot into the left field stands.
– Barnes topped a single over the mound.
– Shawkey relieved Harper.
– Burns singled Barnes to second base.

– Bancroft was a strikeout.
– Frisch flied out to B. Meusel.

3 Runs **4** Hits **0** Errors **2** LOB

GIANTS – 3   **YANKEES – 3**

Second Inning - New York Yankees
– Schang strikeout.
– Shawkey lasered a single into left field.
– Fewster boomed a home run into the left field stands, driving Shawkey home.
– Peckinpaugh out on a ground ball, Frisch to Kelly.
– Miller grounded out to Kelly.

2 Runs **2** Hits **0** Errors **0** LOB

GIANTS – 3   **YANKEES – 5**

Fourth Inning - New York Giants
– Snyder slashed a single into left field.
– Barnes singled Snyder to second base.
– Burns reached first base on McNally's fielding error; bases loaded.
– Bancroft singled into left field, driving in Snyder and Barnes; Burns slid into second base.
– Frisch forced Bancroft at second, Peckinpaugh unassisted; Burns slid into third base; Frisch swiped second base.

– Youngs was a strikeout.
– Kelly singled into right field, driving in Burns and Frisch;
  Kelly caught trying to steal second base, Schang to Ward.

4 Runs **4** Hits **0** Errors **0** LOB

GIANTS – 7   **YANKEES – 5**

Sixth Inning - New York Giants

– Bancroft humpbacked a single into left field.
– Frisch walked Bancroft to second base.
– Youngs was a strikeout; Bancroft thrown out, Schang to
  McNally
– Kelly singled up the middle, driving Frisch home.
– I. Meusel flied out to Fewster.

1 Runs **2** Hits **0** Errors **1** LOB

GIANTS – 8   **YANKEES – 5**

HIGHLIGHTS

- Giants Irish Meusel and Frank Snyder, in the top of the second inning, hammered home runs off of starter Harry Harper
- Meusel's four bagger is the fifth for the Giants franchise
- Jesse Barnes, relieving starter Fred Toney for the second time, hurled 8.1 innings, fanning 10 Bombers, notching his second victory
- Barnes struck out each Yankee at least once
- Giant hitters tagged three Yankee pitchers for 13 hits
- Giants 2B Johnny Rawlings five-game hitting streak ended

DIAMOND DUST

- Meusel and Snyder (Giants), along with Fewster, combined to hit three home runs in the second inning, a first in history
- Barnes is the first reliever to win two games in a single World Series
- Bob and Irish Meusel got hits in their third game and become the first set of brothers to drive in a run in the same game

Game 6 BOX SCORE SUMMARY

NEW YORK GIANTS	AB	R	H	RBI	BB	K	1B	2B	3B	HR	TB	SB
GEORGE BURNS, CF	3	1	1	0	1	0	0	0	0	0	1	0
DAVE BANCROFT, SS	5	0	2	2	0	1	2	0	0	0	2	0
FRANKIE FRISCH, 3B	4	2	0	1	1	2	0	0	0	0	0	1
ROSS YOUNGS, RF	5	0	1	0	0	2	1	0	0	0	1	0
GEORGE KELLY, 1B	4	1	3	2	1	1	3	0	0	0	3	0
IRISH MEUSEL, LF	4	1	2	2	1	0	1	0	0	1	5	0
FRANK SNYDER, C	4	2	2	1	0	0	1	0	0	1	5	0
JESSE BARNES, P	4	1	2	0	0	0	2	0	0	0	2	0
NEW YORK YANKEES	AB	R	H	RBI	BB	K	1B	2B	3B	HR	TB	SB
CHICK FEWSTER, LF	3	2	1	2	2	1	0	0	0	1	4	0
ELMER MILLER, CF	5	1	1	0	0	1	1	0	0	0	1	0
BOB MEUSEL, RF	3	1	1	1	1	1	1	0	0	0	1	0
AARON WARD, 2B	4	0	1	2	0	2	1	0	0	0	1	0
BOB SHAWKEY, P	3	1	1	0	0	1	1	0	0	0	1	0

NEW YORK GIANTS	IP	H	R	ER	HR	K	BB	HBP	ERA
FRED TONEY	0.2	3	3	3	0	0	0	0	23.63
JESSE BARNES W (2-0)	8.1	4	2	2	1	10	4	0	1.65
NEW YORK YANKEES	IP	H	R	ER	HR	K	BB	HBP	ERA
HARRY HARPER	1.1	3	3	3	2	1	2	0	20.25
BOB SHAWKEY L (0-1)	6.2	8	5	3	0	5	2	0	7.00

- Yankees backup outfielder Chick Fewster, who totaled 6 home runs in nearly 2000 career at bats, became the first player in World Series history to homer in his first World Series at bat.

GAME TIME: **2:31**
ATTENDANCE: **34,283**
BEST OF 8:   **GIANTS - 3   YANKEES - 3**

Game 7

NEW YORK YANKEES vs. NEW YORK GIANTS

October 12

LINE SCORE	1	2	3	4	5	6	7	8	9	R	H	E
NEW YORK YANKEES	0	1	0	0	0	0	0	0	0	1	8	1
NEW YORK GIANTS	0	0	0	1	0	0	1	0	X	2	6	0

RECAP

Only three runs crossed the plate over this swiftly played nine-framer. The New York National Leaguers scored two. In the second inning Giants starter Phil Douglas allowed one Yankee run to score and none thereafter. He notched his second victory, extending the team's winning streak to two. The Giants were ahead by one.

SCORING SUMMARY

Second Inning - New York Yankees

– Douglas starting.
– Pipp looped a double into left field.
– Ward sacrificed Pipp to third base, Frisch to Kelly.
– McNally singled into right field, driving Pipp home.
– Schang forced McNally at second base, Bancroft to Rawlings.
– Mays zapped out to Rawlings.

1 Runs **2** Hits **0** Errors **1** LOB

YANKEES – 1   **GIANTS – 0**

Fourth Inning - New York Giants

– Mays starting.
– Frisch bounced back to Mays who fired to Pipp for the out.
– Youngs hot-shotted an infield hit; swiped second base.
– Kelly was a strikeout.
– I. Meusel singled up the middle, driving Youngs home.
– Rawlings tapped out to Kelly.

1 Runs **2** Hits **0** Errors **1** LOB

YANKEES – 1   **GIANTS – 1**

Seventh Inning - New York Giants

– Kelly grounded out, Peckinpaugh to Pipp.
– I. Meusel struck out.
– Rawlings reached first base on Ward's fielding error.
– Snyder doubled into left-center field, driving Rawlings home.
– Douglas was a strikeout.

1 Runs **1** Hits **1** Errors **1** LOB

YANKEES – 1   **GIANTS – 2**

HIGHLIGHTS

• Carl Mays and Phil Douglas started and pitched complete games against each other for the third time in the series
• Mays set a World Series record that still stands with 31.2 consecutive innings without allowing a base on balls (including final 4 IP in 1918 and 1.2 IP in 1922)
• Six doubles were drilled, three in the first three innings, though only Wally Pipp scored
• Frank Snyder's seventh inning double was the game-winning hit
• Douglas wins consecutive starts
• The fifth game of the series in which both starters went the distance

---

DIAMOND DUST

- Mays' 26 innings in the 1921 Series without a base on balls, is part of his all-time World Series record of 31, which began in 1918 and ended after two innings in 1922.

Game 7 BOX SCORE SUMMARY

NEW YORK YANKEES	AB	R	H	RBI	BB	K	1B	2B	3B	HR	TB	SB
WALLY PIPP, 1B	4	1	1	0	0	0	0	1	0	0	2	0
NEW YORK GIANTS	AB	R	H	RBI	BB	K	1B	2B	3B	HR	TB	SB
ROSS YOUNGS, RF	3	1	1	0	0	0	1	0	0	0	1	1
IRISH MEUSEL, LF	3	0	1	1	0	1	1	0	0	0	1	0
JOHNNY RAWLINGS, 2B	3	1	0	0	0	0	0	0	0	0	0	0
FRANK SNYDER, C	3	0	1	1	0	0	0	1	0	0	2	0

NEW YORK YANKEES	IP	H	R	ER	HR	K	BB	HBP	ERA
CARL MAYS L (1-2)	8	6	2	1	0	7	0	0	1.73
NEW YORK GIANTS	IP	H	R	ER	HR	K	BB	HBP	ERA
PHIL DOUGLAS W (2-1)	9	8	1	1	0	3	1	0	2.08

Submarine-style pitcher Carl Mays had his greatest season in 1921, going 27-9 for the Yankees, leading the league with 49 appearances (38 starts) and 336.2 IP. A case can be made for Mays' inclusion in the Hall of Fame, as he went 207-126 in his career (.622) and won 20 games for three different teams. The submariner was not a popular player during his time, to put it mildly, and is best known for throwing the pitch that killed the Indians' Ray Chapman in 1920.

Mays was a tough luck loser in Game 4, allowing an unearned run in the 7th to give the Giants a 2-1 lead they would not relinquish. Mays went 1-2 in the 1921 Series, with 3 complete games, an ERA of 1.73, and zero walks in 26 innings pitched. In 1918, for the Boston Red Sox, Mays had 2 complete-game wins, meaning he had 5 consecutive complete games over the 2 Series, allowing just 30 hits and 3 bases on balls for the 5 games.

GAME TIME:	**1:40**	
ATTENDANCE:	**36,503**	
BEST OF 8:	**GIANTS - 4**	**YANKEES - 3**

NEW YORK GIANTS vs. NEW YORK YANKEES

October 13

LINE SCORE	1	2	3	4	5	6	7	8	9	R	H	E
NEW YORK GIANTS	1	0	0	0	0	0	0	0	0	1	6	0
NEW YORK YANKEES	0	0	0	0	0	0	0	0	0	0	4	1

RECAP

Facing each other twice before in this contest, the Yankees Waite Hoyt had beaten the Giants Art Nehf in both. Hoyt, with the help of a fielding error, was scored upon in the visiting team's very first at-bat. From then on, Hoyt pitched an eight inning shutout. Nehf did better, pitching a nine inning, four hit, final game shutout. Both starters pitched to a 0.00 ERA.

This title was a vindicating triumph for manager John McGraw, who broke a streak of four straight losses in the Fall Classic in the 1910s, bringing his career World Series record to 2-4.

SCORING SUMMARY

First Inning - New York Giants

– Burns bounced out, Baker to Pipp.
– Bancroft trotted to first on a walk.
– Frisch fouled out to Pipp.
– Youngs walked Bancroft to second base.
– Kelly flashed across first base as Bancroft scored on Peckinpaugh's fielding error; Youngs slid into second base.
– I. Meusel grounded out, Baker to Pipp.

1 Runs **0** Hits **1** Errors **2** LOB

GIANTS – 1   **YANKEES – 0**

HIGHLIGHTS

• Art Nehf and Waite Hoyt matched up against each other for the third time
• The third was the charm for Nehf, who finally won when it counted most
• Hoyt lost on an unearned run
• Both starters went the distance
• The Yankees lose their third straight to drop the series

DIAMOND DUST

• Nehf is the seventh pitcher to throw a final-game shutout
• First World Series to end on a double play
• 1921 is the fourth and last best-of-nine Series

Game 8 BOX SCORE SUMMARY

NEW YORK GIANTS	AB	R	H	RBI	BB	SO	1B	2B	3B	HR	TB	SB
DAVE BANCROFT, SS	3	1	0	0	1	1	0	0	0	0	0	0

NEW YORK GIANTS	IP	H	R	ER	HR	K	BB	HBP	ERA
ART NEHF W (1-2)	9	4	0	0	0	0	0	0	0.00

NEW YORK YANKEES	IP	H	R	ER	HR	K	BB	HBP	ERA
WAITE HOYT L (2-1)	9	6	1	0	0	7	4	0	0.00

Roger Peckinpaugh's first-inning error led to the only run of the series-deciding eighth game. Ironically, the long-time shortstop was an outstanding fielder in his career, and was considered a second manager on the field when he was part of the pennant-winning 1925 Washington Senators, resulting in his winning the League Award, equivalent to today's MVP. That team featured several stars, including Goose Goslin and Walter Johnson, the latter of whom won 20 games at age 37 and batted an amazing .433 (42 for 97) and had 20 RBI. Johnson was not eligible for the League Award as he had won it previously.

GAME TIME:	**1:57**	
ATTENDANCE:	**25,410**	
BEST OF 8:	**GIANTS - 5**	**YANKEES - 3**

Babe Ruth drew a crowd wherever he went, but nowhere more than when he was in the batter's box. In a career filled with incredible seasons, 1921 was his most dominating, posting totals that were miles ahead of the game's next best performers. Home runs 59 (+35); RBI 168 (+29), RS 177 (+45), BB 145 (+42), total bases 457 (+92), OPS 1.359 (+.308). And in a tip of the hat to the Dead Ball Era gone by, he even had 4 sacrifice hits!

1921

NEW YORK GIANTS vs. NEW YORK YANKEES

NEW YORK GIANTS

Overall World Series Record: 2 WINS 4 LOSSES, 38 games played (19-18, 1 tie .514)

- Jesse Barnes set a record for most games won by a reliever.
- The staff held the Bombers scoreless over the last 25 innings.
- George Burns, who won his first title in third appearance (1913/17), stroked 11 base hits to lead all players.
- National League home run leader Kelly hit none.
- Frisch, the league stolen base leader, swiped three.
- 1B George Kelly is the first player to strikeout in double digits (10).
- Giants are the first team to rebound from two deficits (0-2 and 2-3).

NEW YORK YANKEES

Overall World Series Record: 0 WINS 1 LOSS, 8 games played (3-5, .375)

- Waite Hoyt, on the mound for 27 innings, gave up 18 hits and zero earned runs, but went only 2-1 due to his tough-luck final-game loss.
- Hoyt pitched three complete games to tie Christy Mathewson's 1905 record.
- Harry Harper allowed both Giants home runs.
- MLB home run leader Babe Ruth (59) hammered one.
- Babe Ruth's first loss in four appearances (Boston Red Sox 1915/16/18).
- Miller Huggins is the ninth skipper to lose debut appearance.
- Eighth team to lose debut appearance.

FUNGOES

- Phil Douglas (Giants) and Carl Mays (Yankees) started against each other in Games 1, 4 and 7; Douglas won Games 4 & 7.
- Phil Douglas (NYG) 2-1 and Carl Mays (NYY) 1-2 both pitched 26 innings and allowed 20 hits in the series.
- Art Nehf (Giants) and Waite Hoyt (Yankees) started against each other in Games 2, 5 and 8; Nehf won Game 8.
- Three of the eight games ended on a double play (two turned by the Giants).
- Six of the eight games were played in less than two hours.
- The American League is now 11-7 in World Series play, though 0-1 in Subway Series.

EIGHT-GAME DATA

TIME	**15:51**	PLAYERS POOL	**$292,522**
ATTENDANCE	**269,976**	SHARES	**NEW YORK GIANTS - $5,265**
			NEW YORK YANKEES - $3,510

1921

NEW YORK GIANTS vs. NEW YORK YANKEES

New York Giants Composite Stats

BATTING	G	AB	R	H	RBI	2B	3B	HR	BB	SO	BA	OBP	SLG	OPS
George Burns	8	33	2	11	2	4	1	0	3	5	.333	.389	.515	.904
Dave Bancroft	8	33	3	5	3	1	0	0	1	5	.152	.176	.182	.358
Frankie Frisch	8	30	5	9	1	0	1	0	4	3	.300	.382	.367	.749
High Pockets Kelly	8	30	3	7	4	1	0	0	3	10	.233	.303	.267	.570
Johnny Rawlings	8	30	2	10	4	3	0	0	0	3	.333	.355	.433	.788
Irish Meusel	8	29	4	10	7	2	1	1	2	3	.345	.387	.586	.973
Ross Youngs	8	25	3	7	4	1	1	0	7	2	.280	.438	.400	.838
Frank Snyder	7	22	4	8	3	1	0	1	0	2	.364	.364	.545	.909
Art Nehf	3	9	0	0	0	0	0	0	1	3	.000	.100	.000	.100
Jesse Barnes	3	9	3	4	0	0	0	0	0	0	.444	.444	.444	.889
Earl Smith	3	7	0	0	0	0	0	0	1	0	.000	.125	.000	.125
Phil Douglas	3	7	0	0	0	0	0	0	0	2	.000	.000	.000	.000
Fred Toney	2	0	0	0	0	0	0	0	0	0				
Totals	**8**	**264**	**29**	**71**	**28**	**13**	**4**	**2**	**22**	**38**	**.269**	**.328**	**.371**	**.699**

PITCHING	G	GS	ERA	W	L	SV	CG	IP	H	R	ER	BB	SO	WHIP
Phil Douglas	3	3	2.08	2	1	0	2	26.0	20	6	6	5	17	0.962
Art Nehf	3	3	1.38	1	2	0	3	26.0	13	6	4	13	8	1.000
Jesse Barnes	3	0	1.65	2	0	0	0	16.1	10	3	3	6	18	0.980
Fred Toney	2	2	23.63	0	0	0	0	2.2	7	7	7	3	1	3.750
Totals	**8**	**8**	**2.54**	**5**	**3**	**0**	**5**	**71.0**	**50**	**22**	**20**	**27**	**44**	**1.085**

1921

NEW YORK GIANTS vs. NEW YORK YANKEES

New York Yankees Composite Stats

BATTING	G	AB	R	H	RBI	2B	3B	HR	BB	SO	BA	OBP	SLG	OPS
Elmer Miller	8	31	3	5	2	1	0	0	2	5	.161	.212	.194	.406
Bob Meusel	8	30	3	6	3	2	0	0	2	5	.200	.250	.267	.517
Roger Peckinpaugh	8	28	2	5	0	1	0	0	4	3	.179	.281	.214	.496
Wally Pipp	8	26	1	4	2	1	0	0	2	3	.154	.214	.192	.407
Aaron Ward	8	26	1	6	4	0	0	0	2	6	.231	.286	.231	.516
Wally Schang	8	21	1	6	1	1	1	0	5	4	.286	.423	.429	.852
Mike McNally	7	20	3	4	1	1	0	0	1	3	.200	.273	.250	.523
Babe Ruth	6	16	3	5	4	0	0	1	5	8	.313	.476	.500	.976
Chick Fewster	4	10	3	2	2	0	0	1	3	3	.200	.385	.500	.885
Waite Hoyt	3	9	0	2	1	0	0	0	0	1	.222	.222	.222	.444
Carl Mays	3	9	0	1	0	0	0	0	0	1	.111	.111	.111	.222
Home Run Baker	4	8	0	2	0	0	0	0	1	0	.250	.333	.250	.583
Bob Shawkey	2	4	2	2	0	0	0	0	0	1	.500	.500	.500	1.000
Jack Quinn	1	2	0	0	0	0	0	0	0	1	.000	.000	.000	.000
Al DeVormer	2	1	0	0	0	0	0	0	0	0	.000	.000	.000	.000
Rip Collins	1	0	0	0	0	0	0	0	0	0				
Harry Harper	1	0	0	0	0	0	0	0	0	0				
Bill Piercy	1	0	0	0	0	0	0	0	0	0				
Tom Rogers	1	0	0	0	0	0	0	0	0	0				
Totals	8	241	22	50	20	7	1	2	27	44	.207	.290	.270	.560

PITCHING	G	GS	ERA	W	L	SV	CG	IP	H	R	ER	BB	SO	WHIP
Waite Hoyt	3	3	0.00	2	1	0	3	27.0	18	2	0	11	18	1.074
Carl Mays	3	3	1.73	1	2	0	3	26.0	20	6	5	0	9	0.769
Bob Shawkey	2	1	7.00	0	1	0	0	9.0	13	9	7	6	5	2.111
Jack Quinn	1	0	9.82	0	1	0	0	3.2	8	4	4	2	2	2.727
Harry Harper	1	1	20.25	0	0	0	0	1.1	3	3	3	2	1	3.750
Tom Rogers	1	0	6.75	0	0	0	0	1.1	3	1	1	0	1	2.250
Bill Piercy	1	0	0.00	0	0	0	0	1.0	2	0	0	0	2	2.000
Rip Collins	1	0	54.00	0	0	0	0	0.2	4	4	4	1	0	7.500
Totals	8	8	3.09	3	5	0	6	70.0	71	29	24	22	38	1.329

1922

NEW YORK GIANTS   VS.   NEW YORK YANKEES

FUNGOES

- ⊚ Best-of-seven format made permanent by the owners.
- ⊚ McGraw (1900) and Huggins (1910-16) both played for the St. Louis Cardinals.
- ⊚ Umpire data: George Hildebrand had a brief 11-game playing career as leftfielder for the 1902 Brooklyn Superbas; Barry McCormick was an infielder for various clubs from 1895-1904.
- ⊚ The Polo Grounds, owned by the Giants and rented by the Yankees, hosts its two home teams for the second time.

SERIES SUMMARY

A New York City rematch, with virtually the same players taking the field. Game 1 was decided in the eighth inning, when the Giants took the lead with a three-run rally. The game's combined 18 base hits included two triples, neither of which crossed home plate. Giants reliever Rosy Ryan pitched a near perfect two innings to get the "W".

Game 2 went 10 innings with the starters going the route. The Giants tallied first in the third inning for all of their runs. The Yankees scored on one-run scoring drives in the first, fourth and eighth frames. Darkness, according to the umpires, though the fans, newspapers and commissioner disagreed, necessitated calling the game. It was the last of three World Series games to end in a tie. (1907/12).

Giants starter Jack Scott pitched the 30th shutout in WS history. It is the fourth shutout in 11 games between the two teams, putting the National Leaguers on a five-game winning streak stretching back to the previous Series.

In Game 4, the Yankees score in the first and seventh, but still come up one run short. The Giants now have won six in a row and are only one win away from a second consecutive championship.

In Game 5, the Yankees put together several rallies, but only three runs. The Giants, on the other hand, put up five in just two rallies, bringing home the title in only five games their third since the advent of the World Series.

THE TEAMS

NEW YORK GIANTS
93 – 61 .604 +7.0 G

The Team
- Subway Series #2; 7th overall appearance.
- First club to capture a pennant without a 20-game winner.

The Players
- 1921 Subway Series returning players (9): Dave Bancroft, Jesse Barnes, Frankie Frisch, George "Highpockets" Kelly, Irish Meusel, Art Nehf, Earl Smith, Frank Snyder and Ross Youngs.
- Three players with prior appearances: Bancroft played on the 1915 pennant-winning Philadelphia Phillies; Casey Stengel played on the 1916 pennant-winning Brooklyn Robins.
- Heinie Groh played on the 1919 title-winning Cincinnati Reds.
- Jesse Barnes threw a no-hitter at the Phillies on May 7th.
- Barnes is the eighth pitcher to throw a no-no to reach the Fall Classic in the same season.

The Manager
- John McGraw, in seventh appearance, is the first to manage in three decades.
- McGraw has made the most managerial appearances.

Top Batters

Pos	Name	AB	R	H	HR	RBI	BA	OPS
1B	High Pockets Kelly	592	96	194	17	107	.328	.860
SS	Dave Bancroft	651	117	209	4	60	.321	.815
OF	Ross Youngs	559	105	185	7	86	.331	.863
OF	Irish Meusel	617	100	204	16	132	.331	.877

Top Pitchers

Pos	Name	W	L	ERA	G	SV	IP	SO
St	Art Nehf	19	13	3.29	37	1	268.1	60
St	Jesse Barnes	13	8	3.51	37	1	212.2	52
St	Phil Douglas	11	4	2.63	24	0	157.2	33
St-R	Rosy Ryan	17	12	3.01	46	2	191.2	75

NEW YORK YANKEES
94 - 60 .610 +1.0 G

The Team
- Subway Series #2; consecutive appearance.
- Bullet Joe Bush (26) and Bob Shawkey (20) are the 20-game winners on the mound staff.

The Players
- 1921 Subway Series returning players (9): Frank "Home Run" Baker, Waite Hoyt, Carl Mays, Bob Meusel, Wally Pipp, Babe Ruth, Wally Schang, Bob Shawkey, and Aaron Ward.
- Players with prior appearances: Frank "Home Run" Baker played on the 1910/11/13/14 Philadelphia Athletics; Wally Schang played on two pennant-winning franchises (1913/14 Philadelphia Athletics and the 1918 Boston Red Sox); Bullet Joe Bush is the first pitcher to start for three different teams (1913/14 Philadelphia Athletics, 1918 Boston Red Sox); Babe Ruth and Everett Scott were teammates on the title-winning 1915/16/18 Boston Red Sox; Elmer Smith played on the 1920 title winning Cleveland Indians, slamming the first Fall Classic grand slam; Smith was a mid-season acquisition from the Boston Red Sox.
- Bob Meusel and Babe Ruth's season did not begin until May 20th due to their playing on a barnstorming tour in the off-season, which was not allowed at the time.

The Manager
- Miller Huggins is the seventh manager to make consecutive appearances. Huggins played 2B for Cincinnati and St. Louis.

Top Batters

Pos	Name	AB	R	H	HR	RBI	BA	OPS
1B	Wally Pipp	577	96	190	9	94	.329	.859
OF	Bob Meusel	473	61	151	16	88	.319	.898
OF	Babe Ruth	406	94	128	35	96	.315	1.106
OF	Whitey Witt	528	98	157	4	37	.297	.763

Top Pitchers

Pos	Name	W	L	ERA	G	SV	IP	SO
St	Bob Shawkey	20	12	2.91	39	1	299.2	130
St	Waite Hoyt	19	12	3.43	37	0	265.0	95
St	Sad Sam Jones	13	13	3.67	45	8	260.0	81
Rel	Bullet Joe Bush	26	7	3.31	39	3	255.1	92

Game 1

NEW YORK YANKEES vs. NEW YORK GIANTS

October 4

LINE SCORE	1	2	3	4	5	6	7	8	9	R	H	E
NEW YORK YANKEES	0	0	0	0	0	1	1	0	0	2	7	0
NEW YORK GIANTS	0	0	0	0	0	0	0	3	X	3	11	2

RECAP

Over the first five innings, both starters - the Yankees Joe Bush and the Giants Art Nehf - gave up hits, got into jams, but allowed no runs.
The American League New Yorkers got to Nehf in the sixth on a Babe Ruth run scoring single and in the seventh on an Aaron Ward sacrifice fly to take a two-run lead. In the eighth, the National League New Yorkers stung Bush with four straight singles. They added a sacrifice fly to take a one-run lead into the final frame. Reliever Rosy Ryan, on the mound since the eighth inning, put the visiting team down in the top of the ninth on two ground balls, one for a double play, giving the Giants the early lead in the series. The Giants have defeated the Yankees in four straight games, dating back to 1921.

SCORING SUMMARY

Sixth Inning - New York Yankees

– Nehf starting.
– Bush out on a ground ball, Bancroft to Kelly.
– Witt triggered a triple into deep left field.
– Dugan safe at first base on a fielder's choice; Witt chased out in a run-down, Bancroft to Groh to Snyder; Dugan slid into second base.
– Ruth singled into right field, driving in Dugan; Ruth slid into second base on Youngs' fumble.
– Pipp dribbled out to Kelly.

1 Runs **2** Hits **1** Errors **1** LOB

YANKEES – 1   **GIANTS – 0**

Seventh Inning - New York Yankees

– B. Meusel singled past the third base bag.
– Schang sacrificed, safe at first base as B. Meusel slid into third base on Nehf's throwing error.
– Ward hoisted a sacrifice fly to Stengel plating B. Meusel; Schang slid into second base.
– Scott flied out to Stengel.
– Bush reached first base on a fielder's choice; Schang tagged out sliding into Groh's tag.

1 Runs **1** Hits **1** Errors **1** LOB

YANKEES – 2   **GIANTS – 0**

Eighth Inning - New York Giants

– Bancroft axed a single into right field.
– Groh singled Bancroft to second base.
– Frisch loaded the bases on a left field single.
– I. Meusel singled over the mound, driving in Bancroft and Groh; Frisch jetted into third base.
– Hoyt relieved Bush.
– Youngs lifted a sacrifice fly to Witt plating Frisch.
– Kelly struck out, I. Meusel held.
– Stengel struck out.

3 Runs **4** Hits **0** Errors **1** LOB

YANKEES – 2   **GIANTS – 3**

HIGHLIGHTS

• Joe Dugan, a mid-season acquisition from the Red Sox, plated the first Yankees run
• Groh and the Yankees CF Whitey Witt torqued triples, but both were stranded
• In openers the Giants are 3-4 while the Yankees are 1-1

— DIAMOND DUST —

- Giants 3B Heinie Groh is the fifth player to stroke a hit in first three at-bats
- C Wally Schang, in the second inning, tied the record for most career passed balls with three (1914/18)
- Bullet Joe Bush is the fourth starter to allow double-digit hits in an opener
- Bush is the first pitcher to start a World Series game for three different teams (1914 Philadelphia Athletics, 1918 Boston Red Sox). He lost all three
- Game One winners have won it all 14 times in 19 World Series

Game 1 BOX SCORE SUMMARY

NEW YORK YANKEES	AB	R	H	RBI	BB	K	1B	2B	3B	HR	TB	SB
JOE DUGAN, 3B	4	1	1	0	0	0	1	0	0	0	1	0
BABE RUTH, RF	4	0	1	1	0	0	1	0	0	0	1	0
BOB MEUSEL, LF	4	1	2	0	0	1	2	0	0	0	2	0
AARON WARD, 2B	1	0	0	1	1	0	0	0	0	0	0	0
NEW YORK GIANTS	AB	R	H	RBI	BB	K	1B	2B	3B	HR	TB	SB
DAVE BANCROFT, SS	4	1	1	0	0	0	1	0	0	0	1	0
HEINIE GROH, 3B	3	1	3	0	0	0	2	0	1	0	5	0
IRISH MEUSEL, LF	4	0	1	2	0	1	1	0	0	0	1	0
ROSS YOUNGS, RF	3	0	0	1	0	1	0	0	0	0	0	0

NEW YORK YANKEES	IP	H	R	ER	HR	K	BB	HBP	ERA
JOE BUSH L (0-1)	7	11	3	3	0	3	1	0	3.86
NEW YORK GIANTS	IP	H	R	ER	HR	BB	K	ERA	HBP
ART NEHF	7	6	2	2	0	3	1	0	1.29
ROSY RYAN W (1-0)	2	1	0	0	0	0	0	0	0.00

Bullet Joe Bush enjoyed his only 20-win season in 1922, on his way to a 196-win career. Bush set a record in 1922 that still stands nearly 100 years later - the most wins in a season (26) without hurling a shutout.

GAME TIME:	**2:08**
ATTENDANCE:	**36,514**
BEST OF 7:	**GIANTS - 1 YANKEES - 0**

NEW YORK GIANTS vs. NEW YORK YANKEES

October 5

LINE SCORE	1	2	3	4	5	6	7	8	9	10	R	H	E
NEW YORK GIANTS	3	0	0	0	0	0	0	0	0	0	3	8	1
NEW YORK YANKEES	1	0	0	1	0	0	0	1	0	0	3	8	0

RECAP

After the first inning, four runs had crossed the plate; three went into the Giants ledger. The Yankees added a run in the fourth and tied the score at 3-3 in the eighth. After the third out in the bottom of the 10th inning home plate umpire George Hildebrand called the game because of darkness. The fans disagreed, believing that there was enough natural light to continue playing. They vented their displeasure with loud booing and by throwing debris onto the field. Some fans personally lambasted Commissioner Kenesaw Landis who did not reverse the decision but did decree that the receipts be donated to a charity.

SCORING SUMMARY

First Inning - New York Giants
– Shawkey starting.
– Bancroft rolled out, Ward to Pipp.
– Groh notched a single into left field.
– Frisch singled Groh to second base.
– I. Meusel clouted a home run into the left field seats, driving home Groh and Frisch.
– Youngs flied out to Witt.
– Kelly fouled out to Schang.

3 Runs **3** Hits **0** Errors **0** LOB

GIANTS – 3   **YANKEES – 0**

First Inning - New York Yankees
– Barnes starting.
– Witt grounded out, Groh to Kelly.
– Dugan reached second base on Bancroft's throwing error.
– Ruth out on a grounder to Kelly; Dugan slid into third base.
– Pipp singled into right field, driving Dugan home.
– B. Meusel flied out to Youngs.

1 Runs **1** Hits **1** Errors **1** LOB

GIANTS – 3   **YANKEES – 1**

Fourth Inning - New York Yankees
– B. Meusel fouled out to Snyder.
– Schang whiffed; third strike dropped, thrown out at first base, Snyder to Kelly.
– Ward slugged a solo shot over the left field fence.
– Scott popped up to Frisch (*great play*).

1 Runs **1** Hits **0** Errors **0** LOB

GIANTS – 3   **YANKEES – 2**

Eighth Inning - New York Yankees
– Dugan bunted out, Barnes to Kelly.
– Ruth doubled against the left field wall.
– Pipp flied out to Cunningham; Ruth slid into third base.
– B. Meusel doubled into left-center field, driving Ruth home.
– Schang squibbed out to Kelly.

1 Runs **2** Hits **0** Errors **1** LOB

GIANTS – 3   **YANKEES – 3**

HIGHLIGHTS

• Both Meusel brothers swatted an extra base hit and an RBI - Irish's first-inning home run plated all of the Giants runs and Bob's eighth-inning double tied the score
• In the Yankees line-up, all but starter Bob Shawkey stroked a hit

DIAMOND DUST

- The eleventh extra-inning game
- Third game in history to end in a tie; the others occurred in 1907 and 1912

Game 2 BOX SCORE SUMMARY

NEW YORK GIANTS	AB	R	H	RBI	BB	K	1B	2B	3B	HR	TB	SB
HEINIE GROH, 3B	4	1	1	0	1	0	1	0	0	0	1	0
FRANKIE FRISCH, 2B	4	1	2	0	0	0	2	0	0	0	2	1
IRISH MEUSEL, LF	4	1	1	3	0	0	0	0	0	1	4	0
NEW YORK YANKEES	AB	R	H	RBI	BB	K	1B	2B	3B	HR	TB	SB
JOE DUGAN, 3B	5	1	2	0	0	1	1	1	0	0	3	0
BABE RUTH, RF	4	1	1	0	1	0	0	1	0	0	2	0
WALLY PIPP, 1B	5	0	1	1	0	0	1	0	0	0	1	0
BOB MEUSEL, LF	4	0	1	1	1	0	0	1	0	0	2	0
AARON WARD, 2B	4	1	1	1	0	2	0	0	0	1	4	0

NEW YORK GIANTS	IP	H	R	ER	HR	K	BB	HBP	ERA
JESSE BARNES	10	8	3	2	1	6	2	0	1.80
NEW YORK YANKEES	IP	H	R	ER	HR	K	BB	HBP	ERA
BOB SHAWKEY	10	8	3	3	1	4	2	0	2.70

A 1922 World Series sew-on patch.

A tie in Game 2 was the best the Yankees could muster in the 1922 World Series, as the Giants came from behind in 3 of their 4 wins, twice in the 8th inning. The next year, the Yankees turned the tables, winning their first title and kicking off the longest sustained stretch of championships and excellence in the history of professional sports.

GAME TIME:	**2:40**	
ATTENDANCE:	**37,020**	
BEST OF 7:	**GIANTS - 1**	**YANKEES - 0**

Game 3

NEW YORK YANKEES vs. NEW YORK GIANTS

October 6

LINE SCORE	1	2	3	4	5	6	7	8	9	R	H	E
NEW YORK YANKEES	0	0	0	0	0	0	0	0	0	0	4	1
NEW YORK GIANTS	0	0	2	0	0	0	1	0	X	3	12	1

RECAP

New York Giants starter Jack Scott pitched a beauty of a game. It was three up and three down for the Yankees in most innings. Scott gave up four hits and extinguished a few rallies all the while completely shutting down the Bombers offense for the Giants second win.

The home team's hit men bounced 12 safeties all over the ballpark. Eight of the nine men in the starting line-up reached first base via a hit. RF Ross Youngs singled three times. SS Dave Bancroft scored two runs. 2B Frankie Frisch drove in two of three runs. The Giants have a commanding two-game lead.

SCORING SUMMARY

Third Inning - New York Giants

– Hoyt starting.
– J. Scott singled up the middle.
– Bancroft reached first base and J. Scott third base on Ward's fielding error.
– Groh safe at first on a fielder's choice; J. Scott chased out in a third base line run-down, Hoyt to Dugan to Pipp to Dugan; both runners moved up.
– Frisch lifted a sacrifice fly to Witt plating Bancroft; Groh advanced.
– I. Meusel singled into right field, driving Groh home.
– Youngs forced I. Meusel at second base, Ward to E. Smith.

2 Runs **2** Hits **1** Errors **1** LOB

YANKEES – 0   **GIANTS – 2**

Seventh Inning - New York Giants

– McNally to 2B.
– Ea. Smith batted back to the mound, Hoyt to Pipp.
– J. Scott bounded out, Dugan to Pipp.
– Bancroft trotted to first on a free pass.
– Groh smoked a hit-and-run single; Bancroft pulled up at third base.
– Frisch singled into right field, driving in Bancroft; Groh moved up.
– I. Meusel out on a grounder, McNally to Pipp.

1 Runs **2** Hits **0** Errors **2** LOB

YANKEES – 0   **GIANTS – 3**

HIGHLIGHTS

- Bomber C Wally Schang drilled the only extra base hit, but was left stranded at second base
- Both Meusel brothers singled, and in the sixth inning, Irish flied out to brother Bob in LF
- SS Dave Bancroft is the only Giant without a base hit but scored two of the three runs
- It is the fifth consecutive win for the Giants over the Yankees, dating back to the previous year
- 15 of the 16 hits in the game were singles

— DIAMOND DUST —

• Giants starter Jack Scott tossed the 30th shutout in World Series history

Game 3 BOX SCORE SUMMARY

NEW YORK GIANTS	AB	R	H	RBI	BB	K	1B	2B	3B	HR	TB	SB
DAVE BANCROFT, SS	3	2	0	0	1	1	0	0	0	0	0	0
HEINIE GROH, 3B	4	1	2	0	0	0	2	0	0	0	2	0
FRANKIE FRISCH, 2B	2	0	2	2	1	0	2	0	0	0	2	0
IRISH MESUEL, LF	4	0	1	1	0	0	1	0	0	0	1	0

NEW YORK YANKEES	IP	H	R	ER	HR	K	BB	HBP	ERA
WAITE HOYT L (0-1)	7	11	3	1	0	2	2	0	1.13

NEW YORK GIANTS	IP	H	R	ER	HR	K	BB	HBP	ERA
JACK SCOTT W (1-0)	9	4	0	0	0	2	1	1	0.00

Ross Youngs collected three hits in Game 3 on his way to 6-for-16 in the Series. His career was cut short four years later at the age of 29 when he contracted kidney disease. He passed away in October, 1927 at the age of 30. Youngs had a career batting average of .322 and OBP of .399. He was elected to the Hall of Fame by the Veteran's Committee in 1972.

• Winning pitcher Jack Scott - a knuckleballing right-hander - was picked up by the Giants in August of 1922, after having been released by Cincinnati earlier that season with a sore arm. Scott became a major contributor, going 8-2 in the final two months of the season. Scott's career had numerous ups and downs. He finished 103-109 in his career, twice losing 20 games in a season. He had one more Fall Classic start, the next year against the same Yankees, this time taking the loss after getting pounded for 9 hits and 4 runs in only 2 IP.

GAME TIME:	**1:48**
ATTENDANCE:	**37,630**
BEST OF 7:	**GIANTS - 2 YANKEES - 0**

Game 4

NEW YORK GIANTS vs. NEW YORK YANKEES

October 7

LINE SCORE	1	2	3	4	5	6	7	8	9	R	H	E
NEW YORK GIANTS	0	0	0	0	4	0	0	0	0	4	9	1
NEW YORK YANKEES	2	0	0	0	0	0	1	0	0	3	8	0

RECAP

The Yankees began as if they wanted to stop their two-game losing streak. Scoring two runs in their first at-bat on four singles and some heads-up base running. From then on Giants starter Hugh McQuillan, hitting his spots, retired nine straight in the middle innings, and held the home team to one run over the remainder of the game. The Giants mounted one scoring drive. In the fifth inning three consecutive hits plated the tying runs. A ground out and another single pushed across two more runs. Those four runs were all the National League New Yorkers would need to extend their winning streak to six games, dating back to 1921, while pushing the Yankees' backs to the wall.

SCORING SUMMARY

First Inning - New York Yankees

- McQuillan starting.
- Witt whipped a single over the second base bag.
- Dugan singled Witt to second base.
- Ruth flied out to Cunningham (great catch); Witt slid into third base.
- Pipp scored Witt on a right field single; Pipp thrown out at second base, Cunningham to Frisch; Dugan braked at third base.
- B. Meusel singled into right field, driving in Dugan; swiped second base; took third on Snyder's throwing error.
- Schang was a strikeout.

2 Runs **4** Hits **1** Errors **1** LOB

GIANTS – 0   **YANKEES – 2**

Fifth Inning - New York Giants

- Snyder stung a sizzler through the shortstop spot.
- McQuillan doubled Snyder to third base.
- Bancroft singled into right field, driving home Snyder and McQuillan.

- Groh singled Bancroft to second base.
- Frisch advanced the runners on a sacrifice, Mays to Pipp.
- I. Meusel scored Bancroft on a ground out, Ward to Pipp; Groh slid into third.
- Youngs singled into left field, driving in Groh; chased out in a run-down, Mays to Pipp to E. Scott to Pipp.

4 Runs **5** Hits **0** Errors **0** LOB

GIANTS – 4   **YANKEES – 2**

Seventh Inning - New York Yankees

- B. Meusel out on a grounder, Groh to Kelly.
- Schang out on a ground ball, Frisch to Kelly.
- Ward slugged a solo shot into the left field stands.
- E. Scott popped up to Kelly.

1 Runs **1** Hits **0** Errors **0** LOB

GIANTS – 4   **YANKEES – 3**

HIGHLIGHTS

- Rain fell all day
- Hugh McQuillan posted the Giants' second consecutive complete game victory
- Mays recorded one strikeout...of counterpart starter McQuillan
- Both Meusel brothers stroked a hit for a third consecutive game

DIAMOND DUST

- Yankee starter Carl Mays is the second pitcher to start a WS game after having a losing record (12-14) in the regular season, and the second to lose
- The Giants are the fourth team to win first three games

Game 4 BOX SCORE SUMMARY

NEW YORK GIANTS	AB	R	H	RBI	BB	K	1B	2B	3B	HR	TB	SB
DAVE BANCROFT, SS	3	1	2	2	1	0	2	0	0	0	2	0
HEINIE GROH, 3B	4	1	1	0	0	0	1	0	0	0	1	0
IRISH MEUSEL, LF	4	0	1	1	0	0	1	0	0	0	1	0
ROSS YOUNGS, RF	4	0	2	1	0	0	2	0	0	0	2	0
FRANK SNYDER, C	4	1	2	0	0	0	2	0	0	0	2	0
HUGH McQUILLAN, P	4	1	1	0	0	1	1	0	0	0	1	0
NEW YORK YANKEES	AB	R	H	RBI	BB	K	1B	2B	3B	HR	TB	SB
WHITEY WITT, CF	4	1	2	0	0	0	1	1	0	0	3	0
JOE DUGAN, 3B	4	1	1	0	0	0	1	0	0	0	1	0
WALLY PIPP, 1B	4	0	2	1	0	0	1	1	0	0	3	0
BOB MEUSEL, LF	4	0	1	1	0	1	1	0	0	0	1	1
AARON WARD, 2B	4	1	1	1	0	1	0	0	0	1	4	1

NEW YORK GIANTS	IP	H	R	ER	HR	K	BB	HBP	ERA
HUGH McQUILLAN W (1-0)	9	8	3	3	1	4	2	0	3.00
NEW YORK YANKEES	IP	H	R	ER	HR	K	BB	HBP	ERA
CARL MAYS L (0-1)	8	9	4	4	0	1	2	0	4.50

Aaron Ward (being tagged out) is one of only four players to have two hits in a World Series that were both home runs. The others are Joe Collins (NYY, 1955), Chuck Essegian (LAD, 1959) and Greg Vaughn (SDP, 1998).

Ward was considered one of the top defensive players in the American League while he was a regular, and he excelled in the field in his 3 Subway Series appearances, too, but his error in Game 7 of the 1921 World Series led to the Giants' second run and a 2-1 loss for the Yankees.

GAME TIME:	1:41
ATTENDANCE:	36,242
BEST OF 7:	GIANTS - 3 YANKEES - 0

Game 5

NEW YORK YANKEES vs. NEW YORK GIANTS

October 8

LINE SCORE	1	2	3	4	5	6	7	8	9	R	H	E
NEW YORK YANKEES	1	0	0	0	1	0	1	0	0	3	5	0
NEW YORK GIANTS	0	2	0	0	0	0	0	3	X	5	10	0

RECAP

Down three games to none, win or wait until next season was what the Yankees faced. They scored three times; once in the first, once in the fifth and once in the seventh inning. It wasn't enough.

Trailing 3-2 the Giants broke the game wide open in the eighth inning. Eight men stepped to the plate, driving in three runs on four base hits. Their offense was wrapped around two RBIs apiece for 1B George Kelly and CF Bill Cunningham and two runs apiece scored by LF Irish Meusel and RF Ross Youngs.

The victory was sweet for Giants skipper John McGraw who became one of the few managers to win consecutive Fall Classics and the manager of the third team to sweep.

SCORING SUMMARY

First Inning - New York Yankees

- Nehf starting.
- Witt zapped out to Bancroft.
- Dugan chipped a single into left field.
- Ruth sacrificed Dugan to second base, Groh to Kelly.
- Pipp singled into left field, driving Dugan home
- B. Meusel forced Pipp at second base, Frisch unassisted.

1 Runs **2** Hits **0** Errors **1** LOB

YANKEES – 1　　　　**GIANTS – 0**

Second Inning - New York Giants

- Bush starting.
- I. Meusel hustled an infield hit to third base.
- Youngs walked I. Meusel to second base.
- Kelly advanced both runners on a sacrifice to Bush.
- Cunningham scored I. Meusel and Youngs on an infield single.
- Snyder singled Cunningham to second base.
- Nehf loaded the bases on a walk.
- Bancroft zapped out to Ward.
- Groh was a strikeout.

2 Runs **3** Hits **0** Errors **3** LOB

YANKEES – 1　　　　**GIANTS – 2**

Fifth Inning - New York Yankees

- Schang struck out; put out at first base, Snyder to Kelly.
- Ward wangled a walk.
- E. Scott singled Ward to second base.
- Bush singled up the middle, driving in Ward; E. Scott chased out in a run-down, Youngs to Frisch to Snyder to Groh to Snyder; Bush took second.
- McMillan PH for Witt, thrown out on a comebacker, Bush to Kelly.

1 Runs **2** Hits **0** Errors **1** LOB

YANKEES – 2　　　　**GIANTS – 2**

Seventh Inning - New York Yankees

- B. Meusel hustled a high-hopper to third base.
- Schang sacrificed B. Meusel to second base, Groh to Frisch; B. Meusel wild pitched to third base.
- Ward given an intentional pass.
- E. Scott lifted a sacrifice fly to Cunningham plating B. Meusel; Ward slid into second.
- Bush out on a ground ball, Frisch to Kelly.

1 Runs **1** Hits **0** Errors **1** LOB

YANKEES – 3　　　　**GIANTS – 2**

Eighth Inning - New York Giants

- Bancroft out on a grounder to Kelly.
- Groh whipsawed a single into left field.
- Frisch doubled Groh to third base.
- I. Meusel reached first base on a fielder's choice; Groh gunned down at the plate, E. Scott to Schang; Frisch and I. Meusel slid into scoring position.
- Youngs intentionally walked to load the bases.
- Kelly singled into left-center field, driving in Frisch and I. Meusel; Youngs scampered into third base.
- King singled into left field, driving home Youngs.
- Snyder flied out to McMillan.

3 Runs **4** Hits **0** Errors **2** LOB

YANKEES – 3   **GIANTS – 5**

— HIGHLIGHTS —

- Both Meusel brothers singled and scored
- In his final Major League at bat, Giants utility OF Lee King drove in the final run of the game
- RF Ross Youngs, after walking in the second and eighth innings, scored the Giants first and last runs
- Bullet Joe Bush lost the first and the final game
- 14 of the combined 15 base hits were singles; all of the Yankees five hits were singles

— DIAMOND DUST —

- Eighth five game set, though one of the games ended in a tie
- Art Nehf is the sixth pitcher to hit a batter and fling a wild pitch in the same game, the third Giant
- Nehf is the first pitcher to win clincher games in consecutive seasons
- The Giants are on two winning streaks, seven straight World Series games won and two consecutive titles
- The third sweep (1907/14), the first in New York

Game 5 BOX SCORE SUMMARY

NEW YORK YANKEES	AB	R	H	RBI	BB	K	1B	2B	3B	HR	TB	SB
JOE DUGAN, 3B	3	1	1	0	0	0	1	0	0	0	1	0
WALLY PIPP, 1B	4	0	1	1	0	0	1	0	0	0	1	0
BOB MEUSEL, LF	4	1	1	0	0	1	1	0	0	0	1	0
AARON WARD, 2B	2	1	0	0	2	0	0	0	0	0	0	0
EVERETT SCOTT, SS	2	0	1	1	0	0	1	0	0	0	1	0
JOE BUSH, P	3	0	1	1	0	0	1	0	0	0	1	0

NEW YORK GIANTS	AB	R	H	RBI	BB	K	1B	2B	3B	HR	TB	SB
FRANKIE FRISCH, 2B	4	1	2	0	0	0	1	1	0	0	3	0
IRISH MEUSEL, LF	4	2	1	0	0	0	1	0	0	0	1	0
ROSS YOUNGS, RF	2	2	0	0	0	0	0	0	0	0	0	0
GEORGE KELLY, 1B	3	0	2	2	0	0	2	0	0	0	2	0
BILL CUNNINGHAM, CF	2	0	1	2	0	0	1	0	0	0	1	0
LEE KING, CF	1	0	1	1	0	0	1	0	0	0	1	0

NEW YORK YANKEES	IP	H	R	ER	HR	K	BB	HBP	ERA
JOE BUSH L (0-2)	9	10	5	5	0	3	4	0	4.80

NEW YORK GIANTS	IP	H	R	ER	HR	K	BB	HBP	ERA
ART NEHF W (1-0)	9	5	3	3	0	3	2	1	2.25

GAME TIME:	**2:00**
ATTENDANCE:	**38,551**
BEST OF 7:	**GIANTS - 4 YANKEES - 0**

The Yankees and Giants shared the Polo Grounds in 1921 and 1922, and both led their respective leagues in attendance both years. Not surprisingly, the Yankees and Babe Ruth outdrew their local rival by more than 337,000 over the two seasons, totaling 1.23M in 1921 and 1.03M in 1922. What is a bit surprising, however, is that in 1923, when the Yankees moved into The House That Ruth Built, their attendance dropped by nearly 20,000 on the season. The Giants' attendance dropped even more in 1923, and the Pinstripers outdrew the Giants by nearly 200,000.

Babe Ruth (shown here in the 1923 World Series) battled a badly infected arm in the 1921 Series, managing only one pinch-hit ground out in the final three games. In 1922, Giants pitchers held Ruth to a 2-for-17 and only two walks. The Babe became The Babe in 1923 (and the other four World Series he appeared in), reaching base via a hit or a walk 15 of his 27 plate appearances, including three home runs.

In this iconic photograph, the New York Giants' Casey Stengel is shown sliding safely into home with a 2-out, inside-the-park home run in the top of the ninth inning that provided the Giants the margin of victory in Game 1 of the 1923 World Series. A long ball by Stengel was the difference for the Giants as well in Game 3's 1-0 victory, this time a blast into the stands in right in the seventh inning. (National Baseball Hall of Fame and Museum)

1922

NEW YORK GIANTS vs. NEW YORK YANKEES

NEW YORK GIANTS

Overall World Series Record: 3 WINS 4 LOSSES, 43 Games Played (23-18, 2 ties, .535)

- 2B Frankie Frisch hit .471 and did not strikeout.
- Groh won his second title with two different National League clubs (1919 Cincinnati Reds).
- Four hurlers on the five-man staff posted a victory.
- 46 of the 50 hits were singles.
- Fourth team to win two straight appearances, second National League franchise (1907/08 Chicago Cubs).
- First New York franchise to win three titles (1905/21).
- Joins the Philadelphia Athletics with three World Series wins.
- The Giants are the first Series champions to be awarded rings--a tradition that continues nearly 100 years later.

NEW YORK YANKEES

Overall World Series Record: 0 WINS 2 LOSSES, 13 Games Played (3- 9, 1 tie, .250)

- RF Bob Meusel is the only .300 hitter in the line-up.
- Schang, Ward, Scott and RF Babe Ruth batted below the Mendoza line.
- 2B Aaron Ward hammered both Yankees home runs (his only hits) and committed the only Yankees error.
- Joe Dugan and Pipp did not draw a walk.
- Bob Meusel and Babe Ruth were fined their full World Series shares for playing in barnstorming tour.
- Miller Huggins is the third skipper to lose two straight.

FUNGOES

- Irish (.250) and Bob Meusel (.300) are the first set of brothers to stroke a hit in each game.
- Four players, two on each club, hit in all five games.
- The composite batting average of both teams was in the low .200s.
- The American League is now 11-8 in World Series play, though 0-2 in Subway Series.

FIVE-GAME DATA

TIME	10:17	PLAYERS POOL	$247,310
ATTENDANCE	185,947	SHARES	NEW YORK GIANTS - $4,546
			NEW YORK YANKEES - $2,843

37

1922

NEW YORK GIANTS vs. NEW YORK YANKEES

New York Giants Composite Stats

BATTING	G	AB	R	H	RBI	2B	3B	HR	BB	SO	BA	OBP	SLG	OPS
Irish Meusel	5	20	3	5	7	0	0	1	0	1	.250	.250	.400	.650
Dave Bancroft	5	19	4	4	2	0	0	0	2	1	.211	.286	.211	.496
Heinie Groh	5	19	4	9	0	0	1	0	2	1	.474	.524	.579	1.103
High Pockets Kelly	5	18	0	5	2	0	0	0	0	3	.278	.278	.278	.556
Frankie Frisch	5	17	3	8	2	1	0	0	1	0	.471	.500	.529	1.029
Ross Youngs	5	16	2	6	2	0	0	0	3	1	.375	.474	.375	.849
Frank Snyder	4	15	1	5	0	0	0	0	0	1	.333	.333	.333	.667
Bill Cunningham	4	10	0	2	2	0	0	0	2	1	.200	.333	.200	.533
Earl Smith	4	7	0	1	0	0	0	0	0	2	.143	.143	.143	.286
Casey Stengel	2	5	0	2	0	0	0	0	0	1	.400	.400	.400	.800
Jesse Barnes	1	4	0	0	0	0	0	0	0	1	.000	.000	.000	.000
Hugh McQuillan	1	4	1	1	0	1	0	0	0	1	.250	.250	.500	.750
Jack Scott	1	4	0	1	0	0	0	0	0	1	.250	.250	.250	.500
Art Nehf	2	3	0	0	0	0	0	0	2	0	.000	.400	.000	.400
Lee King	2	1	0	1	1	0	0	0	0	0	1.000	1.000	1.000	2.000
Rosy Ryan	1	0	0	0	0	0	0	0	0	0				
Totals	**5**	**162**	**18**	**50**	**18**	**2**	**1**	**1**	**12**	**15**	**.309**	**.356**	**.352**	**.708**

PITCHING	G	GS	ERA	W	L	SV	CG	IP	H	R	ER	BB	SO	WHIP
Art Nehf	2	2	2.25	1	0	0	1	16.0	11	5	4	3	6	0.875
Jesse Barnes	1	1	1.80	0	0	0	1	10.0	8	3	2	2	6	1.000
Hugh McQuillan	1	1	3.00	1	0	0	1	9.0	8	3	3	2	4	1.111
Jack Scott	1	1	0.00	1	0	0	1	9.0	4	0	0	1	2	0.556
Rosy Ryan	1	0	0.00	1	0	0	0	2.0	1	0	0	0	2	0.500
Totals	**5**	**5**	**1.76**	**4**	**0**	**0**	**4**	**46.0**	**32**	**11**	**9**	**8**	**20**	**0.870**

1922

NEW YORK GIANTS vs. NEW YORK YANKEES

New York Yankees Composite Stats

BATTING	G	AB	R	H	RBI	2B	3B	HR	BB	SO	BA	OBP	SLG	OPS
Wally Pipp	5	21	0	6	3	1	0	0	0	2	.286	.286	.333	.619
Bob Meusel	5	20	2	6	2	1	0	0	1	3	.300	.333	.350	.683
Joe Dugan	5	20	4	5	0	1	0	0	0	1	.250	.286	.300	.586
Whitey Witt	5	18	1	4	0	1	1	0	1	2	.222	.263	.389	.652
Babe Ruth	5	17	1	2	1	1	0	0	2	3	.118	.250	.176	.426
Wally Schang	5	16	0	3	0	1	0	0	0	3	.188	.188	.250	.438
Everett Scott	5	14	0	2	1	0	0	0	1	0	.143	.200	.143	.343
Aaron Ward	5	13	3	2	3	0	0	2	3	3	.154	.313	.615	.928
Bullet Joe Bush	2	6	0	1	1	0	0	0	0	0	.167	.167	.167	.333
Bob Shawkey	1	4	0	0	0	0	0	0	0	1	.000	.000	.000	.000
Waite Hoyt	2	2	0	1	0	0	0	0	0	0	.500	.500	.500	1.000
Carl Mays	1	2	0	0	0	0	0	0	0	0	.000	.000	.000	.000
Norm McMillan	1	2	0	0	0	0	0	0	0	0	.000	.000	.000	.000
Elmer Smith	2	2	0	0	0	0	0	0	0	2	.000	.000	.000	.000
Home Run Baker	1	1	0	0	0	0	0	0	0	0	.000	.000	.000	.000
Sad Sam Jones	2	0	0	0	0	0	0	0	0	0				
Mike McNally	1	0	0	0	0	0	0	0	0	0				
Totals	**5**	**158**	**11**	**32**	**11**	**6**	**1**	**2**	**8**	**20**	**.203**	**.250**	**.291**	**.541**

PITCHING	G	GS	ERA	W	L	SV	CG	IP	H	R	ER	BB	SO	WHIP
Bullet Joe Bush	2	2	4.80	0	2	0	1	15.0	21	8	8	5	6	1.733
Bob Shawkey	1	1	2.70	0	0	0	1	10.0	8	3	3	2	4	1.000
Waite Hoyt	2	1	1.13	0	1	0	0	8.0	11	3	1	2	4	1.625
Carl Mays	1	1	4.50	0	1	0	0	8.0	9	4	4	2	1	1.375
Sad Sam Jones	2	0	0.00	0	0	0	0	2.0	1	0	0	1	0	1.000
Totals	**5**	**5**	**3.35**	**0**	**4**	**0**	**2**	**43.0**	**50**	**18**	**16**	**12**	**15**	**1.442**

1923

GIANTS

NEW YORK GIANTS   VS.   NEW YORK YANKEES

FUNGOES

- Subway Series between the same two teams for the third straight season.
- Although many teams have appeared in three consecutive World Series, 1921/22/23 marks the only time the same two teams met three years in a row.
- Umpire data: Billy Evans, nicknamed the "Boy Umpire" because at age 22 he was the youngest to umpire a game, and at age 25 became the youngest to umpire a World Series game; author of numerous articles and two books; inducted into the Baseball Hall of Fame (1973). Hank O'Day was a former player (P/LF) on the Toronto Blue Stockings, the Pittsburgh Alleghenys, the Washington Nationals, and the New York Giants, as well as a manager of the Cincinnati Reds and the Chicago Cubs. Bob Hart is a former roller hockey player and a former minor league OF; became a local politician after retirement. Dick Nallin is a former baseball and football player and coach.

SERIES SUMMARY

New York was fast becoming the World Series capital, having hosted half of the 20 Fall Classics played. The opening of Yankee Stadium gave all three New York franchises their own ballpark. In the "House That Ruth Built," Ruth scored the first Yankee World Series run, but Giants' CF Casey Stengel hit the first home run, which was a bases empty, inside-the-park, ninth-inning, tie-breaking, game winner.

The Game 2 combination of Babe Ruth's home run hitting and Herb Pennock's solid mound work evened the match.

Game 3 gave the Giants the Series lead based on another Casey Stengel late-inning home run. Stengel's solo shot was the only run of the game.

The hitters took control of Game 4 with a combined total of 26, of which only five went for extra bases. For the second time in the series, the Giants plated a run in the ninth inning with an inside-the-park home run, but this time they dropped the game.

Game 5 was the second straight for the Bombers to bash out double-digit hits. They took the lead in their first at-bat and never looked back. Yankee starter Bullet Joe Bush's three-hit, complete game allowed the Giants one run on a ground out.

Game 6 was a win or wait for next season situation for the Giants. Both team scored in the opening frame. Next, the Giants put together one-run scoring drives in three consecutive innings. The Yankees' five-run eighth inning, however, eclipsed those rallies, and the World Series flag was raised over Yankee Stadium in its first year.

THE TEAMS

NEW YORK GIANTS
95 - 58 .621 +4.5 G

The Team
- Subway Series #3; 8th overall appearance (3rd consecutive).
- First wire-to-wire pennant-winner.

The Players
- Subway Series players (7) appearing in all three match-ups:
- Dave Bancroft, Frankie Frisch, George 'Highpockets' Kelly, Irish Meusel, Art Nehf, Frank Snyder and Ross Youngs.

The Manager
- John McGraw is the first to appear in eight Classics as well as the first to manage in three decades.
- McGraw is making third straight appearance for the second time (1911/12/13).

Top Batters

Pos	Name	AB	R	H	HR	RBI	BA	OPS
1B	High Pockets Kelly	560	82	172	16	103	.307	.814
2B	Frankie Frisch	641	116	223	12	111	.348	.88
OF	Ross Youngs	596	121	200	3	87	.336	.859
OF	Irish Meusel	595	102	177	19	125	.297	.818

Top Pitchers

Pos	Name	W	L	ERA	G	SV	IP	SO
St	Hugh McQuillan	15	14	3.41	38	0	229.2	75
St-R	Jack Scott	16	7	3.89	40	1	220.0	79
St	Jack Bentley	13	8	4.48	31	2	183.0	80
St-R	Rosy Ryan	16	5	3.49	45	5	172.2	58

NEW YORK YANKEES
98 - 54 .645 +16.0 G

The Team
- Third American League team to win three consecutive pennants (Detroit (07, 08, 09) and Philadelphia (13, 14, 15).

The Players
- Subway Series players appearing in all three match-ups:
- Waite Hoyt, Bob Meusel, Wally Pipp, Babe Ruth, Wally Schang, Bob Shawkey and Aaron Ward.
- Sad Sam Jones threw a no-hitter at the Philadelphia Athletics on September 4th, the first without a strikeout.
- MVP Babe Ruth led the major leagues in runs scored (151) and RBI (130) for the 4th time.
- Ruth's fifth home run title (41).
- Ruth led the league in total bases (399).

The Manager
- Miller Huggins is the fifth manager to make three consecutive appearances.

Top Batters

Pos	Name	AB	R	H	HR	RBI	BA	OPS
1B	Wally Pipp	569	79	173	6	109	.304	.749
3B	Joe Dugan	644	111	182	7	65	.283	.695
OF	Babe Ruth	522	151	205	41	130	.393	1.309
OF	Whitey Witt	596	113	187	6	55	.314	.794

Top Pitchers

Pos	Name	W	L	ERA	G	SV	IP	SO
St	Bullet Joe Bush	19	15	3.43	37	0	275.2	125
St	Sad Sam Jones	21	8	3.63	39	4	243.0	68
St	Waite Hoyt	17	9	3.02	37	1	238.2	60
St	Herb Pennock	19	6	3.13	35	3	238.1	93

Game 1

NEW YORK GIANTS vs. NEW YORK YANKEES

October 10

LINE SCORE	1	2	3	4	5	6	7	8	9	R	H	E
NEW YORK GIANTS	0	0	4	0	0	0	0	0	1	5	8	0
NEW YORK YANKEES	1	2	0	0	0	0	1	0	0	4	12	1

RECAP

The Yankee Stadium Fall Classic debut was a victory for the Giants. Neither starter - the Giants Mule Watson nor the Yankees Waite Hoyt - made it past the third inning. Hoyt was charged with four runs on four hits. Watson was replaced with a one-run lead after giving up three runs on four hits. The Yankees tied the score in the seventh inning on a single and a triple. Stengel's home run in the top of the ninth, the first World Series homer at Yankee Stadium, was the game-winning hit.

SCORING SUMMARY

First Inning - New York Yankees
– Watson starting.
– Witt zapped out to Bancroft.
– Dugan got on on a walk.
– Ruth forced Dugan at second base, Groh to Bancroft.
– B. Meusel doubled into center field, driving Ruth home.
– Pipp flied out to I. Meusel.

1 Runs **1** Hits **0** Errors **1** LOB

GIANTS – 0   **YANKEES – 1**

Second Inning - New York Yankees
– Ward pinged a single into left field.
– Schang singled Ward to second base.
– E. Scott advanced both runners on a sacrifice to Kelly.
– Hoyt was a strikeout.
– Witt singled into center field, driving home Ward and Schang.
– Dugan thrown out on a mounder, Watson to Kelly.

2 Runs **3** Hits **0** Errors **1** LOB

GIANTS – 0   **YANKEES – 3**

Third Inning - New York Giants
– Kelly rippled a single into center field.
– Gowdy walked Kelly to second base.
– Maguire PR for Gowdy.

– Bentley PH for Watson, singled into center field to load the bases.
– Gearin PR for Bentley.
– Bancroft scored Kelly on a force of Gearin at second base, E. Scott to Ward; Maguire slid into third base; Bancroft swiped second base.
– Groh tripled into right field, driving home Maguire and Bancroft.
– Bush relieved Hoyt.
– Frisch singled into right field, driving Groh home.
– Youngs forced Frisch at second base, E. Scott to Ward; thrown out trying to steal second base, Schang to E. Scott.

4 Runs **4** Hits **0** Errors **0** LOB

GIANTS – 4   **YANKEES – 3**

Seventh Inning - New York Yankees
– Bush stroked a single into center field.
– Witt flied out to I. Meusel.
– Dugan tripled into deep right field, driving Bush home.
– Ruth reached first base on a fielder's choice; Dugan gunned down at the plate, Kelly (great stop and throw) to Snyder.
– B. Meusel flied out to Youngs.

1 Runs **2** Hits **0** Errors **1** LOB

GIANTS – 4   **YANKEES – 4**

Ninth Inning - New York Giants

- Johnson to SS.
- Youngs flied out to Witt.
- I. Meusel grounded out, Dugan to Pipp.
- Stengel ran a red-hot rocket to center field into an inside-the-park home run.
- Kelly out on a ground ball, Johnson to Pipp.

1 Runs **1** Hits **0** Errors **0** LOB

GIANTS – 5   **YANKEES – 4**

HIGHLIGHTS

- Yankee starter Mule Watson, a mid-season acquisition from the Boston Braves, allowed three runs on four hits in his only series appearance
- In the third inning the Giants inserted two pinch-runners and one scored
- Giants 1B George Kelly hit into two double plays with Casey Stengel on first
- Giants hurler Rosy Ryan pitched seven innings in relief for the win

DIAMOND DUST

- The New York Giants have won eight straight Fall Classic games, dating back to 1921
- Joe Bush is the first pitcher to lose five consecutive games (1914/18/22 [2])
- Stengel's inside-the-park home run, the first Yankee Stadium World Series home run, was the winning run
- It was the first inside-the-park home run to be a game winner, and the first in an opener

Game 1 BOX SCORE SUMMARY

NEW YORK GIANTS	AB	R	H	RBI	BB	K	1B	2B	3B	HR	TB	SB
DAVE BANCROFT, SS	4	1	1	1	0	0	1	0	0	0	1	1
HEINIE GROH, 3B	4	1	2	2	0	0	1	0	1	0	4	0
FRANKIE FRISCH, 2B	4	0	1	1	0	0	1	0	0	0	1	0
CASEY STENGEL, CF	3	1	2	1	1	0	1	0	0	1	5	0
FRED MAGUIRE, PR	0	1	0	0	0	0	0	0	0	0	0	0
NEW YORK YANKEES	**AB**	**R**	**H**	**RBI**	**BB**	**K**	**1B**	**2B**	**3B**	**HR**	**TB**	**SB**
WHITEY WITT, CF	5	0	1	2	0	1	1	0	0	0	1	0
JOE DUGAN, 3B	4	0	1	1	1	0	0	0	1	0	3	0
BABE RUTH, RF	4	1	1	0	0	0	0	0	1	0	3	0
BOB MEUSEL, LF	4	0	1	1	0	0	0	1	0	0	2	0
AARON WARD, 2B	4	1	2	0	0	0	2	0	0	0	2	0
WALLY SCHANG, C	3	1	2	0	1	0	1	1	0	0	3	0
BULLET JOE BUSH, P	3	1	2	0	0	0	1	1	0	0	3	0

Dave Bancroft, Giants' shortstop, had the first World Series at bat in Yankees Stadium, flying out to right.

NEW YORK GIANTS	IP	H	R	ER	HR	K	BB	HBP	ERA
MULE WATSON	2	4	3	3	0	1	1	0	13.50
ROSY RYAN W (1-0)	7	8	1	1	0	2	1	0	1.29
NEW YORK YANKEES	**IP**	**H**	**R**	**ER**	**HR**	**K**	**BB**	**HBP**	**ERA**
WAITE HOYT	2.1	4	4	4	0	0	1	0	15.43
BULLET JOE BUSH L (0-1)	6.2	4	1	1	1	2	2	0	1.35

GAME TIME:	**2:05**
ATTENDANCE:	**55,307**
BEST OF 7:	**GIANTS - 1 YANKEES - 0**

Game 2

NEW YORK YANKEES vs. NEW YORK GIANTS

October 11

LINE SCORE	1	2	3	4	5	6	7	8	9	R	H	E
NEW YORK YANKEES	0	1	0	2	1	0	0	0	0	4	10	0
NEW YORK GIANTS	0	1	0	0	0	1	0	0	0	2	9	2

RECAP

Solo home runs slugged by 2B Aaron Ward and LF Irish Meusel in both halves of the second inning kept the game tied until RF Babe Ruth slugged the third solo shot in the fourth frame. Ruth did it again in his next at-bat, providing the Yankees with all the runs they needed to even the Series. Babe Ruth had his best day at the plate with a collection of two's; home runs, hits, runs and RBI's. The victory was most satisfying for the Yankees, snapping an eight-game Fall Classic losing streak to the Giants.

SCORING SUMMARY

Second Inning - New York Yankees
– McQuillan starting.
– Pipp tapped out, Groh to Kelly.
– Ward slugged a solo shot into the left field seats.
– Scott popped up to Snyder.
– E. Scott flied out to I. Meusel.

1 Runs **1** Hits **0** Errors **0** LOB

YANKEES – 1   **GIANTS – 0**

Second Inning - New York Giants
– Pennock starting.
– Youngs popped up to Dugan.
– I. Meusel slugged a solo shot into the left field seats.
– Cunningham flied out to Ruth.
– Kelly spanked a single into right field.
– Snyder popped up to Ward.

1 Runs **2** Hits **0** Errors **1** LOB

YANKEES – 1   **GIANTS – 1**

Fourth Inning - New York Yankees
– Ruth slugged a solo shot over the right field roof.
– B. Meusel struck out.
– Pipp spiked a single into right field.
– Ward popped up to Kelly.
– Schang singled Pipp to second; Pipp slid into third base on Youngs fielding error.

– E. Scott singled into left field, driving in Pipp; Schang slid into second base.
– Bentley relieved McQuillan.
– Pennock plunked by a pitch; bases loaded.
– Witt flied out to Cunningham.

2 Runs **4** Hits **1** Errors **3** LOB

YANKEES – 3   **GIANTS – 1**

Fifth Inning - New York Yankees
– Dugan bounded out, Bancroft to Kelly.
– Ruth slugged a solo shot into the lower right field seats.
– B. Meusel stroked a single into right field; moved up on Youngs's juggle.
– Pipp advanced B. Meusel on a grounder to Kelly.
– Ward fouled out to Kelly.

1 Runs **2** Hits **1** Errors **1** LOB

YANKEES – 4   **GIANTS – 1**

Sixth Inning - New York Giants
– Groh safe at first base on a spinner over the second base bag.
– Frisch singled Groh to second base.
– Youngs singled into left field, driving in Groh; Frisch slid into second base.
– I. Meusel forced Youngs at second, E. Scott to Ward; Frisch advanced.

— Cunningham grounded into a double play, E. Scott to Ward to Pipp.

① Runs **③** Hits **⓪** Errors **①** LOB

YANKEES – 4   **GIANTS – 2**

HIGHLIGHTS

- Bomber 2B Aaron Ward solo home run was his third over the last two Classics; he hit 17 in 1922 and 1923 combined
- For the second consecutive game, the Bombers banged out double digit base hits, for a total of 22

DIAMOND DUST

- Yankee RF Babe Ruth is the fourth player to homer twice in the same game
- Babe Ruth is first player to homer in consecutive innings
- Giants PH Travis Jackson, at age 19, is the first teenager to appear in a World Series

Game 2 BOX SCORE SUMMARY

NEW YORK YANKEES	AB	R	H	RBI	BB	K	1B	2B	3B	HR	TB	SB
BABE RUTH, RF	3	2	2	2	2	0	0	0	0	2	8	0
WALLY PIPP, 1B	3	1	1	0	1	0	1	0	0	0	1	0
AARON WARD, 2B	4	1	2	1	0	0	1	0	0	1	5	0
EVERETT SCOTT, SS	4	0	2	1	0	0	2	0	0	0	2	0
NEW YORK GIANTS	AB	R	H	RBI	BB	K	1B	2B	3B	HR	TB	SB
HEINIE GROH, 3B	3	1	1	0	1	0	1	0	0	0	1	0
ROSS YOUNGS, RF	4	0	2	1	0	0	2	0	0	0	2	0
IRISH MEUSEL, LF	2	1	2	1	0	0	1	0	0	1	5	0

NEW YORK YANKEES	IP	H	R	ER	HR	K	BB	HBP	ERA
HERB PENNOCK W (1-0)	9	9	2	2	1	1	1	0	2.00
NEW YORK GIANTS	IP	H	R	ER	HR	K	BB	HBP	ERA
HUGH MCQUILLAN L (0-1)	3.2	5	3	3	2	1	2	0	7.36
JACK BENTLEY	5.1	5	1	1	1	0	2	1	1.69

GAME TIME:	**2:08**	
ATTENDANCE:	**40,402**	
BEST OF 7:	**GIANTS - 1**	**YANKEES - 1**

Game 3

NEW YORK GIANTS vs. NEW YORK YANKEES

October 12

LINE SCORE	1	2	3	4	5	6	7	8	9	R	H	E
NEW YORK GIANTS	0	0	0	0	0	0	1	0	0	1	4	0
NEW YORK YANKEES	0	0	0	0	0	0	0	0	0	0	6	1

RECAP

Pitching and the home run were the dominating factors in this tight struggle. Both starters deserved to win. They matched shutout pitch for shutout pitch over six frames. Yankees mounder Sam Jones had one bad inning. He gave up a home run to Casey Stengel, who also won Game 1 on a home run. Giants starter Art Nehf had no bad innings. He threw a complete game shutout.

SCORING SUMMARY

Seventh Inning - New York Giants

– I. Meusel flied out to B. Meusel.
– Stengel slugged a solo shot into the right field stands.
– Kelly flied out to B. Meusel.
– Snyder out on a ground ball, Ward to Pipp.

1 Runs **1** Hits **0** Errors **0** LOB

GIANTS – 1   **YANKEES – 0**

HIGHLIGHTS

- Stengel's solo shot was the 10th for the franchise, and his second game-winning blast of the Series
- A sold out stadium watched the first 1-0 game in which the only run came on a homer

---

Casey Stengel had a solid major league career, posting a career average of .284 and OPS of 120, meaning he was 20% above average in that important offensive yardstick. A left-handed batter (and thrower), Stengel truly thrived when John McGraw platooned him in his two seasons with the Giants, putting up averages of .368 and .339 (with about 240 AB's per season).

Stengel was even better when it really counted, in the World Series (Bklyn '16, NYG '22, "23), going 11-for-28 overall, with 2 HR and 4 BB, good for a slash line of .393/.469/.607. He had pretty good success in Fall Classics as a manager, too, winning 7 out of 10 appearances.

DIAMOND DUST

- Babe Ruth's move from RF to 1B in the eighth inning made him the first player to appear at five positions (PH/P/RF/LF/1B)
- Giants starter Art Nehf is the second hurler to craft two career shutouts in the World Series (Bill Dinneen, 1903 Boston Red Sox)
- Nehf is the first pitcher to post two complete game 1-0 wins (1921)
- Somewhere in the stands sat the 3 millionth fan to have attended a WS game
- In successive innings, the brothers Meusel each caught a fly ball hit to the other

Game 3 BOX SCORE SUMMARY

NEW YORK GIANTS	AB	R	H	RBI	BB	K	1B	2B	3B	HR	TB	SB
CASEY STENGEL, CF	3	1	1	1	1	0	0	0	0	1	4	0

NEW YORK GIANTS	IP	H	R	ER	HR	K	BB	HBP	ERA
ART NEHF W (1-0)	9	6	0	0	0	4	3	0	0.00
NEW YORK YANKEES	IP	H	R	ER	HR	K	BB	HBP	ERA
SAD SAM JONES L (0-1)	8	4	1	1	1	3	2	0	1.13

A classic photo of the 1923 New York Giants, with John McGraw in the center. Second from the left in the second row is World Series hero Casey Stengel, with young rookie Hack Wilson to his right - seven years ahead of his record-setting 191-RBI season.

GAME TIME:	**2:05**	
ATTENDANCE:	**62,430**	
BEST OF 7:	**GIANTS - 2**	**YANKEES - 1**

Game 4

NEW YORK YANKEES vs. NEW YORK GIANTS

October 13

LINE SCORE	1	2	3	4	5	6	7	8	9	R	H	E
NEW YORK YANKEES	0	6	1	1	0	0	0	0	0	8	13	1
NEW YORK GIANTS	0	0	0	0	0	0	0	3	1	4	13	1

RECAP

The damage was done in the second inning as 10 Yankee batters knocked out two Giant pitchers. Starter Jack Scott faced four, got no outs, giving up four hits and four runs. Reliever Rosy Ryan lasted two-thirds of an inning, facing five, allowing two extra base hits and two tallies. Reliever Hugh McQuillan got the third out but by then the Bombers led by six and the Giants never caught up.

SCORING SUMMARY

Second Inning - New York Yankees
- Pipp pinged a single over the second base bag.
- Ward singled Pipp to second base.
- Schang safe at first base on J. Scott's fielding error; bases loaded.
- E. Scott singled into left field, driving in Pipp and Ward; Schang cruised into third base.
- Ryan relieved J. Scott.
- Shawkey lifted a sacrifice fly to Stengel plating Schang.
- Witt doubled into left-center field, driving E. Scott home.
- Dugan reached first base on a fielder's choice; Witt tagged out at third base by Groh.
- Ruth walked Dugan to second base.
- B. Meusel tripled into deep left field, driving home Dugan and Ruth.
- McQuillan relieved Ryan.
- Pipp flied out to Stengel.

6 Runs **5** Hits **1** Errors **1** LOB

YANKEES – 6   **GIANTS – 0**

Third Inning - New York Yankees
- Ward jogged to first on a walk.
- Schang sacrificed Ward to second base, McQuillan to Kelly.
- E. Scott singled Ward to third base.
- Shawkey fouled out to Snyder.
- Witt doubled into the left field corner, driving in Ward; E. Scott slid into third.

- Dugan flied out to Stengel.

1 Runs **2** Hits **0** Errors **2** LOB

YANKEES – 7   **GIANTS – 0**

Fourth Inning - New York Yankees
- Ruth wangled a free pass.
- B. Meusel struck out.
- Pipp hitched a hit-and-run single; Ruth rushed into third base.
- Ward singled into left field, driving in Ruth; Pipp stormed into second base.
- Schang popped up to Frisch.
- E. Scott popped up to Bancroft.

1 Runs **2** Hits **0** Errors **2** LOB

YANKEES – 8   **GIANTS – 0**

Eighth Inning - New York Giants
- Youngs sprinted across first on a very close play.
- I. Meusel smashed a hit-and-run single; Youngs braked at third base.
- Stengel singled into right field, driving in Youngs; the runners moved up on Ruth's throwing error.
- Kelly scored I. Meusel on a ground out, Ward to Pipp; Stengel took third.
- Snyder scored Stengel on a grounder, E. Scott to Pipp.
- O'Connell PH for Jonnard, clipped by a pitch.

– Bancroft singled O'Connell to second base.
– Groh walked the bases full.
– Pennock relieved Shawkey.
– Frisch popped up to B. Meusel.

3 Runs **4** Hits **1** Errors **3** LOB

YANKEES – 8   **GIANTS – 3**

Ninth Inning - New York Giants

– Youngs ran a red-hot rocket to right field into an inside-the-park home run.
– I. Meusel bounded out, Ward to Pipp.
– Cunningham PH for Stengel, whiffed.
– Kelly flied out to Witt.

1 Runs **1** Hits **0** Errors **0** LOB

YANKEES – 8   **GIANTS – 4**

HIGHLIGHTS

- Yankee 2B Aaron Ward scored, Scott singled, and CF Whitey Witt drilled an RBI double in consecutive frames
- Ross Youngs had a four-hit day
- Both inside-the-park home runs in the series have been slugged in the ninth inning by a Giant
- Yankee starter Bob Shawkey picked up the win, despite allowing 12 hits
- Pennock notched the save, giving him a hand in both Bomber victories
- 26 base hits (13 per team/21 singles) allowed by six pitchers, as a combined 12 runs crossed the plate
- Home runs, all solo shots, hit in four straight games

DIAMOND DUST

- In the second inning, SS Everett Scott singled off of Jack Scott marking a first in same surnames
- In the eighth inning, the Giants scored two runs on ground outs, a first in World Series history
- Giants RF Ross Youngs smacked the sixth inside-the-park home run

Game 4 BOX SCORE SUMMARY

NEW YORK YANKEES	AB	R	H	RBI	BB	K	1B	2B	3B	HR	TB	SB
WHITEY WITT, CF	4	0	3	2	0	0	1	2	0	0	5	0
JOE DUGAN, 3B	5	1	0	0	0	0	0	0	0	0	0	0
BABE RUTH, RF	3	2	1	0	2	2	1	0	0	0	2	0
BOB MEUSEL, LF	5	0	1	2	0	1	0	0	1	0	3	0
WALLY PIPP, 1B	4	1	2	0	1	0	2	0	0	0	2	0
AARON WARD, 2B	4	2	2	1	1	0	2	0	0	0	2	0
WALLY SCHANG, C	3	1	1	0	0	1	1	0	0	0	1	0
NEW YORK GIANTS	AB	R	H	RBI	BB	K	1B	2B	3B	HR	TB	SB
ROSS YOUNGS, RF	5	2	4	1	0	0	3	0	0	1	7	0
IRISH MEUSEL, LF	5	1	1	0	0	1	1	0	0	0	1	0
CASEY STENGEL, CF	2	1	2	1	2	0	2	0	0	0	2	0
GEORGE KELLY, 1B	5	0	2	1	0	0	2	0	0	0	2	0
FRANK SNYDER, C	4	0	0	1	0	0	0	0	0	0	0	0

NEW YORK YANKEES	IP	H	R	ER	HR	K	BB	HBP	ERA
BOB SHAWKEY W (1-0)	7.2	12	3	3	0	2	4	1	3.52
HERB PENNOCK S (1)	1.1	1	1	1	1	1	0	0	2.61
NEW YORK GIANTS	IP	H	R	ER	HR	K	BB	HBP	ERA
JACK SCOTT L (0-1)	1	4	4	3	0	1	0	0	27.00
ROSY RYAN	0.2	2	2	2	0	0	1	0	3.52
HUGH MCQUILLAN	5.1	6	2	2	0	2	2	0	5.00

Frankie Frisch (shown on page 51) went 2-for-4 in Game 4, and and 10-for-25 in the 1923 Series, his second consecutive Series batting .400 or higher. In the Giants' four consecutive WS appearances from 1921 through 1924, Frisch collected 37 hits in 26 games, compiling a BA of .363 and OBA of .428.

Frisch appeared in four World Series for the Cardinals as well, winning two with St. Louis as he did with the Giants.

Frisch is an underrated all-time great. In his career, he collected 2880 hits, 1532 runs scored, and 419 stolen bases. In more than 10,000 career plate appearances, Frisch fanned only 272 times, surpassing 20 in a season only two times.

GAME TIME:	**2:32**	
ATTENDANCE:	**46,302**	
BEST OF 7:	**GIANTS - 2**	**YANKEES - 2**

Game 5

NEW YORK GIANTS vs. NEW YORK YANKEES

October 14

LINE SCORE	1	2	3	4	5	6	7	8	9	R	H	E
NEW YORK GIANTS	0	1	0	0	0	0	0	0	0	1	3	2
NEW YORK YANKEES	3	4	0	1	0	0	0	0	X	8	14	0

RECAP

The Giants had a one-man wrecking crew in Irish Meusel. Meusel stroked all three of the Giants hits and scored the lone run. The Bombers had an eight-man wrecking crew. Five Yankees scored. Three Yankees drove in a run. The home team scored in the first, second and fourth frames. Stroking four hits, driving in three and scoring three was 3B Joe Dugan. Bob Meusel chipped in with three hits and three RBI's. Starter Bullet Joe Bush's mound performance was the perfect complement and the Yankees registered their second straight win.

SCORING SUMMARY

First Inning - New York Yankees
– Bentley starting.
– Witt fouled out to Gowdy.
– Dugan slapped a single into right field.
– Ruth walked Dugan to second base.
– B. Meusel tripled into left-center field, driving home Dugan and Ruth.
– Pipp lofted a sacrifice fly to I. Meusel plating B. Meusel.
– Ward skipped a single into left field; swiped second base.
– Schang was a strikeout.

3 Runs **3** Hits **0** Errors **1** LOB

GIANTS – 0   **YANKEES – 3**

Second Inning - New York Giants
– Bush starting.
– Youngs grounded out, E. Scott to Pipp.
– I. Meusel tattooed a triple into deep left-center field.
– Stengel scored I. Meusel on a ground out, Pipp to Bush.
– Kelly flied out to Witt.

1 Runs **1** Hits **0** Errors **0** LOB

GIANTS – 1   **YANKEES – 3**

Second Inning - New York Yankees
– E. Scott flied out to Stengel.
– Bush socked a single into center field.

– Witt walked Bush to second base.
– Dugan ran a red-hot rocket to deep center field into an inside-the-park home run, driving home Bush and Witt.
– Ruth reached first base on Kelly's fielding error.
– Scott relieved Bentley.
– B. Meusel zinged a hit-and-run single; Ruth chugged into third base.
– Pipp safe at first base on a fielder's choice; Ruth scored on Frisch's bad throw; B. Meusel took second.
– Ward knocked into a double play, Bancroft to Frisch.

4 Runs **3** Hits **2** Errors **1** LOB

GIANTS – 1   **YANKEES – 7**

Fourth Inning - New York Yankees
– Dugan caromed a base hit off of Frisch's shins.
– Ruth smacked a hit-and-run single; Dugan streaked into third base; Ruth picked-off, Youngs to Kelly.
– B. Meusel singled into right field, driving Dugan home.
– Pipp walked B. Meusel to second base.
– Barnes relieved J. Scott.
– Ward was a strikeout.
– Schang forced Pipp at second base, Groh to Frisch.

1 Runs **3** Hits **0** Errors **2** LOB

GIANTS – 1   **YANKEES – 8**

HIGHLIGHTS

- Both Meusel brothers tripled, had three hits and scored a run
- Wally Pipp, in consecutive at-bats, drove in a run sans a hit
- Bombers, in the second inning rally, reached first base in six straight at-bats
- Joe Dugan had a four-hit day at the plate
- Home runs hit in five straight games, one with men on base

DIAMOND DUST

- Yankee 3B Joe Dugan smacked the eighth inside-the-park home run, the third in a Series for the first time, and first with men on base
- Bush broke a personal five-game losing streak and is the second pitcher to win for two different teams (1913 A's). The first was Carl Mays

Game 5 BOX SCORE SUMMARY

NEW YORK GIANTS	AB	R	H	RBI	BB	K	1B	2B	3B	HR	TB	SB
IRISH MEUSEL, LF	4	1	3	0	0	0	1	1	1	0	6	0
CASEY STENGEL, CF	3	0	0	1	0	0	0	0	0	0	0	0
NEW YORK YANKEES	AB	R	H	RBI	BB	K	1B	2B	3B	HR	TB	SB
WHITEY WITT, CF	4	1	1	0	1	0	1	0	0	0	1	0
JOE DUGAN, 3B	5	3	4	3	0	0	3	0	0	1	7	0
BABE RUTH, RF	4	2	1	0	1	1	1	0	0	0	1	0
BOB MEUSEL, LF	5	1	3	3	0	0	2	0	1	0	5	0
WALLY PIPP, 1B	3	0	0	2	1	1	0	0	0	0	0	0
BULLET JOE BUSH, P	4	1	1	0	0	1	1	0	0	0	1	0

NEW YORK GIANTS	IP	H	R	ER	HR	K	BB	HBP	ERA
JACK BENTLEY L (0-1)	1.1	5	7	6	1	1	2	0	9.45
JACK SCOTT	2	5	1	1	0	1	1	0	12.00
NEW YORK YANKEES	IP	H	R	ER	HR	K	BB	HBP	ERA
BULLET JOE BUSH W (1-1)	9	3	1	1	0	3	2	0	1.08

"The Fordham Flash," Hall-of-Famer Frankie Frisch.

GAME TIME:	**1:55**	
ATTENDANCE:	**62,817**	
BEST OF 7:	**GIANTS - 2**	**YANKEES - 3**

NEW YORK YANKEES vs. NEW YORK GIANTS

October 15

LINE SCORE	1	2	3	4	5	6	7	8	9	R	H	E
NEW YORK YANKEES	1	0	0	0	0	0	0	5	0	6	5	0
NEW YORK GIANTS	1	0	0	1	1	1	0	0	0	4	10	1

RECAP

In the top of the first, Yankee RF Babe Ruth slugged a solo home run. In the bottom of the first, the Giants strung together three singles to tie. The National League New Yorkers added single runs in three different at-bats for a lead that held through the seventh inning.

In the top of the eighth inning, nine Pinstripers parlayed three singles and three walks into five runs. Reliever Sam Jones shut down the Giants offense, retiring the last five in a row for the save. The Giants are the first wire-to-wire pennant-winner to lose as the Yankees celebrate their first Fall Classic title.

SCORING SUMMARY

First Inning - New York Yankees

– Nehf starting.
– Witt popped up to Bancroft.
– Dugan grounded out, Frisch to Kelly.
– Ruth slugged a solo shot into the upper right field seats.
– B. Meusel struck out.

1 Runs **1** Hits **0** Errors **0** LOB

YANKEES – 1   **GIANTS – 0**

First Inning - New York Giants

– Pennock starting.
– Bancroft flied out to Witt.
– Groh lasered a line drive single into left field.
– Frisch singled Groh to second base.
– Youngs singled up the middle, driving in Groh; Frisch thrown out trying for third base, Witt to Dugan; Youngs made it to second base.
– I. Meusel was a strikeout.

1 Runs **3** Hits **0** Errors **1** LOB

YANKEES – 1   **GIANTS – 1**

Fourth Inning - New York Giants

– Frisch bunted to first for a base hit.
– Youngs advanced Frisch to second base on a grounder, Ward to Pipp.

– I. Meusel flied out to Witt.
– Cunningham singled into right field, driving Frisch home.
– Kelly out on a ground ball, Ward to Pipp.

1 Runs **2** Hits **0** Errors **1** LOB

YANKEES – 1   **GIANTS – 2**

Fifth Inning - New York Giants

– Snyder slugged a solo shot into the upper left field seats.
– Nehf went down on strikes.
– Bancroft grounded out, E. Scott to Pipp.
– Groh flied out to Ruth.

1 Runs **1** Hits **0** Errors **0** LOB

YANKEES – 1   **GIANTS – 3**

Sixth Inning - New York Giants

– Frisch thumped a triple into deep left-center field.
– Youngs grounded out, Ward to Pipp; Frisch stayed put.
– I. Meusel singled into center field, driving Frisch home.
– Cunningham bounced out to Pipp; I. Meusel slid into second base.
– Kelly was a strikeout.

1 Runs **2** Hits **0** Errors **1** LOB

YANKEES – 1   **GIANTS – 4**

Eighth Inning - New York Yankees

—Ward popped up to Youngs.
—Schang pumped a single into left field.
—E. Scott blistered a single into right field; Schang stormed into third base.
—Hofmann PH for Pennock, stacked the sacks on a walk.
—Haines PR.
—Bush PH for Witt, walked; Schang scored; bases loaded.
—Ryan relieved Nehf.
—Johnson PR for Bush.
—Dugan walked; E. Scott scored; bases loaded.
—Ruth was a strikeout.
—B. Meusel singled through the box, driving in Haines and Johnson; on Cunningham's off-target throw Dugan darted across the plate as B. Meusel slid into third base.
—Pipp nubbed out, Groh to Kelly.

5 Runs **3** Hits **1** Errors **1** LOB

YANKEES – 6 **GIANTS – 4**

HIGHLIGHTS

- Ruth's home run is the 10th for the franchise
- Pinstripers, in the eighth inning, drew consecutive pinch hit walks (a first) and inserted two pinch runners, who both scored
- Bullet Joe Bush as a PH walked with the bases loaded driving in the first run of the eighth-inning rally

DIAMOND DUST

- Fifth six-game set
- Babe Ruth is the first player to hammer three home runs in a Series
- 10 home runs were hammered in the Series for a new record—nine were solo, three were inside the park, five per team
- Yankee starter Herb Pennock is the first pitcher to give up three home runs in a Series (Games 2, 4)
- Art Nehf and reliever Rosy Ryan, in the eighth inning, each walked in a run, the first time in history 2 runs were forced in on walks in one inning
- Giants starter Art Nehf, charged with the loss, is the first pitcher to record the final decision in three straight Fall Classics

Game 6 BOX SCORE SUMMARY

NEW YORK YANKEES	AB	R	H	RBI	BB	K	1B	2B	3B	HR	TB	SB
BULLET JOE BUSH, PH	0	0	0	1	1	0	0	0	0	0	0	0
ERNIE JOHNSON, PR	0	1	0	0	0	0	0	0	0	0	0	0
JOE DUGAN, 3B	0	1	0	1	1	0	0	0	0	0	0	0
BABE RUTH, RF	3	1	1	1	1	2	0	0	0	1	4	0
BOB MEUSEL, LF	4	0	1	2	0	1	1	0	0	0	1	0
WALLY SCHANG, C	4	1	1	0	0	0	1	0	0	0	1	0
EVERETT SCOTT, SS	4	1	1	0	0	0	1	0	0	0	1	0
HINKEY HAINES, PR/CF	0	1	0	0	0	0	0	0	0	0	0	0
NEW YORK GIANTS	AB	R	H	RBI	BB	K	1B	2B	3B	HR	TB	SB
HEINIE GROH, 3B	4	1	1	0	0	0	1	0	0	0	1	0
FRANKIE FRISCH, 2B	4	2	3	0	0	0	2	0	0	1	5	0
ROSS YOUNGS, RF	4	0	2	1	0	0	2	0	0	0	2	0
IRISH MEUSEL, LF	4	0	1	1	0	1	1	0	0	0	1	0
BILL CUNNINGHAM, CF	3	0	1	1	0	0	1	0	0	0	1	0
FRANK SNYDER, C	4	1	2	1	0	1	1	0	0	1	5	0

NEW YORK YANKEES	IP	H	R	ER	HR	K	BB	HBP	ERA
HERB PENNOCK W (2-0)	7	9	4	4	1	6	0	0	3.63
SAD SAM JONES S (1)	2	1	0	0	0	0	0	0	0.90
NEW YORK GIANTS	IP	H	R	ER	HR	K	BB	HBP	ERA
ART NEHF L (1-1)	7.1	4	5	5	1	3	3	0	2.76
ROSY RYAN	1.2	1	1	1	0	1	1	0	3.86

GAME TIME: **2:05**
ATTENDANCE: **34,172**
BEST OF 7:   **GIANTS - 2   YANKEES - 4**

World and Subway Series - Keeping It in the Family

Opponent Brothers in the Same Subway Series			
B	Bob Meusel	NY Yankees - 1921(L)/'22(L)/'23(W)/ '26(L)/'27(W)/'28(W)	
B	Irish Meusel	NY Giants - 1921(W)/'22(W)/'23(L)/'24(L)	
Teammate Brothers Nearly in the Same Subway Series			
B	Jesse Barnes	NY Giants - 1921(W)/1922 (W)	The Barnes' were teammates in 1923, until
B	Virgil Barnes	NY Giants - 1923 (L)/1924 (L)	Jesse was traded to the Braves in June
Opponent Brothers in a World Series			
B	Clete Boyer	New York Yankees, 1960(W)/1963(L)/1964(L)	Clete and Ken both homered in Game 7
B	Ken Boyer	St. Louis Cardinals, 1964	of the 1964 World Series
B	Doc Johnston	Cleveland - 1920(W)	
B	Jimmy Johnston	Brooklyn - 1916(L)/1920(L)	
Brothers Who Both Played in a World Series, One of Whom Played in a Subway Series			
B	Joe DiMaggio	NY Yankees - 1936(W)/'37 (W)/'38 (W)/'39 (W)/'41 (W)/'42 (L)/'49 (W)/'50 (W)/'51 (W)	
B	Dom DiMaggio	Boston - 1946(L)	
B	Orlando Hernandez	NY Yankees - 1998(W)/'99(W)/'00(W), Chicago White Sox - '05(W)	
B	Livan Hernandez	Florida - 1997(W), SF - 2002(L)	
B	Gus Mancuso	St. Louis Cards - '30(L)/'31(W), NY Giants - '33(W)/'36(L)/'37(L)	
B	Frank Mancuso	St. Louis Browns - 1944(L)	
B	Joe Torre (Mgr)	NY Yankees - 1996(W)/'98 (W)/'99(W)/'00(W)/'01(L)	Joe Torre's 2209 games played is the sixth most among players who never appeared in the World Series
B	Frank Torre	Milwaukee - 1957(W)/1958(L)	
B	Dixie Walker	Brooklyn - 1941(L)/1947(L)	
B	Harry Walker	St. Louis Cardinals - 1942(W)/1943(L)/1946(W)	
B	Walker Cooper	St. Louis Cardinals - 1942(W)/1943(L)/1944(W)	Neither Cooper brother appeared in a Subway
B	Mort Cooper	St. Louis Cardinals - 1942(W)/1943(L)/1944(W)	Series, but they both collected an RBI hit in the same inning of the same WS game in 1942
Fathers and Sons Who Both Played in a World Series, One of Whom Played in a Subway Series			
F	Ernie Johnson	NY Yankees - 1923(W)	Johnson hit .447 as a backup (17/38) during the season, but did not bat in the Series
S	Don Johnson	Chicago Cubs - 1945(L)	
F	Clay Bellinger	NY Yankees - 2000(W)	
S	Cody Bellinger	LA Dodgers - 2017(L)/2018(L)	

1923

NEW YORK GIANTS vs. NEW YORK YANKEES

NEW YORK GIANTS

Overall World Series Record: 3 WINS 5 LOSSES. 49 Games Played [25-22 (2 ties) .532]
- Casey Stengel (.417) and Frankie Frisch (.400) were the .400 hitters in the line-up.
- Frisch is the first player to compile a .400+ BA in consecutive Fall Classics (.471 in 1922).
- Frisch did not draw a walk or strikeout.
- Stengel led the team in homers (2), RBIs (4) and walks (4) in addition to tying for most runs scored (3).
- Irish Meusel is the first player to hit for the cycle in a full series twice (1921).
- John McGraw's record falls to 3-5.
- Only MLB team with five World Series losses.

NEW YORK YANKEES

Overall World Series Record: 1 WIN 2 LOSSES, 19 Games Played [7-11 (1 tie) .368]
- Pennock allowed three of the five Giant home runs but had a hand in three of the four victories.
- Bullet Joe Bush and Wally Schang have won four titles for three different teams (1913/14 Philadelphia Athletics/18 Boston Red Sox).
- Babe Ruth and Everett Scott have won four titles for two different clubs 1915/16/18 Boston Red Sox.
- Ruth's three home runs were all solos in the Polo Grounds.
- Ruth, Wally Schang and Aaron Ward stroked a hit in all six games; Schang did not drive in a run.

FUNGOES

- Babe Ruth and Stengel hammered the 10th home run for each franchise.
- Rare for triples (3) to outnumber doubles (2).
- The Bombers both outscored (30-17) and outhit (60-47) the Giants by 13.
- The Yankees' composite BA was .293, compared with .234 for the Giants.
- Game 5 was the only game played in less than two hours.
- First Fall Classic to collect one million dollars in receipts.
- The AL leads the overall World Series Standings 12-8.

SIX-GAME DATA

TIME	**10:17**	PLAYERS POOL	**$368,783**
ATTENDANCE	**301,430**	SHARES	**NEW YORK GIANTS - $4,113**
			NEW YORK YANKEES - $6,143

55

1923

NEW YORK GIANTS vs. NEW YORK YANKEES

New York Giants Composite Stats

BATTING	G	AB	R	H	RBI	2B	3B	HR	BB	SO	BA	OBP	SLG	OPS
Frankie Frisch	6	25	2	10	1	0	1	0	0	0	.400	.400	.480	.880
Irish Meusel	6	25	3	7	2	1	1	1	0	2	.280	.280	.520	.800
Dave Bancroft	6	24	1	2	1	0	0	0	1	2	.083	.120	.083	.203
Ross Youngs	6	23	2	8	3	0	0	1	2	0	.348	.400	.478	.878
Heinie Groh	6	22	3	4	2	0	1	0	3	1	.182	.280	.273	.553
High Pockets Kelly	6	22	1	4	1	0	0	0	1	2	.182	.217	.182	.399
Frank Snyder	5	17	1	2	2	0	0	1	0	2	.118	.118	.294	.412
Casey Stengel	6	12	3	5	4	0	0	2	4	0	.417	.563	.917	1.479
Bill Cunningham	4	7	0	1	1	0	0	0	0	1	.143	.143	.143	.286
Art Nehf	2	6	0	1	0	0	0	0	0	4	.167	.167	.167	.333
Jack Bentley	5	5	0	3	0	1	0	0	0	0	.600	.600	.800	1.400
Hank Gowdy	3	4	0	0	0	0	0	0	1	0	.000	.200	.000	.200
Hugh McQuillan	2	3	0	0	0	0	0	0	0	1	.000	.000	.000	.000
Rosy Ryan	3	2	0	0	0	0	0	0	0	1	.000	.000	.000	.000
Virgil Barnes	2	1	0	0	0	0	0	0	0	1	.000	.000	.000	.000
Travis Jackson	1	1	0	0	0	0	0	0	0	0	.000	.000	.000	.000
Jimmy O'Connell	2	1	0	0	0	0	0	0	0	1	.000	.500	.000	.500
Jack Scott	2	1	0	0	0	0	0	0	0	0	.000	.000	.000	.000
Dinty Gearin	1	0	0	0	0	0	0	0	0	0				
Claude Jonnard	2	0	0	0	0	0	0	0	0	0				
Freddie Maguire	2	0	1	0	0	0	0	0	0	0				
Mule Watson	1	0	0	0	0	0	0	0	0	0				
Totals	**6**	**201**	**17**	**47**	**17**	**2**	**3**	**5**	**12**	**18**	**.234**	**.280**	**.348**	**.629**

PITCHING	G	GS	ERA	W	L	SV	CG	IP	H	R	ER	BB	SO	WHIP
Art Nehf	2	2	2.76	1	1	0	1	16.1	10	5	5	6	7	0.980
Rosy Ryan	3	0	3.86	1	0	0	0	9.1	11	4	4	3	3	1.500
Hugh McQuillan	2	1	5.00	0	1	0	0	9.0	11	5	5	4	3	1.667
Jack Bentley	2	1	9.45	0	1	0	0	6.2	10	8	7	4	1	2.100
Virgil Barnes	2	0	0.00	0	0	0	0	4.2	4	0	0	0	4	0.857
Jack Scott	2	1	12.00	0	1	0	0	3.0	9	5	4	1	2	3.333
Claude Jonnard	2	0	0.00	0	0	0	0	2.0	1	0	0	1	1	1.000
Mule Watson	1	1	13.50	0	0	0	0	2.0	4	3	3	1	1	2.500
Totals	**6**	**6**	**4.75**	**2**	**4**	**0**	**1**	**53.0**	**60**	**30**	**28**	**20**	**22**	**1.509**

1923

NEW YORK GIANTS vs. NEW YORK YANKEES

New York Yankees Composite Stats

BATTING	G	AB	R	H	RBI	2B	3B	HR	BB	SO	BA	OBP	SLG	OPS
Bob Meusel	6	26	1	7	8	1	2	0	0	3	.269	.269	.462	.731
Joe Dugan	6	25	5	7	5	2	1	1	3	0	.280	.357	.560	.917
Whitey Witt	6	25	1	6	4	2	0	0	1	1	.240	.269	.320	.589
Aaron Ward	6	24	4	10	2	0	0	1	1	3	.417	.440	.542	.982
Wally Schang	6	22	3	7	0	1	0	0	1	2	.318	.348	.364	.711
Everett Scott	6	22	2	7	3	0	0	0	0	1	.318	.318	.318	.636
Wally Pipp	6	20	2	5	1	0	0	0	4	1	.250	.375	.250	.625
Babe Ruth	6	19	8	7	3	1	1	3	8	6	.368	.556	1.000	1.556
Bullet Joe Bush	4	7	2	3	1	1	0	0	1	1	.429	.500	.571	1.071
Herb Pennock	3	6	0	0	0	0	0	0	0	2	.000	.143	.000	.143
Bob Shawkey	1	3	0	1	1	0	0	0	0	0	.333	.333	.333	.667
Sad Sam Jones	2	2	0	0	0	0	0	0	0	1	.000	.000	.000	.000
Fred Hofmann	2	1	0	0	0	0	0	0	1	0	.000	.500	.000	.500
Hinkey Haines	2	1	1	0	0	0	0	0	0	0	.000	.000	.000	.000
Harvey Hendrick	1	1	0	0	0	0	0	0	0	0	.000	.000	.000	.000
Waite Hoyt	1	1	0	0	0	0	0	0	0	1	.000	.000	.000	.000
Ernie Johnson	2	0	1	0	0	0	0	0	0	0				
Totals	**6**	**205**	**30**	**60**	**28**	**8**	**4**	**5**	**20**	**22**	**.293**	**.358**	**.444**	**.802**

PITCHING	G	GS	ERA	W	L	SV	CG	IP	H	R	ER	BB	SO	WHIP
Herb Pennock	3	2	3.63	2	0	1	1	17.1	19	7	7	1	8	1.154
Bullet Joe Bush	3	1	1.08	1	1	0	1	16.2	7	2	2	4	5	0.660
Sad Sam Jones	2	1	0.90	0	1	1	0	10.0	5	1	1	2	3	0.700
Bob Shawkey	1	1	3.52	1	0	0	0	7.2	12	3	3	4	2	2.087
Waite Hoyt	1	1	15.43	0	0	0	0	2.1	4	4	4	1	0	2.143
Totals	**6**	**6**	**2.83**	**4**	**2**	**2**	**2**	**54.0**	**47**	**17**	**17**	**12**	**18**	**1.093**

1936

GIANTS   NY

NEW YORK GIANTS   vs.   NEW YORK YANKEES

FUNGOES

- ⚾ 13 years since the last Subway Series, fifth overall.
- ⚾ Both teams in second place at the All-Star break.
- ⚾ Both league MVPs - the Yankees' 1B Lou Gehrig and Giants' Carl Hubbell – are in Series.
- ⚾ Mark Koenig (Giants) and Pat Malone (Yankees) were teammates on the 1932 pennant-winning Chicago Cubs.
- ⚾ One 20-game winner on each staff and three .300 hitters in each line-up.
- ⚾ Umpire data: Harry Geisel was a boxing announcer during the off-season; George Magerkurth was a minor league catcher; Cy Pfirman's start in baseball was as a bat boy. He began umpiring professionally at age 19; Bill Summers was a former boxer, mill worker and road worker. He umpired in high school, semi-pro and industrial league games.

SERIES SUMMARY

Thirteen years had passed since the last Subway Series, during which New York continued to cement its reputation as the World Series capitol of baseball. In that time period, the Yankees appeared in four Fall Classics, winning three, while the Giants went one and one.

1936 was the Yankees' first World Series without Babe Ruth. Their offense was still high-powered, led by Lou Gehrig and four other who surpassed 100 RBI, including a phenomal rookie named Joe DiMaggio. Even so, Hall of Famer Carl Hubbell shut them down in Game 1, allowing only a single run.

Game 2 was a complete reversal. Pinstripers reached base in every inning and scored in five of them, plating a Series record-setting total of 18 runs off five different Giants pitchers. Yankees ace Lefty Gomez collected a complete-game victory on the mound for the Bombers.

Viewers of Game 3 saw a lot of hitting, but only three runs, including a solo home run by each team. Giants starter, the veteran

Freddie Fitzsimmons, threw a complete game, but an infield hit in the bottom of the eighth was the difference in the game.

In Game 4, the Yanks got their revenge against Carl Hubbell. A three-run third inning, led by Lou Gehrig's two-run blast, was all the Bombers needed as Monte Pearson went the distance and allowed only two runs, putting the Giants on the brink of elimination.

The Giants managed to stay alive in Game 5, but it took extra innings. The Yankees' Red Ruffing fell behind by allowing three in the first, and then let the Giants tie it up in the sixth. The National League New Yorkers were led by outfielder Jo-Jo Moore, who scored in the first and last inning after leading them off with a double.

Game 6 was another tight, seesaw battle until the ninth inning when the Yankees took a 1-run lead and turned it into an eight-run difference, putting to rest any doubt that theirs was one of the great teams ever assembled.

--- **THE TEAMS** ---

NEW YORK GIANTS
92 – 62 .597 +5.0 G

The Team
- Subway Series #4, 11th overall appearance.
- Giants are last team to install a public address system.

The Players
- Nine returning players from the 1933 title team - Kiddo Davis, Freddie Fitzsimmons, Carl Hubbell, Travis Jackson, Gus Mancuso, Mel Ott, Hal Schumacher and Bill Terry.
- Mark Koenig makes his fifth appearance with third team (1926/27/28 Yankees/1932 Chicago Cubs), winning titles in 1927/28 and losing to the Yankees in '32; Mancuso played on three pennant-winning franchises (1930/31 St. Louis Cardinals and the 1933 Giants).
- MVP winner Carl Hubbell went 26-6 with a league-leading ERA of 2.31.
- Ott led the National League with 33 home runs.

The Manager
- Bill Terry is the 15th player-manager to appear, the 11th for the same team.
- Six years earlier, Terry hit .401, the last National Leaguer to achieve that mark.

Top Batters

Pos	Name	AB	R	H	HR	RBI	BA	OPS
2B	Burgess Whitehead	632	99	176	4	47	.278	.673
SS	Dick Bartell	510	71	152	8	42	.298	.773
OF	Mel Ott	534	120	175	33	135	.328	1.036
OF	Jo-Jo Moore	649	110	205	7	63	.316	.779

Top Pitchers

Pos	Name	W	L	ERA	G	SV	IP	SO
St	Carl Hubbell	26	6	2.31	42	3	304.0	123
St	Al Smith	14	13	3.78	43	2	209.1	89
R-St	Frank Gabler	9	8	3.12	43	6	161.2	46
R-St	Harry Gumbert	11	3	3.90	39	0	140.2	52

NEW YORK YANKEES
102 – 51 .667 +19.5 G

The Team
- Subway Series #4, 8th overall appearance.
- Fourth season winning 100 games.

The Players
- Fifth appearance for Lou Gehrig and Tony Lazzeri (1926/27/28/32), three titles (1927/28/32).
- First appearance without Babe Ruth - first with rookie Joe DiMaggio.
- Gehrig, Lazzeri, Frank Crosetti, Bill Dickey, Lefty Gomez and Red Ruffing are the six returning players from the 1932 title team.
- MVP winner Lou Gehrig led the major leagues in RBIs, runs scored (167) and home runs (49).
- Gehrig [152], DiMaggio [125], Lazzeri [109], Dickey [107] and George Selkirk [107] combined to drive in 600 runs.

The Manager
- Joe McCarthy's third career appearance, second as a Yankee skipper.
- McCarthy, a former minor league catcher, is the first to manage in both leagues (1929 Cubs).

Top Batters

Pos	Name	AB	R	H	HR	RBI	BA	OPS
1B	Lou Gehrig	579	167	205	49	152	.354	1.174
SS	Frankie Crosetti	632	137	182	15	78	.288	.824
3B	Red Rolfe	568	116	181	10	70	.319	.884
OF	Joe DiMaggio	637	132	206	29	125	.323	.928

Top Pitchers

Pos	Name	W	L	ERA	G	SV	IP	SO
St	Red Ruffing	20	12	3.85	33	0	271.0	102
St	Monte Pearson	19	7	3.71	33	1	223.0	118
St	Lefty Gomez	13	7	4.39	31	0	188.2	105
Rel	Pat Malone	12	4	3.81	35	9	134.2	72

NEW YORK YANKEES vs. NEW YORK GIANTS

September 30

LINE SCORE	1	2	3	4	5	6	7	8	9	R	H	E
NEW YORK YANKEES	0	0	1	0	0	0	0	0	0	1	7	2
NEW YORK GIANTS	0	0	0	0	1	1	0	4	X	6	9	1

RECAP

Until the bottom of the eighth inning, in a face-off between 20-game winners, the Giants had a fragile one-run lead. After the third out, the lead had expanded to five. Eight Giants batted, four crossed home plate. 2B Burgess Whitehead's walk forced home the first run. 3B Travis Jackson's sac fly plated the second run. Carl Hubbell singled home the third, and Yankee SS Frankie Crosetti's throwing error sent home the fourth. Carl Hubbell's third career World Series victory stopped the Bombers 12-game winning streak.

SCORING SUMMARY

Third Inning - New York Yankees
– Hubbell starting.
– Selkirk slugged a solo shot into the right field seats.
– Ruffing bounced a beebee back to the mound, Hubbell to Terry.
– Crosetti popped up to Whitehead.
– Rolfe stroked a single into left field.
– DiMaggio singled Rolfe to second base.
– Gehrig rolled out to the box, Hubbell to Terry

1 Runs **3** Hits **0** Errors **2** LOB

YANKEES – 1   **GIANTS – 0**

Fifth Inning - New York Giants
– Ruffing starting.
– Hubbell out on a ground ball, Lazzeri to Gehrig.
– Moore fouled out to Dickey.
– Bartell slugged a solo shot into the left field seats.
– Terry tapped out, Lazzeri to Gehrig.

1 Runs **1** Hits **0** Errors **0** LOB

YANKEES – 1   **GIANTS – 1**

Sixth Inning - New York Giants
– Gus Mancuso drove home Mel Ott from second base (who had doubled) on a single to left field.

1 Runs **1** Hits **0** Errors **0** LOB

Eighth Inning - New York Giants
– Terry knuckled a single into right field.
– Ott bunted Terry to second base.
– Ripple advanced the runners on a sacrifice, Rolfe to Gehrig.
– Mancuso loaded the bases on an intentional walk.
– Whitehead walked, Terry scored; bases loaded.
– Jackson lofted a sacrifice fly to DiMaggio plating Ott.
– Hubbell singled into left field, driving in Mancuso; on Crosetti's wild throw to the plate Whitehead scored as Hubbell slid into second base; on Dickey's throwing error, Hubbell raced over to third.
– Moore out on a grounder, Crosetti to Gehrig.

4 Runs **3** Hits **2** Errors **1** LOB

YANKEES – 1   **GIANTS – 6**

HIGHLIGHTS

• Pinstripe starter Red Ruffing walked in the first Giants run at the start of the four-run, eighth inning rally
• Both starters went the distance
• Hubbell, in posting his third straight Series victory, had two hits
• Hubbell dominated on the mound. Not one of the Yankees' 27 outs was recorded in the outfield

DIAMOND DUST

- Bomber RF George Selkirk is the fifth player to hit a home run in first at-bat and the third to do so in an opener
- Yankee LF Jake Powell, acquired in a mid-season trade with the Washington Senators, is the 8th player to get a hit in first three at-bats
- In openers, the Giants are 7-4 while the Yankees are 5-3.

Game 1 BOX SCORE SUMMARY

NEW YORK YANKEES	AB	R	H	RBI	BB	K	1B	2B	3B	HR	TB	SB
GEORGE SELKIRK, RF	4	1	1	1	0	1	0	0	0	1	4	0

NEW YORK GIANTS	AB	R	H	RBI	BB	K	1B	2B	3B	HR	TB	SB
DICK BARTELL, SS	4	1	2	1	0	0	1	0	0	1	5	0
BILL TERRY, 1B	4	1	2	0	0	0	2	0	0	0	2	0
MEL OTT, RF	2	2	2	0	2	0	1	1	0	0	3	0
GUS MANCUSO, C	3	1	1	1	1	1	1	0	0	0	1	0
BURGESS WHITEHEAD, 2B	3	1	0	1	1	1	0	0	0	0	0	0
TRAVIS JACKSON, 3B	4	0	0	1	0	0	0	0	0	0	0	0
CARL HUBBELL, P	4	0	2	0	0	0	2	0	0	0	2	0

A 1936 World Series program.

NEW YORK YANKEES	IP	H	R	ER	HR	K	BB	HBP	ERA
RED RUFFING L (0-1)	8	9	6	4	1	5	4	0	5.40
NEW YORK GIANTS	IP	H	R	ER	HR	K	BB	HBP	ERA
CARL HUBBELL W (1-0)	9	7	1	1	1	8	1	1	1.00

Red Ruffing was rescued by the Yankees when the cash-strapped Boston Red Sox traded him in 1930 for a secondary player and $50,000. Ruffing had gone 39-96 (.289) for Boston in the first five years of his career. He was a brilliant 231-124 for the Yankees, along with another 7-2 in 10 World Series starts.

Ruffing's career spanned an era of offensive domination, and his career ERA of 3.80 was the highest among Hall of Fame pitchers until Jack Morris (3.90) surpassed him in 2018. Both are considered among the least deserving members who pitched, though his 273 wins, 45 shutouts, and 353 career complete games tell a very positive story.

Ruffing is famous also for being one of the best hitting pitchers of all time. He totaled 36 home runs in his career with a .269 batting average. He was also a frequent pinch hitter, collecting 53 hits in 188 at-bats for a career average of .282 coming off the bench.

GAME TIME:	**2:40**
ATTENDANCE:	**39,419**
BEST OF 7:	**GIANTS - 1 YANKEES - 0**

Game 2

NEW YORK YANKEES vs. NEW YORK GIANTS

October 2

LINE SCORE	1	2	3	4	5	6	7	8	9	R	H	E
NEW YORK YANKEES	2	0	7	0	0	1	2	0	6	18	17	0
NEW YORK GIANTS	0	1	0	3	0	0	0	0	0	4	6	1

RECAP

After US President Franklin Roosevelt, the 32nd Commander-in-Chief, threw out the first pitch, Yankees batters scored first and often. Ten men went to the plate in the third inning, posting a seven spot, adding to the first two plated in the first. Another run scored in the sixth and two more in the seventh. Six more crossed the plate in the ninth inning, resulting in the most lopsided differential in World Series history.

The Bombers lusty hitting included five runs batted in for Bill Dickey and Tony Lazzeri, four runs scored by Frankie Crosetti, a run scored by every Yankee in the lineup, a base hit ripped by every Yankee in the lineup, an RBI for seven, and a grand slam by Lazzeri.

SCORING SUMMARY

First Inning - New York Yankees

– Schumacher starting.
– Crosetti pumped a single into center field.
– Rolfe walked Crosetti to second base.
– DiMaggio bunted to load the bases.
– Gehrig lifted a sacrifice fly to Ott plating Crosetti; Rolfe took third on the throw home; DiMaggio wild pitched to second base.
– Dickey hoisted a sacrifice fly to Leiber plating Rolfe; DiMaggio thrown out at third base, Leiber to Jackson to Bartell.

2 Runs **2** Hits **0** Errors **0** LOB

YANKEES – 2 **GIANTS – 0**

Second Inning - New York Giants

– Gomez starting.
– Mancuso wangled a walk.
– Whitehead flied out to Selkirk.
– Jackson flied out to Selkirk.
– Schumacher walked Mancuso to second; Mancuso scored on a wild pitch.
– Schumacher slid into third base.
– Moore fouled out to Rolfe.

1 Runs **0** Hits **0** Errors **1** LOB

YANKEES – 2 **GIANTS – 1**

Third Inning - New York Yankees

– Crosetti stroked a single into left field.
– Rolfe walked Crosetti to second base.
– DiMaggio dashed to first to load the bases on Jackson's fumble.
– Smith relieved Schumacher.
– Gehrig singled into right field, driving in Crosetti and Rolfe; DiMaggio glided over to third base.
– Dickey singled into right field, driving in DiMaggio; Gehrig hustled to third.
– Selkirk flied out to Leiber; the runners held.
– Powell walked; bases loaded.
– Coffman relieved Smith.
– Lazzeri slammed a grand slam home run into the right field seats, driving in Gehrig, Dickey and Powell.
– Gomez went down on strikes.
– Crosetti rolled out, Bartell to Terry.

7 Runs **4** Hits **1** Errors **0** LOB

YANKEES – 9 **GIANTS – 1**

Fourth Inning - New York Giants

– Mancuso worked a walk.
– Whitehead whiffed.
– Jackson singled Mancuso to second base.
– Davis PH for Coffman, singled to load the bases.

– Moore was a strike out.
– Bartell walked; Mancuso scored; bases loaded.
– Terry singled into left field, driving in Jackson and Davis; Bartell took second.
– Leiber flied out to Powell.

3 Runs **3** Hits **0** Errors **2** LOB

YANKEES – 9   **GIANTS – 4**

Sixth Inning - New York Yankees

– Gomez out on a ground ball, Bartell to Terry.
– Crosetti jogged to first on a free pass.
– Rolfe smacked a hit-and-run single; Crosetti scampered into third base.
– DiMaggio lifted a sacrifice fly to Moore plating Crosetti.
– Gehrig flied out to Ott.

1 Runs **1** Hits **0** Errors **1** LOB

YANKEES – 10   **GIANTS – 4**

Seventh Inning - New York Yankees

– Dickey coaxed a walk.
– Selkirk singled Dickey to second base.
– Powell singled to left field to load the bases.
– Lazzeri lofted sacrifice fly to Leiber plating Dickey; Selkirk darted to third.
– Gomez scored Selkirk on a grounder, Whitehead to Terry.
– Crosetti flied out to Leiber.

2 Runs **2** Hits **0** Errors **1** LOB

YANKEES – 12   **GIANTS – 4**

Ninth Inning - New York Yankees

– Gumbert on the hill.
– Powell got a walk; swiped second base.

– Lazzeri flied to Leiber; Powell took third base.
– Gomez singled up the middle, driving Powell home.
– Crosetti singled Gomez to second base.
– Rolfe caromed a single off of Jackson's glove, driving in Gomez; Crosetti slid into second base.
– DiMaggio singled off of the left field wall, driving in Crosetti; Rolfe moved up.
– Gehrig advanced both runners on a grounder, Jackson to Terry.
– Dickey clobbered a home run into the right field seats, driving home Rolfe and DiMaggio.
– Selkirk struck out.

6 Runs **5** Hits **0** Errors **0** LOB

YANKEES – 18   **GIANTS – 4**

HIGHLIGHTS

- The Yankees' two sac flies in the first inning was the second two-SF inning in Series history (Yankees, 1927)
- Gus Mancuso scored the Giants' first run from second base on a Lefty Gomez wild pitch
- Mancuso drew lead-off walks in the second and fourth frames and scored the Giants' first two runs
- Second consecutive game in which the Giants scored on a bases loaded walk
- The Yankees received nine walks and were struck out only three times
- 14 of the Yankees 17 hits were singles
- There was a grand total of 23 base hits and 16 walks
- DiMaggio caught the final out of Hank Lieber's 400 ft. line drive while running up the stairs of the clubhouse
- Rain delayed the game for one day, and it was still raining when the game was played

DIAMOND DUST

- Hal Schumacher is the sixth pitcher with a regular season losing record (11-13) to start and the fifth to lose
- 2B Tony Lazzeri's grand slam is the second in history; Elmer Smith of the Cleveland Indians hit the first, in 1920
- Lazzeri and C Bill Dickey are first teammates to drive in five runs each in the same game
- Records were set for most run scored by both teams (22), most runs scored by one team and driven in (18)

Game 2 BOX SCORE SUMMARY

NEW YORK YANKEES	AB	R	H	RBI	BB	K	1B	2B	3B	HR	TB	SB
FRANK CROSETTI, SS	5	4	3	0	1	0	3	0	0	0	3	0
RED ROLFE, 3B	4	3	2	1	2	0	2	0	0	0	2	0
JOE DIMAGGIO, CF	5	2	3	2	0	0	2	1	0	0	4	0
LOU GEHRIG, 1B	5	1	2	3	1	0	2	0	0	0	2	0
BILL DICKEY, C	5	3	2	5	1	0	1	0	0	1	5	0
GEORGE SELKIRK, RF	5	1	1	0	1	1	1	0	0	0	1	0
JAKE POWELL, LF	3	2	2	0	2	0	2	0	0	0	2	0
TONY LAZZERI, 2B	4	1	1	5	1	0	0	0	0	1	4	0
LEFTY GOMEZ, P	5	1	1	2	0	2	1	0	0	0	1	0
NEW YORK GIANTS	AB	R	H	RBI	BB	K	1B	2B	3B	HR	TB	SB
DICK BARTELL, SS	3	0	1	1	2	1	0	1	0	0	2	0
BILL TERRY, 1B	5	0	2	2	0	1	2	0	0	0	2	0
GUS MANCUSO, C	2	2	1	0	2	1	0	1	0	0	2	0
TRAVIS JACKSON, 3B	4	1	1	0	0	0	1	0	0	0	1	0
KIDDO DAVIS, PH	1	1	1	0	0	0	1	0	0	0	1	0

NEW YORK YANKEES	IP	H	R	ER	HR	K	BB	HBP	ERA
LEFTY GOMEZ W (1-0)	9	6	4	4	0	8	7	0	4.00
NEW YORK GIANTS	IP	H	R	ER	HR	K	BB	HBP	ERA
HAL SCHUMACHER L (0-1)	2	3	5	4	0	1	4	0	18.00
AL SMITH	0.1	2	3	3	0	0	1	0	81.00
DICK COFFMAN	1.2	2	1	1	1	1	0	0	5.40
FRANK GABLER	4	5	3	3	0	0	3	0	6.75
HARRY GUMBERT	1	5	6	6	1	1	1	0	54.00

GAME TIME: **2:49**
ATTENDANCE: **43,543**
BEST OF 7:   **GIANTS - 1   YANKEES - 1**

Game 3

NEW YORK GIANTS vs. NEW YORK YANKEES

October 3

LINE SCORE	1	2	3	4	5	6	7	8	9	R	H	E
NEW YORK GIANTS	0	0	0	0	1	0	0	0	0	1	11	0
NEW YORK YANKEES	0	1	0	0	0	0	0	1	X	2	4	0

RECAP

Another sellout crowd watched a game that was the complete opposite of the previous one. Both starters held the opposition scoreless for long stretches, including a number of three up and three down frames. Both starters gave up solo home runs; Yankee 1B Lou Gehrig off of Freddie Fitzsimmons; Giants CF Jimmy Ripple off of hometown hurler Bump Hadley. Hadley gave up 10 hits and that run. Fitzsimmons gave up four hits and two runs. The Pinstripers are on a two-game winning streak.

SCORING SUMMARY

Second Inning - New York Yankees

– Fitzsimmons starting.
– Gehrig slugged a solo shot into the right field seats.
– Dickey trotted to first on a walk.
– Selkirk fouled out to Mancuso.
– Powell tapped into double play, Bartell to Whitehead to Terry.

1 Runs **1** Hits **0** Errors **0** LOB

GIANTS – 0   **YANKEES – 1**

Fifth Inning - New York Giants

– Ripple slugged a solo shot into the right field crowd.
– Mancuso sizzled a single through the shortstop spot.
– Whitehead forced Mancuso at second base, Gehrig to Crosetti; Whitehead thrown out trying to steal second base, Dickey to Crosetti.
– Jackson reached first on a free pass.
– Fitzsimmons blistered a hit-and-run single; Jackson loped into third.
– Moore thrown out on a comebacker, Hadley to Gehrig.

1 Runs **3** Hits **0** Errors **2** LOB

GIANTS – 1   **YANKEES – 1**

Eighth Inning - New York Yankees

– Selkirk stroked a single into right field.
– Powell walked Selkirk to second base.
– Lazzeri moved up both runners on a sacrifice, Jackson to Whitehead.
– Ruffing PH for Hadley, sped to first base on a fielder's choice; Selkirk gunned down at the plate, Fitzsimmons to Mancuso.
– Johnson PR for Ruffing.
– Crosetti cuffed a single off of Fitzsimmons's glove, driving in Powell; Johnson slid into second base.
– Rolfe tapped out, Terry to Fitzsimmons.

1 Runs **2** Hits **0** Errors **2** LOB

GIANTS – 1   **YANKEES – 2**

DIAMOND DUST

• Lou Gehrig is the second player to homer in the Mid-Summer Classic and the Fall Classic in the same season
• Gehrig's homer is the 140th in World Series history

Game 3 BOX SCORE SUMMARY

NEW YORK GIANTS	AB	R	H	RBI	BB	K	1B	2B	3B	HR	TB	SB
JIMMY RIPPLE, CF	4	1	1	1	0	1	0	0	0	1	4	0
NEW YORK YANKEES	AB	R	H	RBI	BB	K	1B	2B	3B	HR	TB	SB
FRANK CROSETTI, SS	4	0	1	1	0	1	1	0	0	0	1	0
JOE DIMAGGIO, CF	3	0	1	0	0	0	0	1	0	0	2	0
LOU GEHRIG, 1B	3	1	1	1	0	0	0	0	0	1	4	0
JAKE POWELL, LF	2	1	0	0	1	1	0	0	0	0	0	0

NEW YORK GIANTS	IP	H	R	ER	HR	K	BB	HBP	ERA
FRED FITZSIMMONS L (0-1)	8	4	2	2	1	5	2	0	2.25
NEW YORK YANKEES	IP	H	R	ER	HR	K	BB	HBP	ERA
BUMP HADLEY W (1-0)	8	10	1	1	1	2	1	0	1.13
PAT MALONE S (1)	1	1	0	0	0	1	0	0	0.00

GAME TIME:	**2:01**
ATTENDANCE:	**64,842**
BEST OF 7:	**GIANTS - 1 YANKEES - 2**

NEW YORK GIANTS vs. NEW YORK YANKEES

October 4

LINE SCORE	1	2	3	4	5	6	7	8	9	R	H	E
NEW YORK GIANTS	0	0	0	1	0	0	0	1	0	2	7	1
NEW YORK YANKEES	0	1	3	0	0	0	0	1	X	5	10	1

RECAP

New York Giants moundsman Carl Hubbell did not have the same stuff he had in the opening game. The Yankees blistered his offerings for eight hits and four runs. Frankie Crosetti, Red Rolfe, Lou Gehrig and Monte Pearson, the winning pitcher, all stroked two hits. The one-run margin bulged to four in the bottom of the third inning when Crosetti doubled, Rolfe singled and Gehrig clocked a home run into the right field seats. On the mound Pearson kept the Giants scoring drives down to two, tallying one run each time. The Yankees, on a three-game roll, have the Giants in a two-game hole.

SCORING SUMMARY

Second Inning - New York Yankees

– Hubbell starting.
– Dickey struck out.
– Powell sped across first base on Jackson's miscue.
– Lazzeri moved Powell up on a ground out, Whitehead to Terry.
– Selkirk singled into left field, driving Powell home.
– Pearson flied out to Ripple.

1 Runs **1** Hits **1** Errors **1** LOB

GIANTS – 0   **YANKEES – 1**

Third Inning - New York Yankees

– Crosetti looped a double into right field.
– Rolfe singled up the middle, driving Crosetti home.
– DiMaggio fouled out to Mancuso; Hubbell wild pitched Rolfe to third base.
– Gehrig clocked a home run into the right field seats, driving Rolfe home.
– Dickey flied out to Moore.
– Powell flied out to Ripple (*great catch*).

3 Runs **3** Hits **0** Errors **0** LOB

GIANTS – 0   **YANKEES – 4**

Fourth Inning - New York Giants

– Pearson starting.
– Bartell cranked a single into right field.
– Terry walked Bartell to second base.
– Ott forced Terry at second base, Crosetti to Lazzeri; Bartell slid into third.
– Ripple singled into left field, driving in Bartell; Ott made it to second.
– Mancuso forced Ripple at second base, Lazzeri to Crosetti; Ott moved up.
– Whitehead popped up to Crosetti.

1 Runs **2** Hits **0** Errors **2** LOB

GIANTS – 1   **YANKEES – 4**

Eighth Inning - New York Giants

- Leslie PH for Hubbell, stroked a single into left field.
- Davis PR.
- Moore singled Davis to second base.
- Bartell advanced both runners on a ground out, Lazzeri to Pearson.
- Terry scored Davis on a grounder, Lazzeri to Gehrig; Moore took third base.
- Ott out on a ground ball, Rolfe to Gehrig.

1 Runs **2** Hits **0** Errors **1** LOB

GIANTS – 2   **YANKEES – 4**

Eighth Inning - New York Yankees

- Gabler pitching.
- Gehrig clubbed a double into right field.
- Dickey grounded out, Bartell to Terry; Gehrig slid into third base.
- Powell singled into left field, driving Gehrig home.
- Lazzeri advanced Powell on a ground ball, Jackson to Terry.
- Selkirk drew a walk.
- Pearson rolled out, Jackson to Terry.

1 Runs **2** Hits **0** Errors **2** LOB

GIANTS – 2   **YANKEES – 5**

HIGHLIGHTS

- 60,000+ crowd again
- Only three Bombers went hitless
- 1B Lou Gehrig drove in two and scored two on two hits, both for extra bases (double/homer)
- Monte Pearson gave up seven hits, all singles
- Pearson's first career World Series win is Carl Hubbell's first career loss

---

DIAMOND DUST

- Pinch hitter Mark Koenig has stroked a hit for three different teams – the Yankees, the Cubs, and the NY Giants
- Gehrig is the seventh player to homer in consecutive games

Game 4 BOX SCORE SUMMARY

NEW YORK GIANTS	AB	R	H	RBI	BB	S0	1B	2B	3B	HR	TB	SB
JO-JO MOORE, LF	3	0	1	0	1	1	1	0	0	0	1	0
BILL TERRY, 1B	3	0	0	1	1	2	0	0	0	0	0	0
JIMMY RIPPLE, CF	4	0	2	1	0	0	2	0	0	0	2	0
KIDDO DAVIS, PR	0	1	0	0	0	0	0	0	0	0	0	0
NEW YORK YANKEES	AB	R	H	RBI	BB	S0	1B	2B	3B	HR	TB	SB
FRANK CROSETTI, SS	4	1	2	0	0	0	1	1	0	0	3	0
RED ROLFE. 3B	3	1	2	1	1	0	2	0	0	0	2	0
LOU GEHRIG, 1B	4	2	2	2	0	0	0	1	0	1	6	0
JAKE POWELL, LF	4	1	1	1	0	0	1	0	0	0	1	0
GEORGE SELKIRK, RF	3	0	1	1	1	1	1	0	0	0	1	0

NEW YORK GIANTS	IP	H	R	ER	HR	K	BB	HBP	ERA
CARL HUBBELL L (1-1)	7	8	4	3	1	2	1	0	2.25
FRANK GABLER	1	2	1	1	0	0	1	0	7.20
NEW YORK YANKEES	IP	H	R	ER	HR	K	BB	HBP	ERA
MONTE PEARSON W (1-0)	9	7	2	2	0	7	2	0	2.00

GAME TIME: **2:12**
ATTENDANCE: **66,669**
BEST OF 7:   **GIANTS - 1   YANKEES - 3**

NEW YORK GIANTS vs. NEW YORK YANKEES

October 4

LINE SCORE	1	2	3	4	5	6	7	8	9	10	R	H	E
NEW YORK GIANTS	3	0	0	0	0	1	0	0	0	1	5	8	3
NEW YORK YANKEES	0	1	1	0	0	2	0	0	0	0	4	10	1

RECAP

In the first inning the Giants jumped out to a three-run lead. The Pinstripers got one back in the second and another in the third. In the sixth the Giants added one and the Yanks added two for a four-all tie. In the top of the 10th, Jo-Jo Moore doubled and was sacrificed home by Dick Bartell and Bill Terry to give the Giants the lead which was sealed in the bottom of the inning when Yankee PR Bob Seeds was caught stealing for the 30th out. Giants starter Hal Schumacher's 10-strikeout performance stopped the National Leaguers' three-game losing streak.

SCORING SUMMARY

First Inning - New York Giants

– Ruffing starting.
– Moore lashed a doubled into left field.
– Bartell doubled into right field, driving Moore home.
– Terry was a strike out.
– Ott grounded out, Crosetti to Gehrig; Bartell slid into third base.
– Ripple singled into left field, driving Bartell home.
– Mancuso smoked a hit-and-run single; Ripple bolted over to third base.
– Whitehead singled into right field, driving in Ripple; Mancuso slid into second.
– Jackson flied out to DiMaggio.

3 Runs **5** Hits **0** Errors **2** LOB

GIANTS – 3   **YANKEES – 0**

Second Inning - New York Yankees

– Schumacher starting.
– Gehrig ripped a single into right field; ended up at third on Ott's fielding error.
– Dickey hit into a double play, Schumacher to Terry to Mancuso.
– Selkirk slugged a solo shot into the right field stands.
– Powell flied out to Ripple.

1 Runs **2** Hits **1** Errors **0** LOB

GIANTS – 3   **YANKEES – 1**

Third Inning - New York Yankees

– Lazzeri sprinted to first on a free pass.
– Ruffing walked Lazzeri to second base; Schumacher advanced both runners on a wild pitch.
– Crosetti crossed first as Lazzeri raced across the plate on Bartell's throwing error; Ruffing stayed put.
– Rolfe bunted to load the bases.
– DiMaggio struck out.
– Gehrig struck out.
– Dickey flied out to Ott.

1 Runs **0** Hits **1** Errors **3** LOB

GIANTS – 3   **YANKEES – 2**

Sixth Inning - New York Giants

– Ott buzzed a single into left field.
– Ripple walked Ott to second base.
– Mancuso advanced the runners on a sacrifice, Ruffing to Lazzeri.
– Whitehead sped across first base, Ott scored as Ripple raced to third base on Crosetti's fielding error.
– Jackson was a strike out.
– Schumacher was a strike out.

1 Runs **1** Hits **1** Errors **2** LOB

GIANTS – 4   **YANKEES – 2**

Sixth Inning - New York Yankees

– Gehrig squibbed out, Whitehead to Terry.
– Dickey fanned.
– Selkirk cued a single into right field.
– Powell safe at first base on an infield single; on Jackson's off-target throw Selkirk slid across the plate; Powell wound up at third base.
– Lazzeri singled up the middle, driving Powell home.
– Johnson PH for Ruffing, struck out.

2 Runs **2** Hits **1** Errors **1** LOB

GIANTS – 4   **YANKEES – 4**

Tenth Inning - New York Giants

– Moore dumped a double into left field.
– Bartell sacrificed Moore to third base, Rolfe to Lazzeri.
– Terry lifted a sacrifice fly to DiMaggio plating Moore.
– Ott popped up to Rolfe.

1 Runs **1** Hits **0** Errors **0** LOB

GIANTS – 5   **YANKEES – 4**

HIGHLIGHTS

- Schumacher, in the third inning, worked out of a bases loaded, no out jam
- Schumacher is the first starter with a losing regular season record to win a Fall Classic game
- SS Frank Crosetti, at the top of the Yankee batting order and Schumacher, at the bottom of the Giants batting order, struck out three times each
- Yankee CF Joe DiMaggio hit into his third double play of the Series

DIAMOND DUST

- 19th extra inning game
- Giants starter Hal Schumacher is the first pitcher with a regular season losing record (11-13) to start twice in a Series
- Pat Malone, who pitched in relief, is the first pitcher to lose in both leagues (Cubs - 1929, 1932)

Game 5 BOX SCORE SUMMARY

NEW YORK GIANTS	AB	R	H	RBI	BB	K	1B	2B	3B	HR	TB	SB
JO-JO MOORE, LF	5	2	2	0	0	0	0	2	0	0	4	0
DICK BARTELL, SS	4	1	1	1	0	2	0	1	0	0	2	0
BILL TERRY, 1B	5	0	0	1	0	1	0	0	0	0	0	0
MEL OTT, RF	5	1	1	0	0	0	1	0	0	0	1	0
JIMMY RIPPLE, CF	2	1	1	1	2	1	1	0	0	0	1	0
BURGESS WHITEHEAD, 2B	4	0	1	1	0	0	1	0	0	0	1	0

NEW YORK YANKEES	AB	R	H	RBI	BB	K	1B	2B	3B	HR	TB	SB
FRANK CROSETTI, SS	5	0	0	1	0	3	0	0	0	0	0	0
GEORGE SELKIRK, RF	4	2	2	1	1	0	1	0	0	1	5	0
JAKE POWELL, LF	4	1	1	0	1	1	1	0	0	0	1	0
TONY LAZZERI, 2B	3	1	1	1	1	0	1	0	0	0	1	0

NEW YORK GIANTS	IP	H	R	ER	HR	K	BB	HBP	ERA
HAL SCHUMACHER W (1-1)	10	10	4	3	1	10	6	0	5.25

NEW YORK YANKEES	IP	H	R	ER	HR	K	BB	HBP	ERA
RED RUFFING	6	7	4	4	0	7	1	0	5.14
PAT MALONE L (0-1)	4	1	1	1	0	1	0	0	1.80

GAME TIME:	**2:45**	
ATTENDANCE:	**50,024**	
BEST OF 7:	**GIANTS - 2**	**YANKEES - 3**

Game 6

NEW YORK YANKEES vs. NEW YORK GIANTS

October 6

LINE SCORE	1	2	3	4	5	6	7	8	9	R	H	E
NEW YORK YANKEES	0	2	1	2	0	0	0	1	7	13	17	2
NEW YORK GIANTS	2	0	0	0	1	0	1	1	0	5	9	1

RECAP

The Yankees line-up battered four Giant pitchers for 17 hits and 13 runs. Four Pinstripers stroked three base hits. Three scored two runs. LF Jake Powell had an outstanding day. In five at-bats, one of his three hits was a two-run home run. He scored three times and drove in four. Still, in the top of the ninth inning, the Giants were only down by one until the Bombers batted around producing seven runs.

Happy eights. Of the 10 Yankees to bat, eight scored at least once, eight had at least one base hit, and eight drove in at least one run. The difference in runs was eight, same as the difference in hits. This was the Yankees eighth title, their won loss record is 5-3.

SCORING SUMMARY

First Inning - New York Giants

– Gomez starting.
– Moore snapped a single over the third base bag.
– Bartell walked Moore to second base.
– Terry sacrificed the runners up, Rolfe to Gehrig.
– Leiber filled the bases on a walk.
– Ott doubled into right field, driving in Moore and Bartell; Leiber slid into third.
– Mancuso fouled out to Rolfe.
– Whitehead nubbed out, Lazzeri to Gehrig.

2 Runs **2** Hits **0** Errors **2** LOB

YANKEES – 0   **GIANTS – 2**

Second Inning - New York Yankees

– Fitzsimmons starting.
– Gehrig flied out to Leiber.
– Dickey flied out to Moore.
– Selkirk tomahawked a triple into deep right-center field.
– Powell powered a home run into the upper left field deck, driving Selkirk home.
– Lazzeri singled up the middle.
– Gomez thrown out on a comebacker, Fitzsimmons to Terry.

2 Runs **3** Hits **0** Errors **1** LOB

YANKEES – 2   **GIANTS – 2**

Third Inning - New York Yankees

– Crosetti struck out.
– Rolfe spun a single into left field.
– DiMaggio hitched a hit-and-run single; Rolfe stopped at third base.
– Gehrig lifted a sacrifice fly to Ott plating Rolfe.
– Dickey flied out to Moore.

1 Runs **1** Hits **0** Errors **1** LOB

YANKEES – 3   **GIANTS – 2**

Fourth Inning - New York Yankees

– Selkirk flied out to Leiber.
– Powell scratched a single into left field.
– Lazzeri singled Powell to second base.
– Gomez singled into left field, driving in Powell; Lazzeri slid into second base.
– Crosetti flied out to Leiber.
– Rolfe singled into right field, driving in Lazzeri; Gomez rumbled into third.
– Castleman relieved Fitzsimmons.
– DiMaggio flied out to Ott.

2 Runs **4** Hits **0** Errors **2** LOB

YANKEES – 5   **GIANTS – 2**

Fifth Inning - New York Giants

– Leiber struck out.
– Ott slugged a solo shot into the top of the left field deck.
– Mancuso flied out to DiMaggio.
– Whitehead tapped out to the mound, Gomez to Gehrig.

1 Runs **1** Hits **0** Errors **0** LOB

YANKEES – 5   **GIANTS – 3**

Seventh Inning - New York Giants

– Bartell chucked a double into left field.
– Terry singled Bartell to third base; Bartell scored as Terry slid into second base on DiMaggio's fumble.
– Leiber sacrificed Terry to third base, Rolfe to Lazzeri.
– Ott jogged to first on a walk.
– Murphy relieved Gomez.
– Leslie PH for Mancuso, fouled out to Rolfe.
– Ripple PH for Whitehead, stacked the sacks on a walk.
– Koenig PH for Jackson, was a strike out.

1 Runs **2** Hits **1** Errors **3** LOB

YANKEES – 5   **GIANTS – 4**

Eighth Inning - New York Yankees

– Castleman pitching.
– Dickey drew a base on balls.
– Selkirk singled to right; Dickey to second.
– Powell struck out.
– Lazzari singled to center, Dickey scored, Selkirk to second.
– Murphy was a strike out.
– Crosetti walked to load the bases.
– Rolfe flied out to right.

YANKEES – 6   **GIANTS – 4**

Eighth Inning - New York Giants

– Davis PH for Castleman, flied out to Powell.
– Moore slugged a solo shot into the right field seats.
– Bartell popped up to Lazzeri.
– Terry tapped out, Lazzeri to Gehrig.

1 Runs **1** Hits **0** Errors **0** LOB

YANKEES – 6   **GIANTS – 5**

Ninth Inning - New York Yankees

– Coffman pitching.
– DiMaggio lopped a single over the third base bag.
– Gehrig smashed a hit-and-run single; DiMaggio ended up at third base.
– Dickey safe at first base on a fielder's choice; on Danning's fielding error DiMaggio dashed across home plate; Gehrig and Dickey advanced.
– Selkirk walked on four purpose pitches; bases loaded.
– Powell singled into left field, driving in Gehrig and Dickey; Selkirk took third.
– Gumbert relieved Coffman.
– Lazzeri drew a walk; bases loaded. Murphy singled into right field, driving in Selkirk; bases loaded.
– Crosetti walked; Powell scored; bases loaded.
– Rolfe scored Lazzeri on a force of Crosetti at second base, Bartell to Koenig.
– Murphy slid into third base.
– DiMaggio singled up the middle, driving in Murphy; Rolfe took second.
– Gehrig walked; bases loaded.
– Dickey was a strike out.
– Selkirk skied out to Ripple.

7 Runs **5** Hits **1** Errors **3** LOB

YANKEES – 13   **GIANTS – 5**

HIGHLIGHTS

• In the ninth inning, the Yankees one-run lead exploded into eight
• 14 men batted, as Joe DiMaggio, Lou Gehrig, Bill Dickey, and George Selkirk batted twice
• DiMaggio singled twice; the bases were loaded five times
• Yankee LF Jake Powell compiled six total bases, drove in four runs, stroked three hits and scored three runs
• A combined 18 runs scored and 26 hits bounced in and out of the ball park with the Yankees racking up double digits in both categories

DIAMOND DUST

• Eighth six-game set; first time two in-a-row
• Gomez's third straight win in last three starts
• The Bombers bombed a home run in every game

Game 6 BOX SCORE SUMMARY

NEW YORK YANKEES	AB	R	H	RBI	BB	K	1B	2B	3B	HR	TB	SB
FRANK CROSETTI, SS	4	0	0	1	2	1	0	0	0	0	0	0
RED ROLFE, 3B	6	1	3	2	0	0	3	0	0	0	3	0
JOE DIMAGGIO, CF	6	1	3	0	0	0	3	0	0	0	3	0
LOU GEHRIG, 1B	5	1	1	1	1	0	1	0	0	0	1	0
BILL DICKEY, C	5	2	0	0	1	1	0	0	0	0	0	0
GEORGE SELKIRK, RF	5	2	2	0	1	0	1	0	1	0	4	0
JAKE POWELL, LF	5	3	3	4	0	2	2	0	0	1	6	0
TONY LAZZERI, 2B	4	2	3	1	1	1	3	0	0	0	3	0
LEFTY GOMEZ. P	3	0	1	1	0	1	1	0	0	0	1	0
JOHNNY MURPHY, P	2	1	1	0	1	1	1	0	0	0	1	0
NEW YORK GIANTS	AB	R	H	RBI	BB	K	1B	2B	3B	HR	TB	SB
JO-JO MOORE, LF	5	2	2	1	0	0	1	0	0	1	5	0
DICK BARTELL, SS	3	2	2	0	2	0	1	1	0	0	3	0
BILL TERRY, 1B	4	0	1	0	0	0	1	0	0	0	1	0
MEL OTT, RF	4	1	2	3	1	0	0	1	0	1	6	0

NEW YORK YANKEES	IP	H	R	ER	HR	K	BB	HBP	ERA
LEFTY GOMEZ W (2-0)	6.1	8	4	4	1	1	4	0	4.70
JOHNNY MURPHY S (1)	2.2	1	1	1	1	1	1	0	3.38
NEW YORK GIANTS	IP	H	R	ER	HR	K	BB	HBP	ERA
FRED FITZSIMMONS L (0-2)	3.2	9	5	5	1	1	0	0	5.40
SLICK CASTLEMAN	4.1	3	1	1	0	5	2	0	2.08
DICK COFFMAN	0	3	5	5	0	0	1	0	32.40
HARRY GUMBERT	1	2	2	2	0	1	3	0	36.00

Hall of Fame Members in the 1936 World Series

Player	Team	Pos
Bill Dickey	NYY	C
Joe DiMaggio	NYY	CF
Lou Gehrig	NYY	1B
Lefty Gomez	NYY	P
Tony Lazzeri	NYY	2B
Red Ruffing	NYY	P
Carl Hubbell	NYG	P
Travis Jackson	NYG	SS/3B
Mel Ott	NYG	RF/3B
Bill Terry	NYG	1B

The 1936 World Series boasted 10 future Hall of Famers, the most of any Subway Series.

Freddy Fitzsimmons (Fat Freddy) dropped two games in the 1936 World Series, but was a solid major league pitcher for many years, compiling a career record of 217-146 for the Giants and then Dodgers. Fitzsimmons won 18 or more games four times for the Giants, and had a remarkable season at age 38 for the Brooklyn Dodgers, compiling a 16-2 record in only 20 appearances (18 starts). He followed that up in 1941 with a 6-1 2.07 in 12 starts, and then made one more in the 1941 WS against the Yankees, hurling 7 shutout innings in a no-decision, making him one of the few players to play in a Subway Series for 2 different teams.

GAME TIME:	**2:50**
ATTENDANCE:	**38,427**
BEST OF 7:	**YANKEES - 4 GIANTS - 2**

1936

NEW YORK GIANTS vs. NEW YORK YANKEES

NEW YORK GIANTS

Overall World Series Record: 4 WINS 7 LOSSES, 67 Games Played [34-31 (2 ties) .507]

- PH/2B Mark Koenig made his fifth appearance with his third team. His record is 2-3, with two wins as a Yankee (1927/28) and one loss each as a Yankee (1926), Cub (1932), and Giant (1936).
- Dick Bartell led the team in runs scored (5) and base hits (8).
- No stolen bases.
- Bill Terry, playing manager, took the field in all six games, scoring once and driving in five.
- Terry, as a player, lost in 1924 and won in 1933 versus the Washington Senators.
- 7 World Series losses by the Giants is the most for any team.

NEW YORK YANKEES

Overall World Series Record: 5 WINS 3 LOSSES, 44 Games Played [26-17 (1 tie) .591]

- Gomez had 2 wins, and in 15.1 innings, gave up 14 hits and 11 walks; the walks tied a 1918 record.
- Jake Powell had the highest batting average (.455) and swiped the only base.
- Powell led both teams with eight runs scored.
- .400 hitters Powell and Red Rolfe (.400) stroked 10 hits each.
- Rolfe's hits were all singles.
- 43 runs set the record for most scored in a six-game set.
- Joe McCarthy's managerial record is 2-1.

FUNGOES

- MVP match-up: Lou Gehrig batted .292 while Carl Hubbell pitched to .500 W/L record.
- Home run champs Gehrig (MLB) and Mel Ott (NL) hit one each.
- Yankees RF George Selkirk and Giants SS Dick Bartell smacked a hit in each game.
- 20-run differential is the second highest in history to this point.
- The Yankees outhit the Giants by 15, while collecting 25 more total bases.
- The eighth straight six-game contest won by the American League.
- The American League is now 20-13 in World Series history.

SIX-GAME DATA

TIME	15:37	PLAYERS POOL	$460,023
ATTENDANCE	302,924	SHARES	NEW YORK GIANTS - $4,656
			NEW YORK YANKEES - $6,431

1936

NEW YORK GIANTS vs. NEW YORK YANKEES

New York Giants Composite Stats

BATTING	G	AB	R	H	RBI	2B	3B	HR	BB	SO	BA	OBP	SLG	OPS
Jo-Jo Moore	6	28	4	6	1	2	0	1	1	4	.214	.241	.393	.634
Bill Terry	6	25	1	6	5	0	0	0	1	4	.240	.269	.240	.509
Mel Ott	6	23	4	7	3	2	0	1	3	1	.304	.385	.522	.906
Dick Bartell	6	21	5	8	3	3	0	1	4	4	.381	.480	.667	1.147
Travis Jackson	6	21	1	4	1	0	0	0	1	3	.190	.227	.190	.418
Burgess Whitehead	6	21	1	1	2	0	0	0	1	3	.048	.091	.048	.139
Gus Mancuso	6	19	3	5	1	2	0	0	3	3	.263	.364	.368	.732
Jimmy Ripple	5	12	2	4	3	0	0	1	3	3	.333	.467	.583	1.050
Hank Leiber	2	6	0	0	0	0	0	0	2	2	.000	.250	.000	.250
Carl Hubbell	2	6	0	2	0	0	0	0	0	0	.333	.333	.333	.667
Hal Schumacher	2	4	0	0	0	0	0	0	1	3	.000	.200	.000	.200
Freddie Fitzsimmons	2	4	0	2	0	0	0	0	0	1	.500	.500	.500	1.000
Mark Koenig	3	3	0	1	0	0	0	0	0	1	.333	.333	.333	.667
Sam Leslie	3	3	0	2	0	0	0	0	0	0	.667	.667	.667	1.333
Slick Castleman	1	2	0	1	0	0	0	0	0	0	.500	.500	.500	1.000
Harry Danning	2	2	0	0	0	0	0	0	0	1	.000	.000	.000	.000
Kiddo Davis	4	2	2	1	0	0	0	0	0	0	.500	.500	.500	1.000
Eddie Mayo	1	1	0	0	0	0	0	0	0	0	.000	.000	.000	.000
Frank Gabler	2	0	0	0	0	0	0	0	1	0		1.000		
Dick Coffman	2	0	0	0	0	0	0	0	0	0				
Harry Gumbert	2	0	0	0	0	0	0	0	0	0				
Al Smith	1	0	0	0	0	0	0	0	0	0				
Totals	**6**	**203**	**23**	**50**	**19**	**9**	**0**	**4**	**21**	**33**	**.246**	**.317**	**.350**	**.667**

PITCHING	G	GS	ERA	W	L	SV	CG	IP	H	R	ER	BB	SO	WHIP
Carl Hubbell	2	2	2.25	1	1	0	1	16.0	15	5	4	2	10	1.063
Hal Schumacher	2	2	5.25	1	1	0	1	12.0	13	9	7	10	11	1.917
F. Fitzsimmons	2	2	5.40	0	2	0	1	11.2	13	7	7	2	6	1.286
Frank Gabler	2	0	7.20	0	0	0	0	5.0	7	4	4	4	0	2.200
Slick Castleman	1	0	2.08	0	0	0	0	4.1	3	1	1	2	5	1.154
Harry Gumbert	2	0	36.00	0	0	0	0	2.0	7	8	8	4	2	5.500
Dick Coffman	2	0	32.40	0	0	0	0	1.2	5	6	6	1	1	3.600
Al Smith	1	0	81.00	0	0	0	0	0.1	2	3	3	1	0	9.000
Totals	**6**	**6**	**6.79**	**2**	**4**	**0**	**3**	**53.0**	**65**	**43**	**40**	**26**	**35**	**1.717**

1936

NEW YORK GIANTS vs. NEW YORK YANKEES

New York Yankees Composite Stats

BATTING	G	AB	R	H	RBI	2B	3B	HR	BB	SO	BA	OBP	SLG	OPS
Frankie Crosetti	6	26	5	7	3	2	0	0	3	5	.269	.345	.346	.691
Joe DiMaggio	6	26	3	9	3	3	0	0	1	3	.346	.370	.462	.832
Bill Dickey	6	25	5	3	5	0	0	1	3	4	.120	.214	.240	.454
Red Rolfe	6	25	5	10	4	0	0	0	3	1	.400	.464	.400	.864
George Selkirk	6	24	6	8	3	0	1	2	4	4	.333	.429	.667	1.095
Lou Gehrig	6	24	5	7	7	1	0	2	3	2	.292	.393	.583	.976
Jake Powell	6	22	8	10	5	1	0	1	4	4	.455	.538	.636	1.175
Tony Lazzeri	6	20	4	5	7	0	0	1	4	4	.250	.375	.400	.775
Lefty Gomez	2	8	1	2	3	0	0	0	0	3	.250	.250	.250	.500
Red Ruffing	3	5	0	0	0	0	0	0	1	2	.000	.167	.000	.167
Monte Pearson	1	4	0	2	0	1	0	0	0	0	.500	.500	.750	1.250
Bump Hadley	1	2	0	0	0	0	0	0	0	1	.000	.000	.000	.000
Johnny Murphy	1	2	1	1	1	0	0	0	0	1	.500	.500	.500	1.000
Roy Johnson	2	1	0	0	0	0	0	0	0	1	.000	.000	.000	.000
Pat Malone	2	1	0	1	0	0	0	0	0	0	1.000	1.000	1.000	2.000
Bob Seeds	1	0	0	0	0	0	0	0	0	0				
Totals	6	215	43	65	41	8	1	7	26	35	.302	.380	.447	.827

PITCHING	G	GS	ERA	W	L	SV	CG	IP	H	R	ER	BB	SO	WHIP
Lefty Gomez	2	2	4.70	2	0	0	1	15.1	14	8	8	11	9	1.630
Red Ruffing	2	2	5.14	0	1	0	1	14.0	16	10	8	5	12	1.500
Monte Pearson	1	1	2.00	1	0	0	1	9.0	7	2	2	2	7	1.000
Bump Hadley	1	1	1.13	1	0	0	0	8.0	10	1	1	1	2	1.375
Pat Malone	2	0	1.80	0	1	1	0	5.0	2	1	1	1	2	0.600
Johnny Murphy	1	0	3.38	0	0	1	0	2.2	1	1	1	1	1	0.750
Totals	6	6	3.50	4	2	2	3	54.0	50	23	21	21	33	1.315

1937

GIANTS

NEW YORK GIANTS   vs.   NEW YORK YANKEES

FUNGOES

- To this point, 17 of 34 Fall Classics have involved a New York team, with the Yankees having won five and the Giants four.
- Umpire data: George Barr opened the first umpiring school in Hot Springs, Arkansas in 1935; Red Ormsby is a WWI veteran and a former minor league pitcher; Bill Stewart - a four sport athlete, a WWI Navy veteran, and as the head coach of the Chicago Blackhawks, won the 1938 Stanley Cup.

SERIES SUMMARY

New York hosting back-to-back Fall Classics again cemented its reputation as the baseball capital of the world. The Giants featured Mel Ott and two 20-game winners, while the Yankees put forth a Murder's Row perhaps even stronger than the 1927 team, led by Joe DiMaggio and Lou Gehrig, who combined for 325 RBI!

Game 1 was all Yankees, as Lefty Gomez held the Giants to one run, while the Bombers broke open a 1-0 game with seven runs in the sixth inning, not built on power, but on five singles, four walks, and two errors.

The Giants struck first in Game 2 as well, but their first-inning run would be the only one they would plate. The Yankees dominated again in the 6th inning, this time scoring four runs, while adding two the inning before and the inning after. When the dust cleared, it was another 8-1 win for the Pinstripers, who got their second straight complete game from their starter.

The Yankees offense was a bit more modest in Game 3, putting up five runs over innings two through 5, but it was more than enough, as 9-game winner Monte Pearson came within one out of another complete-game win, and the Yankees settled for a 5-1 win. In three games, they had outscored their crosstown rivals 21-3.

All-time great Carl Hubbell stopped the bleeding and a six-run second inning for the Giants allowed him to cruise to a 7-3 victory in Game 4. The highlight historically was a ninth-inning home run by the Yankees' Lou Gehrig, the last World Series long ball of his career in the last World Series inning ever pitched by Hubbell.

Lefty Gomez regained control of things for the Yankees in Game 5, who put up a 2-spot in the fifth inning to break a 2-2 tie. The Giants collected 10 hits in all, but could not break through after the third inning, and the Yankees had their second consecutive convincing World Series win over the Giants.

THE TEAMS

NEW YORK GIANTS
95 – 57, .625 +3.0 G

The Team
- Subway Series #5, 12th overall appearance.
- In second place at the All-Star break.

The Players
- 13 players returning from 1936 Subway Series team: Dick Bartell, Dick Coffman, Harry Danning, Harry Gumbert, Carl Hubbell, Hank Leiber, Sam Leslie, Gus Mancuso, Jo-Jo Moore, Mel Ott, Jimmy Ripple, Hal Schumacher and Burgess Whitehead.
- Hubbell lead the major leagues in wins and the National League in strikeouts (159).
- Mel Ott shared the National League home run lead with 31; he also led the previous season with 33.

Top Batters

Pos	Name	AB	R	H	HR	RBI	BA	OPS
SS	Dick Bartell	516	91	158	14	62	.306	.836
OF	Mel Ott	545	99	160	31	95	.294	.931
OF	Jimmy Ripple	426	70	135	5	66	.317	.782
OF	Jo-Jo Moore	580	89	180	6	57	.310	.804

Top Pitchers

Pos	Name	W	L	ERA	G	SV	IP	SO
St	Carl Hubbell	22	8	3.20	39	4	261.2	159
St-R	Cliff Melton	20	9	2.61	46	7	248.0	142
St	Hal Schumacher	13	12	3.60	38	1	217.2	100
St-R	Slick Castleman	11	6	3.31	23	0	160.1	78

NEW YORK YANKEES
102 – 52, .662 +13.0 G

The Team
- Subway Series #5, 9th overall appearance.
- Second consecutive season winning 100 games, fifth overall.
- In first place at the All-Star break.

The Players
- Lou Gehrig and Tony Lazzeri win sixth pennant (1926/27/28/32/36).
- 13 returning players from the 1936 Subway Series. Gehrig, Lazzeri, Frank Crosetti, Bill Dickey, Lefty Gomez, and Red Ruffing were teammates on the 1932 title team as well.
- Lefty Gomez led the league in wins, ERA (2.33), and strikeouts (194) and is the seventh pitching Triple Crown winner to appear.

Top Batters

Pos	Name	AB	R	H	HR	RBI	BA	OPS
C	Bill Dickey	530	87	176	29	133	.332	.987
1B	Lou Gehrig	569	138	200	37	158	.351	1.116
SS	Frankie Crosetti	611	127	143	11	49	.234	.692
3B	Red Rolfe	648	143	179	4	62	.276	.743
OF	Joe DiMaggio	621	151	215	46	167	.346	1.085

Top Pitchers

Pos	Name	W	L	ERA	G	SV	IP	SO
St	Lefty Gomez	21	11	2.33	34	0	278.1	194
St	Red Ruffing	20	7	2.98	31	0	256.1	131
St	Monte Pearson	9	3	3.17	22	1	144.2	71
Rel	Johnny Murphy	13	4	4.17	39	10	110.0	36

NEW YORK GIANTS vs. NEW YORK YANKEES

October 6

LINE SCORE	1	2	3	4	5	6	7	8	9	R	H	E
NEW YORK GIANTS	0	0	0	0	1	0	0	0	0	1	6	2
NEW YORK YANKEES	0	0	0	0	0	7	0	1	X	8	7	0

RECAP

In a stadium sellout, the Giants started the scoring in the fifth inning on two singles and a double play. The Pinstripers broke the game wide open in the sixth inning. They erupted for seven runs on five hits and four walks. Starter Lefty Gomez, Frankie Crosetti, Red Rolfe and Joe DiMaggio batted twice. Six times the Yankees loaded the bases. Singles and walks and an error were the RBI weapons. DiMaggio drove home Gomez and Crosetti, Bill Dickey drove home Rolfe, George Selkirk drove home Lou Gehrig and Dickey, Hoag scored on an error and Selkirk scored on a walk to Rolfe. A force with the bat and on the mound, Gomez posted fourth straight World Series 'W.'

SCORING SUMMARY

Fifth Inning - New York Giants
– Gomez starting.
– Ripple fisted a single to right.
– McCarthy singled to center; Ripple advanced to third.
– Mancuso bounced into a 6-4-3 double play, with Ripple scoring.
– Whitehead doubled down the right field line.
– Hubbell grounded to first unassisted.

1 Runs **3** Hits **0** Errors **1** LOB

GIANTS – 1   **YANKEES – 0**

Sixth Inning - New York Yankees
– Gomez worked a walk.
– Crosetti singled Gomez to second base; Gomez safe at second on a pick-off as Bartell dropped the ball.
– Rolfe loaded the bases on a left field single.
– DiMaggio singled into left-center field, driving in Gomez and Crosetti; runners advanced on the throw to the plate.
– Gehrig got an intentional walk; bases loaded.
– Dickey scored Rolfe on an infield hit; bases loaded.
– Hoag forced DiMaggio at the plate, Ott to Mancuso; bases loaded.

– Selkirk singled up the middle, driving in Gehrig and Dickey; Hoag jetted into third base.
– Gumbert relieved Hubbell.
– Lazzeri flashed to first as Hoag slid across the plate on Whitehead's juggle; Selkirk pulled up at third base.
– Coffman relieved Gumbert.
– Gomez walked; bases loaded.
– Crosetti flied out to Moore.
– Rolfe walked; Selkirk scored; bases loaded.
– DiMaggio flied out to Leiber.

7 Runs **5** Hits **1** Errors **3** LOB

GIANTS – 1   **YANKEES – 7**

Eighth Inning - New York Yankees
– Smith pitching.
– Lazzeri slugged a solo shot into the left field crowd.
– Gomez flied out to Ripple.
– Crosetti zapped out to Ott.
– Rolfe flied out to Moore.

1 Runs **1** Hits **0** Errors **0** LOB

GIANTS – 1   **YANKEES – 8**

HIGHLIGHTS

- 13 Yankees batted in the sixth inning
- Carl Hubbell gave up seven runs in the 6th, tying the World Series record for most runs allowed in one inning set in 1911 by another NY Giant, George Wiltse
- Hubbell won his other World Series opening game start (1936)
- Lefty Gomez has defeated the Giants in consecutive World Series games (Game 6 1936)
- Of the combined 13 base hits in the game, only two were for extra bases

DIAMOND DUST

- Lefty Gomez is the first pitcher to start and win both the All-Star Game and Game 1 in same season.
- Lefty Gomez is the third pitcher to get two at-bats in an inning, the first to walk twice.
- RF Jimmy Ripple, in the fifth inning, scored the only Giants run on a double play, making him the fourth player to score on a double play in World Series history.
- In openers, the Yankees are 6-3 while the Giants are 7-5
- Game One winners have won it all 23 times.

Game 1 BOX SCORE SUMMARY

NEW YORK GIANTS	AB	R	H	RBI	BB	K	1B	2B	3B	HR	TB	SB
JIMMY RIPPLE, RF	3	1	1	0	1	0	1	0	0	0	1	0
GUS MANCUSO, C	3	0	0	1	0	0	0	0	0	0	0	0
CARL HUBBELL, P	4	0	2	0	0	0	2	0	0	0	2	0

NEW YORK YANKEES	AB	R	H	RBI	BB	K	1B	2B	3B	HR	TB	SB
FRANK CROSETTI, SS	4	1	1	0	1	0	1	0	0	0	1	0
RED ROLFE, 3B	4	1	1	1	1	1	1	0	0	0	1	0
JOE DIMAGGIO, CF	4	0	2	2	0	0	2	0	0	0	2	0
LOU GEHRIG, 1B	2	1	0	0	2	1	0	0	0	0	0	0
BILL DICKEY, C	3	1	1	1	1	0	1	0	0	0	1	0
MYRIL HOAG, LF	4	1	0	0	0	0	0	0	0	0	0	0
GEORGE SELKIRK, RF	4	1	1	2	0	1	1	0	0	0	1	0
TONY LAZZERI, 2B	4	1	1	1	0	1	0	0	0	1	4	0
LEFTY GOMEZ, P	2	1	0	0	2	0	0	0	0	0	0	0

NEW YORK GIANTS	IP	H	R	ER	HR	K	BB	HBP	ERA
CARL HUBBELL L (0-1)	5.1	6	7	4	0	3	3	0	6.75
AL SMITH	1	1	1	1	1	0	0	0	9.00
NEW YORK YANKEES	IP	H	R	ER	HR	K	BB	HBP	ERA
LEFTY GOMEZ W (1-0)	9	6	1	1	0	2	1	0	1.00

Lefty Gomez was 6-0 in his World Series career, the most wins ever by a pitcher with zero defeats.

Gomez won 20 games 4 times in the 1930s, including a 26-5 mark in 1934 when he won the first of his 2 pitching Triple Crowns. He finished his career 189-102, a sparkling .649 W-L percentage.

GAME TIME:	**2:20**
ATTENDANCE:	**60,573**
BEST OF 7:	**GIANTS - 0 YANKEES - 1**

Game 2

NEW YORK GIANTS vs. NEW YORK YANKEES

October 7

LINE SCORE	1	2	3	4	5	6	7	8	9	R	H	E
NEW YORK GIANTS	1	0	0	0	0	0	0	0	0	1	7	0
NEW YORK YANKEES	0	0	0	0	2	4	2	0	X	8	12	0

RECAP

The Giants offense produced one run in the first inning on a Dick Bartell double and a Mel Ott single. It was the only run they scored. New York Yankees starter Red Ruffing pitched a shutout over the next eight innings. Ruffing and his teammates mounted attacks in three straight frames. In the fifth, Tony Lazzeri and Ruffing drove in two runs. In the sixth, Ruffing, George Selkirk and Frankie Crosetti drove in a total of four. In the seventh, both Bill Dickey and Myril Hoag drove in a run. In the first 2 games, the Yankees have outscored the Giants 16-2.

SCORING SUMMARY

First Inning - New York Giants

- Ruffing starting.
- Moore struck out.
- Bartell drilled a double into left field.
- Ott singled into right field, driving in Bartell; Ott slid into second base on the throw home.
- Ripple was a strikeout.
- McCarthy was a strikeout.

1 Runs **2** Hits **0** Errors **1** LOB

GIANTS – 1   **YANKEES – 0**

Fifth Inning - New York Yankees

- Hoag laced a double into right field.
- Selkirk singled into right field, driving Hoag home.
- Lazzeri singled Selkirk to second base.
- Ruffing singled into left field, driving in Selkirk; Lazzeri slid into second base.
- Gumbert relieved Melton.
- Crosetti flied out to Moore.
- Rolfe forced Ruffing at second base, Whitehead to Bartell; Lazzeri advanced.
- DiMaggio was a strikeout.

2 Runs **4** Hits **0** Errors **2** LOB

GIANTS – 1   **YANKEES – 2**

Sixth Inning - New York Yankees

- Gehrig hustled a hit to the hot corner.
- Dickey singled Gehrig to second base.
- Hoag forced Gehrig at third base, McCarthy to Ott.
- Selkirk doubled off of McCarthy's leg, driving home Dickey and Hoag.
- Lazzeri reached on an intentional walk.
- Ruffing doubled into left field, driving home Selkirk and Lazzeri.
- Coffman relieved Gumbert.
- Crosetti advanced Ruffing on a sacrifice fly to Chiozza.
- Rolfe bounced out, Whitehead to McCarthy.

4 Runs **4** Hits **0** Errors **1** LOB

GIANTS – 1   **YANKEES – 6**

Seventh Inning - New York Yankees

- DiMaggio jammed a single into left field.
- Gehrig walked DiMaggio to second base.
- Dickey singled into center field, driving in DiMaggio; Gehrig slid into second.
- Hoag lifted a sacrifice fly to Chiozza plating Gehrig.
- Selkirk forced Dickey at second base, Bartell to Whitehead.
- Lazzeri tapped out, Ott to McCarthy.

2 Runs **2** Hits **0** Errors **1** LOB

GIANTS – 1   **YANKEES – 8**

HIGHLIGHTS

- Yankee starter Red Ruffing drove in three runs, as did RF George Selkirk
- In the 5th inning, Giant hurler Cliff Melton gave up four straight hits and two runs before Harry Gumbert put out the fire in 1-2-3 fashion
- Five Bombers had a two-hit day at the plate
- Frank Crosetti and Red Rolfe, batting first and second in the line-up, are the only Yankees to not score a run, stroke a hit, or drive in a run
- Back-to-back complete games pitched by the Yankee starters who also contributed on offense

DIAMOND DUST

- Giants hurler Cliff Melton is the 14th rookie to start and the sixth to lose

Game 2 BOX SCORE SUMMARY

NEW YORK GIANTS	AB	R	H	RBI	BB	K	1B	2B	3B	HR	TB	SB
DICK BARTELL, SS	4	1	2	0	0	2	1	1	0	0	3	0
MEL OTT, 3B	4	0	1	1	0	0	1	0	0	0	1	0
NEW YORK YANKEES	**AB**	**R**	**H**	**RBI**	**BB**	**K**	**1B**	**2B**	**3B**	**HR**	**TB**	**SB**
JOE DIMAGGIO, CF	4	1	2	0	0	1	2	0	0	0	2	0
LOU GEHRIG, 1B	2	1	1	0	2	0	1	0	0	0	1	0
BILL DICKEY, C	4	1	2	1	0	1	2	0	0	0	2	0
MYRIL HOAG, LF	4	2	1	1	0	0	0	1	0	0	2	0
GEORGE SELKIRK, RF	4	2	2	3	0	0	1	1	0	0	3	0
TONY LAZZERI, 2B	3	1	2	0	1	0	2	0	0	0	2	0
RED RUFFING, P	4	0	2	3	0	0	1	1	0	0	3	0

NEW YORK GIANTS	IP	H	R	ER	HR	K	BB	HBP	ERA
CLIFF MELTON L (0-1)	4	6	2	2	0	2	1	0	4.50
HARRY GUMBERT	1.1	4	4	4	0	1	1	0	27.00
DICK COFFMAN	2.2	2	2	2	0	1	1	0	4.15
NEW YORK YANKEES	**IP**	**H**	**R**	**ER**	**HR**	**K**	**BB**	**HBP**	**ERA**
RED RUFFING W (1-0)	9	7	1	1	0	8	3	0	1.00

Mel Ott (shown above) led the NL in home runs in 1937 for the 4th of 6 times in his career and in bases on balls for the 5th of 6 times. He drove in 95, the first time he had fewer than 100 since 1928, when he collected 77 at age 19. 1937 was Ott's third and last trip to the World Series, where he totaled 4 HR and 10 RBI in 61 career at-bats.

Ott was a member of the Giants at age 17, as manager McGraw wanted to protect his phenom from bad minor league managers and other negative influences. Ott had not developed his power swing at that age, as he failed to homer in 60 at-bats, but he did collect 23 hits, for an amazing average of .383. By age 20, Ott was one of the top stars in baseball, collecting 42 HR and 151 RBI (along with 113 BB and only 38 K),

Ott was one of the game's most popular players during his long career and after, and his death at age 49 in a car crash is regarded as one of the true tragedies in the annals of the game.

GAME TIME:	**2:49**
ATTENDANCE:	**43,543**
BEST OF 7:	**GIANTS - 0 YANKEES - 2**

Game 3

NEW YORK YANKEES vs. NEW YORK GIANTS

October 8

LINE SCORE	1	2	3	4	5	6	7	8	9	R	H	E
NEW YORK YANKEES	0	1	2	1	1	0	0	0	0	5	9	0
NEW YORK GIANTS	0	0	0	0	0	0	1	0	0	1	5	4

RECAP

Yankee starter Monte Pearson pitched a no-hitter through four frames. He lost the shutout in the seventh inning. Pearson allowed the Giants' third hit in the seventh inning when 1B Johnny McCarthy doubled home RF Jimmy Ripple with their only run. Pearson wavered in the bottom of the ninth inning leaving a bases loaded, two-out situation to the bullpen. Johnny Murphy got the last out for the save.

Giants starter Hal Schumacher had no such luck. The Bombers tagged him for all nine hits and all five runs. His second straight World Series loss was the Yankees third straight win.

SCORING SUMMARY

Second Inning - New York Yankees

– Schumacher starting.
– Dickey flied out to Chiozza.
– Selkirk got a free pass.
– Hoag singled Selkirk to second base.
– Lazzeri singled into center field, driving in Selkirk; Hoag pulled up at third.
– Pearson drew a walk to load the bases.
– Crosetti forced Hoag at the plate, Ott to Danning.
– Rolfe fouled out to Danning.

1 Runs **2** Hits **0** Errors **3** LOB

YANKEES – 1   **GIANTS – 0**

Third Inning - New York Yankees

– DiMaggio flied out to Chiozza.
– Gehrig rebounded a single off of the right field fence; took second base on the throw to first base.
– Dickey tripled off of the left field fence, driving Gehrig home.
– Selkirk singled into right field, driving Dickey home.
– Hoag advanced Selkirk on a sacrifice, Ott to McCarthy.
– Lazzeri intentionally walked.
– Pearson was a strikeout.

2 Runs **3** Hits **0** Errors **2** LOB

YANKEES – 3   **GIANTS – 0**

Fourth Inning - New York Yankees

– Crosetti out on a grounder, Ott to McCarthy.
– Rolfe looped a double into right field.
– DiMaggio singled Rolfe to third base.
– Gehrig lifted a sacrifice fly to Moore plating Rolfe.
– Dickey forced DiMaggio at second base, Whitehead to Bartell.

1 Runs **2** Hits **0** Errors **1** LOB

YANKEES – 4   **GIANTS – 0**

Fifth Inning - New York Yankees

– Selkirk safe at first base on McCarthy's fielding error; slid into second base on McCarthy's throwing error.
– Hoag singled Selkirk to third base; Selkirk scored on Chiozza's juggle.
– Lazzeri struck out.
– Pearson bounced out to the mound, Schumacher to McCarthy.
– Crosetti flied out to Moore.

1 Runs **1** Hits **3** Errors **1** LOB

YANKEES – 5   **GIANTS – 0**

Seventh Inning - New York Giants

– Ott popped up to Lazzeri.
– Ripple whacked a wicked single into right field.
– McCarthy doubled off of the right field wall, driving Ripple home.
– Chiozza sacrificed McCarthy to third base, Lazzeri to Gehrig.
– Danning tapped out, Crosetti to Gehrig.

1 Runs **2** Hits **0** Errors **1** LOB

YANKEES – 5   **GIANTS – 1**

HIGHLIGHTS

• Giants 1B Johnny McCarthy committed two of the three Giants' errors in the fifth inning
• The Yankees mounted scoring drives in four consecutive innings
• Only Frank Crosetti and the Yankee two pitchers went hitless
• The Giants plated just one run for the third straight game
• The Bombers have outscored the Giants 21-3 over 27 innings

DIAMOND DUST

• The Pinstripers are the eighth team to win the first three games, first team to do so four times
• Giants starter Hal Schumacher, in the first inning, fired his fifth career wild pitch to set a new WS record

Game 3 BOX SCORE SUMMARY

NEW YORK YANKEES	AB	R	H	RBI	BB	K	1B	2B	3B	HR	TB	SB
RED ROLFE, 3B	4	1	2	0	1	0	1	1	0	0	3	0
LOU GEHRIG, 1B	5	1	1	1	0	0	1	0	0	0	1	0
BILL DICKEY, C	5	1	1	1	0	0	0	0	1	0	3	0
GEORGE SELKIRK, RF	4	2	1	1	1	0	1	0	0	0	1	0
TONY LAZZERI, 2B	2	0	1	1	2	1	1	0	0	0	1	0
NEW YORK GIANTS	AB	R	H	RBI	BB	K	1B	2B	3B	HR	TB	SB
JIMMY RIPPLE, RF	4	1	1	0	0	0	1	0	0	0	1	0
JOHNNY McCARTHY, 1B	3	0	1	1	0	0	0	1	0	0	2	0

NEW YORK YANKEES	IP	H	R	ER	HR	K	BB	HBP	ERA
MONTE PEARSON W (1-0)	8.2	5	1	1	0	4	2	0	1.04
JOHNNY MURPHY S (1)	0.1	0	0	0	0	0	0	0	0.00
NEW YORK GIANTS	IP	H	R	ER	HR	K	BB	HBP	ERA
HAL SCHUMACHER L (0-1)	6	9	5	4	0	3	4	0	6.00

Lou Gehrig is one of the greatest performers in World Series history. In seven Series with the Yankees (of which NY won six), Gehrig went 43-for-119 (.368), had an OBA of .483 and slugged .731. Gehrig belted 10 homers and drove in 35 in 34 games.
In 1928, when the Yankees overwhelmed the Cardinals in 4 games, Gehrig hit 4 home runs and drove in 9. In his next World Series appearance, in 1932, he hit 3 more home runs and drove in 8 in a 4-game sweep of the Cubs, giving him 7 homers, 17 RBI and a batting average of .535 for the eight games.

GAME TIME:	2:07
ATTENDANCE:	37,385
BEST OF 7:	GIANTS - 0 YANKEES - 3

Game 4

NEW YORK YANKEES vs. NEW YORK GIANTS

October 9

LINE SCORE	1	2	3	4	5	6	7	8	9	R	H	E
NEW YORK YANKEES	1	0	1	0	0	0	0	0	1	3	6	0
NEW YORK GIANTS	0	6	0	0	0	0	1	0	X	7	12	3

RECAP

In the second inning, Yankee starter Bump Hadley and reliever Ivy Andrews faced 11 Giants and were stung for seven singles and six runs. CF Hank Leiber and 1B Johnny McCarthy batted twice. Leiber singled twice, drove in two runs and scored a run. McCarthy singled, scored and made the last out. Over the final frames the lead shrunk and expanded but was never overcome. Carl Hubbell, the only batter in the line-up who was hitless, stopped the Giants' slide by holding the visiting bats to six hits and three runs. Hubbell delivered a complete game win in what would turn out to be his last World Series start.

SCORING SUMMARY

First Inning - New York Yankees

- Hubbell starting.
- Crosetti popped up to Whitehead.
- Rolfe torched a triple into deep center field.
- DiMaggio hoisted a sacrifice fly to Ripple plating Rolfe.
- Gehrig fouled out to McCarthy.

1 Runs **1** Hits **0** Errors **0** LOB

YANKEES – 1   **GIANTS – 0**

Second Inning - New York Giants

- Leiber rapped a single into center field.
- McCarthy singled Leiber to second base.
- Danning singled into right field, driving in Leiber; McCarthy cruised into third.
- Whitehead's single hit Danning for an automatic out; McCarthy held.
- Hubbell sprinted to first, McCarthy scored and Whitehead slid into second on Lazzeri's wide throw.
- Moore singled into right field, driving in Whitehead; Hubbell slid into second.
- Andrews relieved Hadley.
- Bartell singled into center field, driving in Hubbell; Moore moved up.
- Ott was a strikeout.

- Ripple stacked the sacks on a walk.
- Leiber singled into left field, driving in Moore and Bartell; Ripple made third.
- McCarthy nubbed out, Lazzeri to Gehrig.

6 Runs **7** Hits **1** Errors **2** LOB

YANKEES – 1   **GIANTS – 6**

Third Inning - New York Yankees

- Andrews reached first base on Bartell's bobble.
- Crosetti forced Andrews at second base, Whitehead to Bartell; Crosetti slid into second base on Bartell's throwing error.
- Rolfe flied out to Moore.
- DiMaggio darted into second as Crosetti scored on Ott's throwing error, their third of the inning.
- Gehrig grounded out to McCarthy.

1 Runs **0** Hits **3** Errors **1** LOB

YANKEES – 2   **GIANTS – 6**

Seventh Inning - New York Giants

- Ott fouled out to Dickey.
- Ripple slapped a single into center field; thrown out trying to steal second base, Dickey to Lazzeri.

84

– Leiber got to first base on a walk.
– McCarthy singled Leiber to second base.
– Danning doubled into right field, driving in Leiber; McCarthy busted into third.
– Whitehead given an intentional pass; bases loaded.
– Hubbell flied out to Hoag.

1 Runs **3** Hits **0** Errors **3** LOB

YANKEES – 2   **GIANTS – 7**

Ninth Inning - New York Yankees
– DiMaggio fouled out to Ott.
– Gehrig slugged a solo shot into the right field crowd.
– Dickey flied out to Ripple.
– Hoag hot-wired a single up the middle.
– Selkirk skied out to Leiber.

1 Runs **2** Hits **0** Errors **1** LOB

YANKEES – 3   **GIANTS – 7**

HIGHLIGHTS

- In the second inning rally, Carl Hubbell plated the second run and scored the fourth without getting a hit
- SS Dick Bartell, in the third inning, committed two of the three errors
- Gehrig has homered off of Hubbell in consecutive World Series
- Hubbell gave up Gehrig's 10th and final World Series home run

DIAMOND DUST

- Giants' CF Hank Leiber is the 8th player to get two hits in an inning
- The Giants' seven singles in one inning tied a team record
- The eight singles in the second inning tied the record for two teams
- Lou Gehrig is the first player to homer in both the Midsummer Classic and the Fall Classic in the same season
- Gehrig is the player first to do so twice (1936)

Game 4 BOX SCORE SUMMARY

NEW YORK YANKEES	AB	R	H	RBI	BB	K	1B	2B	3B	HR	TB	SB
FRANK CROSETTI, SS	4	1	0	0	0	0	0	0	0	0	0	0
RED ROLFE, 3B	4	1	2	0	0	0	1	0	1	0	4	0
JOE DIMAGGIO, CF	4	0	0	1	0	0	0	0	0	0	0	0
LOU GEHRIG, 1B	4	1	1	1	0	1	0	0	0	1	4	0
NEW YORK GIANTS	AB	R	H	RBI	BB	K	1B	2B	3B	HR	TB	SB
JO-JO MOORE, LF	5	1	1	1	0	0	1	0	0	0	1	0
DICK BARTELL, SS	5	1	1	1	0	0	1	0	0	0	1	0
HANK LEIBER, CF	3	2	2	2	1	0	2	0	0	0	2	0
JOHNNY MCCARTHY, 1B	4	1	2	0	0	0	2	0	0	0	2	0
HARRY DANNING, C	4	0	3	2	0	0	2	1	0	0	5	0
BURGESS WHITEHEAD, 2B	3	1	1	0	1	0	1	0	0	0	1	1
CARL HUBBELL, P	4	1	0	1	0	0	0	0	0	0	0	0

NEW YORK YANKEES	IP	H	R	ER	HR	K	BB	HBP	ERA
BUMP HADLEY L (0-1)	1.1	6	5	5	0	0	0	0	33.75
IVY ANDREWS	5.2	6	2	2	0	1	4	0	3.18
NEW YORK GIANTS	IP	H	R	ER	HR	K	BB	HBP	ERA
CARL HUBBELL W (1-1)	9	6	3	2	1	4	1	0	3.77

GAME TIME:	**1:57**
ATTENDANCE:	**44,293**
BEST OF 7:	**GIANTS - 1 YANKEES - 3**

85

NEW YORK YANKEES vs. NEW YORK GIANTS

October 10

LINE SCORE	1	2	3	4	5	6	7	8	9	R	H	E
NEW YORK YANKEES	0	1	1	0	2	0	0	0	0	4	8	0
NEW YORK GIANTS	0	0	2	0	0	0	0	0	0	2	10	0

RECAP

After three frames with home runs hammered by Yankees Myril Hoag, Joe DiMaggio, and the Giants' Mel Ott, the teams were deadlocked at 2-2. In the fifth, ace Lefty Gomez singled home Tony Lazzeri with the tie breaker, and two batters later, Lou Gehrig doubled him home with the Yankees' fourth run. Over the final six innings, the Giants offense was done. The loss was the second straight for the Giants at the hands of the Pinstripers. The Yankees now have won more titles, six, than any other team, one more than the Philadelphia A's.

SCORING SUMMARY

Second Inning - New York Yankees
– Melton starting.
– Hoag slugged a solo shot into the right field stands.
– Selkirk out on a grounder, Whitehead to McCarthy.
– Lazzeri struck out.
– Gomez went down on strikes.

1 Runs **1** Hits **0** Errors **2** LOB

YANKEES – 1   **GIANTS – 0**

Third Inning - New York Yankees
– Crosetti dribbled out, Ott to McCarthy.
– Rolfe fanned.
– DiMaggio slugged a solo shot into the left field crowd.
– Gehrig struck out.

1 Runs **1** Hits **0** Errors **0** LOB

YANKEES – 2   **GIANTS – 0**

Third Inning - New York Giants
– Moore popped up to Crosetti.
– Bartell blooped a single into left field.

– Ott yanked a home run into the upper right field seats, driving Bartell home.
– Ripple popped up to Crosetti.
– Lieber flied out to DiMaggio.

2 Runs **2** Hits **0** Errors **0** LOB

YANKEES – 2   **GIANTS – 2**

Fifth Inning - New York Yankees
– Lazzeri lashed a double into center field.
– Gomez caromed a single off of Whitehead's glove, driving Lazzeri home.
– Crosetti flied out to Ripple.
– Rolfe walked Gomez to second base.
– DiMaggio popped up to Danning.
– Gehrig doubled into center field, driving in Gomez; Rolfe bolted over to third.
– Dickey got a bases loading walk.
– Hoag fouled out to Danning.

2 Runs **3** Hits **0** Errors **3** LOB

YANKEES – 4   **GIANTS – 2**

HIGHLIGHTS

- Giants hurler Cliff Melton faced two wily veterans, Red Ruffing and Lefty Gomez, and lost both games
- Cliff Melton gave up solo shots in consecutive frames, the first pitcher in World Series history to do so
- SS Frank Crosetti and C Bill Dickey went hitless
- Gomez is the first pitcher in World Series history to field the final out (a comebacker he threw to Gehrig)

DIAMOND DUST

- Giants hurler Cliff Melton is the sixth rookie to start twice in a World Series
- LF Jo-Jo Moore tied the five-game record for most hits with nine
- Joe DiMaggio's first World Series home run is the 150th in World Series history
- Lou Gehrig hit his last home run and DiMaggio hit his first in consecutive games
- Gomez is the third pitcher to win Games 1 and 5, as well as the third pitcher to win a clincher in consecutive Fall Classics
- New York teams have the distinction of winning and losing the milestone 200th World Series game

Game 5 BOX SCORE SUMMARY

NEW YORK YANKEES	AB	R	H	RBI	BB	K	1B	2B	3B	HR	TB	SB
JOE DIMAGGIO, CF	5	1	1	1	0	1	1	0	0	0	1	0
LOU GEHRIG, 1B	4	0	2	1	1	2	0	1	1	0	5	0
MYRIL HOAG, LF	4	1	1	1	0	0	0	0	0	1	4	0
TONY LAZZERI, 2B	3	1	1	0	0	1	0	1	0	0	2	0
LEFTY GOMEZ, P	4	1	1	1	0	1	1	0	0	0	1	0
NEW YORK GIANTS	AB	R	H	RBI	BB	K	1B	2B	3B	HR	TB	SB
DICK BARTELL, SS	4	1	1	0	0	0	1	0	0	0	1	0
MEL OTT, 3B	3	1	1	2	1	1	0	0	0	1	4	0

NEW YORK YANKEES	IP	H	R	ER	HR	K	BB	HBP	ERA
LEFTY GOMEZ W (2-0)	9	10	2	2	1	6	1	0	1.50
NEW YORK GIANTS	IP	H	R	ER	HR	K	BB	HBP	ERA
CLIFF MELTON L (0-2)	5	6	4	4	2	5	3	0	4.91

Frank "Home Run" Baker earned his nickname for the Philadelphia Athletics where he led the league in dingers four years in a row. But Baker played nearly half his career for the Yankees, who acquired him in the winter of 1916 for $37,500.

Baker is one of 6 players to collect 9 hits in a 5-game WS. New York Giants' left fielder Jo Jo Moore did the same in 1937.

BAKER, PHILADELPHIA AMER.

Players Who Collected 9 Hits in a 5-Game Series

1910 - Eddie Collins, Philadelphia Athletics
1910 - Frank Baker, Philadelphia Athletics
1913 - Eddie Collins, Philadelphia Athletics
1922 - Heinie Groh, New York Giants
1937 - Jo-Jo Moore, New York Giants
1961 - Bobby Richardson, New York Yankees

GAME TIME:	**2:06**
ATTENDANCE:	**38,216**
BEST OF 7:	**GIANTS - 1 YANKEES - 4**

Pitching Triple Crown Winners in the World Series

WS	PITCHERS	TEAM	Regular Season				World Series			
			W	L	SO	ERA	W	L	SO	ERA
1905	CHRISTY MATHEWSON	NY(NL)	31	9	206	1.27	3	0	18	0.00
1915	GROVER ALEXANDER	PHI(NL)	31	10	241	1.22	1	1	1	1.53
1918	HIPPO VAUGHN	CHI(NL)	22	10	148	1.74	1	2	17	1.00
1924	WALTER JOHNSON	WAS	23	7	158	2.72	1	2	20	2.25
1930	LEFTY GROVE	PHI(AL)	28	5	209	2.54	2	1	10	1.42
1931	LEFTY GROVE	PHI(AL)	31	4	175	2.06	2	1	16	2.42
1937	**LEFTY GOMEZ**	**NY(AL)**	**21**	**11**	**194**	**2.33**	**2**	**0**	**8**	**1.50**
1939	BUCKY WALTERS	CIN	27	11	137	2.29	0	2	6	4.91
1945	HAL NEWHOUSER	DET	25	9	212	1.81	2	1	22	6.10
1963	SANDY KOUFAX	LAD	25	5	306	1.88	2	0	23	1.50
1965	SANDY KOUFAX	LAD	26	6	382	2.04	2	1	29	0.38
1966	SANDY KOUFAX	LAD	27	9	382	1.73	0	1	2	1.50

Batting Triple Crowns in the World Series

YR	HITTER	TEAM	Regular Season				World Series			
			BA	HR	RBI	RS	BA	HR	RBI	RS
1909	TY COBB	DET	.377	9	107	115	.231	0	5	3
1956	MICKEY MANTLE	NYY	.353	52	130	132	.250	3	4	6
1966	FRANK ROBINSON	BAL	.316	49	122	122	.286	2	3	4
1967	CARL YASTRZEMSKI	BOS(AL)	.326	44	121	112	.400	3	5	4
2012	MIGUEL CABRERA	DET	.330	44	139	109	.231	1	3	1

1937

NEW YORK GIANTS vs. NEW YORK YANKEES

NEW YORK GIANTS

Overall World Series Record: 4 WINS 8 LOSSES. 72 Games Played [35 – 35 (2 ties) .500]

- Cliff Melton is the fourth rookie to lose two games.
- Carl Hubbell gave up 12 hits and 10 runs in 14.1 innings.
- Jo-Jo Moore smacked a hit in each game, and led team with 9 hits.
- Bill Terry's managerial record ends at 1-2, with two consecutive losses after an initial win in 1933.
- Third team to lose consecutive series, the first to do so twice (1923/24). The Yankees are the other (1921/22).
- Long-time slugger Wally Berger went 0-for-3 as a pinch hitter and followed that up with an 0-for-15 for the Reds in 1939, making him 0-for-18 with zero walks in his World Series career.

NEW YORK YANKEES

Overall World Series Record: 6 WINS 3 LOSSES. 49 Games Played [30-18 (1 tie) .625]

- Pitching Triple Crown winner Lefty Gomez's two victories tied Herb Pennock for most career World Series wins with five.
- Gomez is the sixth pitcher to post a decision in the final game of consecutive World Series.
- Johnny Murphy is the first reliever to notch saves in consecutive Fall Classic games.
- Lou Gehrig and Tony Lazzeri win their fifth title (1927/28/32/36).
- George Selkirk scored five runs while driving in six to lead both teams; he also did not strikeout.
- Zero stolen bases.
- The Yankees are the first team to not commit an error in a World Series.
- First franchise to earn six championships.

FUNGOES

- Joe DiMaggio (Yankees) and Mel Ott (Giants), home run champs, hit one each.
- The Yankees outscored the Giants by 16 runs over the five games.
- Combined with the previous Series, the Yankees outscored the Giants 71-35.
- The AL now leads the all-time World Series standings 21-13.

FIVE-GAME DATA

TIME	10:40	PLAYERS POOL	$459,629
ATTENDANCE	238,142	SHARES	NEW YORK GIANTS - $4,490
			NEW YORK YANKEES - $6,471

1937

NEW YORK GIANTS vs. NEW YORK YANKEES

New York Giants Composite Stats

BATTING	G	AB	R	H	RBI	2B	3B	HR	BB	SO	BA	OBP	SLG	OPS
Jo-Jo Moore	5	23	1	9	1	1	0	0	0	1	.391	.391	.435	.826
Dick Bartell	5	21	3	5	1	1	0	0	0	3	.238	.238	.286	.524
Mel Ott	5	20	1	4	3	0	0	1	1	4	.200	.238	.350	.588
Johnny McCarthy	5	19	1	4	1	1	0	0	1	2	.211	.250	.263	.513
Jimmy Ripple	5	17	2	5	0	0	0	0	3	1	.294	.400	.294	.694
Burgess Whitehead	5	16	1	4	0	2	0	0	2	0	.250	.333	.375	.708
Harry Danning	3	12	0	3	2	1	0	0	0	2	.250	.250	.333	.583
Hank Leiber	3	11	2	4	2	0	0	0	1	1	.364	.417	.364	.780
Gus Mancuso	3	8	0	0	1	0	0	0	0	1	.000	.000	.000	.000
Lou Chiozza	2	7	0	2	0	0	0	0	1	1	.286	.375	.286	.661
Carl Hubbell	2	6	1	0	1	0	0	0	0	0	.000	.000	.000	.000
Wally Berger	3	3	0	0	0	0	0	0	0	1	.000	.000	.000	.000
Cliff Melton	3	2	0	0	0	0	0	0	1	1	.000	.333	.000	.333
Sam Leslie	2	1	0	0	0	0	0	0	1	0	.000	.500	.000	.500
Dick Coffman	2	1	0	0	0	0	0	0	0	1	.000	.000	.000	.000
Blondy Ryan	1	1	0	0	0	0	0	0	0	1	.000	.000	.000	.000
Hal Schumacher	1	1	0	0	0	0	0	0	0	1	.000	.000	.000	.000
Don Brennan	2	0	0	0	0	0	0	0	0	0				
Harry Gumbert	2	0	0	0	0	0	0	0	0	0				
Al Smith	2	0	0	0	0	0	0	0	0	0				
Totals	**61**	**169**	**12**	**40**	**12**	**6**	**0**	**1**	**11**	**21**	**.237**	**.283**	**.290**	**.573**

PITCHING	G	GS	ERA	W	L	SV	CG	IP	H	R	ER	BB	SO	WHIP
Carl Hubbell	2	2	3.77	1	1	0	1	14.1	12	10	6	4	7	1.116
Cliff Melton	3	2	4.91	0	2	0	0	11.0	12	6	6	6	7	1.636
Hal Schumacher	1	1	6.00	0	1	0	0	6.0	9	5	4	4	3	2.167
Dick Coffman	2	0	4.15	0	0	0	0	4.1	2	2	2	5	1	1.615
Don Brennan	2	0	0.00	0	0	0	0	3.0	1	0	0	1	1	0.667
Al Smith	2	0	3.00	0	0	0	0	3.0	2	1	1	0	1	0.667
Harry Gumbert	2	0	27.00	0	0	0	0	1.1	4	4	4	1	1	3.750
Totals	**5**	**5**	**4.81**	**1**	**4**	**0**	**1**	**43.0**	**42**	**28**	**23**	**21**	**21**	**1.465**

1937

NEW YORK GIANTS vs. NEW YORK YANKEES

New York Yankees Composite Stats

BATTING	G	AB	R	H	RBI	2B	3B	HR	BB	SO	BA	OBP	SLG	OPS
Joe DiMaggio	5	22	2	6	4	0	0	1	0	3	.273	.273	.409	.682
Frankie Crosetti	5	21	2	1	0	0	0	0	3	2	.048	.167	.048	.214
Red Rolfe	5	20	3	6	1	2	1	0	3	2	.300	.391	.500	.891
Myril Hoag	5	20	4	6	2	1	0	1	0	1	.300	.300	.500	.800
Bill Dickey	5	19	3	4	3	0	1	0	2	2	.211	.286	.316	.602
George Selkirk	5	19	5	5	6	1	0	0	2	0	.263	.333	.316	.649
Lou Gehrig	5	17	4	5	3	1	1	1	5	4	.294	.455	.647	1.102
Tony Lazzeri	5	15	3	6	2	0	1	1	3	3	.400	.526	.733	1.260
Lefty Gomez	2	6	2	1	1	0	0	0	2	1	.167	.375	.167	.542
Red Ruffing	1	4	0	2	3	1	0	0	0	0	.500	.500	.750	1.250
Monte Pearson	1	3	0	0	0	0	0	0	1	1	.000	.250	.000	.250
Ivy Andrews	1	2	0	0	0	0	0	0	0	1	.000	.000	.000	.000
Jake Powell	1	1	0	0	0	0	0	0	0	1	.000	.000	.000	.000
Bump Hadley	1	0	0	0	0	0	0	0	0	0				
Johnny Murphy	1	0	0	0	0	0	0	0	0	0				
Kemp Wicker	1	0	0	0	0	0	0	0	0	0				
Totals	**49**	**169**	**28**	**42**	**25**	**6**	**4**	**4**	**21**	**21**	**.249**	**.335**	**.402**	**.737**

PITCHING	G	GS	ERA	W	L	SV	CG	IP	H	R	ER	BB	SO	WHIP
Lefty Gomez	2	2	1.50	2	0	0	2	18.0	16	3	3	2	8	1.000
Red Ruffing	1	1	1.00	1	0	0	1	9.0	7	1	1	3	8	1.111
Monte Pearson	1	1	1.04	1	0	0	0	8.2	5	1	1	2	4	0.808
Ivy Andrews	1	0	3.18	0	0	0	0	5.2	6	2	2	4	1	1.765
Bump Hadley	1	1	33.75	0	1	0	0	1.1	6	5	5	0	0	4.500
Kemp Wicker	1	0	0.00	0	0	0	0	1.0	0	0	0	0	0	0.000
Johnny Murphy	1	0	0.00	0	0	0	1	0.1	0	0	0	0	0	0.000
Totals	**5**	**5**	**2.45**	**4**	**1**	**1**	**3**	**44.0**	**40**	**12**	**12**	**11**	**21**	**1.159**

1941

 vs.

BROOKLYN DODGERS vs. NEW YORK YANKEES

FUNGOES

- Subway Series #6.
- Ninth same city contest.
- Both teams in first place at the All-Star break.
- 100-game pennant-winners compete for the fourth time.
- Umpire update: Larry Goetz had a career after umpiring as a radio commentator; appeared in the Norman Rockwell painting "Bottom of the Sixth" with Lou Jorda and Beans Reardon. Bill McGowan first umpired at age 17; served in the US Armed Forces during WWI; spent the off season writing newspaper articles about baseball. Babe Pinelli was a catcher for the Cincinnati Reds (1922-27). Eddie Rommel pitched for the Philadelphia Athletics from 1920-32, winning titles in 1929/30.

SERIES SUMMARY

After five battles between the Yankees and the Giants, Brooklyn took its first turn in a Subway Series in their third appearance ever in the Fall Classic, having lost in 1916 and 1920. The Yankees, meanwhile, had been in two of the three Series since the last Subway Series, defeating the Cubs and the Reds.

The Yankees rarely lose a Game 1, and Red Ruffing had three opening-game wins coming in, and both traditions were continued as Ruffing pitched a complete-game six-hitter in a tight 3-2 victory. Joe Gordon was the hero on offense.

The Dodgers turned the tables in Game 2 with a 3-2 victory of their own, as 22-game winner Whitlow Wyatt went the distance. Brooklyn pushed across the lead run in the sixth inning with the help of an error by Game 1 hero Joe Gordon.

Game 3 was another hard-fought, low-scoring affair. After an injury to Brooklyn starter Freddie Fitzsimmons forced the Dodgers to go to their bullpen, the Yankees broke a scoreless tie in the eighth inning with two runs, the first of which was driven in on a single by Joe DiMaggio. As would become the norm, the Dodgers' comeback would come up short and the Yankees prevailed 2-1.

Brooklyn was on the verge of evening the Series at two games apiece when a game-ending third strike to Tommy Henrich was muffed and the Yankees' hopes were kept alive. Two walks and three hits later the Yankees were 7-4 winners rather than 4-3 losers and held a commanding 3-1 lead in the Series.

THE TEAMS

BROOKLYN DODGERS
100 – 54, .649 +2.5 G

The Team
- Subway Series debut; 3rd overall appearance (first since 1920).
- A National League franchise since 1884.
- Known in the early years as the Atlantics, the Grays, the Bridegrooms (Grooms), the Trolley Dodgers, the Ward Wonders, the Superbas.
- Name officially changed from the Robins to the Dodgers in 1931.
- First season winning 100 or more games.
- Facing third different American League pennant winner.

The Players
- Seven players with prior Fall Classic appearances: Johnny Allen, 1932 New York Yankees; Billy Herman 1932/35/38 Chicago Cubs, who lost all three; Freddie Fitzsimmons is the first player to appear in the World Series for both New York National League franchises. He pitched for the New York Giants in 1933 and 1936; Joe "Ducky" Medwick played on the 1934 title-winning St. Louis Cardinals; Larry French and Augie Galan were teammates on the 1935/38 pennant-winning Chicago Cubs; Lew Riggs as a Cincinnati Reds player defeated the Tigers in the 1940 Classic; MVP Dolph Camilli led the National League with 34 homers and 120 RBIs.

The Manager
- Leo Durocher is the 33rd manager to debut.
- Durocher played on two pennant-winning teams (1928 New York Yankees/1934 St. Louis Cardinals), winning titles in both leagues.

Top Batters

Pos	Name	AB	R	H	HR	RBI	BA	OPS
1B	Dolph Camilli	529	92	151	34	120	.285	.962
2B	Billy Herman	572	81	163	3	41	.285	.732
OF	Pete Reiser	536	117	184	14	76	.343	.964
OF	Joe Medwick	538	100	171	18	88	.318	.881

Top Pitchers

Pos	Name	W	L	ERA	G	SV	IP	SO
St	Kirby Higbe	22	9	3.14	48	3	298.0	121
St	Whit Wyatt	22	10	2.34	38	1	288.1	176
St	Curt Davis	13	7	2.97	28	2	154.1	50
Rel	Hugh Casey	14	11	3.89	45	7	162.0	61

NEW YORK YANKEES
101 – 53, .656 +17.0 G

The Team
- Subway Series # 6; 12th overall appearance.
- Seventh season winning 100 games.

The Players
- Six returning players from the 1936/37 Subway Series: Bill Dickey, Joe DiMaggio, Johnny Murphy, Red Rolfe, Red Ruffing and George Selkirk.
- Dickey and Ruffing played on the 1932/36/37/38/39 title-winning teams.
- Joe DiMaggio named American League MVP for second time (1939).
- DiMaggio led the major leagues in total bases (348) and runs batted in (125).

The Manager
- Joe McCarthy's seventh career appearance, sixth as Yankees skipper.

Top Batters

Pos	Name	AB	R	H	HR	RBI	BA	OPS
2B	Joe Gordon	588	104	162	24	87	.276	.824
OF	Charlie Keller	507	102	151	33	122	.298	.996
OF	Tommy Henrich	538	106	149	31	85	.277	.895
OF	Joe DiMaggio	541	122	193	30	125	.357	1.083

Top Pitchers

Pos	Name	W	L	ERA	G	SV	IP	SO
St	Marius Russo	14	10	3.09	28	1	209.2	105
St	Red Ruffing	15	6	3.54	23	0	185.2	60
St	Lefty Gomez	15	5	3.74	23	0	156.1	76
Rel	Johnny Murphy	8	3	1.98	35	15	77.1	29

Game 1

BROOKLYN DODGERS vs. NEW YORK YANKEES

October 1

LINE SCORE	1	2	3	4	5	6	7	8	9	R	H	E
BROOKLYN DODGERS	0	0	0	0	1	0	1	0	0	2	6	0
NEW YORK YANKEES	0	1	0	1	0	1	0	0	X	3	6	1

RECAP

SS Pee Wee Reese played a big part in the Dodgers two scoring drives. In the fifth inning he rode home on a triple torqued by C Mickey Owen. Two innings later, Reese singled 3B Cookie Lavagetto to second base who was later singled home by PH Lew Riggs.
Yankee extra base hits produced their first two runs. 2B Joe Gordon slugged a second inning solo shot. Two innings later C Bill Dickey double home Charlie Keller with the second run. In the sixth Keller, Dickey and Gordon collaborated to produce the winning run. The Pinstripers are on a 10-game World Series winning streak.

SCORING SUMMARY

Second Inning - New York Yankees
– Davis starting.
– Keller flied out to Reiser.
– Dickey out on a grounder, Herman to Camilli.
– Gordon slugged a solo shot into the lower left field deck.
– Rizzuto flied out to Medwick.

1 Runs **1** Hits **0** Errors **0** LOB

DODGERS – 0   **YANKEES – 1**

Fourth Inning - New York Yankees
– Henrich popped up to Reese.
– DiMaggio flied out to Medwick (*great catch*).
– Keller drew a free pass.
– Dickey doubled off of the right-center field wall, driving Keller home.
– Gordon purposely walked.
– Rizzuto rolled out, Herman to Camilli.

1 Runs **1** Hits **0** Errors **1** LOB

DODGERS – 0   **YANKEES – 2**

Fifth Inning - Brooklyn Dodgers
– Ruffing starting.
– Medwick flied out to DiMaggio.
– Lavagetto flied out to DiMaggio.

– Reese stroked a single into left field.
– Owen tripled into the left-center field corner, driving Reese home.
– Davis out on a grounder, Rizzuto to Sturm.

1 Runs **2** Hits **0** Errors **1** LOB

DODGERS – 1   **YANKEES – 2**

Sixth Inning - New York Yankees
– DiMaggio tapped out, Reese to Camilli.
– Keller drew a walk.
– Dickey smacked a hit-and-run single; Keller bolted over to third base.
– Gordon singled up the middle, driving in Keller; Dickey advanced.
– Casey relieved Davis.
– Rizzuto flied out to Reiser.
– Ruffing flied out to Walker.

1 Runs **2** Hits **0** Errors **2** LOB

DODGERS – 1   **YANKEES – 3**

Seventh Inning - Brooklyn Dodgers
– Lavagetto flew across first base on Rizzuto's throwing error.
– Reese singled Lavagetto to second base.

– Riggs PH for Owen, singled up the middle, driving in
  Lavagetto; Reese slid into second base.
– Wasdell PH for Casey, fouled out to Rolfe who uncorked
  a straight arrow to Rizzuto who tagged out a sliding
  Reese.
– Walker grounded out, Gordon to Sturm.

1 Runs **2** Hits **1** Errors **1** LOB

DODGERS – 2   **YANKEES – 3**

HIGHLIGHTS

- Brooklyn 1B Dolph Camilli struck out in his first three
  at-bats
- Yankee LF Charlie Keller walked and scored in
  consecutive at-bats
- Five scoring drives netted one run each, four occurred
  in consecutive innings

DIAMOND DUST

- New York starter Red Ruffing posted his fourth opening game "W" (1932/38/39)
- Ruffing joined Chief Bender, Waite Hoyt, and Lefty Gomez as winners of six games
- Bender won all as a Philadelphia Athletic; Gomez and Hoyt won all as a Yankee
- In openers, the Yankees are 9-3 while the Dodgers are 0-3
- Game One winners have won it all 26 of 38 World Series

Game 1 BOX SCORE SUMMARY

BROOKLYN DODGERS	AB	R	H	RBI	BB	K	1B	2B	3B	HR	TB	SB
COOKIE LAVAGETTO, 3B	4	1	0	0	0	0	0	0	0	0	0	0
PEE WEE REESE, SS	4	1	3	0	0	0	3	0	0	0	3	0
MICKEY OWEN, C	2	0	1	1	0	0	0	0	1	0	3	0
LEW RIGGS, PH	1	0	1	1	0	0	0	0	0	0	1	0
NEW YORK YANKEES	AB	R	H	RBI	BB	K	1B	2B	3B	HR	TB	SB
CHARLIE KELLER, LF	2	2	0	0	2	0	0	0	0	0	0	0
BILL DICKEY, C	4	0	2	1	0	0	1	1	0	0	3	0
JOE GORDON, 2B	2	1	2	2	2	0	1	0	0	1	4	0

BROOKLYN DODGERS	IP	H	R	ER	HR	K	BB	HBP	ERA
CURT DAVIS L (0-1)	5.1	6	3	3	1	1	3	0	5.06
NEW YORK YANKEES	IP	H	R	ER	HR	K	BB	HBP	ERA
RED RUFFING W (1-0)	9	6	2	1	0	5	1	0	1.00

GAME TIME:	**2:08**	
ATTENDANCE:	**68,540**	
BEST OF 7:	**DODGERS - 0**	**YANKEES - 1**

Game 2

BROOKLYN DODGERS vs. NEW YORK YANKEES

October 2

LINE SCORE	1	2	3	4	5	6	7	8	9	R	H	E
BROOKLYN DODGERS	0	0	0	0	2	1	0	0	0	3	6	2
NEW YORK YANKEES	0	1	1	0	0	0	0	0	0	2	9	1

—— RECAP ——

Another 65,000+ fans rocked the Stadium. The final score was the same as Game 1, but the winner was not, as Brooklyn evened the Series. Winner Whitlow Wyatt, going the distance, did not have an easy time with the home team. He gave up nine safeties. Most innings he pitched with Pinstripers on base, often in scoring position, but only two crossed the plate. Wyatt was charged with one run less than his counterpart, Spud Chandler.

—— SCORING SUMMARY ——

Second Inning - New York Yankees
– Wyatt starting.
– Keller topped a single into center field.
– Dickey struck out.
– Gordon walked Keller to second base.
– Rizzuto moved up the runners on a ground out, Herman to Camilli.
– Chandler scored Keller on an infield single; Gordon thrown out at the plate, Camilli to Owen.

1 Runs **2** Hits **0** Errors **1** LOB

DODGERS – 0   **YANKEES – 1**

Third Inning - New York Yankees
– Sturm skied out to Camilli.
– Rolfe dribbled out to Camilli.
– Henrich doubled against the right field wall.
– DiMaggio trotted to first on a walk.
– Keller singled into right field, driving in Henrich; DiMaggio dashed into third.
– Dickey out on a ground ball, Herman to Camilli.

1 Runs **2** Hits **0** Errors **2** LOB

DODGERS – 0   **YANKEES – 2**

Fifth Inning - Brooklyn Dodgers
– Camilli got a free pass.
– Medwick doubled Camilli to third base.

– Lavagetto walked the bases full.
– Reese scored Camilli on a force of Lavagetto at second base, Rizzuto to Gordon; Medwick moved up.
– Owen singled into left field, driving in Medwick; Reese made third.
– Wyatt whammed into a double play, Gordon to Rizzuto to Sturm.

2 Runs **2** Hits **0** Errors **1** LOB

DODGERS – 2   **YANKEES – 2**

Sixth Inning - Brooklyn Dodgers
– Walker flew to first base on Gordon's throwing error.
– Herman blistered a hit-and-run single; Walker rumbled into third base.
– Murphy relieved Chandler.
– Reiser was a strikeout.
– Camilli singled into right field, driving in Walker; Herman took third.
– Medwick flashed across first base on a fielder's choice. Herman nailed at the plate, Rizzuto to Dickey; Camilli slid into second base.
– Lavagetto flied out to DiMaggio.

1 Runs **2** Hits **1** Errors **2** LOB

DODGERS – 3   **YANKEES – 2**

┌─ HIGHLIGHTS ─┐

- Yankee 2B Joe Gordon was thrown out at the plate in the second inning
- Bums' 2B Billy Herman was thrown out at the plate in the sixth inning
- Pee Wee Reese made two errors in the eighth inning but the Yankees did not score
- Frenchy Bordagaray is the first player to pinch run in the World Series for both leagues ('41 Yankees and '39 Reds)
- Joe Gordon drew three walks but did not score
- Wyatt hit into two inning-ending double plays

DIAMOND DUST

- Dodgers' starter Whitlow Wyatt was the starting pitcher in the All-Star Game
- Brooklyn stops the Yankees' 10-game winning streak

Game 2 BOX SCORE SUMMARY

BROOKLYN DODGERS	AB	R	H	RBI	BB	K	1B	2B	3B	HR	TB	SB
DIXIE WALKER, RF	4	1	0	0	0	1	0	0	0	0	0	0
DOLPH CAMILLI, 1B	3	1	1	1	1	0	1	0	0	0	1	0
JOE MEDWICK, LF	4	1	2	0	0	0	1	1	0	0	3	0
PEE WEE REESE, SS	4	0	0	1	0	0	0	0	0	0	0	0
MICKEY OWEN, C	2	0	1	1	0	0	1	0	0	0	1	0
NEW YORK YANKEES	AB	R	H	RBI	BB	K	1B	2B	3B	HR	TB	SB
TOMMY HENRICH, RF	4	1	1	0	1	1	0	1	0	0	2	0
CHARLIE KELLER, LF	4	1	2	1	0	0	2	0	0	0	2	0
SPUD CHANDLER, P	2	0	1	1	0	0	1	0	0	0	1	0

BROOKLYN DODGERS	IP	H	R	ER	HR	K	BB	HBP	ERA
WHITLOW WYATT W (1-0)	9	9	2	2	0	5	5	0	2.00
NEW YORK YANKEES	IP	H	R	ER	HR	K	BB	HBP	ERA
SPUD CHANDLER L (0-1)	5	4	3	2	0	2	2	0	3.60
JOHNNY MURPHY	4	2	0	0	0	2	1	0	0.00

Spud Chandler (pictured above) took the loss in Game 2 for the Yankees, a situation he rarely found himself in during his career. Chandler finished his career - spent entirely with the Yankees - with a record of 109-43 (.717), the highest winning percentage in major league history for pitchers with at least 100 victories.

Due to injuries and a loaded parent club, Chandler did not make the majors until age 29, but he won 20 games in a season twice and was 2-2 in the Fall Classic with an ERA of 1.62 in 33.1 innings.

Somewhat surprisingly, Spud Chandler did not get his nickname for being from Idaho or anything having to do with potatoes. His given name was Spurgeon Ferdinand Chandler, and as a boy became known as "Spud."

GAME TIME:	**2:31**	
ATTENDANCE:	**66,248**	
BEST OF 7:	**DODGERS - 1**	**YANKEES - 1**

NEW YORK YANKEES vs. BROOKLYN DODGERS

October 4

LINE SCORE	1	2	3	4	5	6	7	8	9	R	H	E
NEW YORK YANKEES	0	0	0	0	0	0	0	2	0	2	8	0
BROOKLYN DODGERS	0	0	0	0	0	0	0	1	0	1	4	0

RECAP

Play resumed after a one-day rain delay. This scoreless pitching duel between the starters ended in the top of the seventh inning when Marius Russo, the Yankees starter, broke Dodgers starter Freddie Fitzsimmons' knee cap with a line drive that was caught on the fly by the shortstop. Facing reliever Hugh Casey in their next at-bat, New York strung together four straight singles, scoring two runs and knocking Casey out of the game. In the bottom of the same frame, Russo's shutout bid ended when Pee Wee Reese singled in a run. Russo set the Dodgers down in order in the ninth to earn the win.

SCORING SUMMARY

Eighth Inning - New York Yankees

– Casey pitching.
– Sturm flied out to Reiser.
– Rolfe ripped a single into right field.
– Herman singled Rolfe to second base.
– DiMaggio singled up the middle, driving in Rolfe; Henrich scooted to third.
– Keller singled up the middle, driving in Henrich; DiMaggio jetted to third.
– French relieved Casey.
– Dickey rolled into a double play, Reese to Camilli.

2 Runs **4** Hits **0** Errors **1** LOB

YANKEES – 2   **DODGERS – 0**

Eighth Inning - Brooklyn Dodgers

– Walker drilled a double into right field.
– Owen thrown out on a comebacker, Russo to Sturm.
– Galan PH for French, was a strikeout.
– Reese singled into right field, driving Walker home.
– Coscarart popped up to Rolfe.

1 Runs **2** Hits **0** Errors **1** LOB

YANKEES – 2   **DODGERS – 1**

HIGHLIGHTS

- Freddy Fitzsimmons' lone strikeout was of his counterpart Marius Russo
- Six Yankee batters stroked eight base hits
- All three games have been decided by one run
- Marius Russo is the third starter in the series to throw a complete game victory

Game 3 BOX SCORE SUMMARY

NEW YORK YANKEES	AB	R	H	RBI	BB	K	1B	2B	3B	HR	TB	SB
RED ROLFE, 3B	4	1	2	0	0	0	2	0	0	0	2	0
TOMMY HENRICH, RF	3	1	1	0	1	0	1	0	0	0	1	0
JOE DIMAGGIO, CF	4	0	2	1	0	0	2	0	0	0	2	0
CHARLIE KELLER, LF	4	0	1	1	0	0	1	0	0	0	1	0
BROOKLYN DODGERS	AB	R	H	RBI	BB	K	1B	2B	3B	HR	TB	SB
PEE WEE REESE, SS	4	0	1	1	0	0	1	0	0	0	1	0
DIXIE WALKER, RF	3	1	1	0	0	0	0	1	0	0	2	0

NEW YORK YANKEES	IP	H	R	ER	HR	K	BB	HBP	ERA
MARIUS RUSSO W (1-0)	9	4	1	1	0	5	2	0	1.00
BROOKLYN DODGERS	IP	H	R	ER	HR	K	BB	HBP	ERA
FREDDY FITZSIMMONS	7	4	0	0	0	1	3	0	0.00
HUGH CASEY L (0-1)	0.1	4	2	2	0	0	0	0	18.00

Marius Russo enjoyed the best year of his brief career in 1941, collecting 14 wins and 17 complete games in only 27 starts. Arm injuries limited the Brooklyn native to six seasons and only 120 games pitched in his career, all for the Yankees. Russo was already on the way out in 1943, when he went 5-10 as a reliever and spot starter. Yankees' manager Joe McCarthy, perhaps considering Russo's success in the 1941 series, started Russo in Game 4 of the 1943 World Series, in which the Yankees held a 2-1 advantage over the St. Louis Cardinals.

Russo justified McCarthy's confidence in him, pitching a complete-game victory, allowing only 1 unearned run. The all-but-forgotten left-handed pitcher finished his World Series career with a 2-0 record and 0.50 ERA.

GAME TIME: **2:22**
ATTENDANCE: **33,100**
BEST OF 7: **DODGERS - 1   YANKEES - 2**

NEW YORK YANKEES vs. BROOKLYN DODGERS

October 5

LINE SCORE	1	2	3	4	5	6	7	8	9	R	H	E
NEW YORK YANKEES	1	0	0	2	0	0	0	0	4	7	12	0
BROOKLYN DODGERS	0	0	0	2	2	0	0	0	0	4	9	1

RECAP

This game is considered one of the most memorable in World Series history because of an error. Brooklyn was leading by one run in the top of the ninth inning. Yankee RF Tommy Henrich was struck out for the third out but the ball was mishandled by C Mickey Owen. Henrich reached first base and the next four batters - Joe DiMaggio, Charlie Keller, Bill Dickey and Joe Gordon - produced four runs. The decisions went to the relievers; Hugh Casey, charged with those four runs, got the "L." Johnny Murphy, putting down the six Dodgers he faced, got the "W."

SCORING SUMMARY

First Inning - New York Yankees
– Higbe starting.
– Sturm squibbed out, Reese to Camilli.
– Rolfe buzzed a single into left field.
– Henrich flied out to Medwick.
– DiMaggio walked Rolfe to second base.
– Keller singled into right field, driving in Rolfe; DiMaggio slid into third base.
– Dickey grounded out, Coscarat to Camilli.

1 Runs **2** Hits **0** Errors **2** LOB

YANKEES – 1   **DODGERS – 0**

Fourth Inning - New York Yankees
– Keller split the gap in left-center field for a double.
– Dickey wangled a walk.
– Gordon singled into left field to stack the sacks.
– Rizzuto forced Keller at the plate, Riggs to Owen; bases loaded.
– Donald was a strikeout.
– Sturm singled into left field, driving in Dickey and Gordon; Rizzuto slid into second base.
– French relieved Higbe; on a passed ball, Rizzuto tagged out, Owen to Reese.

2 Runs **3** Hits **0** Errors **1** LOB

YANKEES – 3   **DODGERS – 0**

Fourth Inning - Brooklyn Dodgers
– Riggs popped up to Gordon.
– Medwick flied out to DiMaggio.
– Owen worked a free pass.
– Coscarat walked Owen to second base.
– Wasdell PH for French, doubled into left field, driving home Owen and Coscarat.
– Reese out on a grounder, Rizzuto to Sturm.

2 Runs **1** Hits **0** Errors **1** LOB

YANKEES – 3   **DODGERS – 2**

Fifth Inning - Brooklyn Dodgers
– Walker laced a double into left field.
– Reiser yanked a home run over the scoreboard, driving Walker home.
– Breuer relieved Donald.
– Camilli flied out to Henrich.
– Riggs struck out.
– Casey cut a single over the second-base bag.
– Owen flied out to DiMaggio.

2 Runs **3** Hits **0** Errors **1** LOB

YANKEES – 3   **DODGERS – 4**

Ninth Inning - New York Yankees

– Sturm out on a grounder, Coscarat to Camilli.
– Rolfe rolled out to the mound, Casey to Camilli.
– Henrich whiffed; hustled across first base on Owens' passed ball.
– DiMaggio singled Henrich to second base.
– Keller doubled off of the right field wall, driving home Henrich and DiMaggio.
– Dickey walked; Keller held.
– Gordon doubled off of the left field wall, driving home Keller and Dickey.
– Rizzuto walked; Gordon held.
– Murphy bounced out, Reese to Camilli.

4 Runs **3** Hits **1** Errors **2** LOB

YANKEES – 7   DODGERS – 4

HIGHLIGHTS

• Yankee LF Charlie Keller and 2B Joe Gordon drove home four runs on consecutive doubles after Owens' passed ball
• Charlie Keller stroked four hits, four other Yankees stroked two hits each
• Keller drove in three, two other Yankees drove in two each
• Dodger PH/LF Jimmy Wasdell drove in two
• Yankee C Bill Dickey walked three times, scored twice
• Hugh Casey, hurling 4.2 innings over two games, has allowed nine hits and six runs, though all four in game four were unearned

DIAMOND DUST

• Brooklyn's C Mickey Owens' dropped third strike is considered one of the biggest muffs in World Series history
• Casey is the third pitcher to lose consecutive games. Deacon Phillippe, Pit (1903, G7,G8) and Christy Mathewson, NYG (1911, G3,G4) are the other two.

Game 4 BOX SCORE SUMMARY

NEW YORK YANKEES	AB	R	H	RBI	BB	K	1B	2B	3B	HR	TB	SB
JOHNNY STURM, 1B	5	0	2	2	0	0	2	0	0	0	2	0
RED ROLFE, 3B	5	1	2	0	0	0	2	0	0	0	2	0
TOMMY HENRICH, RF	4	1	0	0	0	1	0	0	0	0	0	0
JOE DIMAGGIO, CF	4	1	2	0	1	0	2	0	0	0	2	0
CHARLIE KELLER, LF	5	1	4	3	0	0	2	2	0	0	6	0
BILL DICKEY, C	2	2	0	0	3	0	0	0	0	0	0	0
JOE GORDON, 2B	5	1	2	2	0	0	1	1	0	0	3	0
BROOKLYN DODGERS	AB	R	H	RBI	BB	K	1B	2B	3B	HR	TB	SB
DIXIE WALKER, RF	5	1	2	0	0	0	1	1	0	0	3	0
PETE REISER, CF	5	1	2	2	0	1	1	0	0	1	5	0
MICKEY OWEN, C	2	1	0	0	2	0	0	0	0	0	0	0
PETE COSCARAT, 2B	3	1	0	0	1	2	0	0	0	0	0	0
JIMMY WASDELL, PH/LF	3	0	1	2	0	0	0	1	0	0	2	0

NEW YORK YANKEES	IP	H	R	ER	HR	K	BB	HBP	ERA
ATLEY DONALD	4	6	4	4	1	2	3	0	9.00
JOHNNY MURPHY W (1-0)	2	0	0	0	0	1	0	0	0.00
BROOKLYN DODGERS	IP	H	R	ER	HR	K	BB	HBP	ERA
KIRBY HIGBE	3.2	6	3	3	0	1	2	0	7.36
HUGH CASEY L (0-2)	4.1	5	4	0	0	1	2	0	3.38

Pete Reiser's 2-run homer in the 5th inning of Game 4 gave the Dodgers a 1-run lead that held up until the fateful 9th inning. Reiser hit only .200 in the Series, collecting only 4 hits, driving in 3, and scoring only 1 run. It was a disappointing finish to a phenomenal season in which the 22-year-old led the league in batting average, runs scored, total bases and slugging average, double, triples, and hit by pitch. Reiser finished second in the MVP voting to teammate Dolph Camilli. Three seasons in his prime lost to WWII and numerous collisions with concrete walls rendered Reiser a shadow of his former self, and he never approached his 1941 level of production again.

GAME TIME:	**2:54**
ATTENDANCE:	**33,813**
BEST OF 7:	**DODGERS - 1 YANKEES - 3**

Game 5

NEW YORK YANKEES vs. BROOKLYN DODGERS

October 6

LINE SCORE	1	2	3	4	5	6	7	8	9	R	H	E
NEW YORK YANKEES	0	2	0	0	1	0	0	0	0	3	6	0
BROOKLYN DODGERS	0	0	1	0	0	0	0	0	0	1	4	1

RECAP

Both Whitlow Wyatt from Brooklyn, in his second start, and Ernie Bonham from the Bronx, in his first, hurled complete games. Each pitched well enough to win. Neither had an easy time, pitching with runners on base more often than not. Wyatt gave up six hits, Bonham four. Wyatt allowed three runs on a wild pitch, a single and a solo home run. Bonham yielded one run on a sacrifice fly. Over the final six innings Bonham shut down the Dodgers, giving up one hit and one walk. Bonham's first victory results in the Yankees' ninth title.

(National Baseball Hall of Fame and Museum)

Tommy Henrich heads to first on what could have been a game-ending strikeout. Mickey Owen was one of the top defensive catchers of his time, making the All-Star team four times despite being at best an average hitter. In 1941, his first season with the Dodgers, he set an NL record for consecutive putouts by a catcher without an error (476). He was successful at throwing out just over 50% of would-be base stealers in his career.

But his name will always be associated with the passed ball that allowed the Yankees to come back and win Game 4 of the 1941 World Series. The judgment seems particularly harsh considering a Dodgers' win would have made the series only 2-2, and considering the Yankees took Game 5, Brooklyn would have had to be considered an underdog even had they successfully evened the Series after four.

Dodgers fans awaiting entry into Ebbets Field before the start of Game 3. No doubt many were filled with optimism, fresh off a Game 2 win, with the next three to be played in their friendly confines.

It had been 21 years since Da Bums had been in a World Series; they had gone 100-54 during the regular season, and the long Fall Classic losing streak to the Yankees had yet to begin.

But it was not meant to be for the Dodgers, as they were held to 1 run and 4 hits in Games 3 and 5, and blew a 9th inning lead in Game 4.

(National Baseball Hall of Fame and Museum)

SCORING SUMMARY

Second Inning - New York Yankees
– Wyatt starting.
– Keller legged it to first on a free pass.
– Dickey hitched a hit-and-run single; Keller braked at third base.
– Wyatt heaved a wild pitch, Keller scored; Dickey slid into second base.
– Gordon singled into right field, driving Dickey home.
– Rizzuto forced Gordon at second base, Riggs to Coscarart.
– Bonham went down on strikes.
– Sturm bunted out, Riggs to Camilli.

2 Runs **2** Hits **0** Errors **1** LOB

YANKEES – 2   **DODGERS – 0**

Third Inning - Brooklyn Dodgers
– Wyatt rattled a double into the left field corner.
– Walker flied out to DiMaggio.
– Riggs cuffed a single off of Bonham's ankle; Wyatt slid into third base.
– Reiser lifted a sacrifice fly to Henrich plating Wyatt.
– Camilli struck out.

1 Runs **1** Hits **0** Errors **0** LOB

YANKEES – 2   **DODGERS – 1**

Fifth Inning - New York Yankees
– Rolfe out on a grounder, Camilli to Wyatt.
– Henrich slugged a solo shot over the right field wall.
– DiMaggio flied out to Reiser.
– Keller struck out.

1 Runs **1** Hits **0** Errors **0** LOB

YANKEES – 3   **DODGERS – 1**

HIGHLIGHTS

• Dodger starter Whitlow Wyatt, in the second inning, wild pitched Charlie Keller home for the first run of the day
• Wyatt, in the next frame, got the run back, scoring on a sacrifice fly after drilling a lead off double
• Pinstripers hit into three double plays
• Yankee starter Ernie Bonham retired the side on three pitches in the seventh inning
• Ernie Bonham struck out in all four trips to the plate

GAME TIME:	2:13
ATTENDANCE:	34,072
BEST OF 7:	**DODGERS - 1 YANKEES - 4**

Game 5

NEW YORK YANKEES vs. BROOKLYN DODGERS

DIAMOND DUST

- Bonham is the first pitcher to win a clincher in his first World Series start
- The 12th five-game set

Game 5 BOX SCORE SUMMARY

NEW YORK YANKEES	AB	R	H	RBI	BB	K	1B	2B	3B	HR	TB	SB
TOMMY HENRICH, RF	3	1	1	1	1	1	0	0	0	1	4	0
CHARLIE KELLER, LF	3	1	0	0	1	1	0	0	0	0	0	0
BILL DICKEY, C	4	1	1	0	0	0	1	0	0	0	1	0
JOE GORDON, 2B	3	0	1	1	1	0	1	0	0	0	1	0
BROOKLYN DODGERS	AB	R	H	RBI	BB	K	1B	2B	3B	HR	TB	SB
PETE REISER, CF	4	0	1	0	0	1	0	0	1	0	0	1
WHITLOW WYATT, P	3	1	1	0	0	0	0	1	0	0	2	0

NEW YORK YANKEES	IP	H	R	ER	HR	K	BB	HBP	ERA
ERNIE BONHAM W (1-0)	9	4	1	1	0	2	2	0	1.00
BROOLYN DODGERS	IP	H	R	ER	HR	K	BB	HBP	ERA
WHITLOW WYATT L (1-1)	9	6	3	3	1	9	5	0	2.50

Ernie "Tiny" Bonham won the clincher in the 1941 World Series, and became the Yankees' top pitcher the following season, going 21-5 with a league-leading 22 complete games. Bonham racked up 34 more CGs the next two seasons and won a total of 103 games for the Yankees and Pirates in solid 10-year career, one that was marred by serious back troubles.

On August 27, 1949, Bonham pitched a complete-game win for Pittsburgh and drove in two runs with his only hit of the season. Shortly thereafter he was admitted to the hospital for an emergency appendectomy. During surgery it was discovered that Bonham had advanced intestinal cancer. On September 15th, less than three weeks after his final major league appearance, he succumbed to the disease at the very young age of 36.

104

1941

BROOKLYN DODGERS vs. NEW YORK YANKEES

BROOKLYN DODGERS

Overall World Series Record: 0 WINS 3 LOSSES. 17 Games Played (4-13 .235)
- No hitter compiled a .300 batting average or stroked more than four hits.
- Billy Herman has lost four Fall Classics, the other 3 while playing for the Cubs.
- Lost all three games at home.
- Composite batting average of .182 is one of the lowest in history.
- 20 players took the field (7 pitchers).
- Durocher is the second manager to lose in debut Subway Series appearance (1921).
- "Wait 'till next year" was coined after this Series.

NEW YORK YANKEES

Overall World Series Record: 9 WINS 3 LOSSES. 62 Games Played [42-19 (1 tie) .677]
- Johnny Murphy, Ernie Bonham, Red Ruffing and Marius Russo won one game each, pitching to a 1.00 ERA.
- Spud Chandler took the only loss for the Yankees.
- Atley Donald yielded the only Dodger home run.
- Joe Gordon, hitting for the cycle, is the only player to bat .400 in the Series (.500 7/14).
- Charlie Keller and Gordon stroked seven base hits and drove in five runs to lead both teams.
- Gordon tied the record for most walks in a five-game set with seven.
- Joe McCarthy is the first manager to win six Fall Classics (6-1).
- The Yankees' nine World Series wins tops all teams.

FUNGOES

220 games have been played since 1903
- MVP match-up: Joe DiMaggio batted .263 and Dolph Camilli batted .167.
- Joe Gordon and Pete Reiser hit for the cycle.
- At least one starter went the distance in four of the five games.
- 10 different players hit into 12 double plays.
- A double play was turned in every game.
- A grand total of 38 players (14 pitchers) took the field.
- Midsummer Classic and the Fall Classic won by the same league for the fifth season.
- National League's winning streak stopped at one.
- The all-time World Series record now stands at American League 24-14.

FIVE-GAME DATA

TIME	11:08	PLAYERS POOL	$474,185
ATTENDANCE	235,773	SHARES	BROOKLYN DODGERS - $4,829
			NEW YORK YANKEES - $5,943

105

1941

BROOKLYN DODGERS vs. NEW YORK YANKEES

Brooklyn Dodgers Composite Stats

BATTING	G	AB	R	H	RBI	2B	3B	HR	BB	SO	BA	OBP	SLG	OPS
Pete Reiser	5	20	1	4	3	1	1	1	1	6	.200	.238	.500	.738
Pee Wee Reese	5	20	1	4	2	0	0	0	0	0	.200	.200	.200	.400
Dixie Walker	5	18	3	4	0	2	0	0	2	1	.222	.300	.333	.633
Dolph Camilli	5	18	1	3	1	1	0	0	1	6	.167	.211	.222	.433
Joe Medwick	5	17	1	4	0	1	0	0	1	2	.235	.278	.294	.572
Mickey Owen	5	12	1	2	2	0	1	0	3	0	.167	.333	.333	.667
Cookie Lavagetto	3	10	1	1	0	0	0	0	2	0	.100	.250	.100	.350
Billy Herman	4	8	0	1	0	0	0	0	2	0	.125	.300	.125	.425
Lew Riggs	3	8	0	2	1	0	0	0	1	1	.250	.333	.250	.583
Pete Coscarart	3	7	1	0	0	0	0	0	1	2	.000	.125	.000	.125
Whit Wyatt	2	6	1	1	0	1	0	0	0	1	.167	.167	.333	.500
Jimmy Wasdell	3	5	0	1	2	1	0	0	0	0	.200	.200	.400	.600
Augie Galan	2	2	0	0	0	0	0	0	0	1	.000	.000	.000	.000
Freddie Fitzsimmons	1	2	0	0	0	0	0	0	0	0	.000	.000	.000	.000
Curt Davis	1	2	0	0	0	0	0	0	0	0	.000	.000	.000	.000
Hugh Casey	3	2	0	1	0	0	0	0	0	1	.500	.500	.500	1.000
Kirby Higbe	1	1	0	1	0	0	0	0	0	0	1.000	1.000	1.000	2.000
Herman Franks	1	1	0	0	0	0	0	0	0	0	.000	.000	.000	.000
Larry French	2	0	0	0	0	0	0	0	0	0				
Johnny Allen	3	0	0	0	0	0	0	0	0	0				
Totals	**5**	**159**	**11**	**29**	**11**	**7**	**2**	**1**	**14**	**21**	**.182**	**.249**	**.270**	**.519**

PITCHING	G	GS	ERA	W	L	SV	CG	IP	H	R	ER	BB	SO	WHIP
Whit Wyatt	2	2	2.50	1	1	0	2	18.0	15	5	5	10	14	1.389
F. Fitzsimmons	1	1	0.00	0	0	0	0	7.0	4	0	0	3	1	1.000
Hugh Casey	3	0	3.38	0	2	0	0	5.1	9	6	2	2	1	2.063
Curt Davis	1	1	5.06	0	1	0	0	5.1	6	3	3	3	1	1.688
Johnny Allen	3	0	0.00	0	0	0	0	3.2	1	0	0	3	0	1.091
Kirby Higbe	1	1	7.36	0	0	0	0	3.2	6	3	3	2	1	2.182
Larry French	2	0	0.00	0	0	0	0	1.0	0	0	0	0	0	0.000
Totals	**5**	**5**	**2.66**	**1**	**4**	**0**	**2**	**44.0**	**41**	**17**	**13**	**23**	**18**	**1.455**

1941

BROOKLYN DODGERS vs. NEW YORK YANKEES

New York Yankees Composite Stats

BATTING	G	AB	R	H	RBI	2B	3B	HR	BB	SO	BA	OBP	SLG	OPS
Johnny Sturm	5	21	0	6	2	0	0	0	0	2	.286	.318	.286	.604
Red Rolfe	5	20	2	6	0	0	0	0	2	1	.300	.364	.300	.664
Joe DiMaggio	5	19	1	5	1	0	0	0	2	2	.263	.333	.263	.596
Bill Dickey	5	18	3	3	1	1	0	0	3	1	.167	.286	.222	.508
Tommy Henrich	5	18	4	3	1	1	0	1	3	3	.167	.318	.389	.707
Charlie Keller	5	18	5	7	5	2	0	0	3	1	.389	.476	.500	.976
Phil Rizzuto	5	18	0	2	0	0	0	0	3	1	.111	.238	.111	.349
Joe Gordon	5	14	2	7	5	1	1	1	7	0	.500	.667	.929	1.595
Tiny Bonham	1	4	0	0	0	0	0	0	0	4	.000	.000	.000	.000
Marius Russo	1	4	0	0	0	0	0	0	0	1	.000	.000	.000	.000
Red Ruffing	1	3	0	0	0	0	0	0	0	0	.000	.000	.000	.000
Spud Chandler	1	2	0	1	1	0	0	0	0	0	.500	.500	.500	1.000
Atley Donald	1	2	0	0	0	0	0	0	0	1	.000	.000	.000	.000
Johnny Murphy	2	2	0	0	0	0	0	0	0	1	.000	.000	.000	.000
George Selkirk	2	2	0	1	0	0	0	0	0	0	.500	.500	.500	1.000
Marv Breuer	1	1	0	0	0	0	0	0	0	0	.000	.000	.000	.000
Frenchy Bordagaray	1	0	0	0	0	0	0	0	0	0				
Buddy Rosar	1	0	0	0	0	0	0	0	0	0				
Totals	**5**	**166**	**17**	**41**	**16**	**5**	**1**	**2**	**23**	**18**	**.247**	**.346**	**.325**	**.671**

PITCHING	G	GS	ERA	W	L	SV	CG	IP	H	R	ER	BB	SO	WHIP
Marius Russo	1	1	1.00	1	0	0	1	9.0	4	1	1	2	5	0.667
Red Ruffing	1	1	1.00	1	0	0	1	9.0	6	2	1	3	5	1.000
Tiny Bonham	1	1	1.00	1	0	0	1	9.0	4	1	1	2	2	0.667
Johnny Murphy	2	0	0.00	1	0	0	0	6.0	2	0	0	1	3	0.500
Spud Chandler	1	1	3.60	0	1	0	0	5.0	4	3	2	2	2	1.200
Atley Donald	1	1	9.00	0	0	0	0	4.0	6	4	4	3	2	2.250
Marv Breuer	1	0	0.00	0	0	0	0	3.0	3	0	0	1	2	1.333
Totals	**5**	**5**	**1.80**	**4**	**1**	**0**	**3**	**45.0**	**29**	**11**	**9**	**14**	**21**	**0.956**

1947

BROOKLYN DODGERS vs. NEW YORK YANKEES

FUNGOES

- ⚾ Dixie Walker's brother Harry (St. Louis Cardinals) defeated Joe DiMaggio's brother Dom (Boston Red Sox) in the 1946 Classic.
- ⚾ Six umpires deployed for the first time.
- ⚾ Two umpires were former players - Babe Pinelli played 3B for various teams (1918-27) and Eddie Rommel pitched for the Philadelphia Athletics from 1920-32, winning titles in 1929/30.
- ⚾ Both teams started a pitcher with a regular season losing record [Yankees - Bill Bevens (7-13); Dodgers - Hal Gregg (4-5)].

SERIES SUMMARY

The Yankees won the Series opener, as they had, amazingly, in their previous 11 World Series. A 5-run fifth inning (after the first 12 batters made out) eclipsed Brooklyn's 3 1-run rallies. Three walks and a HBP did in the Dodgers. Joe Page pitched the final four innings.

Game 2 was also close through four innings, but the Bronx Bombers lived up to their nickname the next three frames, in which they piled on seven more runs, totaling 10 in all, on 15 hits. It was truly a team effort, with seven different Yankees driving in and scoring at least one run. Allie Reynolds coasted to a complete-game victory.

The Yankees added eight more runs in Game 3, but the Dodgers, on the strength of a 6-run third, tallied nine, taking a 7-2 lead and hanging on for the win. Hugh Casey notched a clutch eight-out save, while Brooklyn spread out its offense, matching the Yankees with seven players recording RBI and seven crossing the plate.

Game 4 was the setting for one of the most dramatic moments in World Series history. Yankees' starter took a no-hitter and 2-1 lead into the bottom of the ninth inning. After Bevens's ninth and tenth walks of the game, Cookie Lavagetto broke up the no-hitter and gave the Dodgers a stunning victory to even the series with a 2-run double. Hal Gregg was the unlikely hero on the mound, allowing just one run in seven innings after posting an ERA of 5.87 during the regular season.

More good pitching was the theme of Game 5, as Yankees rookie Spec Shea pitched a complete game 4-hitter for a 2-1 win. DiMaggio's homer in the fifth proved to be the difference, after Shea had driven in the Yankees' first run the inning before.

The bats took over again in Game 6, which saw a total of 14 runs and 27 hits off a total of 10 pitchers. The frequently invincible Allie Reynolds and Joe Page of the Yankees gave up all eight runs in Brooklyn's 8-6 series-saving victory, with Peewee Reese doing the most damage with three hits, 2 RBI, and 2 RS.

Game 7 once again showed why the Yankees are the Yankees as clutch 2-out hits accounted for four of their five runs and Hugh Casey shut down Brooklyn on one hit and no runs over the final five innings. The 5-2 victory gave New York their second of what would turn out to be three World Series wins against the Dodgers of the decade.

THE TEAMS

BROOKLYN DODGERS
94–60 .610 +5.0 G

The Team
- Subway Series #2; fourth overall appearance.
- In first place at the All-Star break.

The Players
- 1941 Subway Series returning players: Hugh Casey, Cookie Lavagetto, Pee Wee Reese, Pete Reiser and Dixie Walker.
- Ralph Branca won as many games (21) as his years on the planet, the only 20-game winner on the staff.
- Dixie Walker (.306) is the only .300 hitter in the line-up.
- Walker's brother Harry played on the 1942/43/46 National League pennant-winning St. Louis Cardinals, winning then losing to the Yankees in 1942 and 1943 and defeating the Boston Red Sox in '46.
- Jackie Robinson, as the first African-American player, ended racial apartheid in this Fall Classic.
- Robinson won the Rookie of the Year award, leading the league with 29 stolen bases, batting .297 and scoring 125 runs.

The Manager
- Manager Burt Shotton played the outfield for the St. Louis Cardinals and the Washington Senators.
- Shotton is the second skipper to manage in street clothes (Connie Mack).
- Shotton is the third manager to debut in the Subway Series (Miller Huggins 1921, Leo Durocher 1941).

Top Batters

Pos	Name	AB	R	H	HR	RBI	BA	OPS
1B	Jackie Robinson	590	125	175	12	48	.297	.810
2B	Eddie Stanky	559	97	141	3	53	.252	.702
SS	Pee Wee Reese	476	81	135	12	73	.284	.841
OF	Dixie Walker	529	77	162	9	94	.306	.842

Top Pitchers

Pos	Name	W	L	ERA	G	SV	IP	SO
St	Ralph Branca	21	12	2.67	43	1	280.0	148
St	Joe Hatten	17	8	3.63	42	0	225.1	76
St	Vic Lombardi	12	11	2.99	33	3	174.2	72
Rel	Hugh Casey	10	4	3.99	46	18	76.2	40

NEW YORK YANKEES
97–57 .630 +12.0 G

The Team
- Subway Series #7; 15th overall appearance.
- In second place at the All-Star break.

The Players
- 1941 Subway Series returning players: Spud Chandler, Joe DiMaggio, Tommy Henrich and Phil Rizzuto.
- DiMaggio played on the 1936/37/38/39/41/42 pennant-winning teams, winning five titles.
- Phil Rizzuto played on the 1941/42 pennant-winning teams, winning title in '41.
- Chandler played on the 1941/42/43 pennant-winning teams, winning two titles.
- DiMaggio was named the MVP of the American League for the third time (1939/41).
- DiMaggio (.315) and George McQuinn (.304) are the .300 hitters in the line-up.

The Manager
- Bucky Harris' third career appearance, in two different decades, debut appearance as a Yankee manager.
- Harris was the player-manager (2B) for the 1924/25 pennant-winning Washington Senators, capturing the 1924 title from the New York Giants.
- Harris's 2158 wins as a manager (against 2219 losses) rank seventh all time; he was elected to the Hall of Fame by the Veteran's Committee in 1975.

Top Batters

Pos	Name	AB	R	H	HR	RBI	BA	OPS
1B	George McQuinn	517	84	157	13	80	.304	.832
2B	Snuffy Stirnweiss	571	102	146	5	41	.256	.700
OF	Joe DiMaggio	534	97	168	20	97	.315	.913
OF	Tommy Henrich	550	109	158	16	98	.287	.857

Top Pitchers

Pos	Name	W	L	ERA	G	SV	IP	SO
St	Allie Reynolds	19	8	3.20	34	2	241.2	129
St	Spec Shea	14	5	3.07	27	1	178.2	89
St	Spud Chandler	9	5	2.46	17	0	128.0	68
Rel	Joe Page	14	8	2.48	56	17	141.1	116

Game 1

BROOKLYN DODGERS vs. NEW YORK YANKEES

September 30

LINE SCORE	1	2	3	4	5	6	7	8	9	R	H	E
BROOKLYN DODGERS	1	0	0	0	0	1	1	0	0	3	6	0
NEW YORK YANKEES	0	0	0	0	5	0	0	0	X	5	4	0

RECAP

Down by one run in the bottom of the fifth inning the Yankees sent 10 men to the plate. Dodger starter Ralph Branca and reliever Hank Behrman allowed seven New Yorkers to reach base via a hit batter, three walks and three base hits. The four Bombers - George McQuinn, Billy Johnson, Phil Rizzuto and Bobby Brown - who reached base without a hit, all scored.

Brooklyn fought back against Yankee reliever Joe Page scoring single runs in sixth and seventh innings. However, in the eighth and ninth frames, Page found his rhythm, retiring six of the last seven Dodgers to notch the save.

SCORING SUMMARY

First Inning - Brooklyn Dodgers

– Shea starting.
– Stanky skied out to Lindell.
– J. Robinson jogged to first on a walk; swiped second base.
– Reiser crossed first base on a fielder's choice; J. Robinson chased out in a run-down, Shea to Rizzuto; Reiser took second on the play.
– Walker singled into left field, driving Reiser home.
– Herman struck out.

1 Runs **1** Hits **0** Errors **1** LOB

DODGERS – 1   **YANKEES – 0**

Fifth Inning - New York Yankees

– DiMaggio one-hopped a single into left field.
– McQuinn walked DiMaggio to second base.
– Johnson clipped by a pitch; bases loaded.
– Lindell doubled into left field, driving in DiMaggio and McQuinn; Johnson chugged into third base.
– Rizzuto walked; bases loaded.
– Brown PH for Shea, reached a two-ball count, Behrman relieved Branca, walked; Johnson scored; bases loaded.
– Stirnweiss safe at first on a fielder's choice; Lindell forced at home. J. Robinson to Edwards; bases loaded.

– Henrich singled into left field, driving in Rizzuto and Brown; Stirnweiss slid into second base.
– Berra flied out to Walker.
– DiMaggio flied out to Hermanski.

5 Runs **3** Hits **0** Errors **2** LOB

DODGERS – 1   **YANKEES – 5**

Sixth Inning - Brooklyn Dodgers

– Page pitching.
– Stanky stroked a single into center field.
– J. Robinson forced Stanky at second base, Rizzuto to Stirnweiss.
– Reiser sped across first base on a bang-bang play, J. Robinson slid into second base.
– Walker flied out to Henrich.
– Furillo PH for Hermanski, singled into center field, driving in J. Robinson.
– Reiser streaked into third base.
– Edwards forced Furillo at second base, Rizzuto to Stirnweiss.

1 Runs **2** Hits **0** Errors **2** LOB

DODGERS – 2   **YANKEES – 5**

Seventh Inning - Brooklyn Dodgers

– Lavagetto PH for Jorgensen, popped up to Stirnweiss.
– Reese picked up a right field single.
– Miksis PH for Behrman, struck out; Reese swiped second base; Page flung a wild pitch, Reese scored from second.
– Stanky bounced back to the box, Page to McQuinn.

1 Runs **1** Hits **0** Errors **0** LOB

DODGERS – 3   **YANKEES – 5**

HIGHLIGHTS

- Dodger starter Ralph Branca retired the first 12 Bombers
- Then, in the 5th, Branca allowed the first five batters to reach base, and was relieved two balls into the sixth batter
- Behrman completed the bases-loaded walk to Brown, which was charged to Branca
- Joe DiMaggio, batting twice in the fifth inning, got the first hit, scored the first run, and made the last out
- DiMaggio has batted twice in an inning in three Classics (1936/37)
- Unusual for a balk (Shea), a hit batter (Branca) and a wild pitch (Page) to occur in the same game

DIAMOND DUST

- 73,365 fans set a new attendance record, in addition to the millions more watching on television for the first time
- Frank 'Spec' Shea and Yogi Berra comprised the first rookie battery in World Series history.
- Shea is the fourth rookie to start an opener, the second to pitch a complete game, as well as the second to win (Babe Adams, 1909)
- Jackie Robinson, in the sixth inning, became the first African-American player to score a World Series run, on a Carl Furillo pinch-hit single
- Shea is the third pitcher to win in both the Mid-Summer Classic and the Fall Classic in the same season
- Page is the first pitcher to notch a save in both the Mid-Summer Classic and the Fall Classic in the same season
- In openers, the Yankees are 12-3 while the Dodgers are 0-4
- Game One winners have won it all 28 times out of 44 World Series
- New York has not lost an opener since 1936 (seven wins in a row)

Game 1 BOX SCORE SUMMARY

BROOKLYN DODGERS	AB	R	H	RBI	BB	K	1B	2B	3B	HR	TB	SB
JACKIE ROBINSON, 1B	2	1	0	0	2	0	0	0	0	0	0	1
PETE REISER, CF/LF	4	1	1	0	0	0	1	0	0	0	1	0
DIXIE WALKER, RF	4	0	2	1	0	0	2	0	0	0	2	0
CARL FURILLO, PH/CF	1	0	1	1	1	0	1	0	0	0	1	0
PEE WEE REESE, SS	4	1	1	0	0	0	1	0	0	0	1	1
NEW YORK YANKEES	AB	R	H	RBI	BB	K	1B	2B	3B	HR	TB	SB
TOMMY HENRICH, RF	4	0	1	2	0	1	1	0	0	0	1	0
JOE DIMAGGIO, CF	4	1	1	0	0	0	1	0	0	0	1	0
GEORGE MCQUINN, 1B	3	1	0	0	1	1	0	0	0	0	0	0
BILLY JOHNSON, 3B	2	1	0	0	0	0	0	0	0	0	0	0
JOHNNY LINDELL, LF	3	0	1	2	0	1	0	1	0	0	2	0
PHIL RIZZUTO, SS	2	1	1	0	1	0	1	0	0	0	1	0
BOBBY BROWN, PH	0	1	0	1	1	0	0	0	0	0	0	0

BROOKLYN DODGERS	IP	H	R	ER	HR	K	BB	HBP	ERA
RALPH BRANCA L (0-1)	4	2	5	5	0	0	0	1	11.25
HANK BEHRMAN	2	1	0	0	0	0	0	0	0.00
HUGH CASEY	2	1	0	0	0	1	0	0	0.00
NEW YORK YANKEES	IP	H	R	ER	HR	K	BB	HBP	ERA
FRANK SHEA W (1-0)	5	2	1	1	0	3	2	0	1.80
JOE PAGE S (1)	4	4	2	2	0	2	1	0	4.50

GAME TIME:	2:20
ATTENDANCE:	73,365
BEST OF 7:	DODGERS - 0 YANKEES - 1

Game 2

BROOKLYN DODGERS vs. NEW YORK YANKEES

October 1

LINE SCORE	1	2	3	4	5	6	7	8	9	R	H	E
BROOKLYN DODGERS	0	0	1	1	0	0	0	0	1	3	9	2
NEW YORK YANKEES	1	0	1	1	2	1	4	0	X	10	15	1

RECAP

Taking the field in the friendly atmosphere of Yankee Stadium, the Bronx Bombers bombed four Dodgers pitchers for 15 base hits and 10 tallies. The Yankees mounted scoring drives in all but two innings. Of the starting nine, eight stroked a hit and/or scored a run, and seven drove in a run.

Allie Reynolds was a standout on both sides of the ball. As a batter he had two hits, scored two runs and drove in one. As a pitcher he went the distance, allowing nine hits and single runs in three frames.

SCORING SUMMARY

First Inning - New York Yankees
– Lombardi starting.
– Stirnweiss notched a single into right field.
– Henrich hitched a hit-and-run single; Stirnweiss motored into third.
– Lindell scored Stirnweiss on a double play, Jorgensen to Stanky to J.Robinson.
– DiMaggio struck out.

1 Runs **1** Hits **0** Errors **1** LOB

DODGERS – 0   **YANKEES – 1**

Third Inning - Brooklyn Dodgers
– Reynolds starting.
– Reese sprinted to first on a walk.
– Jorgensen flied out to Henrich; Reese swiped second base.
– Lombardi flied out to DiMaggio.
– Stanky singled Reese to third base.
– J. Robinson singled into left field, driving in Reese; Stanky slid into second.
– Reiser was a strikeout.

1 Runs **2** Hits **0** Errors **1** LOB

DODGERS – 1   **YANKEES – 1**

Third Inning - New York Yankees
– Reynolds grounded out, Jorgensen to J. Robinson.

– Stirnweiss triggered a triple into the right-center field alley.
– Henrich fouled out to Jorgensen.
– Lindell tripled to deepest center field, driving Stirnweiss home.
– DiMaggio walked on purpose; runners on the corners.
– McQuinn was a strikeout.

1 Runs **2** Hits **0** Errors **2** LOB

DODGERS – 1   **YANKEES – 2**

Fourth Inning - Brooklyn Dodgers
– Walker slugged a first pitch solo shot into the right field crowd.
– Hermanski out on a grounder, McQuinn to Reynolds.
– Edwards popped up to McQuinn.
– Reese thrown out trying to stretch a single, Berra to Rizzuto.

1 Runs **2** Hits **0** Errors **0** LOB

DODGERS – 2   **YANKEES – 2**

Fourth Inning - New York Yankees
– Johnson tattooed a triple into dead-center field.
– Rizzuto doubled into left field, driving Johnson home.
– Berra advanced Rizzuto on a fly to Reiser.

– Reynolds sped to first base on a fielder's choice; Rizzuto tagged out in a run-down, Edwards to Jorgensen; Reynolds slid into second.

– Stirnweiss was a strikeout.

1 Runs **2** Hits **0** Errors **1** LOB

DODGERS – 2   **YANKEES – 3**

Fifth Inning - New York Yankees

– Henrich slugged a solo shot into the right-center field seats.

– Lindell one-hopped a ground rule double into the left field stands.

– DiMaggio got to a 1-0 count; Gregg relieved Lombardi; out on a ground ball, Jorgensen to J. Robinson.

– McQuinn singled up the middle, driving Lindell home.

– Johnson flew to first as McQuinn slid into second on Stanky's fumble.

– Rizzuto flied out to Reiser.

– Berra was a strikeout.

2 Runs **3** Hits **1** Errors **2** LOB

DODGERS – 2   **YANKEES – 5**

Sixth Inning - New York Yankees

– Reynolds cut a single over the third base bag into left field.

– Stirnweiss walked Reynolds to second base.

– Henrich advanced both runners on a sacrifice, Gregg to Stanley.

– Lindell lifted a sacrifice fly to Hermanski plating Reynolds.

– DiMaggio singled off of Reese's outstretched glove.

– McQuinn struck out.

1 Runs **1** Hits **0** Errors **1** LOB

DODGERS – 2   **YANKEES – 6**

Seventh Inning - New York Yankees

– Behrman pitching.

– McQuinn hooked a single into right field; wild pitched to second.

– Johnson singled into center field, driving in McQuinn; Johnson made third as Reiser lost the ball in the sun.

– Rizzuto popped up to Stanky.

– Berra given an intentional pass; runners on the corners.

– Reynolds scored Johnson on a squeeze bunt single; Berra barreled into third base.

– Barney relieved Behrman.

– Stirnweiss scored Berra on an infield hit; Reynolds slid into second base.

– Henrich advanced Reynolds on a fly to Reiser; on a wild pitch Reynolds scored; Stirnweiss slid into second base.

– Lindell got a free pass; Stirnweiss held.

– DiMaggio forced Stirnweiss at third base, Jorgensen unassisted.

4 Runs **3** Hits **1** Errors **2** LOB

DODGERS – 2   **YANKEES – 10**

Ninth Inning - Brooklyn Dodgers

– Hermanski hurried to first base on a walk.

– Edwards flied out to Lindell.

– Reese blistered a hit-and-run single; Hermanski scrambled into third.

– Jorgensen scored Hermanski on a force of Reese at second base, Stirnweiss to Rizzuto.

– Gionfriddo PH for Barney, forced Jorgensen at second base, Johnson to Stirnweiss.

1 Runs **1** Hits **0** Errors **1** LOB

DODGERS – 3   **YANKEES – 10**

HIGHLIGHTS

- Allie Reynolds, in the seventh inning, bunted home a run, and two batters later he scored on a wild pitch
- Brooklyn relievers Hank Behrman and Rex Barney fired wild pitches in the 7th inning, leading to two scores
- Tommy Henrich, Stirnweiss and Lindell each swatted five total bases
- Bombers pounded out 15 hits, including three triples

DIAMOND DUST

- Brooklyn starter Vic Lombardi is the first pitcher in 29 years to allow two triples in an inning (3rd)
- Snuffy Stirnweiss and Johnny Lindell-tattooed three-baggers, the eighth time a team hit two triples in a World Series game
- Somewhere in the stands sat the nine millionth fan
- Jackie Robinson, in the third inning, became the first African-American player to drive in a run, scoring Pee Wee Reese

Game 2 BOX SCORE SUMMARY

BROOKLYN DODGERS	AB	R	H	RBI	BB	K	1B	2B	3B	HR	TB	SB
JACKIE ROBINSON, 1B	4	0	2	1	0	0	1	1	0	0	3	0
DIXIE WALKER, RF	4	1	1	1	0	0	0	0	0	1	4	0
GENE HERMANSKI, LF	3	1	0	0	0	0	0	0	0	0	0	0
PEE WEE REESE, SS	3	1	2	0	0	0	2	0	0	0	2	1
SPIDER JORGENSON, 3B	4	0	1	1	0	0	1	0	0	0	1	0
NEW YORK YANKEES	AB	R	H	RBI	BB	K	1B	2B	3B	HR	TB	SB
SNUFFY STIRNWEISS, 2B	4	2	3	1	1	1	2	0	1	0	5	0
TOMMY HENRICH, RF	4	1	2	1	0	0	1	0	0	1	5	0
JOHNNY LINDELL, LF	4	1	2	2	1	0	0	1	1	0	5	0
GEORGE MCQUINN, 1B	5	1	2	1	0	2	2	0	0	0	2	0
BILLY JOHNSON, 3B	5	2	2	1	0	0	1	0	1	0	4	0
PHIL RIZZUTO, SS	5	0	1	1	0	0	0	1	0	0	2	0
YOGI BERRA, C	3	1	0	0	1	1	0	0	0	0	0	0
ALLIE REYNOLDS, P	4	2	2	1	0	0	2	0	0	0	2	0

Phil Rizzuto (seen with Al Gionfriddo sliding into second) played in 9 World Series in his 13 seasons in the majors. He collected 45 hits and 30 walks in 52 games, (.355 OBP) and struck out only 11 times in 219 plate appearances. (National Baseball Hall of Fame and Museum)

BROOKLYN DODGERS	IP	H	R	ER	HR	K	BB	HBP	ERA
VIC LOMBARDI L (0-1)	4	9	5	5	1	3	1	0	11.25
HAL GREGG	2	2	1	1	0	2	1	0	4.50
HANK BEHRMAN	0.1	3	4	4	0	0	1	0	15.43
NEW YORK YANKEES	IP	H	R	ER	HR	K	BB	HBP	ERA
ALLIE REYNOLDS W (1-0)	9	9	3	3	1	6	2	0	3.00

GAME TIME:	2:36	
ATTENDANCE:	69,865	
BEST OF 7:	**DODGERS - 0**	**YANKEES - 2**

Game 3

NEW YORK YANKEES vs. BROOKLYN DODGERS

October 2

LINE SCORE	1	2	3	4	5	6	7	8	9	R	H	E
NEW YORK YANKEES	0	0	2	2	2	1	1	0	0	8	13	0
BROOKLYN DODGERS	0	6	1	2	0	0	0	0	X	9	13	1

--- **RECAP** ---

A one-run differential built on 26 base hits and scoring in six of the nine frames. The home team plated six in the second inning and then added three more in the next two frames. The visitors battled back with three successive rallies to get the deficit down to two. New York rookie PH Yogi Berra, in the seventh inning, made history by belting the first pinch-hit home run, off of Brooklyn hurler Ralph Branca. That first ended the scoring for the day, and the Dodgers two-game losing streak ended as well.

--- **SCORING SUMMARY** ---

Second Inning - Brooklyn Dodgers
– Walker out on a ground ball, Rizzuto to McQuinn.
– Hermanski finagled a free pass.
– Edwards doubled into right field, driving Hermanski home.
– Reese singled up the middle, driving Edwards home.
– Jorgensen flied out to DiMaggio.
– Hatten singled Reese to second base; both runners advanced on a Lollar passed ball.
– Stanky doubled into right field, driving home Reese and Hatten.
– Raschi relieved Newsom.
– J. Robinson singled Stanky to third base.
– Furillo PH for Reiser, doubled off of the center field score board, driving home Stanky and J. Robinson.
– Walker grounded out, Rizzuto to McQuinn.

6 Runs **5** Hits **0** Errors **1** LOB

YANKEES – 0   **DODGERS – 6**

Third Inning - New York Yankees
– Furillo to CF.
– Lollar short-hopped a single into center field.
– Clark PH for Raschi, walked Lollar to second base.
– Stirnweiss was a strikeout.
– Henrich flied out to Hermanski.

– Lindell singled up the middle, driving in Lollar; Clark advanced.
– DiMaggio singled through the box, driving in Clark; Lindell slid into second.
– McQuinn was a strikeout.

2 Runs **3** Hits **0** Errors **2** LOB

YANKEES – 2   **DODGERS – 6**

Third Inning - Brooklyn Dodgers
– Drews pitching.
– Hermanski plunked by a pitch; slid into second on a wild pitch.
– Edwards back to the box, Drews to McQuinn; Hermanski moved up.
– Reese out on a mounder, Drews to McQuinn; Hermanski held.
– Jorgensen singled up the middle, driving Hermanski home.
– Hatten forced Jorgensen at second base, Rizzuto to Stirnweiss.

1 Runs **1** Hits **0** Errors **1** LOB

YANKEES – 2   **DODGERS – 7**

Fourth Inning - New York Yankees
– Johnson jogged to first on a walk.
– Rizzuto flied out to Hermanski.
– Lollar doubled into right field, driving Johnson home.

- Phillips PH for Drews, flied out to Hermanski.
- Stirnweiss singled up the middle, driving in Lollar; Stirnweiss slid into second base on Furillo's throwing error.
- Henrich squibbed out, Stanky to J. Robinson.

2 Runs **2** Hits **1** Errors **1** LOB

YANKEES – 4   **DODGERS – 7**

Fourth Inning - Brooklyn Dodgers
- Chandler on the mound.
- Stanky drew a walk.
- J. Robinson sacrificed Stanky to second base, McQuinn to Stirnweiss.
- Furillo worked a walk.
- Walker singled into center field, driving in Stanky; Furillo flashed into third.
- Hermanski singled up the middle, driving in Furillo; Walker slid into second.
- Edwards was a strikeout.
- Reese walked; bases loaded.
- Jorgensen grounded out to McQuinn.

2 Runs **2** Hits **0** Errors **3** LOB

YANKEES – 4   **DODGERS – 9**

Fifth Inning - New York Yankees
- Lindell wangled a walk.
- DiMaggio powered a home run into the left field seats, driving Lindell home.
- McQuinn nubbed out, Jorgensen to J. Robinson.
- Branca relieved Hatten.

- Johnson struck out.
- Rizzuto stung a sizzler over the first base bag.
- Lollar forced Rizzuto at second base, Reese to Stanky.

2 Runs **2** Hits **0** Errors **1** LOB

YANKEES – 6   **DODGERS – 9**

Sixth Inning - New York Yankees
- Brown PH for Chandler, rattled a double into the right field corner.
- Stirnweiss pushed Brown to third base on a grounder, Reese to J. Robinson.
- Henrich doubled off of Stanky's glove, driving Brown home.
- Lindell fouled out to Jorgensen.
- DiMaggio got on on a walk.
- McQuinn walked; bases loaded.
- Johnson popped up to Stanky.

1 Runs **1** Hits **0** Errors **3** LOB

YANKEES – 7   **DODGERS – 9**

Seventh Inning - New York Yankees
- Rizzuto flied out to Hermanski.
- Berra PH for Lollar, slugged a solo shot high off of the scoreboard.
- Casey relieved Branca.
- Page out on a grounder, Reese to J. Robinson.
- Stirnweiss struck out.

1 Runs **1** Hits **0** Errors **0** LOB

YANKEES – 8   **DODGERS – 9**

HIGHLIGHTS

- Jackie Robinson and Pete Reiser were both thrown out trying to steal second base in the first inning
- 10 men batted in the Brooklyn second inning rally, as RF Dixie Walker made the first and the last out
- Bobo Newsom, acquired in mid-season from the Washington Senators, gave up five hits and five runs in his only Series appearance
- Seven different players drilled doubles—Dodgers (4) Yankees (3)—and all but one resulted in a run scored or a run batted in
- Eight of the nine starters on both teams got a hit
- All eight pitchers Yankees (5) Dodgers (3) gave up base hits; six of the eight gave up runs

Bobo Newsom started and lost Game 3. He was purchased by the Yankees in July of 1947 and released the following February. Newsom played in one other World Series—for the 1940 Tigers—in which he won Games 1 and 5 and lost Game 7, 2-1, when Cincinnati rallied for 2 runs in the bottom of the seventh inning. Newsom, who played for 9 of the original 16 major league teams, went 211-222 in his career, and remains one of only 2 pitchers in major league history to win at least 200 games in his career but finish with a losing record.

DIAMOND DUST

- Yankees reliever Karl Drews is the sixth pitcher to hit a batter and throw a wild pitch in the same frame
- Three pinch-hits (all for extra bases) ties a record
- Yogi Berra's seventh inning PH solo shot was the first hit and the first run batted of his long World Series career
- Three Dodgers doubles in the second inning tied a team record
- Carl Furillo collected his second pinch hit of the series—a single and a double—good for three RBI

Game 3 BOX SCORE SUMMARY

NEW YORK YANKEES	AB	R	H	RBI	BB	K	1B	2B	3B	HR	TB	SB
SNUFFY STIRNWEISS, 2B	5	0	2	1	0	2	2	0	0	0	2	0
TOMMY HENRICH, RF	4	0	1	1	1	0	0	1	0	0	2	0
JOHNNY LINDELL, LF	4	1	2	1	1	0	2	0	0	0	2	0
JOE DIMAGGIO, CF	4	1	2	3	1	0	1	0	0	1	5	0
BILLY JOHNSON, 3B	4	1	1	0	1	1	1	0	0	0	1	0
SHERM LOLLAR, C	3	2	2	1	0	0	1	1	0	0	3	0
YOGI BERRA, PH/C	2	1	1	1	0	0	0	0	0	1	4	0
ALLIE CLARK, PH	0	1	0	0	1	0	0	0	0	0	0	0
BOBBY BROWN, PH	1	1	1	0	0	0	0	1	0	0	2	0

BROOKLYN DODGERS	AB	R	H	RBI	BB	K	1B	2B	3B	HR	TB	SB
EDDIE STANKY, 2B	4	2	1	2	1	0	0	1	0	0	2	0
JACKIE ROBINSON, 1B	4	1	2	0	0	0	2	0	0	0	2	1
CARL FURILLO, PH/CF	3	1	2	2	1	0	1	1	0	0	3	0
DIXIE WALKER, RF	5	0	2	1	0	0	2	0	0	0	2	1
GENE HERMANSKI, LF	3	2	1	1	1	1	1	0	0	0	1	0
BRUCE EDWARDS, C	4	1	1	1	1	1	0	1	0	0	2	0
PEE WEE REESE, SS	3	1	1	1	1	1	1	0	0	0	1	0
SPIDER JORGENSON, 3B	4	0	2	1	0	0	1	1	0	0	3	0
JOE HATTEN, P	2	1	1	0	0	0	1	0	0	0	1	0

22-year old Yogi Berra was backup catcher to Aaron Robinson during the 1947 season, but in the Series that year he started 4 games behind the plate, along with 2 others in right field. He hit only .158 in the Series, but went on to appear in 13 more, an all-time record, finishing with a record 75 games, 259 at bats, a solid slash line of .274/.359/452, and 12 home runs. (National Baseball Hall of Fame and Museum)

NEW YORK YANKEES	IP	H	R	ER	HR	K	BB	HBP	ERA
BOBO NEWSOM L (0-1)	1.2	5	5	5	0	0	2	0	27.00
VIC RASCHI	0.1	2	1	1	0	0	0	0	27.00
KARL DREWS	1	1	1	1	0	0	0	1	9.00
SPUD CHANDLER	2	2	2	2	0	1	3	0	9.00

BROOKLYN DODGERS	IP	H	R	ER	HR	K	BB	HBP	ERA
JOE HATTEN	4.1	8	6	6	1	3	3	0	12.46
RALPH BRANCA	2	4	2	2	1	1	2	0	10.50
HUGH CASEY W (1-0)	2.2	1	0	0	0	1	1	0	0.00

GAME TIME:	**3:05**
ATTENDANCE:	**33,098**
BEST OF 7:	**DODGERS - 1 YANKEES - 2**

Game 4

NEW YORK YANKEES vs. BROOKLYN DODGERS

October 3

LINE SCORE	1	2	3	4	5	6	7	8	9	R	H	E
NEW YORK YANKEES	1	0	0	1	0	0	0	0	0	2	8	1
BROOKLYN DODGERS	0	0	0	0	1	0	0	0	2	3	1	3

RECAP

A near-no-hitter, coupled with bottom-of-the-ninth dramatics, marked this game as a classic. For eight and two-thirds innings Yankee starter Floyd (Bill) Bevens held the Brooklynites hitless. Bevens was nursing a one-run lead in the bottom of the ninth with one out to go. The Dodgers had two men on base via their ninth and 10th walks. PH Cookie Lavagetto stepped to the plate. On Bevens' 137th pitch, he lost the no-hitter and the game to a Lavagetto double that scored Al Gionfriddo with the tying run and Eddie Miksis with the winning run.

SCORING SUMMARY

First Inning - New York Yankees
– Taylor starting.
– Stirnweiss cracked a single into left field.
– Henrich singled Stirnweiss to second base.
– Berra sprinted across first base on Reese's fumble; bases loaded.
– DiMaggio walked; Stirnweiss scored; bases loaded.
– Gregg relieved Taylor.
– McQuinn popped up to Reese.
– Johnson knocked into a double play, Reese to Stanky to J. Robinson.

1 Runs **2** Hits **1** Errors **2** LOB

YANKEES – 1   **DODGERS – 0**

Fourth Inning - New York Yankees
– Johnson torqued a triple into deepest center field.
– Lindell doubled into right field, driving Johnson home.
– Rizzuto out on a ground ball to J. Robinson; Lindell slid into third base.
– Bevens grounded out, Reese to J. Robinson.
– Stirnweiss was a strikeout.

1 Runs **2** Hits **0** Errors **1** LOB

YANKEES – 2   **DODGERS – 0**

Fifth Inning - Brooklyn Dodgers
– Jorgensen walked.
– Gregg walked; Jorgensen advanced.
– Stanky sacrificed the runners up, Berra to Stirnweiss.
– Reese reached first base on a fielder's choice; Jorgensen scored.
– Gregg tagged out at third base, Rizzuto to Johnson; Reese swiped second base; slid into third base on Berra's errant throw.
– J. Robinson was a strikeout.

1 Runs **0** Hits **1** Errors **1** LOB

YANKEES – 2   **DODGERS – 1**

Ninth Inning - Brooklyn Dodgers
– Edwards flied out to DiMaggio.
– Furillo walked.
– Jorgensen fouled out to McQuinn.
– Gionfriddo PR; swiped second base.
– Reiser PH for Casey, walked.
– Miksis PR.
– Lavagetto PH for Stanky, doubled, breaking up Beven's no-hit bid, driving home Gionfriddo and Miksis for the win.

2 Runs **1** Hits **0** Errors **1** LOB

YANKEES – 2   **DODGERS – 3**

HIGHLIGHTS

- Dodger starter Harry Taylor is the 21st rookie to start, but he did not record an out, facing only four batters
- Taylor gave up a lead-off single to Snuffy Stirnweiss, and two batters later, walked in Stirnweiss with the first run
- Hal Gregg hurled 7 innings of one-run relief
- Tommy Henrich hit into two rally-killing double plays
- Dodger reliever Hugh Casey threw one pitch in the top of the ninth, inducing an inning-ending double play to notch the win
- Brooklyn gets their first walk-off win in World Series history, while the Yankees go to 2-1 in such games

DIAMOND DUST

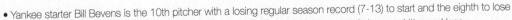
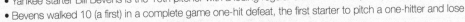
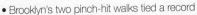

- Yankee starter Bill Bevens is the 10th pitcher with a losing regular season record (7-13) to start and the eighth to lose
- Bevens walked 10 (a first) in a complete game one-hit defeat, the first starter to pitch a one-hitter and lose
- Brooklyn's two pinch-hit walks tied a record
- Casey is the sixth pitcher to post consecutive wins, the second reliever to win two games
- Ironically, Casey LOST Games 3 and 4 in the 1941 World Series
- It is the 16th walk-off win in WS history (5 have been series-ending)

Game 4 BOX SCORE SUMMARY

NEW YORK YANKEES	AB	R	H	RBI	BB	K	1B	2B	3B	HR	TB	SB
SNUFFY STIRNWEISS, 2B	4	1	2	0	1	2	2	0	0	0	2	0
JOE DIMAGGIO, CF	2	0	0	1	2	0	0	0	0	0	0	0
BILLY JOHNSON, 3B	4	1	1	0	0	0	0	0	1	0	3	0
JOHNNY LINDELL, LF	3	0	2	1	1	0	1	1	0	0	3	0
BROOKLYN DODGERS	AB	R	H	RBI	BB	K	1B	2B	3B	HR	TB	SB
COOKIE LAVAGETTO, PH	1	0	1	2	0	0	0	1	0	0	2	0
PEE WEE REESE, SS	4	0	0	1	0	0	0	0	0	0	0	0
AL GIONFRIDDO, PR	0	1	0	0	0	0	0	0	0	0	0	0
SPIDER JORGENSEN, 3B	2	1	0	0	2	0	0	0	0	0	0	0
EDDIE MIKSIS, PR	0	1	0	0	0	0	0	0	0	0	0	0

Bill Bevens injured his arm during his epic Game 4 performance. He managed to put up 2.2 crucial scoreless innings of relief in the Yankees' Game 7 victory, but permanent damage had been done, and Bevens never again pitched in the major leagues.

Ironically, two other key players in the busted-up Bevens no-hitter—Cookie Lavagetto and Al Gionfriddo—also never appeared in a major league game after the 1947 World Series.

NEW YORK YANKEES	IP	H	R	ER	HR	K	BB	HBP	ERA
BILL BEVENS L (0-1)	8.2	1	3	3	0	5	10	0	3.12
BROOKLYN DODGERS	IP	H	R	ER	HR	K	BB	HBP	ERA
HARRY TAYLOR	0	2	1	0	0	0	1	0	0.00
HAL GREGG	7	4	1	1	0	5	3	0	2.00
HUGH CASEY W (2-0)	0.2	0	0	0	0	0	0	0	0.00

GAME TIME: **2:20**
ATTENDANCE: **33,443**
BEST OF 7: **DODGERS - 2   YANKEES - 2**

NEW YORK YANKEES vs. BROOKLYN DODGERS

October 4

LINE SCORE	1	2	3	4	5	6	7	8	9	R	H	E
NEW YORK YANKEES	0	0	0	1	1	0	0	0	0	2	5	0
BROOKLYN DODGERS	0	0	0	0	0	1	0	0	0	1	4	1

RECAP

A low scoring, one-run difference game featuring stingy pitching and near flawless fielding. The odd fact was that of the nine free passes issued by Dodger starter Rex Barney, only one led to a score. Brooklyn produced one run with their four hits. In the sixth, losing by two, Jackie Robinson singled home Al Gionfriddo. The Yankees produced two runs with their five safeties. In the third inning starter Frank Shea singled home Aaron Robinson to break the ice. In the fifth, Joe DiMaggio slugged a solo home run to put his team ahead for good. Shea posted his second win with a last out strikeout.

SCORING SUMMARY

Fourth Inning - New York Yankees
—McQuinn flied out to Hermanski.
—Johnson struck out.
—A. Robinson wangled a free pass.
—Rizzuto walked A. Robinson to second base.
—Shea singled into left field, driving in A. Robinson; Rizzuto slid into second.
—Stirnweiss stacked the sacks on a walk.
—Henrich grounded out, Reese to J. Robinson.

1 Runs **1** Hits **0** Errors **3** LOB

YANKEES – 1   **DODGERS – 0**

Fifth Inning - New York Yankees
—Lindell grounded out, Reese to J. Robinson.
—DiMaggio slugged a solo shot into the left field crowd.
—McQuinn popped up to Stanky.
—Johnson got a free pass.
—Hatten relieved Barney.
—A. Robinson popped up to Jorgensen.

1 Runs **1** Hits **0** Errors **1** LOB

YANKEES – 2   **DODGERS – 0**

Sixth Inning - Brooklyn Dodgers
—Gionfriddo PH for Hatten, sprinted to first on a walk.
—Stanky struck out.
—Reese walked Gionfriddo to second base.
—J. Robinson singled into center field, driving in Gionfriddo; both runners moved upon the throw in.
—Walker fouled out to Johnson.
—Hermanski skied out to DiMaggio.

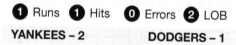

1 Runs **1** Hits **0** Errors **2** LOB

YANKEES – 2   **DODGERS – 1**

HIGHLIGHTS

- Dodger starter Rex Barney pitched into and out of a bases-loaded jam in the first inning
- DiMaggio hit into his third double play of the series
- 10 Yankees walked, only one scored
- Dodgers two pinch-hit walks matched a record
- The two staffs combined to issue 29 free passes over the previous 18 innings
- Pinstripers Snuffy Stirnweiss, in the first, and Tommy Henrich, in the ninth, were thrown out at the plate
- 18 Dodgers took the field

DIAMOND DUST

- Rex Barney gave up the 200th home run in World Series history, to Joe DiMaggio
- Joe DiMaggio also hit milestone home run 150 (1937)
- Brooklyn's Bruce Edwards is the fifth catcher charged with two passed balls in a game, though no runs scored
- Bomber starter Frank "Spec" Shea is only the fourth rookie to win two games. The others were Dickie Kerr (ChW 1919), Paul Dean (StLC 1934), Johnny Beazley (StLC, 1942)

Game 5 BOX SCORE SUMMARY

NEW YORK YANKEES	AB	R	H	RBI	BB	K	1B	2B	3B	HR	TB	SB
JOE DIMAGGIO, CF	4	1	1	1	1	1	0	0	0	1	4	0
AARON ROBINSON, C	3	1	0	0	1	0	0	0	0	0	0	0
FRANK "SPEC" SHEA, P	4	0	2	1	0	2	1	2	0	0	3	0
BROOKLYN DODGERS	AB	R	H	RBI	BB	K	1B	2B	3B	HR	TB	SB
JACKIE ROBINSON, 1B	4	0	1	1	0	1	1	0	0	0	1	0
AL GIONFRIDDO, PH	0	1	0	0	1	0	0	0	0	0	0	0

NEW YORK YANKEES	IP	H	R	ER	HR	K	BB	HBP	ERA
"SPECS" SHEA W (2-0)	9	4	1	1	0	7	5	0	1.29
BROOKLYN DODGERS	IP	H	R	ER	HR	K	BB	HBP	ERA
REX BARNEY L (0-1)	4.2	3	2	2	1	3	9	0	9.53
JOE HATTEN	1.1	0	0	0	0	1	0	0	0.00
HUGH CASEY	2	1	0	0	0	1	0	0	0.00

Fireballer Rex Barney came into the majors in 1943 at age 18 with a much-heralded fastball. He spent the next two years in the military, returning to the Dodgers for the 1946 season. Barney's one good year came in 1948, when he went 15-13 with an ERA of 3.10 in 246.2 IP.

Control prevented Barney from achieving any ongoing success in the majors. In only one season of his 6-year career did he strikeout more than he walked, finishing with 410 bases on balls in just under 600 career innings pitched.

Barney walked 9 in 4.2 innings in Game 5, and finished his career with 16 BB in 9.1 innings in the Fall Classic.

(National Baseball Hall of Fame and Museum)

GAME TIME:	**2:46**
ATTENDANCE:	**34,379**
BEST OF 7:	**DODGERS - 2 YANKEES - 3**

Game 6

BROOKLYN DODGERS vs. NEW YORK YANKEES

October 5

LINE SCORE	1	2	3	4	5	6	7	8	9	R	H	E
BROOKLYN DODGERS	2	0	2	0	0	4	0	0	0	8	12	1
NEW YORK YANKEES	0	0	4	1	0	0	0	0	1	6	15	2

RECAP

The Dodgers won this memorable Game 6, not because of a brilliant pitching performance or a game-winning hit, but because of a spectacular catch. Brooklyn scored two in the first and then two more in the fourth. The Yankees countered with four in the third and the go-ahead run in the fifth. In the top of the sixth, Brooklyn plated four for the second time, taking the lead by three. In the bottom of the sixth, the Bombers were threatening with men on first and second when Joe DiMaggio cracked a sure home run to left field. Al Gionfriddo, just in as a replacement, turned his back to the plate and sprinted to the low railing. The ball was about to land 415 feet into the bullpen until it dropped into Gionfriddo's outstretched glove for the third out. From there, Joe Hatten and Hugh Casey shut the door on the Yankees.

SCORING SUMMARY

First Inning - Brooklyn Dodgers
– Reynolds starting.
– Stanky rippled a single into left field.
– Reese singled Stanky to second base.
– J. Robinson loaded the bases on an infield bouncer.
– Walker scored Stanky on a double play, Rizzuto to Phillips; Reese slid into third base; Reese scored on a Lollar passed ball.
– Hermanski drew a walk.
– Edwards nubbed out, Johnson to Phillips.

2 Runs **3** Hits **0** Errors **1** LOB

DODGERS – 2   **YANKEES – 0**

Third Inning - Brooklyn Dodgers
– Stanky flied out to DiMaggio.
– Reese clubbed a double into left field.
– J. Robinson one-hopped a ground rule double into the left field stands, driving Reese home.
– Walker doubled into right field, driving J. Robinson home.
– Drews relieved Reynolds.

– Hermanski advanced Walker on a ground out, Stirnweiss to Phillips.
– Edwards flied out to DiMaggio.

2 Runs **3** Hits **0** Errors **1** LOB

DODGERS – 4   **YANKEES – 0**

Third Inning - New York Yankees
– Lollar lashed a double into left field.
– Drews was a strikeout; Lollar wild pitched to third base.
– Stirnweiss safe at first base as Lollar scored on Jorgensen's juggle.
– Henrich stroked a single into center field; Stirnweiss thrown out at third on a bulls-eye throw from Furillo to Jorgensen.
– Lindell singled up the middle, driving Henrich home.
– DiMaggio singled Lindell to second base.
– Branca relieved Lombardi.
– Johnson singled into right field, driving Lindell home; DiMaggio slid into third.

– Brown PH for Phillips, singled into right field, driving DiMaggio home; Johnson raced into third base.
– Rizzuto zapped out to Stanky.

4 Runs **6** Hits **1** Errors **2** LOB

DODGERS – 4   **YANKEES – 4**

Fourth Inning - New York Yankees
– A. Robinson high-hopped a beebee through the middle.
– Drews went down on strikes.
– Stirnweiss struck out.
– Henrich singled A. Robinson to second base.
– Berra singled into right field, driving in A. Robinson; Henrich hustled to third.
– DiMaggio forced Berra at second base, Jorgensen to Stanky.

1 Runs **3** Hits **0** Errors **2** LOB

DODGERS – 4   **YANKEES – 5**

Sixth Inning - Brooklyn Dodgers
– Edwards guided a single into right field.
– Furillo doubled Edwards to third base.
– Lavagetto PH for Jorgensen, lifted a sacrifice fly to Berra plating Edwards.
– Bragan PH for Branca, doubled into left field, driving Furillo home.
– Bankhead PR.
– Stanky smoked a hit-and-run single; Bankhead flew to third base; on A. Robinson's fielding error Stanky took second.
– Newsom relieved Page.
– Reese singled into left field, driving home Bankhead and Stanky.

– J. Robinson flied out to Lindell.
– Walker fouled out to Johnson.

4 Runs **5** Hits **1** Errors **1** LOB

DODGERS – 8   **YANKEES – 5**

Ninth Inning - New York Yankees
– Johnson stroked a single into left field.
– McQuinn walked Johnson to second base.
– Casey relieved Hatten.
– Rizzuto flied out to Furillo.
– A. Robinson hustled an infield hit; bases loaded.
– Frey PH for Wensloff, forced A. Robinson at second, J. Robinson to Reese; Johnson scored; McQuinn moved to third.
– Stirnweiss out on a mounder, Casey to J. Robinson.

1 Runs **2** Hits **0** Errors **2** LOB

DODGERS – 8   **YANKEES – 6**

HIGHLIGHTS

• Brooklyn scored their first two runs on a double play and a passed ball
• Dodger Al Gionfriddo, acquired in mid-season from the Pittsburgh Pirates, scored the tying run in Game 4 and saved a run with his glove in the sixth inning
• 38 players (21 Yankees) took the field
• The clubs combined to bang out 27 base hits (21 singles)
• 14 of the 15 Yankee base hits were singles
• Hugh Casey recorded the save after winning two games

DIAMOND DUST

• Reliever Dan Bankhead become the second African-American to appear in the World Series when he pinch ran (and scored) in the sixth inning
• Allie Reynolds, in the top half of the third, is the second pitcher to give up three straight doubles. Walter Johnson, in 1925, was the first
• Brooklyn is the first team to drill three doubles in an inning twice in one World Series (Game 3)
• Four doubles tied a record for most doubles drilled by both teams
• Three pinch-hits matched a record tied in Game 3
• The teams combined to set a new World Series record for wild pitches thrown, with 8, with the Dodgers' 5 in a Series also record. Both figures still stand

Game 6 BOX SCORE SUMMARY

BROOKLYN DODGERS	AB	R	H	RBI	BB	K	1B	2B	3B	HR	TB	SB
EDDIE STANKY, 2B	5	2	2	0	0	0	2	0	0	0	2	0
PEE WEE REESE, SS	4	2	3	2	1	0	2	1	0	0	4	0
JACKIE ROBINSON, 1B	5	1	2	1	0	0	1	1	0	0	3	0
DIXIE WALKER, RF	5	0	1	1	0	1	0	1	0	0	2	0
BRUCE EDWARDS, C	4	1	1	0	0	1	1	0	0	0	1	0
CARL FURILLO, RF	4	1	2	0	0	1	1	0	0	0	3	0
COOKIE LAVAGETTO, PH/3B	2	0	0	1	0	0	0	0	0	0	0	0
BOBBY BRAGAN, PH	1	0	1	1	0	0	0	1	0	0	2	0
DAN BANKHEAD, PR	0	1	0	0	0	0	0	0	0	0	0	0

NEW YORK YANKEES	AB	R	H	RBI	BB	K	1B	2B	3B	HR	TB	SB
SNUFFY STIRNWEISS, 2B	5	0	0	1	1	1	0	0	0	0	0	0
TOMMY HEINRICH, RF/LF	5	1	2	0	0	2	0	0	0	0	2	0
JOHNNY LINDELL, LF	2	1	2	1	0	0	2	0	0	0	2	0
YOGI BERRA, RF	3	0	2	1	0	0	2	0	0	0	2	0
JOE DIMAGGIO, CF	5	1	1	0	0	0	1	0	0	0	1	0
BILLY JOHNSON, 3B	5	1	2	1	0	1	2	0	0	0	2	0
BOBBY BROWN, PH	1	0	1	1	0	0	1	0	0	0	1	0
SHERM LOLLAR, C	1	1	1	0	0	0	0	1	0	0	2	0
AARON ROBINSON, C	4	1	2	0	0	0	2	0	0	0	2	0

BROOKLYN DODGERS	IP	H	R	ER	HR	K	BB	HBP	ERA
VIC LOMBARDI	2.2	5	4	4	0	2	0	0	12.15
RALPH BRANCA W 1-0	2.1	6	1	1	0	2	0	0	8.64
JOE HATTEN	3	3	1	1	0	0	4	0	7.27
HUGH CASEY S (1)	1	1	0	0	0	0	0	0	0.00

NEW YORK YANKEES	IP	H	R	ER	HR	K	BB	HBP	ERA
ALLIE REYNOLDS	2.1	6	4	3	0	0	1	0	4.76
JOE PAGE L (0-1)	1	4	4	4	0	0	0	0	6.75

- Yankees' third baseman Billy Johnson ripped 3 triples in the 1947 World Series, and 4 in his WS career, which ties him for the most in Fall Classic history. The other two with 4 both played during the Dead Ball era, when triples were more common: Tommy Leach (Pitt. 1903) and Tris Speaker (Boston AL 1912, 1915; Cleveland, 1920). Johnson also scored 8 runs in the series, tied for the most ever for a player in a Subway Series, with Babe Ruth (1923) and Jake Powell (1936).

GAME TIME:	**3:19**
ATTENDANCE:	**74,065**
BEST OF 7:	**DODGERS - 3 YANKEES - 3**

Game 7

BROOKLYN DODGERS vs. NEW YORK YANKEES

October 6

LINE SCORE	1	2	3	4	5	6	7	8	9	R	H	E
BROOKLYN DODGERS	0	2	0	0	0	0	0	0	0	2	7	0
NEW YORK YANKEES	0	1	0	2	0	1	1	0	X	5	7	0

--- RECAP ---

Consecutive sell-out crowds watched the Yankees overwhelm Brooklyn with four scoring drives. Phil Rizzuto singled home the first run in the second inning. In the fourth frame PH Bobby Brown and RF Tommy Henrich drove in two. Another pinch-hitter, Allie Clark, plated the fourth run. C Aaron Robinson's sacrifice fly put the last run on the board.

The Dodgers scored two runs in the second inning with four straight hits that knocked starter Frank Shea out of the game. They never scored again. Yankee reliever Joe Page took over in the fifth inning. He retired 13 consecutive Brooklyn batters. The 14th Dodger, Eddie Miksis, broke the string with a one-out, ninth inning single. Page induced the 15th batter, Bruce Edwards, to hit into a double play to end a Game Seven.

--- SCORING SUMMARY ---

Second Inning - Brooklyn Dodgers

– Walker fouled out to McQuinn.
– Hermanski triggered a triple into the deepest part of right field.
– Edwards singled into left field, driving Hermanski home.
– Furillo singled Edwards to second base.
– Bevens relieved Shea.
– Jorgensen doubled into right field, driving in Edwards; Furillo sprinted to third.
– Gregg safe at first base on a fielder's choice; Furillo gunned down at the plate.
– Rizzuto to A. Robinson; Jorgensen took third base.
– Stanky popped up to Rizzuto.

2 Runs **4** Hits **0** Errors **2** LOB

DODGERS – 2   **YANKEES – 0**

Second Inning - New York Yankees

– DiMaggio flied out to Furillo.
– McQuinn worked a walk.
– Johnson popped up to Stanky.
– A. Robinson walked McQuinn to second base.
– Rizzuto singled into left field, driving in McQuinn; A. Robinson took second.
– Bevens was a strikeout.

1 Runs **1** Hits **0** Errors **2** LOB

DODGERS – 2   **YANKEES – 1**

Fourth Inning - New York Yankees

– McQuinn struck out.
– Johnson coaxed a walk.
– A. Robinson fanned.
– Rizzuto singled Johnson to second base.
– Brown PH for Bevens, doubled into left field, driving in Johnson; Rizzuto raced over to third base.
– Behrman relieved Gregg.
– Stirnweiss loaded the bases on a walk.
– Henrich singled into right field, driving in Rizzuto; bases loaded.
– Berra out on a grounder, J. Robinson to Behrman.

2 Runs **3** Hits **0** Errors **3** LOB

DODGERS – 2   **YANKEES – 3**

Sixth Inning - New York Yankees

– Miksis to LF.
– Rizzuto spun a successful home plate bunt; swiped second base.
– Page was a strikeout.
– Stirnweiss got a walk; Rizzuto held.

—Hatten relieved Behrman.

—Henrich was a strikeout.

—Clark PH for Berra, singled up the middle, driving in Rizzuto; Stirnweiss slid into second base.

—Barney relieved Hatten.

—DiMaggio flied out to Furillo

1 Runs **2** Hits **0** Errors **2** LOB

DODGERS – 2   **YANKEES – 4**

Seventh Inning - New York Yankees

—Casey pitching. Lavagetto to 3B.

—McQuinn out on a ground ball, Reese to J. Robinson.

—Johnson torched a triple into the left field corner.

—A. Robinson lifted a sacrifice fly to Hermanski plating Johnson.

—Rizzuto popped up to Stanky.

1 Runs **1** Hits **0** Errors **0** LOB

DODGERS – 2   **YANKEES – 5**

HIGHLIGHTS

- Eleventh seven-game set, third straight; first seven-game Subway Series struggle
- SRO crowd of 70,000 plus for the third straight game, for a grand total of 218, 978 for the final 3
- Eddie Stanky and Pee Wee Reese were caught stealing in the first inning, the second time in the Series the Dodgers had 2 CS in the first inning
- Yankee reliever Joe Page took over in the fifth inning and hurled five shutout innings, allowing one hit and collecting the win
- Page set the record for most scoreless innings in relief in one game
- Game Seven team stats: the Yankees are 1-1, while the Dodgers are 0-1
- Game Seven league stats: National League 7 - American League 4

DIAMOND DUST

- Shea is the third rookie to start three games, including a Game 7
- Bomber PH Bobby Brown doubled in the fourth inning for his third pinch hit of the series, setting a record
- Brooklyn hurler Hal Gregg is the 11th pitcher with a losing regular season record to start, and the ninth to lose
- Gregg is also the first pitcher with a losing record to start and lose a Game Seven
- Only game of the series without either a hit batter, a wild pitch, or a balk
- The second final game (1921) to end in a double play, the first Game 7

Game 7 BOX SCORE SUMMARY

BROOKLYN DODGERS	AB	R	H	RBI	BB	K	1B	2B	3B	HR	TB	SB
GENE HERMANSKI, LF	2	1	1	0	0	0	0	0	1	0	3	0
BRUCE EDWARDS, C	4	1	2	1	0	0	2	0	0	0	2	0
SPIDER JORGENSON, 3B	2	0	1	1	0	0	0	1	0	0	2	0
NEW YORK YANKEES	AB	R	H	RBI	BB	K	1B	2B	3B	HR	TB	SB
TOMMY HENRICH, LF	5	0	1	1	0	1	1	0	0	0	1	0
ALLIE CLARK, PH/RF	1	0	1	1	0	0	1	0	0	0	1	0
GEORGE MCQUINN, 1B	2	1	0	0	1	1	0	0	0	0	0	0
BILLY JOHNSON, 3B	3	2	1	0	1	0	0	0	1	0	3	0
AARON ROBINSON, C	3	0	0	1	1	1	0	0	0	0	0	0
PHIL RIZZUTO, SS	4	2	3	1	0	0	0	1	0	0	3	1

BROOKLYN DODGERS	IP	H	R	ER	HR	K	BB	HBP	ERA
HAL GREGG L (0-1)	3.2	3	3	3	0	3	4	0	2.55
HANK BEHRMAN	1.1	2	1	1	0	1	3	0	7.11
HUGH CASEY	2	1	1	1	0	0	0	0	0.87
NEW YORK YANKEES	IP	H	R	ER	HR	K	BB	HBP	ERA
FRANK "SPECS" SHEA	1.1	4	2	2	0	0	1	0	2.35
JOE PAGE W (1-1)	5	1	0	0	0	1	0	0	4.15

GAME TIME:	**2:19**
ATTENDANCE:	**71,548**
BEST OF 7:	**DODGERS - 3 YANKEES - 4**

1947

BROOKLYN DODGERS vs. NEW YORK YANKEES

--- **BROOKLYN DODGERS** ---

Overall World Series Record (0 WINS 4 LOSSES). 24 Games Played (7-17 .292)

- Hugh Casey is the second reliever to win two games (Jesse Barnes, NYG 1921, who pitched to a 1.65 ERA over 16.1 innings).
- Casey, on the mound for 10.1 innings, crafted an 0.87 ERA.
- Bert Shotton is the 20th skipper to lose debut appearance.
- Shotton is the second manager to lose debut appearance in the Subway Series (Durocher, 1941).

--- **NEW YORK YANKEES** ---

Overall World Series Record (11 WINS 4 LOSSES) 79 Games Played [51-27 (1 tie) .654]

- Joe Page saved Game 1, lost Game 6, and won Game 7.
- Page is the first pitcher to save Game 1 and then win Game 7.
- Page is the first pitcher to lose Game 6 then win Game 7.
- Tommy Henrich, the only player with 30 plus at-bats, smacked a hit in each game, amassing 10 hits.
- Johnny Lindell drove in seven runs in six games, the most of any player on either team.
- Bobby Brown, pinch hitting in four games, drilled two doubles, stroked a single, walked, drove in three and scored two.
- Bucky Harris (2-1) wins final Classic in managerial career; 23 years between first and last victory.
- Eleven Fall Classic championships are the most in MLB, leading the St. Louis Cardinals by five.

--- **FUNGOES** ---

- Record set for most pinch hits at 11, Yankees (6) Dodgers (5).
- Both National League New York franchises now have four World Series losses.
- First Fall Classic to produce total receipts over two million dollars.
- The American League is now 27-17 overall in World Series.

--- **SEVEN-GAME DATA** ---

TIME	**18:45**	PLAYERS POOL	**$493,675**
ATTENDANCE	**389,763**	SHARES	**BROOKLYN DODGERS - $4,081**
			NEW YORK YANKEES - $5,830

127

1947

BROOKLYN DODGERS vs. NEW YORK YANKEES

Brooklyn Dodgers Composite Stats

BATTING	G	AB	R	H	RBI	2B	3B	HR	BB	SO	BA	OBP	SLG	OPS
Dixie Walker	7	27	1	6	4	1	0	1	3	1	.222	.300	.370	.670
Bruce Edwards	7	27	3	6	2	1	0	0	2	7	.222	.276	.259	.535
Jackie Robinson	7	27	3	7	3	2	0	0	2	4	.259	.310	.333	.644
Eddie Stanky	7	25	4	6	2	1	0	0	3	2	.240	.321	.280	.601
Pee Wee Reese	7	23	5	7	4	1	0	0	6	3	.304	.448	.348	.796
Spider Jorgensen	7	20	1	4	3	2	0	0	2	4	.200	.273	.300	.573
Gene Hermanski	7	19	4	3	1	0	1	0	3	3	.158	.304	.263	.568
Carl Furillo	6	17	2	6	3	2	0	0	3	0	.353	.450	.471	.921
Pete Reiser	5	8	1	2	0	0	0	0	3	1	.250	.455	.250	.705
Cookie Lavagetto	5	7	0	1	3	1	0	0	0	2	.143	.143	.286	.429
Ralph Branca	3	4	0	0	0	0	0	0	0	1	.000	.000	.000	.000
Eddie Miksis	5	4	1	1	0	0	0	0	0	1	.250	.250	.250	.500
Al Gionfriddo	4	3	2	0	0	0	0	0	1	0	.000	.250	.000	.250
Hal Gregg	3	3	0	0	0	0	0	0	1	1	.000	.250	.000	.250
Joe Hatten	4	3	1	1	0	0	0	0	0	0	.333	.333	.333	.667
Vic Lombardi	3	3	0	0	0	0	0	0	0	0	.000	.000	.000	.000
Arky Vaughan	3	2	0	1	0	1	0	0	1	0	.500	.667	1.000	1.667
Rex Barney	3	1	0	0	0	0	0	0	0	0	.000	.000	.000	.000
Bobby Bragan	1	1	0	1	1	1	0	0	0	0	1.000	1.000	2.000	3.000
Hugh Casey	6	1	0	0	0	0	0	0	0	1	.000	.000	.000	.000
Gil Hodges	1	1	0	0	0	0	0	0	0	1	.000	.000	.000	.000
Dan Bankhead	1	0	1	0	0	0	0	0	0	0				
Hank Behrman	5	0	0	0	0	0	0	0	0	0				
Harry Taylor	1	0	0	0	0	0	0	0	0	0				
Totals	**7**	**226**	**29**	**52**	**26**	**13**	**1**	**1**	**30**	**32**	**.230**	**.323**	**.310**	**.633**

PITCHING	G	GS	ERA	W	L	SV	CG	IP	H	R	ER	BB	SO	WHIP
Hal Gregg	3	1	3.55	0	1	0	0	12.2	9	5	5	8	10	1.342
Hugh Casey	6	0	0.87	2	0	1	0	10.1	5	1	1	1	3	0.581
Joe Hatten	4	1	7.00	0	0	0	0	9.0	12	7	7	7	5	2.111
Ralph Branca	3	1	8.64	1	1	0	0	8.1	12	8	8	5	8	2.040
Rex Barney	3	1	2.70	0	1	0	0	6.2	4	2	2	10	3	2.100
Vic Lombardi	2	2	12.15	0	1	0	0	6.2	14	9	9	1	5	2.250
Hank Behrman	5	0	7.11	0	0	0	0	6.1	9	5	5	5	3	2.211
Harry Taylor	1	1	~	0	0	0	0	0.0	2	1	0	1	0	
Totals	**7**	**7**	**5.55**	**3**	**4**	**1**	**0**	**60.0**	**67**	**38**	**37**	**38**	**37**	**1.750**

1947

BROOKLYN DODGERS vs. NEW YORK YANKEES

New York Yankees Composite Stats

BATTING	G	AB	R	H	RBI	2B	3B	HR	BB	SO	BA	OBP	SLG	OPS
Tommy Henrich	7	31	2	10	5	2	0	1	2	3	.323	.364	.484	.848
Snuffy Stirnweiss	7	27	3	7	3	0	1	0	8	8	.259	.429	.333	.762
Joe DiMaggio	7	26	4	6	5	0	0	2	6	2	.231	.375	.462	.837
Phil Rizzuto	7	26	3	8	2	1	0	0	4	0	.308	.400	.346	.746
Billy Johnson	7	26	8	7	2	0	3	0	3	4	.269	.367	.500	.867
George McQuinn	7	23	3	3	1	0	0	0	5	8	.130	.286	.130	.416
Yogi Berra	6	19	2	3	2	0	0	1	1	2	.158	.200	.316	.516
Johnny Lindell	6	18	3	9	7	3	1	0	5	2	.500	.625	.778	1.403
Aaron Robinson	3	10	2	2	1	0	0	0	2	1	.200	.333	.200	.533
Spec Shea	3	5	0	2	1	1	0	0	0	2	.400	.400	.600	1.000
Bill Bevens	2	4	0	0	0	0	0	0	0	2	.000	.000	.000	.000
Sherm Lollar	2	4	3	3	1	2	0	0	0	0	.750	.750	1.250	2.000
Joe Page	4	4	0	0	0	0	0	0	0	1	.000	.000	.000	.000
Allie Reynolds	2	4	2	2	1	0	0	0	0	0	.500	.500	.500	1.000
Bobby Brown	4	3	2	3	3	2	0	0	1	0	1.000	1.000	1.667	2.667
Allie Clark	3	2	1	1	1	0	0	0	1	0	.500	.667	.500	1.167
Karl Drews	2	2	0	0	0	0	0	0	0	2	.000	.000	.000	.000
Jack Phillips	2	2	0	0	0	0	0	0	0	0	.000	.000	.000	.000
Lonny Frey	1	1	0	0	1	0	0	0	0	0	.000	.000	.000	.000
Ralph Houk	1	1	0	1	0	0	0	0	0	0	1.000	1.000	1.000	2.000
Spud Chandler	1	0	0	0	0	0	0	0	0	0				
Bobo Newsom	2	0	0	0	0	0	0	0	0	0				
Vic Raschi	2	0	0	0	0	0	0	0	0	0				
Butch Wensloff	1	0	0	0	0	0	0	0	0	0				
Totals	89	238	38	67	36	11	5	4	38	37	.282	.385	.420	.805

PITCHING	G	GS	ERA	W	L	SV	CG	IP	H	R	ER	BB	SO	WHIP
Spec Shea	3	3	2.35	2	0	0	1	15.1	10	4	4	8	10	1.174
Joe Page	4	0	4.15	1	1	1	0	13.0	12	6	6	2	7	1.077
Allie Reynolds	2	2	4.76	1	0	0	1	11.1	15	7	6	3	6	1.588
Bill Bevens	2	1	2.38	0	1	0	1	11.1	3	3	3	11	7	1.235
Karl Drews	2	0	3.00	0	0	0	0	3.0	2	1	1	1	0	1.000
Bobo Newsom	2	1	19.29	0	1	0	0	2.1	6	5	5	2	0	3.429
Spud Chandler	1	0	9.00	0	0	0	0	2.0	2	2	2	3	1	2.500
Butch Wensloff	1	0	0.00	0	0	0	0	2.0	0	0	0	0	0	0.000
Vic Raschi	2	0	6.75	0	0	0	0	1.1	2	1	1	0	1	1.500
Totals	7	7	4.09	4	3	1	3	61.2	52	29	28	30	32	1.330

1949

 VS.

BROOKLYN DODGERS VS. NEW YORK YANKEES

FUNGOES

- ⑩ Third Subway Series meeting between the two clubs, and of the decade.
- ⑩ Joe DiMaggio and Pee Wee Reese have played in all three.
- ⑩ Both in first place at the All-Star break.
- ⑩ Both teams won the pennant by one game.
- ⑩ First time in World Series history the opponents ended the season with the same won-loss record.
- ⑩ Twenty-two returning players, 11 per team, from the 1947 Subway Series.
- ⑩ No travel days.
- ⑩ Umpire info: Cal Hubbard played professional football from 1927-36. Hubbard is the only member of the Baseball Hall of Fame, the Football Hall of Fame, and the College Football Hall of Fame; Art Passarella was also a movie and television actor.

SERIES SUMMARY

After a one-year interruption of a New York team in the World Series, the Yankees and Dodgers met again for the eighth Subway Series in 1949. The cast of characters was much the same as the 1947 clash.

Game 1 featured two powerful lineups against two hard-throwing righties. Allie Reynolds and Don Newcombe faced off after posting a combined regular-season record of 34-14. Each time managed some base runners through the first eight innings, but the aces left them all stranded. Newcombe finally broke, his fifth hit allowed being a walk-off home run to Tommy Henrich.

Pitching dominated again in Game 2, as again only one run crossed the plate, this time by the Dodgers in the second inning on a sacrifice fly. After that, Vic Raschi and Preacher Roe shut the door to even the Series at one.

Zeros abounded in Game 3 as well, until the ninth inning when in the top half the Yankees broke through with three runs. The Dodgers came back with two solo home runs in the bottom half, but came up one short.

The Yankees defeated Don Newcombe again in Game 4, this time knocking him out in the fourth inning. Hometown local reliever Joe Hatten got similar treatment, and the Yankees found themselves ahead by six. The Dodger put together a powerful rally in the bottom of the sixth, with four runs on seven hits, but that was all they could manage for the remainder of the game and they fell into a 3-1 hole.

In Game 5, two in the first and three more in the third gave the Yankees a 5-0 lead. The Bombers plated another five in the next three innings and the Dodgers could manage only two. As in the previous game, Brooklyn put up a four spot to make the score more respectable, but the game ended 10-6 and the Yankees had another World Series title.

THE TEAMS

BROOKLYN DODGERS
97 - 57 .630 +1.0 G

The Team
• Third Subway Series. Fifth appearance overall.
• The Dodgers went 20-7 in September to edge the Cards by 1 game.

The Players
• 1947 Subway Series returning players (11): Rex Barney, Ralph Branca, Bruce Edwards, Carl Furillo, Joe Hatten, Gene Hermanski, Gil Hodges, Spider Jorgensen, Eddie Miksis, Jackie Robinson, and Pee Wee Reese.
• Reese is the only player to also appear on the 1941 pennant-winning team.
• Mike McCormick's third appearance with third team (1940 Cincinnati Reds [W]/1948 Boston Braves [L]).
• 2B Robinson is the 16th batting champ (.342) and 15th MVP to appear in the World Series.
• Robinson stroked 203 base hits while leading the majors in stolen bases with 37.

The Manager
Burt Shotton is making second managerial appearance. Shotton played the outfield for the St. Louis Cardinals and the Washington Senators. Shotton is the second to manage in street clothes.

Top Batters

Pos	Name	AB	R	H	HR	RBI	BA	OPS
1B	Gil Hodges	596	94	170	23	115	.285	.813
2B	Jackie Robinson	593	122	203	16	124	.342	.960
SS	Pee Wee Reese	617	132	172	16	73	.279	.806
OF	Carl Furillo	549	95	177	18	106	.322	.875

Top Pitchers

Pos	Name	W	L	ERA	G	SV	IP	SO
St	Don Newcombe	17	8	3.17	38	1	244.1	149
St	Preacher Roe	15	6	2.79	30	1	212.2	109
St	Ralph Branca	13	5	4.39	34	1	186.2	109
Rel	Jack Banta	10	6	3.37	48	3	152.1	97

NEW YORK YANKEES
97 - 57 .630 +1.0 G

The Team
• Subway Series #8, 16th overall appearance in third straight decade.

The Players
• 1947 Subway Series returning players (11): Yogi Berra, Bobby Brown, Joe DiMaggio, Tommy Henrich, Billy Johnson, Johnny Lindell, Joe Page, Vic Raschi, Allie Reynolds, Phil Rizzuto and Snuffy Stirnweiss.
• DiMaggio played on the 1936/37/38/39/41/42/47 pennant-winning teams, winning six titles.
• Several other players were part of multiple Yankees championship teams as well.
• Johnny Mize came to the Yankees in a mid-season trade from the New York Giants.

The Manager
Casey Stengel is the 40th manager to make debut appearance. Stengel is the fourth manager to debut in the Subway Series (1921/1941/1947).
Stengel played in the Fall Classic on two New York based teams - the 1916 Brooklyn Robins and the 1921/22 New York Giants.
Stengel is the only man to play on two different New York teams and manage the third.

Top Batters

Pos	Name	AB	R	H	HR	RBI	BA	OPS
C	Yogi Berra	415	59	115	20	91	.277	.802
1B	Tommy Henrich	411	90	118	24	85	.287	.942
SS	Phil Rizzuto	614	110	169	5	65	.275	.711
3B	Bobby Brown	343	61	97	6	61	.283	.759

Top Pitchers

Pos	Name	W	L	ERA	G	SV	IP	SO
St	Vic Raschi	21	10	3.34	38	0	274.2	124
St	Eddie Lopat	15	10	3.26	31	1	215.1	70
St	Allie Reynolds	17	6	4.00	35	1	213.2	105
Rel	Joe Page	13	8	2.59	60	27	135.1	99

Game 1

BROOKLYN DODGERS vs. NEW YORK YANKEES

October 5

LINE SCORE	1	2	3	4	5	6	7	8	9	R	H	E
BROOKLYN DODGERS	0	0	0	0	0	0	0	0	0	0	2	0
NEW YORK YANKEES	0	0	0	0	0	0	0	0	1	1	5	1

RECAP

A sellout crowd watched a classic 1-0 pitching duel. Rookie Don Newcombe, the first African-American to start, was matched against veteran hurler Allie Reynolds. Newcombe could have just as easily been the winning pitcher. Reynolds yielded two base hits while hurling a shutout. Newcombe blanked the Yankees on four base hits over eight frames, striking out 11. Facing the 29th Bomber in the bottom of the ninth inning, Newcombe gave up their fifth and final hit, a solo shot to 1B Tommy Henrich.

SCORING SUMMARY

Ninth Inning - New York Yankees
– Henrich cannonaded a solo shot into the right field stands.

1 Runs **1** Hits **0** Errors **0** LOB

DODGERS – 0　　　　**YANKEES – 1**

HIGHLIGHTS

- 20 batters struck out and one hitter on each team fanned three times
- Cliff Mapes struck out in three straight at-bats
- Reynolds retired the side in order in only four of the nine frames
- The second consecutive 1-0 Game 1 in World Series

132

DIAMOND DUST

- In openers the Yankees are 13-3 while the Dodgers are 0-5
- The Yankees have not lost an opener since 1936 (eight appearances)
- Dodgers' Don Newcombe is the fifth rookie to start an opener and the third to lose
- Newcombe is the 10th Game One starter to record double-digit strikeouts
- Newcombe is the fourth pitcher to strikeout 11 batters, the second to lose
- Don Newcombe is second pitcher, first rookie, to strikeout 11 batters without giving up a free pass
- Newcombe is the third hurler to lose the Mid-Summer Classic and Game One of the Fall Classic in the same season
- The game was the second in WS history in which the only run was a solo home run (1923, Casey Stengel NYG vs. NYY)
- Yankee starter Allie Reynolds is the seventh pitcher to hurl an opening game shutout and the 11th to throw a two-hitter
- Second opener won on a walk-off hit – both Yankee victories (Bill Dickey singled in Charlie Keller in 1939)
- New York is 3-1 while the Brooklynites are 1-1 in walk-offs

Game 1 BOX SCORE SUMMARY

NEW YORK YANKEES	AB	R	H	RBI	BB	K	1B	2B	3B	HR	TB	SB
TOMMY HENRICH, 1B	4	1	1	1	0	0	0	0	0	1	4	0

BROOKLYN DODGERS	IP	H	R	ER	HR	K	BB	HBP	ERA
DON NEWCOMBE L (0-1)	8	5	1	1	1	11	0	0	1.13

NEW YORK YANKEES	IP	H	R	ER	HR	K	BB	HBP	ERA
ALLIE REYNOLDS W (1-0)	9	2	0	0	0	9	4	0	0.00

Tommy Henrich's game-ending hit in Game 1 of the 1949 World Series was the first walk-off home run in World Series history. Known for his timely hitting, it is a fitting accomplishment for Henrich.

Henrich had a great season in 1949, driving in 85 runs in only 411 at-bats, and also walking 86 times against only 34 strikeouts, good for an OBA of .416. The year before Henrich had probably his greatest season (at age 35), batting .308, driving in 100 and scoring a major league-leading 138 runs.

Destined to play in the shadows of greats like DiMaggio, Rizzuto, and Berra, Henrich nonetheless was a critical member of four World Champion Yankees teams. Henrich was not a regular player until age 25, he missed three seasons in his prime to World War II, and he had knee problems throughout his career. These factors limited his lifetime totals to 1284 games and 4603 at bats, but his career slash line of .282/.382/.491 (and an OPS of 132) demonstrate what an excellent hitter he was.

(National Baseball Hall of Fame and Museum)

GAME TIME:	2:24
ATTENDANCE:	66,224
BEST OF 7:	DODGERS - 0 YANKEES - 1

Game 2

BROOKLYN DODGERS vs. NEW YORK YANKEES

October 6

LINE SCORE	1	2	3	4	5	6	7	8	9	R	H	E
BROOKLYN DODGERS	0	1	0	0	0	0	0	0	0	1	7	2
NEW YORK YANKEES	0	0	0	0	0	0	0	0	0	0	6	1

--- **RECAP** ---

Second consecutive sell-out crowd watched another nine-inning pitcher's duel with the same 1-0 score, but with opposite winners and losers. The starting mound combatants were the Yankees Vic Raschi and the Dodgers Preacher Roe. Raschi worked the first eight innings, Roe the full nine. Two of the six hits Raschi allowed plated the lone tally. Roe, in scattering six Yankee singles, did not issue a walk and only once did he pitch with two runners on base in the same frame. His whitewash evened the Series at one apiece.

--- **SCORING SUMMARY** ---

Second Inning - Brooklyn Dodgers

- Robinson rammed a rocket double into left field.
- Hermanski fouled out to Coleman; Robinson tagged and advanced to third base.
- Rackley bounced out, Johnson to Henrich. Robinson held at third.
- Hodges singled into left field, driving in Robinson; on Lindell's miscue, Hodges slid into second base.
- Campanella given an intentional pass; Hodges held.
- Roe was a strikeout.

1 Runs **2** Hits **1** Errors **2** LOB

DODGERS – 1   **YANKEES – 0**

HIGHLIGHTS

- SRO crowd of 70,000+ in Yankee Stadium for the fourth time - all versus the Dodgers.
- Roy Campanella drew the only walk (intentional) in the game.
- In three consecutive frames, runners were thrown out thwarting potential scoring chances: (Top 4) Dodger LF Gene Hermanksi, on third via a triple, was nabbed at the plate; (Bot 4) Leading off , Yankee RF Hank Bauer was thrown out trying to stretch a single; and leading off the top of the 5th, Campanella did the same.
- Preacher Roe struck out three batters and was struck out three times.

134

— DIAMOND DUST —

- Roe is the 12th pitcher to allow zero walks in a shutout.
- Consecutive 1-0 pitching duels a Fall Classic first.
- Back-to-back shutouts – one by each team – for the sixth time in history.

Game 2 BOX SCORE SUMMARY

BROOKLYN DODGERS	AB	R	H	RBI	BB	K	1B	2B	3B	HR	TB	SB
JACKIE ROBINSON, 2B	3	1	1	0	0	0	0	1	0	0	2	0
GIL HODGES, 1B	3	0	1	1	0	0	1	0	0	0	1	0

BROOKLYN DODGERS	IP	H	R	ER	HR	K	BB	HBP	ERA
PREACHER ROE W (1-0)	9	6	0	0	0	3	0	0	0.00
NEW YORK YANKEES	IP	H	R	ER	HR	K	BB	HBP	ERA
VIC RASCHI L (0-1)	8	6	1	1	0	4	1	0	1.13

Christy Mathewson famously hurled 3 consecutive shutouts against the Philadelphia Athletics in the 1905 World Series. Mathewson walked a total of one batter in the series, Ralph Orlando "Socks" Seybold, not to be confused with Harry "Socks" Seibold, who pitched for the Athletics between 1916-1919.

WORLD SERIES PITCHERS WITH SHUTOUTS AND ZERO BASES ON BALLS			
Year	Gm	Pitcher	Team
1905	1	Christy Mathewson	New York Giants
1905	5	Christy Mathewson	New York Giants
1908	4	"Three Finger" Brown	Chicago Cubs
1917	3	Rube Benton	New York Giants
1920	7	Stan Coslevski	Cleveland Indians
1921	1	Carl Mays	New York Yankees
1934	7	Dizzy Dean	St. Louis Cardinals
1935	1	Lon Warnke	Chicago Cubs
1942	3	Ernie White	St. Louis Cardinals
1948	1	Johnny Sain	Boston Braves
1948	3	Gene Bearden	Cleveland Indians
1949	2	Preacher Roe	Brooklyn Dodgers
1956	5	Don Larsen	New York Yankees
1957	5	Lew Burdette	Milwaukee Braves
1985	7	Bret Saberhagen	Kansas City Royals
2014	5	Madison Bumbarner	San Francisco Giants

GAME TIME:	**2:30**
ATTENDANCE:	**70,053**
BEST OF 7:	**DODGERS - 1 YANKEES - 1**

Game 3

NEW YORK YANKEES vs. BROOKLYN DODGERS

October 7

LINE SCORE	1	2	3	4	5	6	7	8	9	R	H	E
NEW YORK YANKEES	0	0	1	0	0	0	0	0	3	4	5	0
BROOKLYN DODGERS	0	0	0	1	0	0	0	0	2	3	5	0

RECAP

After the eighth inning, the game was deadlocked at 1-1. The ninth inning turned the tide. In the top half, the Yankees put together a three-run scoring drive led by Yogi Berra, Bobby Brown, Gene Woodling, Johnny Mize and Jerry Coleman. All of the runs scored after two were out and with only a runner at first. In the bottom, the Dodgers fell one run short on solo shots slugged by Luis Olmo and Roy Campanella. Five frames of relief were in jeopardy for New York reliever Joe Page until he notched a strikeout for the last out to cement the win.

SCORING SUMMARY

Third Inning - New York Yankees
– Mapes sprinted to first on a walk.
– Coleman struck out.
– Byrne zinged a hit-and-run single; Mapes stopped at third base.
– Rizzuto lifted a sacrifice fly to Furillo plating Mapes.
– Henrich walked Byrne to second base.
– Berra popped up to Robinson.

1 Runs **1** Hits **0** Errors **2** LOB

YANKEES – 1   **DODGERS – 0**

Fourth Inning - Brooklyn Dodgers
– Reese slugged a solo shot into the left-center field crowd.
– Miksis skied out to DiMaggio.
– Furillo cranked a single into left field.
– Robinson walked Furillo to second base.
– Hodges walked; bases loaded.
– Page relieved Byrne.
– Olmo fouled out to Henrich.
– Snider bounded out, Coleman to Henrich.

1 Runs **2** Hits **0** Errors **3** LOB

YANKEES – 1   **DODGERS – 1**

Ninth Inning - New York Yankees
– Henrich grounded out, Robinson to Hodges,
– Berra walked.

– DiMaggio fouled out to Miksis.
– B. Brown singled Berra to second base.
– Woodling walked; bases jammed.
– Mize PH for Mapes, singled into right field, driving in Berra and B. Brown; Woodling rumbled into third base; runners on the corners.
– Banta relieved Branca.
– Bauer PR for Mize.
– Coleman singled up the middle, driving in Woodling; Bauer moved up.
– Page was a strikeout.

3 Runs **3** Hits **0** Errors **2** LOB

YANKEES – 4   **DODGERS – 1**

Ninth Inning - Brooklyn Dodgers
– Bauer to RF.
– Hodges tapped out, Coleman to Henrich.
– Olmo slugged a solo shot into the left field seats.
– Snider struck out.
– Campanella slugged a solo shot into the left field crowd.
– Edwards PH for Banta, fanned.

2 Runs **2** Hits **0** Errors **0** LOB

YANKEES – 4   **DODGERS – 3**

HIGHLIGHTS

- Dodgers starter Ralph Branca retired 14 straight Bombers between the fifth and ninth innings
- Brooklyn slugged three solo home runs
- Yankee reliever Joe Page entered the game in the fourth inning with the game tied and pitched out of a one out, bases loaded jam
- PH Johnny Mize, a mid-season acquisition from the New York Giants, broke the 1-1 tie
- Both teams stroked five safeties - three of the Dodger hits were home runs, four of the Yankees hits were singles

DIAMOND DUST

- Pee Wee Reese, in the fourth inning, slugged the 210th home run in World Series history
- Branca's first loss at home

Game 3 BOX SCORE SUMMARY

NEW YORK YANKEES	AB	R	H	RBI	BB	K	1B	2B	3B	HR	TB	SB
PHIL RIZZUTO, SS	4	0	0	1	0	0	0	0	0	0	0	0
YOGI BERRA, C	3	1	0	0	1	1	0	0	0	0	0	0
BOBBY BROWN, 3B	4	1	1	0	0	0	1	0	0	0	1	0
GENE WOODLING, LF	3	1	1	0	1	0	0	1	0	0	2	0
CLIFF MAPES, RF	2	1	0	0	1	0	0	0	0	0	0	0
JOHNNY MIZE, PH	1	0	1	2	0	0	1	0	0	0	1	0
JERRY COLEMAN, 2B	4	0	1	1	0	2	1	0	0	0	1	0
BROOKLYN DODGERS	AB	R	H	RBI	BB	K	1B	2B	3B	HR	TB	SB
PEE WEE REESE, SS	2	1	1	1	1	0	0	0	0	1	4	0
LUIS OLMO, LF	4	1	1	1	0	0	0	0	0	1	4	0
ROY CAMPANELLA, C	4	1	1	1	0	0	0	0	0	1	4	0

NEW YORK YANKEES	IP	H	R	ER	HR	K	BB	HBP	ERA
TOMMY BYRNE	3.1	2	1	1	1	1	2	0	2.70
JOE PAGE W (1-0)	5.2	3	2	2	2	4	2	0	2.70
BROOKLYN DODGERS	IP	H	R	ER	HR	K	BB	HBP	ERA
RALPH BRANCA L (0-1)	8.2	4	4	4	0	6	4	0	4.15

GAME TIME:	2:30	
ATTENDANCE:	32,788	
BEST OF 7:	DODGERS - 1	YANKEES - 2

NEW YORK YANKEES vs. BROOKLYN DODGERS

October 8

LINE SCORE	1	2	3	4	5	6	7	8	9	R	H	E
NEW YORK YANKEES	0	0	0	3	3	0	0	0	0	6	10	0
BROOKLYN DODGERS	0	0	0	0	0	4	0	0	0	4	9	1

RECAP

The Dodgers didn't score until they were down by six runs. In the sixth inning, starter Eddie Lopat faced eight men and was tagged for seven singles that produced four runs. After that outburst, Yankee reliever Allie Reynolds retired, consecutively, the last 10 home team batters.

Brooklyn starter Don Newcombe survived a first inning, bases loaded Bomber scoring threat but did not do so in the fourth. Three Yankee doubles sandwiched around a walk put three runs on the scoreboard. In their next at bat, the Yankees expanded their lead to six against reliever Joe Hatten, which held up for the victory.

SCORING SUMMARY

Fourth Inning - New York Yankees

– DiMaggio flied out to Snider.
– B. Brown ricochet a double off of the left-center field wall.
– Woodling worked a walk.
– Mapes doubled into left field, driving home B. Brown and Woodling.
– Coleman flied out to Olmo.
– Lopat doubled off of the left field wall, driving Mapes home.
– Hatten relieved Newcombe.
– Rizzuto singled into left field; Lopat tagged out at the plate on a bulls-eye throw from Olmo to Campanella.

3 Runs **4** Hits **0** Errors **1** LOB

YANKEES – 3   **DODGERS – 0**

Fifth Inning - New York Yankees

– Henrich coaxed a walk.
– Berra singled Henrich to second base; Miksis' miscue advanced the runners.
– DiMaggio loaded the bases on an intentional walk.
– B. Brown tripled into deep center field, driving home Henrich, Berra and DiMaggio.
– Woodling flied out to Snider.
– Bauer PH for Mapes, flied out to Hermanski.
– Coleman rolled out, Reese to Hodges.

3 Runs **2** Hits **1** Errors **1** LOB

YANKEES – 6   **DODGERS – 0**

Sixth Inning - Brooklyn Dodgers

– Reese stroked a single into center field.
– Cox PH for Miksis, hustled an infield hit as Reese slid into second base.
– Snider grounded into a double play, Rizzuto to Henrich; Reese advanced.
– Robinson singled into left field, driving Reese home.
– Hodges blistered a hit-and-run single; Robinson eased into third base.
– Olmo singled up the middle, driving in Robinson; Hodges advanced.
– Campanella singled into left field, driving in Hodges; Olmo slid into second.
– Hermanski singled into right field, driving in Olmo; Campanella cruised into third base.
– Reynolds relieved Lopat.
– Jorgensen PH for Erskine, was a strikeout.

4 Runs **7** Hits **0** Errors **2** LOB

YANKEES – 6   **DODGERS – 4**

HIGHLIGHTS

- Pinstripe starter Ed Lopat doubled in the final run in the fourth inning scoring drive and was thrown out at the plate for the last out
- Bobby Brown, in consecutive innings, doubled and tripled (scoring in the fourth and driving in three in the fifth)
- Runs were scored in bunches, as New York mounted two drives of three runs while Brooklyn had one that netted four

DIAMOND DUST

- Dodgers rookie starter Don Newcombe is the eighth rookie to start twice and the sixth to lose both
- Brooklyn's seven singles in the sixth inning, four-run rally tied the record for most in an inning
- New York drilled three doubles in the fourth inning to tie a record achieved twice by the Brooklyn Dodgers in 1947

Game 4 BOX SCORE SUMMARY

NEW YORK YANKEES	AB	R	H	RBI	BB	K	1B	2B	3B	HR	TB	SB
TOMMY HENRICH, 1B	4	1	3	0	1	0	3	0	0	0	3	0
YOGI BERRA, C	5	1	1	0	0	0	1	0	0	0	1	0
JOE DIMAGGIO, CF	3	1	0	0	2	1	0	0	0	0	0	0
BOBBY BROWN, 3B	3	1	2	3	1	0	0	1	1	0	5	0
GENE WOODLING, LF	3	1	0	0	1	0	0	0	0	0	0	0
CLIFF MAPES, RF	2	1	1	2	0	0	0	1	0	0	2	0
EDDIE LOPAT, P	3	0	1	1	0	0	0	1	0	0	2	0
BROOKLYN DODGERS	**AB**	**R**	**H**	**RBI**	**BB**	**K**	**1B**	**2B**	**3B**	**HR**	**TB**	**SB**
PEE WEE REESE, SS	4	1	2	0	0	0	1	1	0	0	3	0
JACKIE ROBINSON, 2B	3	1	1	1	1	0	1	0	0	0	1	0
GIL HODGES, 1B	4	1	1	0	0	1	1	0	0	0	1	0
LUIS OLMO, LF	4	1	1	1	0	1	1	0	0	0	1	0
ROY CAMPANELLA, C	4	0	1	1	0	0	1	0	0	0	1	0
GENE HERMANSKI, RF	4	0	2	1	0	2	2	0	0	0	2	0

Jackie Robinson, seen here upending Phil Rizzuto on a hard slide into second, scored the only run of Game 2, though it was one of only 2 runs he scored in the series, in which he hit .188 (3/16).

NEW YORK YANKEES	IP	H	R	ER	HR	K	BB	HBP	ERA
EDDIE LOPAT W (1-0)	5.2	9	4	4	0	4	1	0	6.35
ALLIE REYNOLDS S (1)	3.1	0	0	0	0	5	0	0	0.00
BROOKLYN DODGERS	**IP**	**H**	**R**	**ER**	**HR**	**K**	**BB**	**HBP**	**ERA**
DON NEWCOMBE L (0-2)	3.2	5	3	3	0	0	3	0	3.09
JOE HATTEN	1.1	3	3	3	0	0	2	0	20.25

GAME TIME:	**2:42**
ATTENDANCE:	**33,934**
BEST OF 7:	**DODGERS - 1 YANKEES - 3**

Game 5

NEW YORK YANKEES vs. BROOKLYN DODGERS

October 9

LINE SCORE	1	2	3	4	5	6	7	8	9	R	H	E
NEW YORK YANKEES	2	0	3	1	1	3	0	0	0	10	11	1
BROOKLYN DODGERS	0	0	1	0	0	1	4	0	0	6	11	2

─────────────────────── **RECAP** ───────────────────────

Bats lit up the field for the first time in the series. By the end of the third inning the Yankees had five runs, and by the end of the sixth they had ten and led by 8. The Dodgers' 4-run seventh was too little, too late. Multiple Bronx Bombers had outstanding days at the plate. Stroking three hits were 3B Bobby Brown and LF Gene Woodling. 2B Joe Coleman drove in three. Brown and Woodling drove in two. 1B Tommy Henrich - each crossed home plate twice. Four players - Brown, Woodling, SS Phil Rizzuto and The 11 hits and 10 runs off of six Brooklyn pitchers ensured the Yankees' third straight win for their 12th Fall Classic victory.

─────────────────── **SCORING SUMMARY** ───────────────────

First Inning - New York Yankees
– Barney starting.
– Rizzuto drew a free pass.
– Henrich walked Rizzuto to second base; both runners advanced on Barney's errant pick-off throw.
– Berra was a strikeout.
– DiMaggio hoisted a sacrifice fly to Snider plating Rizzuto; Henrich took third.
– B. Brown singled up the middle, driving Henrich home.
– Woodling walked B. Brown to second base.
– Mapes was a strikeout.

② Runs   **①** Hits   **①** Errors   **②** LOB

YANKEES – 2   **DODGERS – 0**

Third Inning - New York Yankees
– Berra tapped back to the box, Barney to Hodges.
– DiMaggio flied out to Snider.
– B. Brown managed a walk.
– Woodling hitched a hit-and-run single; B. Brown scooted to third.
– Mapes jammed the bases on a walk.
– Coleman singled into left field, driving in B. Brown and Woodling; Mapes slid into second base.
– Banta relieved Barney.

– Raschi singled up the middle, driving in Mapes; Coleman slid into second.
– Rizzuto flied out to Snider.

③ Runs   **③** Hits   **⓪** Errors   **②** LOB

YANKEES – 5   **DODGERS – 0**

Third Inning - Brooklyn Dodgers
– Rackley struck out.
– Campanella pounded a double into left field.
– Banta pushed Campanella up on a grounder to Henrich.
– Reese singled into right field, driving Campanella home.
– Jorgensen popped up to Rizzuto.

① Runs   **②** Hits   **⓪** Errors   **①** LOB

YANKEES – 5   **DODGERS – 1**

Fourth Inning - New York Yankees
– Henrich rolled out, Robinson to Hodges.
– Berra zapped out to Hodges.
– DiMaggio slugged a solo shot into the left field crowd.
– B. Brown struck out.

① Runs   **①** Hits   **⓪** Errors   **⓪** LOB

YANKEES – 6   **DODGERS – 1**

Fifth Inning - New York Yankees

– Woodling rammed a double off of the right field scoreboard.
– Mapes sacrificed Woodling to third base, Banta to Hodges.
– Coleman scored Woodling on a ground out to Hodges.
– Raschi went down on strikes.

1 Runs **1** Hits **0** Errors **0** LOB

YANKEES – 7   **DODGERS – 1**

Sixth Inning - New York Yankees

– Erskine pitching.
– Rizzuto reached first base on a free pass.
– Henrich zinged a hit-and-run single; Rizzuto cruised into third base.
– Berra lifted a sacrifice fly to Rackley plating Rizzuto.
– DiMaggio popped up to Robinson.
– B. Brown tripled into the right field corner, driving in Henrich; on Robinson's wild throw B. Brown scored.
– Hatten relieved Erskine.
– Woodling doubled high off of the left field wall.
– Mapes flied out to Rackley.

3 Runs **3** Hits **1** Errors **1** LOB

YANKEES – 10   **DODGERS – 1**

Sixth Inning - Brooklyn Dodgers

– Snider doubled to the base of the right field wall.
– Robinson reached on a walk.
– Hermanski singled into right field, driving in Snider; Robinson made second; on Mapes throwing error, Robinson slid into third base.
– Hodges was a strikeout.
– Rackley out on a ground ball to Henrich; Hermanski slid into second.
– Campanella walked the bases full.
– Cox PH for Hatten and was a strikeout.

1 Runs **2** Hits **1** Errors **3** LOB

YANKEES – 10   **DODGERS – 2**

Seventh Inning - Brooklyn Dodgers

– Reese flied out to Woodling.
– Jorgensen managed a walk.
– Snider smacked a hit-and-run single; Jorgensen braked at third base.
– Robinson lifted a sacrifice fly to Woodling plating Jorgensen.
– Hermanski walked Snider to second base.
– Hodges clouted a home run into the left field seats, driving home Snider and Hermanski.
– Page relieved Raschi.
– Olmo PH for Rackley, whiffed.

4 Runs **2** Hits **0** Errors **0** LOB

YANKEES – 10   **DODGERS – 6**

HIGHLIGHTS

- Dodgers starter Rex Barney walked six in 2.2 innings; three scored
- Phil Rizzuto, on base via a walk twice, scored both times via a sac fly
- Yankee starter Vic Raschi gave up six runs but the Dodgers mound staff gave up 10
- Six of the nine Yankees hitters scored and/or drove in a run
- Five of the Dodgers hitters scored and/or drove in a run
- Joe Page, in 2.1 innings of relief, faced nine Brooklyn batters striking out four
- Page struck out the first and last batters he faced

DIAMOND DUST

- Fifteenth five-game set
- Raschi notched an All-Star Game save and a Fall Classic victory in the same season
- New York has defeated Brooklyn in three straight meetings

Game 5 BOX SCORE SUMMARY

NEW YORK YANKEES	AB	R	H	RBI	BB	K	1B	2B	3B	HR	TB	SB
PHIL RIZZUTO, SS	3	2	0	0	2	1	0	0	0	0	0	0
TOMMY HENRICH, 1B	4	2	1	0	1	0	1	0	0	0	1	0
YOGI BERRA, C	5	0	0	1	0	1	0	0	0	0	0	0
JOE DIMAGGIO, CF	4	1	1	2	1	0	0	0	0	1	4	0
BOBBY BROWN, 3B	4	2	3	2	1	1	2	0	1	0	5	0
GENE WOODLING, LF	4	2	3	0	1	0	1	2	0	0	5	0
CLIFF MAPES, RF	3	1	0	0	1	1	0	0	0	0	0	0
JERRY COLEMAN, 2B	5	0	2	3	0	0	1	1	0	0	3	0
VIC RASCHI, P	3	0	1	1	1	1	1	0	0	0	1	0
BROOKLYN DODGERS	AB	R	H	RBI	BB	K	1B	2B	3B	HR	TB	SB
PEE WEE REESE, SS	5	0	2	1	0	0	2	0	0	0	2	0
SPIDER JORGENSON, 3B	3	1	0	0	1	0	0	0	0	0	0	0
DUKE SNIDER, CF	5	2	2	0	0	3	1	1	0	0	3	0
JACKIE ROBINSON, 2B	4	0	1	1	1	1	1	0	0	0	1	0
GENE HERMANSKI, LF	3	1	1	1	2	0	1	0	0	0	1	0
GIL HODGES, 1B	5	1	2	3	0	2	1	0	0	1	5	0
ROY CAMPANELLA, C	3	1	1	0	1	0	0	1	0	0	2	0

NEW YORK YANKEES	IP	H	R	ER	HR	K	BB	HBP	ERA
VIC RASCHI W (1-1)	6.2	9	6	6	1	7	4	0	4.30
JOE PAGE S (1)	2.1	2	0	0	0	4	1	0	2.00
BROOKLYN DODGERS	IP	H	R	ER	HR	K	BB	HBP	ERA
REX BARNEY L (0-1)	2.2	3	5	5	0	2	6	0	16.88
JACK BANTA	2.1	3	2	2	1	2	0	0	3.18
CARL ERSKINE	0.2	2	3	3	0	0	1	0	16.20

(National Baseball Hall of Fame and Museum)

Joe Page's save in Game 5 was his only of the series (though he did win G3 with 5.2 inning of 2-run relief.) Page collected 27 saves in 1949 for the Yankees' new manager, Casey Stengel. Page's 27 saves set a new single-season record, surpassing Firpo Marberry's 22, a record that had stood for 27 years. (Marberry held the all-time record for career saves with 99 from 1926-1945.) At the time, of course, saves had not yet been invented, so neither Page nor Stengel had any idea of the reliever's accomplishment.

But Stengel knew how to win ballgames, and having the tall, fire-balling lefty in at the end of the game proved to be a great strategy. Page pitched in a league-leading 60 games in 1949 and threw 135.1 innings, all in relief. His greatest performance, and certainly one of the most clutch in baseball history, came in the final game of the season, when he pitched 6.1 innings of 1-hit relief against the Boston Red Sox to complete a 3-game sweep to end the season and win the pennant by 1 game.

GAME TIME:	**3:04**	
ATTENDANCE:	**33,711**	
BEST OF 7:	**DODGERS - 1**	**YANKEES - 4**

1949

BROOKLYN DODGERS vs. NEW YORK YANKEES

--- **BROOKLYN DODGERS** ---

Overall World Series Record: 0 WINS 5 LOSSES: 29 Games Played (8 - 21 .276)
- Jackie Robinson, regular season batting champ, batted below the Mendoza line.
- Duke Snider, also batting below the Mendoza line, did not drive in a run nor draw a walk.
- Three of the four home runs were solo shots.
- Brooklyn is the fourth team to lose three Fall Classics in a decade (all to the Yankees)

--- **NEW YORK YANKEES** ---

Overall World Series Record 12 WINS 4 LOSSES: 84 Games Played [55 - 28 [1 tie] .663]
- Allie Reynolds was on the mound for 12.1 innings and compiled an ERA of 0.00.
- Reynolds posted one win, one save, and struck out 14.
- Page struck out the last batter to end a Series for the second time (1947).
- Brown and Woodling combined to score eight runs, Brown drove in five, batting .500.
- Henrich has homered in all four Series appearances (1938/41/47).
- Casey Stengel is the 19th manager to win debut appearance, winning as a player and as a manager.
- Stengel is the fourth manager (1921/1941/1947) to win debut in the Subway Series.
- New York is the first team to win four Fall Classics in a decade (Cardinals, 1943, along with 3 vs Brooklyn).

--- **FUNGOES** ---

- Both teams had two players who batted below the Mendoza line.
- A grand total of 45 players (14 pitchers) took the field.
- Overall World Series tally now stands at American League 29-17.

--- **A QUICK LOOK AT THE FIFTH DECADE** ---

- 10 different teams appeared...the Detroit Tigers broke even in their two appearances...the New York Yankees made five appearances, winning four, three from the Brooklyn Dodgers...the New York Yankees and the St. Louis Cardinals traded victories in consecutive seasons...the intra-city duel in St. Louis was won by the Cardinals in the Browns' only Fall Classic appearance...the St. Louis Cardinals made four appearances, winning three...the two leagues traded victories in the first eight contests...apartheid against African-Americans players ended in 1947...this was the final World Series appearances for the Boston Braves...there were two sweeps...the American League won six of the 10.

--- **FIVE-GAME DATA** ---

TIME	**13:10**	PLAYERS POOL	**$490,856**
ATTENDANCE	**716,236**	SHARES	**BROOKLYN DODGERS - $4,273**
			NEW YORK YANKEES - $5,627

1949

BROOKLYN DODGERS vs. NEW YORK YANKEES

Brooklyn Dodgers Composite Stats

BATTING	G	AB	R	H	RBI	2B	3B	HR	BB	SO	BA	OBP	SLG	OPS
Duke Snider	5	21	2	3	0	1	0	0	0	8	.143	.143	.190	.333
Pee Wee Reese	5	19	2	6	2	1	0	1	1	0	.316	.381	.526	.907
Gil Hodges	5	17	2	4	4	0	0	1	1	4	.235	.278	.412	.690
Jackie Robinson	5	16	2	3	2	1	0	0	4	2	.188	.350	.250	.600
Roy Campanella	5	15	2	4	2	1	0	1	3	1	.267	.389	.533	.922
Gene Hermanski	4	13	1	4	2	0	1	0	3	3	.308	.438	.462	.899
Spider Jorgensen	4	11	1	2	0	2	0	0	2	2	.182	.308	.364	.671
Luis Olmo	4	11	2	3	2	0	0	1	0	2	.273	.273	.545	.818
Carl Furillo	3	8	0	1	0	0	0	0	1	0	.125	.222	.125	.347
Eddie Miksis	3	7	0	2	0	1	0	0	0	1	.286	.286	.429	.714
Marv Rackley	2	5	0	0	0	0	0	0	0	2	.000	.000	.000	.000
Don Newcombe	2	4	0	0	0	0	0	0	0	3	.000	.000	.000	.000
Ralph Branca	1	3	0	0	0	0	0	0	0	3	.000	.000	.000	.000
Billy Cox	2	3	0	1	0	0	0	0	0	1	.333	.333	.333	.667
Preacher Roe	1	3	0	0	0	0	0	0	0	3	.000	.000	.000	.000
Tommy Brown	2	2	0	0	0	0	0	0	0	1	.000	.000	.000	.000
Bruce Edwards	2	2	0	1	0	0	0	0	0	1	.500	.500	.500	1.000
Jack Banta	3	1	0	0	0	0	0	0	0	0	.000	.000	.000	.000
Dick Whitman	1	1	0	0	0	0	0	0	0	1	.000	.000	.000	.000
Rex Barney	1	0	0	0	0	0	0	0	0	0				
Carl Erskine	2	0	0	0	0	0	0	0	0	0				
Joe Hatten	2	0	0	0	0	0	0	0	0	0				
Mike McCormick	1	0	0	0	0	0	0	0	0	0				
Paul Minner	1	0	0	0	0	0	0	0	0	0				
Erv Palica	1	0	0	0	0	0	0	0	0	0				
Totals	**5**	**162**	**14**	**34**	**14**	**7**	**1**	**4**	**15**	**38**	**.210**	**.281**	**.340**	**.620**

PITCHING	G	GS	ERA	W	L	SV	CG	IP	H	R	ER	BB	SO	WHIP
Don Newcombe	2	2	3.09	0	2	0	1	11.2	10	4	4	3	11	1.114
Preacher Roe	1	1	0.00	1	0	0	1	9.0	6	0	0	0	3	0.667
Ralph Branca	1	1	4.15	0	1	0	0	8.2	4	4	4	4	6	0.923
Jack Banta	3	0	3.18	0	0	0	0	5.2	5	2	2	1	4	1.059
Rex Barney	1	1	16.88	0	1	0	0	2.2	3	5	5	6	2	3.375
Erv Palica	1	0	0.00	0	0	0	0	2.0	1	0	0	1	1	1.000
Carl Erskine	2	0	16.20	0	0	0	0	1.2	3	3	3	1	0	2.400
Joe Hatten	2	0	16.20	0	0	0	0	1.2	4	3	3	2	0	3.600
Paul Minner	1	0	0.00	0	0	0	0	1.0	1	0	0	0	0	1.000
Totals	**5**	**5**	**4.30**	**1**	**4**	**0**	**2**	**44.0**	**37**	**21**	**21**	**18**	**27**	**1.250**

1949

BROOKLYN DODGERS vs. NEW YORK YANKEES

New York Yankees Composite Stats

BATTING	G	AB	R	H	RBI	2B	3B	HR	BB	SO	BA	OBP	SLG	OPS
Jerry Coleman	5	20	0	5	4	3	0	0	0	4	.250	.250	.400	.650
Tommy Henrich	5	19	4	5	1	0	0	1	3	0	.263	.364	.421	.785
Joe DiMaggio	5	18	2	2	2	0	0	1	3	5	.111	.238	.278	.516
Phil Rizzuto	5	18	2	3	1	0	0	0	3	1	.167	.286	.167	.452
Yogi Berra	4	16	2	1	1	0	0	0	1	3	.063	.118	.063	.180
Bobby Brown	4	12	4	6	5	1	2	0	2	2	.500	.571	.917	1.488
Gene Woodling	3	10	4	4	0	3	0	0	3	0	.400	.538	.700	1.238
Cliff Mapes	4	10	3	1	2	1	0	0	2	4	.100	.250	.200	.450
Billy Johnson	2	7	0	1	0	0	0	0	0	2	.143	.143	.143	.286
Johnny Lindell	2	7	0	1	0	0	0	0	0	2	.143	.143	.143	.286
Hank Bauer	3	6	0	1	0	0	0	0	0	0	.167	.167	.167	.333
Vic Raschi	2	5	0	1	1	0	0	0	1	1	.200	.333	.200	.533
Joe Page	3	4	0	0	0	0	0	0	0	2	.000	.000	.000	.000
Allie Reynolds	2	4	0	2	0	1	0	0	0	1	.500	.500	.750	1.250
Eddie Lopat	1	3	0	1	1	1	0	0	0	0	.333	.333	.667	1.000
Johnny Mize	2	2	0	2	2	0	0	0	0	0	1.000	1.000	1.000	2.000
Charlie Silvera	1	2	0	0	0	0	0	0	0	0	.000	.000	.000	.000
Tommy Byrne	1	1	0	1	0	0	0	0	0	0	1.000	1.000	1.000	2.000
Gus Niarhos	1	0	0	0	0	0	0	0	0	0				
Snuffy Stirnweiss	1	0	0	0	0	0	0	0	0	0				
Totals	**5**	**164**	**21**	**37**	**20**	**10**	**2**	**2**	**18**	**27**	**.226**	**.302**	**.348**	**.650**

PITCHING	G	GS	ERA	W	L	SV	CG	IP	H	R	ER	BB	SO	WHIP
Vic Raschi	2	2	4.30	1	1	0	0	14.2	15	7	7	5	11	1.364
Allie Reynolds	2	1	0.00	1	0	1	1	12.1	2	0	0	4	14	0.486
Joe Page	3	0	2.00	1	0	1	0	9.0	6	2	2	3	8	1.000
Eddie Lopat	1	1	6.35	1	0	0	0	5.2	9	4	4	1	4	1.765
Tommy Byrne	1	1	2.70	0	0	0	0	3.1	2	1	1	2	1	1.200
Totals	**5**	**5**	**2.80**	**4**	**1**	**2**	**1**	**45.0**	**34**	**14**	**14**	**15**	**38**	**1.089**

1951

GIANTS

NEW YORK GIANTS VS. NEW YORK YANKEES

FUNGOES

- Subway Series #9 is the sixth meeting between the two clubs.
- The second (and most famous) of four seasons in which there was a tie for the pennant that was broken by a best-of-three series (1946, StL over Bklyn 2-0; 1959, LAD over Milw 2-0; 1962, SFG over LAD 2-1). In 1948, Cleveland defeated Boston in a 1-game playoff to take the AL crown.
- Rookie-of-the-Year match-up for the first time (Willie Mays, Gil McDougald).
- No travel days.
- Umpire Info: Al Barlick is known for strong voice in calling balls and strikes, 1989 Hall of Fame inductee; Lee Ballanfant was a former minor league player and manager; Artie Gore was a minor league shortstop; Bill Summers is a former boxer, mill worker and road worker; umpired in high school, semi-pro and industrial league games.

SERIES SUMMARY

The Giant made their return to the Subway Series after a 14-year absence. And playing off the momentum of their incredible pennant-winning drive and "Shot Heard Round the World" playoff win against the Dodgers, they rolled over the Yankees 5-1 in the opener of the Series. It was the first time in 10 World Series that the Yankees had lost the first game. Surprise starter Dave Koslo went the distance, and the offense was led by a 3-run homer by Alvin Dark in the sixth that put the Giants ahead by four.

"Steady Eddie" Lopat restored the natural order with a 5-hit complete game win in Game 2. Three of the hits were by Monte Irvin (who had four in Game 1), but the Giants scored only one run, while the Yankees scratched out single runs in the first, second, and eighth innings.

The Giants got the upper hand once more in Game 3 with a 6-2 win. Two Yankees errors were costly, and Whitey Lockman belted a 3-run homer in the bottom of the fifth to break the game wide open. The Giants' Jim Hearn, who won a career-high 17 games in 1951, pitched into the eighth inning.

The Yankees were equally as dominating in Game 4, as Allie Reynolds went the route, allowing just two runs. Joe DiMaggio, playing in the final game of his career, broke out of an 0-for-12 slump with a single and a two-run home run.

In the critical Game 5, the Yankees made sure there was no suspense, turning a 1-0 deficit in the first inning to a 7-1 lead after four and a 13-1 annihilation. Numerous walks and errors contributed to the Giants' demise, while DiMaggio had his second straight strong game, with three hits and three RBI.

Game 6 was a tight battle for the first five innings, with each team scoring one run. The Yankees broke through with three in the last of the sixth, in which all three runs were driven in on a two-out triple by Hank Bauer. The Giants came back with two in the ninth, but that was one too few, and the Yankees were winners again.

THE TEAMS

NEW YORK GIANTS
98 - 59 .624 +1.0 G

The Team
- Subway Series #6 appearance; 13th overall (14-year hiatus).
- In second place at the All-Star break.
- Defeated the Brooklyn Dodgers in a three-game playoff after tying them with a 96-58 mark during the regular season.

The Players
- Eddie Stanky's third appearance for third National League pennant-winner (1947 Brooklyn Dodgers/1948 Boston Braves).
- Al Dark and Stanky were teammates on the 1948 pennant-winning Boston Braves.
- Willie Mays was NL Rookie of the Year, batting .274 with 20 homers and 68 RBI.

The Manager
- Leo Durocher, after a 10-year hiatus, is making second managerial appearance.
- Durocher lost to the Yankees in the 1941 Subway Series as the manager of the Brooklyn Dodgers.
- Durocher is the only skipper to manage two National League franchises in the Subway Series.

Top Batters

Pos	Name	AB	R	H	HR	RBI	BA	OPS
C	Wes Westrum	361	59	79	20	70	.219	.818
SS	Al Dark	646	114	196	14	69	.303	.805
OF	Monte Irvin	558	94	174	24	121	.312	.929
OF	Willie Mays	464	59	127	20	68	.274	.828

Top Pitchers

Pos	Name	W	L	ERA	G	SV	IP	SO
St	Sal Maglie	23	6	2.93	42	4	298.0	146
St	Larry Jansen	23	11	3.04	39	0	278.2	145
St	Jim Hearn	17	9	3.62	34	0	211.1	66
Rel	George Spencer	10	4	3.75	57	6	132.0	36

NEW YORK YANKEES
98 - 56 .636 +5.0 G

The Team
- Subway Series #9; 18th overall appearance (third consecutive).
- In third place at the All-Star break.

The Players
- 1949 Subway Series returning players (11): Hank Bauer, Yogi Berra, Bobby Brown, Jerry Coleman, Joe DiMaggio, Eddie Lopat, Johnny Mize, Vic Raschi, Allie Reynolds, Phil Rizzuto, Gene Woodling.
- DiMaggio played on the 1936/37/38/39/41/42/47/49/50 pennant-winning teams, winning eight titles.
- DiMaggio is appearing in sixth Subway Series.
- DiMaggio's final appearance as Mickey Mantle debuts.
- Rizzuto played on the 1941/42/47/49/50 pennant-winning teams, winning four titles.
- Berra, Brown, Raschi and Reynolds played on 3 title-winning teams, while 5 other Yankees played on the last two.
- Allie Reynolds is the first pitcher to hurl two no-hitters in the same season to appear in the World Series.
- Reynolds, on July 12th, no-hit Cleveland and on September 28, the last day of the season, did the same to the Red Sox in Yankee Stadium.
- Yogi Berra won the Most Valuable Player award.
- Gil McDougald named the Rookie of the Year, the first American Leaguer. (From 1947-1950, was only one winner for both leagues.)

The Manager
- Casey Stengel is the 10th manager to make three straight appearances, and the third Yankee skipper.

Top Batters

Pos	Name	AB	R	H	HR	RBI	BA	OPS
C	Yogi Berra	547	92	161	27	88	.294	.842
SS	Phil Rizzuto	540	87	148	2	43	.274	.696
OF	Gene Woodling	420	65	118	15	71	.281	.835
OF	Joe DiMaggio	415	72	109	12	71	.263	.787

Top Pitchers

Pos	Name	W	L	ERA	G	SV	IP	SO
St	Vic Raschi	21	10	3.27	35	0	258.1	164
St	Eddie Lopat	21	9	2.91	31	0	234.2	93
St	Allie Reynolds	17	8	3.05	40	6	221.0	126
St-R	Tom Morgan	9	3	3.68	27	2	124.2	57

NEW YORK GIANTS vs. NEW YORK YANKEES

October 4

LINE SCORE	1	2	3	4	5	6	7	8	9	R	H	E
NEW YORK GIANTS	2	0	0	0	0	3	0	0	0	5	10	1
NEW YORK YANKEES	0	1	0	0	0	0	0	0	0	1	7	1

RECAP

The fans were hardly in their seats when the Giants took a first inning, two-run lead. The second run was a steal of home plate by Giants LF Monte Irvin. The Giants never lost that lead. In the sixth inning they added three more on a home run by SS Alvin Dark. The star Giants players were Irvin, who had a four-hit day, Dark who drove in three, and Dave Koslo, the surprise starter, who pitched a complete game, seven-hit, one-run gem.

SCORING SUMMARY

First Inning - New York Giants
- Reynolds starting.
- Stanky grounded out, Rizzuto to Collins.
- Dark flied out to Mantle.
- Thompson sprinted to first base on a walk.
- Irvin zinged a hit-and-run single; Thompson streaked into third.
- Lockman bounced a ground-rule double into the left field seats, driving in Thompson; Irvin motored into third base.
- Irvin stole home plate.
- Thomson got to first on a free pass; Lockman held.
- Mays flied out to Mantle.

2 Runs **2** Hits **0** Errors **2** LOB

GIANTS – 2   **YANKEES – 0**

Second Inning - New York Yankees
- Berra squibbed out to Lockman.
- McDougald rattled a double into the left field corner.
- Coleman singled McDougald to third base; on Thompson's juggle McDougald slid across the plate.
- Collins forced Coleman at second base, Thomson to Stanky.
- Reynolds singled Collins to second base.
- Mantle put a runner on each base on a walk.
- Rizzuto grounded out, Lockman to Koslo.

1 Runs **3** Hits **1** Errors **3** LOB

GIANTS – 2   **YANKEES – 1**

Sixth Inning - New York Giants
- Mays flied out to Mantle.
- Westrum lobbed a single into left field.
- Koslo sacrificed Westrum to second base, Berra to Collins.
- Stanky worked a walk.
- Dark belted a home run into the lower left field seats, driving home Westrum and Stanky.
- Thomson drew a walk.
- Irvin blistered a hit-and-run single; Thompson high-tailed it into third.
- Lockman out on a ground ball, Coleman to Collins.

3 Runs **3** Hits **0** Errors **2** LOB

GIANTS – 5   **YANKEES – 1**

HIGHLIGHTS

- Monte Irvin got a hit in his first 4 WS at-bats, and collected 11 overall in the series, good for a .458 BA
- SS Al Dark drove in three of the five runs
- Dark's third inning home run is the 25th in New York Giants history
- Pinstripe starter Allie Reynolds charged with first loss in third start

— DIAMOND DUST —

- Giants LF Monte Irvin, CF Willie Mays, and RF Hank Thompson comprised the first all African-American outfield in World Series history
- Irvin is the 11th player to steal home, the first since 1934
- First steal of home since 1928 that was not part of a double steal and the third in a Game One
- In openers the Giants are 8-5 while the Yankees are 14-4
- Yankees lose first opening game since 1936

Game 1 BOX SCORE SUMMARY

NEW YORK GIANTS	AB	R	H	RBI	BB	K	1B	2B	3B	HR	TB	SB
EDDIE STANKY, 2B	4	1	0	0	1	0	0	0	0	0	0	0
AL DARK, SS	5	1	2	3	0	1	1	0	0	1	5	0
HANK THOMPSON, RF	3	1	0	0	2	0	0	0	0	0	0	0
MONTE IRVIN, LF	5	1	4	0	0	0	3	0	1	0	6	1
WHITEY LOCKMAN, 1B	4	0	1	1	1	0	0	1	0	0	2	0
WES WESTRUM, C	3	1	2	0	2	0	2	0	0	0	2	0
NEW YORK YANKEES	AB	R	H	RBI	BB	K	1B	2B	3B	HR	TB	SB
GIL MCDOUGALD, 3B	4	1	1	0	0	0	0	1	0	0	2	0

NEW YORK GIANTS	IP	H	R	ER	HR	K	BB	HBP	ERA
DAVE KOSLO W (1-0)	9	7	1	1	0	3	3	0	1.00
NEW YORK YANKEES	IP	H	R	ER	HR	K	BB	HBP	ERA
ALLIE REYNOLDS L (0-1)	6	8	5	5	1	1	7	0	7.50

World Series Appearances in 3 Decades

Player	Decades
Joe DiMaggio	1930s, 1940s, 1950s
Yogi Berra	1940s, 1950s, 1960s
Eddie Murray	1970s, 1980s, 1990s
Matt Williams	1980s, 1990s, 2000s
Edgar Rentaria	1990s, 2000s, 2010s

Monte Irvin got the Giants off to a fast start, stealing home in the top of the first inning. Irvin had his finest year in 1951, with 24 HR, a league-leading 121 RBI, and a slash line of .312/.415/.514, and finishing third in MVP balloting.

Irvin was a phenomenal high school athlete in Orange, NJ, earning 16 letters. He went on to star in the Negro Leagues in the late 30's and early 40's, batting over .400 several seasons. He then lost 3 prime seasons to WWII, when he was stationed in Europe and did not have a chance to play any baseball.

"I was a .400 hitter when I went into the army and a .300 hitter when I came out." Irvin finally made it to the majors at age 30. Said sometime opponent and sometime teammate Roy Campanella, "Monty was the best all-around player I have ever seen. As great as he was in 1951, he was twice as good 10 years earlier in the Negro Leagues."

(National Baseball Hall of Fame and Museum)

GAME TIME:	**2:58**	
ATTENDANCE:	**65,673**	
BEST OF 7:	**GIANTS - 1**	**YANKEES - 0**

Game 2

NEW YORK GIANTS vs. NEW YORK YANKEES

October 5

LINE SCORE	1	2	3	4	5	6	7	8	9	R	H	E
NEW YORK GIANTS	0	0	0	0	0	0	1	0	0	1	5	1
NEW YORK YANKEES	1	1	0	0	0	0	0	1	X	3	6	0

RECAP

For the second straight game the first team to score won. The home team, on the strength of two perfectly placed bunts laid down by Mickey Mantle and Phil Rizzuto, took the lead by one in their first at bat. 1B Joe Collins's solo home run in the next frame extended the Yankees lead. Starting mounder Eddie Lopat pitched a shut out for six innings, lost it in the seventh, drove in a run in the eighth and resumed his dominance for the last two innings.

SCORING SUMMARY

First Inning - New York Yankees

– Jansen starting.
– Mantle pushed a perfect bunt past the mound.
– Rizzuto bunted Mantle to second base; on Lockman's throwing error Mantle raced into third base.
– McDougald singled into right field, driving in Mantle; Rizzuto slid into second.
– DiMaggio bounded into a double play, Dark to Stanky to Lockman; Rizzuto took third base.
– Berra was a strike out.

1 Runs **3** Hits **1** Errors **1** LOB

GIANTS – 0   **YANKEES – 1**

Second Inning - New York Yankees

– Woodling flied out to Irvin.
– Brown grounded out, Stanky to Lockman.
– Collins slugged a solo shot into the right field crowd.
– Lopat bounded out to Lockman.

1 Runs **1** Hits **0** Errors **0** LOB

GIANTS – 0   **YANKEES – 2**

Seventh Inning - New York Giants

– Irvin one-hopped a beebee up the middle.
– Lockman singled Irvin to second base.
– Mays forced Lockman at second, Brown to Rizzuto; Irvin slid into third base.
– Westrum walked to put runners on each base.
– Schenz PR for Westrum.
– Rigney PH for Thomson, lifted a sacrifice fly to Bauer plating Irvin; Mays slid into third base.
– Noble PH for Jansen, fouled out to Berra.

1 Runs **2** Hits **0** Errors **2** LOB

GIANTS – 1   **YANKEES – 2**

Eighth Inning - New York Yankees

– Brown chopped a single into center field.
– Martin PR.
– Collins moved Martin up on a ground out, Thomson to Lockman.
– Lopat singled up the middle, driving Martin home.
– Bauer flied out to Irvin.
– Rizzuto flied out to Mays.

1 Runs **2** Hits **0** Errors **1** LOB

GIANTS – 1   **YANKEES – 3**

HIGHLIGHTS

- Mickey Mantle laid down a perfectly executed, lead-off bunt for his first hit, which led to his first run scored
- Giants starter Larry Jansen retired 13 Yankees in a row in the middle innings
- Eddie Lopat held the Giants to one tally, and as a hitter Lopat drove in a run
- 10 of the combined 11 base hits were singles; Yankees' 1B Joe Collins's solo shot was the lone extra base hit
- The Giants mound staff issued no walks, the Yankees mound staff recorded one strike out
- 60,000 plus fans in attendance in consecutive games

DIAMOND DUST

- Mantle, at age 19, is the third teenager to get a hit (Freddie Linstrom, 1924; Phil Cavaretta, 1935)
- Giants LF Monte Irvin is the third player (1906/24) to stroke a total of seven hits in two consecutive games
- In the fifth inning, Mantle sustained a knee injury that hampered him his entire career

Game 2 BOX SCORE SUMMARY

NEW YORK GIANTS	AB	R	H	RBI	BB	K	1B	2B	3B	HR	TB	SB
MONTE IRVIN, LF	4	1	3	0	0	0	3	0	0	0	3	1
BILL RIGNEY, PH	1	0	0	1	0	0	0	0	0	0	0	0
NEW YORK YANKEES	AB	R	H	RBI	BB	K	1B	2B	3B	HR	TB	SB
MICKEY MANTLE, RF	2	1	1	0	0	1	1	0	0	0	1	0
GIL MCDOUGALD, 2B/3B	3	0	1	1	0	1	1	0	0	0	1	0
BILLY MARTIN, PR	0	1	0	0	0	0	0	0	0	0	0	0
JOE COLLINS, 1B	3	1	1	1	0	0	0	0	0	1	4	0
EDDIE LOPAT, P	3	0	1	1	0	1	1	0	0	0	1	0

NEW YORK GIANTS	IP	H	R	ER	HR	K	BB	HBP	ERA
LARRY JANSEN L (0-1)	6	4	2	2	1	5	0	0	3.00
GEORGE SPENCER	2	2	1	1	0	0	0	0	4.50
NEW YORK YANKEES	IP	H	R	ER	HR	K	BB	HBP	ERA
EDDIE LOPAT W (1-0)	9	5	1	1	0	1	2	0	1.00

Teenagers in the World Series

Season	Tm	Age	Name	Performance
1923	NYG	19	Travis Jackson*	PH F7 to end Gm 2
1924	NYG	18	Freddie Lindstrom	10-for-30 in Series, including 4-for-5 against Walter Johnson in G5
1935	ChC	19	Phil Cavarretta	3-for-24 in Series
1951	NYY	19	Mickey Mantle*	Batted lead-off and went 0-for-3 with 2 BB in first game
1955	NYY	19	Tom Carroll*	Appeared in 2 games, 0 at-bats
1965	LAD	19	Willie Crawford	Pinch hit single in G1
1967	BOS	19	Ken Brett	1.1 scoreless innings in 2 games
1970	CIN	19	Don Gullet	1.35 ERA in 3 games (6.2 IP)
1996	ATL	19	Andruw Jones	3 hits, 2 HR, 5 RBI in first WS game

*Subway Series

GAME TIME:	**2:05**	
ATTENDANCE:	**66,018**	
BEST OF 7:	**GIANTS - 1**	**YANKEES - 1**

Game 3

NEW YORK YANKEES vs. NEW YORK GIANTS

October 6

LINE SCORE	1	2	3	4	5	6	7	8	9	R	H	E
NEW YORK YANKEES	0	0	0	0	0	0	0	1	1	2	5	2
NEW YORK GIANTS	0	1	0	0	5	0	0	0	X	6	7	2

--- RECAP ---

For the third straight game, the first team to score won. The Giants tallied first in the second inning and in the fifth sent eight men to the plate. The rally was ignited by the scrappy play of 2B Eddie Stanky. On first via a walk, Stanky, attempting to steal second base, was out on a perfect throw from Yogi Berra to Phil Rizzuto. However, Stanky kicked the ball out of Rizzuto's glove and wound up on third. Two singles, two errors and a three-run home run hammered by Whitey Lockman put five runs on the board.

--- SCORING SUMMARY ---

Second Inning - New York Giants
– Raschi starting.
– Thomson looped a double into left field.
– Mays singled into right field, driving Thomson home.
– Westrum popped up to Rizzuto.
– Hearn popped up to McDougald.
– Stanky struck out.

1 Runs **2** Hits **0** Errors **1** LOB
YANKEES – 0   **GIANTS – 1**

Fifth Inning - New York Giants
– Hearn went down on strikes.
– Stanky jogged to first on a free pass; swiped second base; stormed into third base on Rizzuto's fielding error.
– Dark singled into left field, driving Stanky home.
– Thompson smoked a hit-and-run single; Dark dashed over to third base.
– Irvin made it to first on a fielder's choice; Dark scored on Berra's fielding error; Thompson and Irvin moved into scoring position.
– Lockman hammered a home run into the lower left field seats, driving home Thompson and Irvin.
– Hogue relieved Raschi.
– Thomson fouled out to Berra.
– Mays flied out to DiMaggio.

5 Runs **3** Hits **2** Errors **0** LOB
YANKEES – 0   **GIANTS – 6**

Eighth Inning - New York Yankees
– Rizzuto plunked by a pitch.
– McDougald singled Rizzuto to second base.
– DiMaggio popped up to Thomson.
– Berra advanced both runners on a mounder, Hogue to Lockman.
– Brown walked; bases loaded.
– Collins walked; Rizzuto scored; bases loaded.
– Jones relieved Hearn.
– Bauer thrown out on a comebacker, Jones to Lockman.

1 Runs **1** Hits **0** Errors **1** LOB
YANKEES – 1   **GIANTS – 6**

Ninth Inning - New York Yankees
– Mize PH for Ostrowski, flied out to Thompson.
– Woodling slugged a solo shot into the lower right field seats.
– Rizzuto flied out deep to Mays.
– McDougald fouled out to Lockman.

1 Runs **1** Hits **0** Errors **0** LOB
YANKEES – 2   **GIANTS – 6**

152

HIGHLIGHTS

- Giants 1B Whitey Lockman drove in half of the six runs
- Jim Hearn, after hurling seven innings of shutout ball, walked in the first Yankee run
- Hearn allowed eight free passes in the win

DIAMOND DUST

- Gene Woodling's ninth inning solo shot is the 220th in New York Yankees history
- Phil Rizzuto's error in the Giants' big fifth inning rally ended an 18-game errorless streak
- Giants 2B Eddie Stanky stroked a WS hit for third National League pennant-winner (1947 Dodgers/1948 Braves)

Game 3 BOX SCORE SUMMARY

NEW YORK YANKEES	AB	R	H	RBI	BB	K	1B	2B	3B	HR	TB	SB
GENE WOODLING, LF	4	1	1	1	1	0	0	0	0	1	4	0
PHIL RIZZUTO, SS	4	1	1	0	0	0	1	0	0	0	1	0
JOE COLLINS, 1B	3	0	0	1	1	0	0	0	0	0	0	0

NEW YORK GIANTS	AB	R	H	RBI	BB	K	1B	2B	3B	HR	TB	SB
EDDIE STANKY, 2B	2	1	1	0	1	1	1	0	0	0	1	0
AL DARK, SS	4	1	1	1	0	0	1	0	0	0	1	0
HANK THOMPSON, RF	3	1	1	0	1	1	1	0	0	0	1	0
MONTE IRVIN, LF	3	1	0	0	1	0	0	0	0	0	0	0
WHITEY LOCKMAN, 1B	4	1	1	3	0	1	0	0	0	1	4	0
BOBBY THOMSON, 3B	4	1	1	0	0	0	0	1	0	0	2	0
WILLE MAYS, CF	4	0	2	1	0	0	2	0	0	0	2	0

NEW YORK YANKEES	IP	H	R	ER	HR	K	BB	HBP	ERA
VIC RASCHI L (0-1)	4.1	5	6	1	1	3	3	1	2.08
JOE OSTROWSKI	2	1	0	0	0	1	0	0	0.00

NEW YORK GIANTS	IP	H	R	ER	HR	K	BB	HBP	ERA
JIM HEARN W (1-0)	7.2	4	1	1	0	1	8	0	1.17
SHELDON JONES S (1)	1.1	1	1	1	1	0	0	0	6.75

No fewer than 9 players on the 2 teams' rosters in the 1951 Series became big league managers. Many were long-time skippers through the 1960s and 1970s.

Manager	tm	Yrs Mgr	WS
George Bamberger	NYG	7	0
Hank Bauer	NYY	8	1
Yogi Berra	NYY	7	2
Alvin Dark	NYG	13	1
Ralph Houk	NYY	20	3
Billy Martin	NYY	16	2
Bill Rigney	NYG	18	0
Eddie Stanky	NYG	8	0
Wes Westrum	NYG	5	0

GAME TIME:	**2:42**	
ATTENDANCE:	**52,035**	
BEST OF 7:	**GIANTS - 2**	**YANKEES - 1**

Game 4

NEW YORK YANKEES vs. NEW YORK GIANTS

October 8

LINE SCORE	1	2	3	4	5	6	7	8	9	R	H	E
NEW YORK YANKEES	0	1	0	1	2	0	2	0	0	6	12	0
NEW YORK GIANTS	1	0	0	0	0	0	0	0	1	2	8	2

─────────── **RECAP** ───────────

The rest caused by a one-day rain delay benefited the Yankee hitters rather than the Giants pitchers. The visitors out-hit the home team 12 to 8. Eight of the nine Pinstripers stroked at least one base hit. The Yankees tied the game in the second, broke the tie in the fourth, surged ahead in the fifth and increased the lead by two more in the seventh. The trend of the winning team scoring first came to an end. After the Giants' one run in the first scored, set up by the first of Al Dark's three doubles, double plays did them in. As a team they hit into four, three by Willie Mays. Yankee starter Allie Reynolds pitched a complete game to rack up the 'W'.

─────────── **SCORING SUMMARY** ───────────

First Inning - New York Giants
– Reynolds starting.
– Stanky zapped out to Rizzuto.
– Dark ricochet a double off of the left field wall.
– Thompson grounded out, McDougald to Collins; Dark slid into third.
– Irvin singled into left field, driving in Dark; Irvin thrown out trying to steal second base, Berra to Rizzuto.

1 Runs **2** Hits **0** Errors **0** LOB

YANKEES – 0   **GIANTS – 1**

Second Inning - New York Yankees
– Maglie starting.
– Woodling clubbed a double into left field.
– McDougald safe at first base on Thompson's fielding error; Woodling held.
– Brown advanced Woodling on a fly to DiMaggio; McDougald held.
– Collins singled into right field, driving in Woodling; McDougald made second.
– Reynolds flied out to Irvin.

– Bauer's single hit McDougald for an automatic out (Dark got the putout).

1 Runs **3** Hits **1** Errors **1** LOB

YANKEES – 1   **GIANTS – 1**

Fourth Inning - New York Yankees
– McDougald flied out to Mays.
– Brown hustled an infield hit.
– Collins walked Brown to second base.
– Reynolds singled up the middle, driving in Brown; Collins scrambled over to third base; Reynolds thrown out, Mays to Dark to Lockman.
– Bauer grounded out, Thomson to Lockman.

1 Runs **2** Hits **0** Errors **1** LOB

YANKEES – 2   **GIANTS – 1**

Fifth Inning - New York Yankees
– Rizzuto popped up to Stanky.
– Berra blooped a single into right field.
– DiMaggio yanked a home run into the upper left field deck, driving Berra home.

154

- Woodling popped up to Dark.
- McDougald struck out.

② Runs **②** Hits **⓪** Errors **⓪** LOB

YANKEES – 4   **GIANTS – 1**

Seventh Inning - New York Yankees

- Rizzuto hopped a single into right field.
- Berra flied out to Mays.
- DiMaggio popped up to Stanky.
- Woodling walked Rizzuto to second base.
- Stanky missed pick-off throw, Rizzuto went to third and then scored when Thomson's throw hits him.
- McDougald singled into left field, driving in Woodling; McDougald slid into second on the play at the plate.
- Brown flied out to Mays.

② Runs **②** Hits **①** Errors **①** LOB

YANKEES – 6   **GIANTS – 1**

Ninth Inning - New York Giants

- Thompson trotted to first on a walk.
- Irvin singled Thompson to second base.
- Lockman lined out to Woodling; the runners held.
- Thomson singled into left field, driving in Thompson; Irvin slid into third base.
- Mays grounded into a double play, Rizzuto to Coleman to Collins.

① Runs **②** Hits **⓪** Errors **①** LOB

YANKEES – 6   **GIANTS – 2**

HIGHLIGHTS

- Joe DiMaggio broke out of a 0-for-12 slump with a single and a home run
- In the fourth frame Allie Reynolds was doubled off in an unusual play · CF Willie Mays to SS Al Dark to 1B Whitey Lockman
- 3B Bobby Thomson was on first base for all three of Willie Mays's GIDP
- The Giants hit into four double plays for a four-game total of six
- The Bombers starting nine each stroked at least one hit

DIAMOND DUST

- DiMaggio homered in his third decade
- Giants SS Al Dark is the first player to drill a double in three consecutive at-bats
- Dark is the third player in history to double three times in a game
- Willie Mays is the second player to hit into three double plays in a game. Charlie Deal of the 1914 Boston Braves was the first
- Bobby Thomson was on first for all 3 of them
- Reynolds tied the record for most walks in a Series with 11

Game 4 BOX SCORE SUMMARY

NEW YORK YANKEES	AB	R	H	RBI	BB	K	1B	2B	3B	HR	TB	SB
PHIL RIZZUTO, SS	5	1	1	0	0	2	1	0	0	0	1	0
YOGI BERRA, C	5	1	1	0	0	0	1	0	0	0	1	0
JOE DIMAGGIO, CF	5	1	2	2	0	2	1	0	0	1	5	0
GENE WOODLING, LF	4	2	1	0	1	1	0	1	0	0	2	0
GIL MCDOUGALD, 2B/3B	4	0	1	1	0	1	1	0	0	0	1	0
BOBBY BROWN, 3B	4	1	2	0	0	0	1	1	0	0	3	0
JOE COLLINS, 1B	3	0	1	1	1	0	1	0	0	0	1	0
ALLIE REYNOLDS, P	4	0	1	0	1	0	1	0	0	0	1	0
NEW YORK GIANTS	AB	R	H	RBI	BB	K	1B	2B	3B	HR	TB	SB
AL DARK, SS	4	1	3	0	0	0	0	3	0	0	6	0
HANK THOMPSON, RF	3	1	0	0	1	0	0	0	0	0	0	0
MONTE IRVIN, LF	4	0	2	1	0	1	2	0	0	0	2	0
BOBBY THOMSON, 3B	2	0	2	1	2	0	2	0	0	0	2	0

NEW YORK YANKEES	IP	H	R	ER	HR	K	BB	HBP	ERA
ALLIE REYNOLDS W (1-1)	9	8	2	2	0	7	4	0	4.20
NEW YORK GIANTS	IP	H	R	ER	HR	K	BB	HBP	ERA
SAL MAGLIE L (0-1)	5	8	4	4	1	3	2	0	7.20
SHELDON JONES	3	4	2	0	0	2	1	0	2.08

GAME TIME:	**2:57**
ATTENDANCE:	**49,010**
BEST OF 7:	**GIANTS - 2 YANKEES - 2**

Game 5

NEW YORK YANKEES vs. NEW YORK GIANTS

October 9

LINE SCORE	1	2	3	4	5	6	7	8	9	R	H	E
NEW YORK YANKEES	0	0	5	2	0	2	4	0	0	13	12	1
NEW YORK GIANTS	1	0	0	0	0	0	0	0	0	1	5	3

RECAP

A New York Yankee blow out produced a five-run rally in the third and a four-run rally in the seventh inning. In between the Bombers scored two runs in the fourth and sixth innings for a lucky total of 13. Gene Woodling, Phil Rizzuto, Joe DiMaggio and Gil McDougald had great days with the bat. Woodling and Rizzuto each scored three runs. Rizzuto and DiMaggio each drove in three runs. DiMaggio poked three hits. McDougald slammed the third World Series grand slam home run. Hurling his second complete game, Eddie Lopat notched his second win, allowing only one earned run.

SCORING SUMMARY

First Inning - New York Giants
– Lopat starting.
– Stanky out on a grounder, McDougald to Mize.
– Dark lasered a single into left field.
– Thomson flied out to DiMaggio.
– Irvin hitched a hit-and-run single; Dark stormed into third base; on Woodling's fielding error Dark scored, Irvin slid into second base.
– Lockman flied out to DiMaggio.

1 Runs **2** Hits **1** Errors **1** LOB

YANKEES – 0   **GIANTS – 1**

Third Inning - New York Yankees
– Jansen starting.
– Lopat thrown out on a come-backer, Jansen to Lockman.
– Woodling drew a free pass.
– Rizzuto walked Woodling to second base.
– Berra forced Rizzuto at second, Lockman to Dark; Woodling slid into third.
– DiMaggio singled into left field, driving in Woodling; Irvin's fielding error advanced the runners.
– Mize walked intentionally to load the bases.
– McDougald slammed the 3rd World Series grand slam home run into the left field seats, driving in Berra, DiMaggio and Mize.

– Brown flogged a single into center field.
– Collins flied out to Mays.

5 Runs **3** Hits **1** Errors **1** LOB

YANKEES – 5   **GIANTS – 1**

Fourth Inning - New York Yankees
– Kennedy pitching.
– Lopat went down on strikes.
– Woodling got first on a walk.
– Rizzuto blasted a home run into the right field crowd, driving Woodling home.
– Berra popped up to Dark.
– DiMaggio rifled a single into left field.
– Mize fouled out to Westrum.

2 Runs **2** Hits **0** Errors **1** LOB

YANKEES – 7   **GIANTS – 1**

Sixth Inning - New York Yankees
– Spencer came in to pitch.
– Woodling tapped out, Stanky to Lockman.
– Rizzuto whacked a wicked single into left field.
– Berra smashed a hit-and-run single; Rizzuto jetted into third base; on Hartung's fielding error Rizzuto scored; Berra slid into second base.

– DiMaggio flied out to Hartung.
– Mize doubled into center field, driving Berra home.
– McDougald grounded out, Thomson to Lockman.

2 Runs **3** Hits **1** Errors **1** LOB

YANKEES – 9 **GIANTS – 1**

Seventh Inning - New York Yankees

– Brown worked a walk.
– Coleman pinch ran for Brown.
– Collins bunt single; Brown advanced to second.
– Lopat advanced the runners on a mounder, Spencer to Lockman.
– Woodling walked; bases full.
– Rizzuto walked; Coleman scored; bases loaded.
– Corwin relieved Spencer; on a wild pitch Collins scored as the runners advanced.
– Berra flied out to Irvin.
– DiMaggio doubled into left field, driving home Woodling and Rizzuto.
– Bauer flew across first on a fielder's choice; DiMaggio tagged out at third base, Dark to Thomson.

4 Runs **2** Hits **0** Errors **1** LOB

YANKEES – 13 **GIANTS – 1**

HIGHLIGHTS

- McDougal's grand slam is the first in 15 years, with the last also having been hit by the Yankees against the Giants (1936)
- Gil McDougal's grand slam is the 75th home run in franchise history
- George Spencer is the second Giants reliever in the Series to force home a run on a walk (Game 3)
- Gene Woodling and Phil Rizzuto, the first two batters in the line-up, scored three times each
- Only three Pinstripers went hitless and a different three did not score
- The Giants have hit into seven double plays in series

George Spencer collected 10 of his career 16 wins in 1951, going 10-4 with a respectable ERA of 3.75 in 132 IP, mostly in relief. But Spencer struggled in the Series, allowing 7 runs in 3.1 IP, for an ERA of 18.90. He did retire Joe DiMaggio twice in the Series and joked later "I always thought I was a big contributor to his retirement in 1951 because I faced him twice and got him out both times. He must be saying, if I can't hit that guy, I must be through."

DIAMOND DUST

- The fourth blow-out game in World Series history (winning by 10 or more runs); the second in which the Yankees blew out the Giants.

Game 5 BOX SCORE SUMMARY

NEW YORK YANKEES	AB	R	H	RBI	BB	K	1B	2B	3B	HR	TB	SB
GENE WOODLING, LF	3	3	1	0	3	1	0	0	1	0	3	0
PHIL RIZZUTO, SS	4	3	2	3	0	0	1	0	0	1	5	0
YOGI BERRA, C	4	2	1	0	1	0	1	0	0	0	1	0
JOE DIMAGGIO, CF	5	1	3	3	0	0	2	1	0	0	4	0
JOHNNY MIZE, 1B	3	1	1	1	1	0	0	1	0	0	2	0
GIL MCDOUGALD, 2B/3B	5	1	1	4	0	0	0	0	0	1	4	0
JERRY COLEMAN, PR/2B	1	1	0	0	0	1	0	0	0	0	0	0
JOE COLLINS, RF/1B	5	1	1	0	0	1	1	0	0	0	1	0
NEW YORK GIANTS	AB	R	H	RBI	BB	K	1B	2B	3B	HR	TB	SB
AL DARK, SS	4	1	2	0	0	0	2	0	0	0	2	0

NEW YORK YANKEES	IP	H	R	ER	HR	K	BB	HBP	ERA
EDDIE LOPAT, W (2-0)	9	5	1	0	0	3	1	0	0.50
NEW YORK GIANTS	IP	H	R	ER	HR	K	BB	HBP	ERA
LARRY JANSEN L (0-2)	3	3	5	5	1	1	4	0	7.00
MONTY KENNEDY	2	3	2	2	1	2	1	0	6.00
GEORGE SPENCER	1.1	4	6	6	0	0	3	0	18.90

GAME TIME:	2:31
ATTENDANCE:	47,530
BEST OF 7:	GIANTS - 2 YANKEES - 3

Game 6

NEW YORK GIANTS vs. NEW YORK YANKEES

October 10

LINE SCORE	1	2	3	4	5	6	7	8	9	R	H	E
NEW YORK GIANTS	0	0	0	0	1	0	0	0	2	3	11	1
NEW YORK YANKEES	1	0	0	0	0	3	0	0	X	4	7	0

RECAP

The offensive weapons of the day were four run-scoring sacrifice flies and a bases loaded triple. The Giants managed three sacrifice flies. The Yankees torqued the triple.

By the end of the fifth inning, the game was knotted at 1-1 on sacrifice flies lifted by each team. In the sixth inning, Hank Bauer tripled in three forging a three run-lead.

The top of the ninth inning had New York fans on both sides expecting the worst, hoping for the best. On the mound, Yankees reliever Bob Kuzava was facing a no-out, bases-loaded situation. Kuzava got the first two outs on sacrifice flies that narrowed the lead to one. The third out was a low line drive to right field that settled into a sliding Hank Bauer's glove mere inches from the ground. The victory gave the Yankees their 14th Fall Classic title; the only North American sports team with double-digit championships.

SCORING SUMMARY

First Inning - New York Yankees
– Koslo starting.
– Rizzuto flied out to Irvin.
– Coleman stroked a single into center field.
– Berra doubled Coleman to third base.
– DiMaggio purposely walked to load the bases.
– McDougald lifted a sacrifice fly to Mays plating Coleman.
– Mize zapped out to Stanky.

1 Runs **2** Hits **0** Errors **2** LOB

GIANTS – 0 **YANKEES – 1**

Fifth Inning - New York Giants
– Raschi starting.
– Mays singled up the middle; slid into second base on Berra's passed ball.
– Koslo flied out to Bauer; Mays crossed over to third base.
– Stanky hoisted a sacrifice fly to Woodling plating Mays.
– Dark legged it to first on a walk.

– Lockman singled Dark to second base.
– Irvin grounded out, McDougald to Mize.

1 Runs **2** Hits **0** Errors **2** LOB

GIANTS – 1 **YANKEES – 1**

Sixth Inning - New York Yankees
– Coleman struck out.
– Berra stroked a single into right field; slid into second base on Thompson's fielding error.
– DiMaggio walked intentionally; the runners advanced on Koslo's wild pitch.
– McDougald lined out to Thomson.
– Mize stacked the sacks on a walk.
– Bauer tripled into left field, driving home Berra, DiMaggio and Mize.
– Woodling bounded out, Stanky to Lockman.

3 Runs **2** Hits **1** Errors **1** LOB

GIANTS – 1 **YANKEES – 4**

158

Ninth Inning - New York Giants

- Stanky plugged a single into center field.
- Dark's bunt single advanced Stanky to second.
- Lockman loaded the bases on a right field single.
- Kuzava relieved Sain.
- Irvin lofted a sacrifice fly to Woodling plating Stanky; both runners advanced.
- Thomson lifted a sacrifice fly to Woodling plating Dark; Lockman held.
- Yvars PH for Thompson, flied out to Bauer (diving catch).

2 Runs **2** Hits **0** Errors **1** LOB

GIANTS – 3   **YANKEES – 4**

HIGHLIGHTS

- The Giants hit into inning-ending double plays in the third and fourth innings
- Over the six games Giants hit into 10 double plays
- Vic Raschi wins second clincher game (1949)
- In winning final three games, the Yankees outscored the Giants 23-6

DIAMOND DUST

- Joe DiMaggio, in consecutive at-bats, scored his last run and drilled his last hit, an RBI double
- The Yankees are the only team to win three Fall Classics in row twice (1936/37/38)

Game 6 BOX SCORE SUMMARY

NEW YORK GIANTS	AB	R	H	RBI	BB	K	1B	2B	3B	HR	TB	SB
EDDIE STANKY, 2B	5	1	1	1	0	0	1	0	0	0	1	0
AL DARK, SS	3	1	1	0	2	2	1	0	0	0	1	0
MONTE IRVIN, LF	4	0	0	1	1	0	0	0	0	0	0	0
BOBBY THOMSON, 3B	4	0	1	1	1	0	1	0	0	0	1	0
WILLIE MAYS, CF	3	1	2	0	1	0	2	0	0	0	2	0

NEW YORK YANKEES	AB	R	H	RBI	BB	K	1B	2B	3B	HR	TB	SB
JERRY COLEMAN, 2B	4	1	1	0	1	0	1	0	0	0	1	0
YOGI BERRA, C	4	1	2	0	0	0	1	1	0	0	3	0
JOE DIMAGGIO, CF	2	1	1	0	2	0	0	1	0	0	2	0
JOHNNY MIZE, 1B	2	1	1	0	1	0	1	0	0	0	1	0
HANK BAUER, RF	3	0	1	3	0	0	0	0	1	0	3	0

NEW YORK GIANTS	IP	H	R	ER	HR	K	BB	HBP	ERA
DAVE KOSLO L (1-1)	6	5	4	4	0	3	4	0	3.00

NEW YORK YANKEES	IP	H	R	ER	HR	K	BB	HBP	ERA
VIC RASCHI W (1-1)	6	7	1	0	0	1	5	0	0.87
JOHNNY SAIN	2	4	2	2	0	2	2	0	9.00
BOB KUZAVA S (1)	1	0	0	0	0	0	0	0	0.00

Joltin' Joe Says Goodbye

Joe DiMaggio doubled to right-center in the bottom of the 8th inning in what was his final World Series at-bat, and as it turned out, the final at-bat of his major league career. He was also intentionally walked twice in the game, coming around to score once.

DiMaggio appeared in 10 World Series in his 13-year career. Interestingly, his performance in October was a mere shadow of his regular season production. Overall, in 51 World Series games, DiMaggio had a slash line of just .271/.338/.422, and hit only 8 home runs and drove in 30 in 199 at bats. By contrast, his career numbers were .325/.398/.579, and he drove home 1537 runs in only 6821 at bats, an amazing rate of 1 every 4.4 at bats.

GAME TIME:	**2:59**
ATTENDANCE:	**61,711**
BEST OF 7:	**GIANTS - 2 YANKEES - 4**

(National Baseball Hall of Fame and Museum)

1951 was not only the year of the "Shot Heard Round the World, it also marked the debut of inner circle Hall of Famers Willie Mays and Mickey Mantle. Neither thrived in the 1951 Fall Classic, as Mays managed only 4 singles in 22 AB's and Mantle was 1-for-5 before his devastating injury in Game 2. Overall, Mays was not at his best in his 4 WS appearances, collecting only 17 hits in 71 AB's (.239) with no home runs and only 6 RBI. Mantle batted just .257 in 230 WS at bats, but his 18 home runs and 40 RBI and 42 RS still stand as all-time highs.

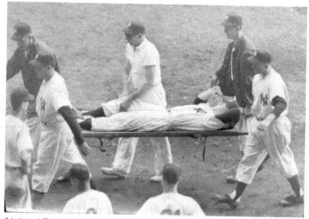

(National Baseball Hall of Fame and Museum)

(Top) 20-year old Willie Mays flanked by teammates Monty Irvin and Hank Thompson. The trio was the first all-African-American outfield to play in the World Series. Thompson put together a solid big league career, hitting 20+ HR in 3 seasons and finishing with a career OBA of .377. (Above) Mantle is carried off the field after the Game 2 injury. Mantle drove in 65 runs in only 341 at bats as a 19-year-old rookie. (Left) Edward "Whitey" Ford missed the 1951 (and 1952) World Series due to military service. Ford had gone a remarkable 9-1 in his 1950 rookie season (20 app, 12 starts) and was 18-6 upon his return in 1953. It seems safe to assume that had Ford not missed those 2 seasons, he would have added at least 30 wins to his career total of 236, still the most for any Yankees pitcher all time.

1951

NEW YORK YANKEES vs. NEW YORK GIANTS

NEW YORK GIANTS

Overall World Series Record: 4 WINS 9 LOSSES. 77 Games Played [36 - 39 (2 ties) .480]

- LF Monte Irvin (.458) and SS Al Dark (.417) were the only .400 hitters on either club.
- Irvin (11) and Dark (10) combined to stroke 21 of the Giants' 46 hits.
- 10 of Irvin's 11 hits were singles; Irvin was the only base stealer (2).
- Willie Mays, Eddie Stanky, and Hank Thompson all batted below the Mendoza line.
- Eddie Stanky has played on three losing National League pennant-winners (1947/48), twice to the Yankees.
- Durocher has lost as a manager for both New York National League franchises.
- Giants are only team with nine World Series losses.

NEW YORK YANKEES

Overall World Series Record: 14 WINS 4 LOSSES. 94 Games Played [63 – 30 (1 tie) .677]

- Eddie Lopat won two games and had an ERA of 0.50, allowing only 10 hits and 2 runs over 18 innings.
- Reynolds has earned a win in four consecutive WS appearances (1947/49/50).
- Bob Kuzava, a mid-season acquisition from the Washington Senators, notched the only save.
- Joe DiMaggio played in 51 games on 10 pennant-winning and nine championships teams spanning three decades.
- Gene Woodling, in 18 at-bats, scored six runs, the most by any player on either team.
- Gil McDougald drove in seven runs, the most by any player on either team.
- No stolen bases.
- The infielders turned a record-setting 10 double plays.

FUNGOES

- Both shortstops, Phil Rizzuto and Al Dark, got a hit in all six games.
- Neither catcher, Yogi Berra nor Wes Westrum, drove in a run.
- 51 walks combined were issued, establishing a new record.
- American League's winning streak is at five.
- New York City is the first to host a World Series and the NBA Finals in the same calendar year.
- AL now leads the overall series 31-17.

SIX-GAME DATA

TIME	16:12	PLAYERS POOL	$560,562
ATTENDANCE	341,977	SHARES	NEW YORK GIANTS - $4,951
			NEW YORK YANKEES - $6,446

1951

NEW YORK GIANTS vs. NEW YORK YANKEES

New York Giants Composite Stats

BATTING	G	AB	R	H	RBI	2B	3B	HR	BB	SO	BA	OBP	SLG	OPS
Whitey Lockman	6	25	1	6	4	2	0	1	1	2	.240	.269	.440	.709
Al Dark	6	24	5	10	4	3	0	1	2	3	.417	.462	.667	1.128
Monte Irvin	6	24	3	11	2	0	1	0	2	1	.458	.500	.542	1.042
Eddie Stanky	6	22	3	3	1	0	0	0	3	2	.136	.269	.136	.406
Willie Mays	6	22	1	4	1	0	0	0	2	2	.182	.250	.182	.432
Bobby Thomson	6	21	1	5	2	1	0	0	5	0	.238	.385	.286	.670
Wes Westrum	6	17	1	4	0	1	0	0	5	3	.235	.409	.294	.703
Hank Thompson	5	14	3	2	0	0	0	0	5	2	.143	.368	.143	.511
Dave Koslo	2	5	0	0	0	0	0	0	0	2	.000	.000	.000	.000
Clint Hartung	2	4	0	0	0	0	0	0	0	0	.000	.000	.000	.000
Bill Rigney	4	4	0	1	1	0	0	0	0	1	.250	.250	.250	.500
Jim Hearn	2	3	0	0	0	0	0	0	0	1	.000	.000	.000	.000
Larry Jansen	3	2	0	0	0	0	0	0	0	0	.000	.000	.000	.000
Jack Lohrke	2	2	0	0	0	0	0	0	0	1	.000	.000	.000	.000
Ray Noble	2	2	0	0	0	0	0	0	0	1	.000	.000	.000	.000
Sal Maglie	1	1	0	0	0	0	0	0	0	1	.000	.000	.000	.000
Davey Williams	2	1	0	0	0	0	0	0	0	0	.000	.000	.000	.000
Sal Yvars	1	1	0	0	0	0	0	0	0	0	.000	.000	.000	.000
Al Corwin	1	0	0	0	0	0	0	0	0	0				
Sheldon Jones	2	0	0	0	0	0	0	0	0	0				
Monty Kennedy	2	0	0	0	0	0	0	0	0	0				
Alex Konikowski	1	0	0	0	0	0	0	0	0	0				
Hank Schenz	1	0	0	0	0	0	0	0	0	0				
George Spencer	2	0	0	0	0	0	0	0	0	0				
Totals	**6**	**194**	**18**	**46**	**15**	**7**	**1**	**2**	**25**	**22**	**.237**	**.327**	**.314**	**.642**

PITCHING	G	GS	ERA	W	L	SV	CG	IP	H	R	ER	BB	SO	WHIP
Dave Koslo	2	2	3.00	1	1	0	1	15.0	12	5	5	7	6	1.267
Larry Jansen	3	2	6.30	0	2	0	0	10.0	8	7	7	4	6	1.200
Jim Hearn	2	1	1.04	1	0	0	0	8.2	5	1	1	8	1	1.500
Sal Maglie	1	1	7.20	0	1	0	0	5.0	8	4	4	2	3	2.000
Sheldon Jones	2	0	2.08	0	0	0	1	4.1	5	3	1	1	2	1.385
George Spencer	2	0	18.90	0	0	0	0	3.1	6	7	7	3	0	2.700
Monty Kennedy	2	0	6.00	0	0	0	0	3.0	3	2	2	1	4	1.333
Al Corwin	1	0	0.00	0	0	0	0	1.2	1	0	0	0	1	0.600
Alex Konikowski	1	0	0.00	0	0	0	0	1.0	1	0	0	0	0	1.000
Totals	**6**	**6**	**4.67**	**2**	**4**	**1**	**1**	**52.0**	**49**	**29**	**27**	**26**	**23**	**1.442**

1951

NEW YORK GIANTS vs. NEW YORK YANKEES

New York Yankees Composite Stats

BATTING	G	AB	R	H	RBI	2B	3B	HR	BB	SO	BA	OBP	SLG	OPS
Phil Rizzuto	6	25	5	8	3	0	0	1	2	3	.320	.393	.440	.833
Yogi Berra	6	23	4	6	0	1	0	0	2	1	.261	.320	.304	.624
Joe DiMaggio	6	23	3	6	5	2	0	1	2	4	.261	.320	.478	.798
Gil McDougald	6	23	2	6	7	1	0	1	2	2	.261	.320	.435	.755
Gene Woodling	6	18	6	3	1	1	1	1	5	3	.167	.348	.500	.848
Joe Collins	6	18	2	4	3	0	0	1	2	1	.222	.300	.389	.689
Hank Bauer	6	18	0	3	3	0	1	0	1	1	.167	.211	.278	.488
Bobby Brown	5	14	1	5	0	1	0	0	2	1	.357	.438	.429	.866
Jerry Coleman	5	8	2	2	0	0	0	0	1	2	.250	.333	.250	.583
Eddie Lopat	2	8	0	1	1	0	0	0	0	2	.125	.125	.125	.250
Johnny Mize	4	7	2	2	1	1	0	0	2	0	.286	.444	.429	.873
Allie Reynolds	2	6	0	2	1	0	0	0	0	1	.333	.333	.333	.667
Mickey Mantle	2	5	1	1	0	0	0	0	2	1	.200	.429	.200	.629
Vic Raschi	2	2	0	0	0	0	0	0	2	1	.000	.500	.000	.500
Johnny Sain	1	1	0	0	0	0	0	0	0	0	.000	.000	.000	.000
Johnny Hopp	1	0	0	0	0	0	0	0	1	0		1.000		
Bobby Hogue	2	0	0	0	0	0	0	0	0	0				
Bob Kuzava	1	0	0	0	0	0	0	0	0	0				
Billy Martin	1	0	1	0	0	0	0	0	0	0				
Tom Morgan	1	0	0	0	0	0	0	0	0	0				
Joe Ostrowski	1	0	0	0	0	0	0	0	0	0				
Totals	**6**	**199**	**29**	**49**	**25**	**7**	**2**	**5**	**26**	**23**	**.246**	**.336**	**.377**	**.713**

PITCHING	G	GS	ERA	W	L	SV	CG	IP	H	R	ER	BB	SO	WHIP
Eddie Lopat	2	2	0.50	2	0	0	2	18.0	10	2	1	3	4	0.722
Allie Reynolds	2	2	4.20	1	1	0	1	15.0	16	7	7	11	8	1.800
Vic Raschi	2	2	0.87	1	1	0	0	10.1	12	7	1	8	4	1.935
Bobby Hogue	2	0	0.00	0	0	0	0	2.2	1	0	0	0	0	0.375
Tom Morgan	1	0	0.00	0	0	0	0	2.0	2	0	0	1	3	1.500
Joe Ostrowski	1	0	0.00	0	0	0	0	2.0	1	0	0	0	1	0.500
Johnny Sain	1	0	9.00	0	0	0	0	2.0	4	2	2	2	2	3.000
Bob Kuzava	1	0	0.00	0	0	1	0	1.0	0	0	0	0	0	0.000
Totals	**6**	**6**	**1.87**	**4**	**2**	**1**	**3**	**53.0**	**46**	**18**	**11**	**25**	**22**	**1.340**

1952

BROOKLYN DODGERS vs. NEW YORK YANKEES

FUNGOES

- ⑪ Both teams in first place at the All-Star break.
- ⑪ Johnny Sain (Yankees) and Tommy Holmes (Dodgers) were teammates on the 1948 pennant-winning Boston Braves.
- ⑪ Third time the Yankees have faced the same New York National League pennant-winner in consecutive seasons.
- ⑪ No travel days.
- ⑪ Umpire data:
- ⑪ Dusty Boggers played every position for the St. Louis Cardinals in the minor leagues; was a minor league manager and owner.
- ⑪ Larry Goetz had a career after umpiring as a radio commentator; was depicted in the Norman Rockwell painting - "Bottom of the Sixth" with Lou Jorda and Beans Reardon; Jim Honochick served in the US Navy during WWII; Bill McKinley is the first graduate of an umpiring school to reach the majors; Art Passarella served in the US Army during WWII; began umpiring in the Cotton States League whose players were mostly African American; after umpiring had a career in television and the movies; Babe Pinelli is a former 3B with various teams, wrote magazine articles and was elected to the Italian American Sports Hall of Fame (2000); Dressen and Pinelli were Cincinnati Reds teammates (1925-27).

SERIES SUMMARY

The Casey Stengel-led Yankees reached their fourth straight World Series, three of which were against a New York Team. This time their opponent was the Dodgers, led by a powerful lineup and rookie phenom reliever Joe Black. The result was one of the most dramatic of all Subway Series.

Game 1 went to the Dodgers, behind Black, who had started only two games in the regular season, but fired a complete game victory against the mighty Yankees. The Brooklynites smashed three home runs to account for all four of their runs, the first off the bat of Jackie Robinson, one of only two he hit in the World Series in his entire career.

The Yankees evened the score in Game 2 with a 7-1 drubbing. They were led by three hits by Mantle and two more by Billy Martin, who drove in four. Vic Raschi pitched a complete-game three-hitter.

Game 3 was a battle—2-1 Dodgers after seven, 3-2 after eight, ultimately winning 5-3. Brooklyn's final tallies came on a 2-run passed ball by Yogi Berra that scored Peewee Reese and Jackie Robinson, who had just pulled off a double steal.

Game 4 was a rematch between the opening-game starters, but this time Reynolds got the better of Black, hurling a brilliant four-hit shutout. Black was the tough-luck loser, allowing just one run in seven innings before the Bombers put up an insurance run in the eighth on a Mantle triple.

Carl Erskine's gutsy 11-inning, complete-game win put the Dodgers back in the driver's seat in Game 3. All the Yankees' scoring came in the fifth inning when they broke through with five runs. Brooklyn tied it in the seventh and then put across the winner in the 11th on a Duke Snider double.

The Yankees evened things up again in Game 6 with a tight 3-2 victory. Raschi went 7.2 innings and then Stengel brought on starter Allie Reynolds, who struck out Roy Campanella with a runner on second and then closed the door in the ninth. The Yankees got solo homers from Berra and Mantle.

Brooklyn and New Yorked matched each other through the first five innings of Game 7, each scoring single runs in the fourth and fifth. The Yankees took the lead in the sixth on a Mantle home run and tacked on another in the seventh on a Mantle single. Bob Kuzava got the final eight outs of the game for the Bombers, who celebrated once again.

THE TEAMS

BROOKLYN DODGERS
96 - 57 .627 +4.5 G

The Team
- Subway Series #4; 6th overall appearance.
- National League leader in runs scored (775), home runs (153) and stolen bases (90).

The Players
- 9 players remain from the 1949 Subway Series team: Roy Campanella, Billy Cox, Carl Erskine, Carl Furillo, Gil Hodges, Pee Wee Reese, Jackie Robinson, Preacher Roe and Duke Snider.
- Reese played on the 1941/47/49 pennant-winning teams, appearing in all four Subway Series.
- Furillo, Hodges, and Robinson played on the 1947/49 pennant-winning teams.
- Carl Erskine threw a no-hitter at the Chicago Cubs on June 19th.
- Black is the third African American ROY (1947 Jackie Robinson/1949 Don Newcombe).

The Manager
- Chuck Dressen is the 42nd manager to debut.
- Dressen is the fifth manager (1921/1941/1947/1949) to debut in the Subway Series.
- Dressen played 3B on the 1933 New York Giants but did not appear in the World Series.

Top Batters

Pos	Name	AB	R	H	HR	RBI	BA	OPS
C	Roy Campanella	468	73	126	22	97	.269	.805
1B	Gil Hodges	508	87	129	32	102	.254	.886
2B	Jackie Robinson	510	104	157	19	75	.308	.904
SS	Pee Wee Reese	559	94	152	6	58	.272	.734

Top Pitchers

Pos	Name	W	L	ERA	G	SV	IP	SO
St	Carl Erskine	14	6	2.70	33	2	206.2	131
St	Billy Loes	13	8	2.69	39	1	187.1	115
St	Preacher Roe	11	2	3.12	27	0	158.2	83
Rel	Joe Black	15	4	2.15	56	15	142.1	85

NEW YORK YANKEES
95 - 59 .617 +2.0 G

The Team
- Subway Series #10, 19th overall appearance.
- Second time making four straight appearances (1936-39).

The Players
- 14 players returning from 1951 Subway Series: Hank Bauer, Yogi Berra, Joe Collins, Bob Kuzava, Eddie Lopat, Mickey Mantle, Billy Martin, Gil McDougald, Johnny Mize, Vic Raschi, Allie Reynolds, Phil Rizzuto, Johnny Sain, Gene Woodling.
- Rizzuto played on the 1941/42/47/49/50/51 pennant-winning teams, capturing five titles.
- Berra, Raschi, Reynolds played on the 1947/49/50/51 title-winning teams.
- Bauer, Lopat, Mize, Woodling played on the 1949/50/51 title-winning teams.
- Allie Reynolds, 20-8, led the majors in ERA (2.08) and strikeouts (160).

The Manager
- Casey Stengel is the third manager to make four straight WS appearances (Joe McCarthy, 1936-1939, who was in seven of eight, and John McGraw, 1921-1924).

Top Batters

Pos	Name	AB	R	H	HR	RBI	BA	OPS
C	Yogi Berra	534	97	146	30	98	.273	.835
SS	Phil Rizzuto	578	89	147	2	43	.254	.678
OF	Hank Bauer	553	86	162	17	74	.293	.818
OF	Mickey Mantle	549	94	171	23	87	.311	.924

Top Pitchers

Pos	Name	W	L	ERA	G	SV	IP	SO
St	Allie Reynolds	20	8	2.06	35	6	244.1	160
St	Vic Raschi	16	6	2.78	31	0	223.0	127
St	Eddie Lopat	10	5	2.53	20	0	149.1	56
R-St	Johnny Sain	11	6	3.46	35	7	148.1	57

NEW YORK YANKEES vs. BROOKLYN DODGERS

October 1

LINE SCORE	1	2	3	4	5	6	7	8	9	R	H	E
NEW YORK YANKEES	0	0	1	0	0	0	0	1	0	2	6	2
BROOKLYN DODGERS	0	1	0	0	0	2	0	1	X	4	6	0

RECAP

The scoring started via lead-off home runs; Dodger 2B Jackie Robinson greeted Allie Reynolds in the second; Bombers 3B Gil McDougald greeted Joe Black in the third. That tie was broken by Brooklyn in the sixth as Duke Snider's first home run sailed over the right field scoreboard. In the top of the eighth inning the Yanks scored on a pinch-hit triple and sac fly. Pee Wee Reese, in the bottom of the eighth, hammered the Dodgers' third four-bagger. Meanwhile rookie hurler Joe Black, who started only two games during the regular season, pitched a complete game that gave Brooklyn their first opening game win in the history of the franchise.

SCORING SUMMARY

Second Inning - Brooklyn Dodgers
– Reynolds starting.
– J. Robinson slugged a solo shot into the left field seats.
– Campanella rebounded a single off of the right field wall; tagged out trying to steal second base, Berra to Martin.
– Pafko rolled out, McDougald to Collins.
– Hodges thrown out on a comebacker, Reynolds to Collins.

1 Runs **2** Hits **0** Errors **1** LOB

YANKEES – 0   **DODGERS – 1**

Third Inning - New York Yankees
– Black starting.
– McDougald slugged a solo shot into the left field crowd.
– Martin struck out.
– Reynolds went down on strikes.
– Bauer struck out.

1 Runs **1** Hits **0** Errors **0** LOB

YANKEES – 1   **DODGERS – 1**

Sixth Inning - Brooklyn Dodgers
– Black went down on strikes (#2).
– Cox fouled out to Berra.

– Reese stroked single into left field; wild pitched to second base.
– Snider orbited a home run over the right field scoreboard, driving in Reese.
– J. Robinson raced across first on McDougald's fielding error; on Reynolds's throwing error J. Robinson slid into second base.
– Campanella grounded out, Rizzuto to Collins.

2 Runs **2** Hits **2** Errors **1** LOB

YANKEES – 1   **DODGERS – 3**

Eighth Inning - New York Yankees
– Woodling PH for Reynolds, tattooed a triple off of the right field screen.
– Bauer lifted a sacrifice fly to Snider plating Woodling.
– Rizzuto flied out to Furillo.
– Mantle fanned.

1 Runs **1** Hits **0** Errors **0** LOB

YANKEES – 2   **DODGERS – 3**

Eighth Inning - Brooklyn Dodgers
– Scarborough pitching.
– Black went down on strikes

- Cox squibbed out, McDougald to Collins.
- Reese slugged a solo shot into the lower left field seats.
- Snider thrown out on a comebacker, Scarborough to Collins.

1 Runs **1** Hits **0** Errors **0** LOB

YANKEES – 2 **DODGERS – 4**

HIGHLIGHTS

- Duke Snider's first career World Series home run allowed by Yankee starter Allie Reynolds
- All four Dodger runs were driven in on the long ball
- Every Brooklyn fielder recorded a putout
- Allie Reynolds in seventh career start (fifth straight) loses for the second time (1951)

DIAMOND DUST

- Joe Black is the first African American pitcher to win a Fall Classic game
- Black is the 26th rookie to start and the 11th to win
- Black is the sixth rookie to start an opener and the third to win with a complete game
- Jackie Robinson is the fifth player to homer in both the Mid-Summer Classic and the Fall Classic in the same season
- Robinson's All Star game blast came off the Yankees' Vic Raschi
- Brooklyn is 1-5 while the Yankees are 14-5 in openers
- Yankee lose consecutive Game Ones for the second time (1921/22)

Game 1 BOX SCORE SUMMARY

NEW YORK YANKEES	AB	R	H	RBI	BB	K	1B	2B	3B	HR	TB	SB
HANK BAUER, RF	4	0	0	1	0	1	0	0	0	0	0	0
GIL MCDOUGALD, 3B	2	1	1	1	1	0	0	0	0	1	4	0
GENE WOODLING, PH	1	1	1	0	0	0	0	0	1	0	3	0
BROOKLYN DODGERS	AB	R	H	RBI	BB	K	1B	2B	3B	HR	TB	SB
PEE WEE REESE, SS	4	2	2	1	0	1	1	0	0	1	5	0
DUKE SNIDER, CF	4	1	2	2	0	0	0	1	0	1	6	0
JACKIE ROBINSON, 2B	2	1	1	1	1	0	0	0	0	1	4	0

NEW YORK YANKEES	IP	H	R	ER	HR	K	BB	HBP	ERA
ALLIE REYNOLDS L (0-1)	7	5	3	3	2	4	2	0	3.86
RAY SCARBOROUGH	1	1	1	1	1	1	0	0	9.00
BROOKLYN DODGERS	IP	H	R	ER	HR	K	BB	HBP	ERA
JOE BLACK W (1-0)	9	6	2	2	1	6	2	0	2.00

(National Baseball Hall of Fame and Museum)

Joe Black was a phenomenal 15-4 in 1952, with an ERA of 2.15 and 102 hits allowed in 71 games and 141.1 innings pitched. He won the Rookie of the Year and finished third in NL MVP voting. Black was never the same after that, collecting only another 15 wins in his career, which ended in 1957.

GAME TIME:	**2:21**
ATTENDANCE:	**34,861**
BEST OF 7:	**DODGERS - 1 YANKEES - 0**

Game 2

NEW YORK YANKEES vs. BROOKLYN DODGERS

October 2

LINE SCORE	1	2	3	4	5	6	7	8	9	R	H	E
NEW YORK YANKEES	0	0	0	1	1	5	0	0	0	7	10	0
BROOKLYN DODGERS	0	0	1	0	0	0	0	0	0	1	3	1

RECAP

The Bronx Bombers had a one-run lead at the beginning of the sixth inning and a six-run lead at the end. Carl Erskine was gone after the first three Pinstripers loaded the bases. Reliever Billy Loes got the first out on a fielder's choice, but could not get the second out until the Yankees had scored five times. Mickey Mantle had a three-hit day, scoring twice. Billy Martin homered and drove in four runs.

Yankee starter Vic Raschi complemented the 10-hit offense with a three-hit, complete game outing. All of the Dodgers singles were stroked in the third inning, plating their lone run. After that outburst, Raschi faced 21 batters, in one stretch retiring 12 in a row.

SCORING SUMMARY

Third Inning - Brooklyn Dodgers
– Raschi starting.
– Cox struck out.
– Reese singled past the left side of the mound.
– Snider's bunt single moved Reese to second base.
– J. Robinson forced Snider at second, Collins to Rizzuto; Reese slid into third.
– Campanella singled into left field, driving in Reese; J. Robinson took third.
– Pafko was a strikeout.

1 Runs **3** Hits **0** Errors **2** LOB

YANKEES – 0   **DODGERS – 1**

Fourth Inning - New York Yankees
– Erskine starting.
– Mantle split the right-center field gap for a double.
– Woodling moved Mantle to third on a grounder, J. Robinson to Hodges.
– Berra hoisted a sacrifice fly to Furillo plating Mantle.
– Collins thrown out on a comebacker, Erskine to Hodges.

1 Runs **1** Hits **0** Errors **0** LOB

YANKEES – 1   **DODGERS – 1**

Fifth Inning - New York Yankees
– McDougald drew a walk; swiped second base.
– Martin singled into left field, driving in McDougald; Martin took second.
– Raschi was a strikeout.
– Bauer walked; Martin caught trying to steal third base, Campanella to Cox; Bauer advanced.
– Reynolds out on a grounder, Reese to Hodges.

1 Runs **1** Hits **0** Errors **1** LOB

YANKEES – 2   **DODGERS – 1**

Sixth Inning - New York Yankees
– Mantle bunted wide of the mound for a single.
– Woodling singled Mantle to second; both runners advanced on a wild pitch.
– Berra walked; bases jammed.
– Loes relieved Erskine.
– Collins safe at first on a fielder's choice; Berra tagged out by J. Robinson; on Hodges fielding error Mantle scored; Woodling slid into third.
– McDougald dragged a bunt up the first base line, driving in Woodling; Collins slid into second base.

168

– Martin clocked a home run into the left field crowd, driving home Collins and McDougald.
– Raschi went down on strikes.
– Bauer struck out.

5 Runs   **3** Hits   **1** Errors   **0** LOB

YANKEES – 7   **DODGERS – 1**

DIAMOND DUST

- Duke Snider struck out three times
- Billy Martin and Mickey Mantle are the only Yankees who did not receive a free pass
- Raschi allowed just 3 hits along with 5 walks in his complete-game victory, his fourth straight WS win overall.
- Raschi's second game-ending strikeout (1950)

Game 2 BOX SCORE SUMMARY

NEW YORK YANKEES	AB	R	H	RBI	BB	K	1B	2B	3B	HR	TB	SB
MICKEY MANTLE, CF	5	2	3	0	0	1	2	1	0	0	4	0
GENE WOODLING, LF	4	1	1	0	1	0	1	0	0	0	1	0
YOGI BERRA, C	3	0	2	1	1	0	2	0	0	0	2	0
JOE COLLINS, 1B	3	1	0	0	1	1	0	0	0	0	0	0
GIL McDOUGALD, 3B	3	2	1	1	1	1	1	0	0	0	1	1
BILLY MARTIN, 2B	4	1	2	4	0	0	1	0	0	1	5	0
BROOKLYN DODGERS	AB	R	H	RBI	BB	K	1B	2B	3B	HR	TB	SB
PEE WEE REESE, SS	3	1	1	0	1	1	1	0	0	0	1	0
ROY CAMPANELLA, C	4	0	1	1	0	0	1	0	0	0	1	0

NEW YORK YANKEES	IP	H	R	ER	HR	K	BB	HBP	ERA
VIC RASCHI W (1-0)	9	3	1	1	0	9	5	0	1.00
BROOKLYN DODGERS	IP	H	R	ER	HR	K	BB	HBP	ERA
CARL ERSKINE L (0-1)	5	6	5	4	0	4	6	0	7.20
BILLY LOES	2	2	2	2	1	2	0	0	9.00

GAME TIME:	**2:47**	
ATTENDANCE:	**33,792**	
BEST OF 7:	**DODGERS - 1**	**YANKEES - 1**

Game 3

BROOKLYN DODGERS vs. NEW YORK YANKEES

October 3

LINE SCORE	1	2	3	4	5	6	7	8	9	R	H	E
BROOKLYN DODGERS	0	0	1	0	1	0	0	1	2	5	11	0
NEW YORK YANKEES	0	1	0	0	0	0	0	1	1	3	6	2

RECAP

Until the final inning, five runs had scored most conventionally. The Dodgers' three tallies were plated on sacrifice flies and an RBI single. The Yankees two came home on an RBI single and a solo home run. In the top the ninth, Brooklyn plated two runs most unconventionally. After Pee Wee Reese and Jackie Robinson cracked consecutive singles, starter Eddie Lopat was out and reliever Tom Gorman was in. Immediately, Reese and Robinson executed a double steal. One out later, they both scored on a Yogi Berra passed ball. Brooklyn gained the victory in the game and the Series lead as well.

SCORING SUMMARY

Second Inning - New York Yankees

– Roe starting.
– Berra fouled out to Campanella.
– Bauer got a walk.
– McDougald moved Bauer up on a ground out, Cox to Hodges.
– Martin intentionally walked.
– Lopat singled in to right-center field, driving in Bauer; Martin slid into second.
– Rizzuto grounded out, J. Robinson to Hodges.

1 Runs **1** Hits **0** Errors **2** LOB

DODGERS – 0   **YANKEES – 1**

Third Inning - Brooklyn Dodgers

– Lopat starting.
– Furillo bounced a ground-rule double for the right field fans.
– Reese bunted Furillo to third base on a single.
– J. Robinson lifted a sacrifice fly to Mantle plating Furillo; Reese advanced.
– Campanella lined into a double play, Rizzuto to Martin.

1 Runs **2** Hits **0** Errors **0** LOB

DODGERS – 1   **YANKEES – 1**

Fifth Inning - Brooklyn Dodgers

– Cox roped a single into left field.
– Roe sacrificed Cox to second base, Berra to Martin.
– Furillo grounded out, Rizzuto to Mize; Cox held.
– Reese singled into right field, driving Cox home.
– J. Robinson flied out to Woodling.

1 Runs **2** Hits **0** Errors **1** LOB

DODGERS – 2   **YANKEES – 1**

Eighth Inning - Brooklyn Dodgers

– J. Robinson stroked a single into center field.
– Campanella smacked a hit-and-run single; J. Robinson glided into third.
– Pafko lifted a sacrifice fly to Woodling plating J. Robinson; Campanella slid into second base.
– Snider got a second life when Berra dropped his foul pop; popped up to Rizzuto.
– Hodges intentionally walked.
– Cox purposely walked to load the bases.
– Roe bounced out, Martin to Collins.

1 Runs **2** Hits **0** Errors **3** LOB

DODGERS – 3   **YANKEES – 1**

Eighth Inning - New York Yankees

Woodling whiffed.
Berra slugged a solo shot into the left field seats.
Bauer out on a grounder, Cox to Hodges.
McDougald flied out to Snider.

1 Runs **1** Hits **0** Errors **0** LOB

DODGERS – 3   **YANKEES – 2**

Ninth Inning - Brooklyn Dodgers

Furillo out on a ground ball, Rizzuto to Collins.
Reese drove a single into right field.
J. Robinson singled Reese to second base.
Gorman relieved Lopat; Reese and J. Robinson double steal.
Campanella popped up to Rizzuto; on Berra's passed ball
  Reese and J. Robinson scored.
Pafko singled past the right side of the mound.
Snider fouled out to Berra.

2 Runs **3** Hits **0** Errors **1** LOB

DODGERS – 5   **YANKEES – 2**

Ninth Inning - New York Yankees

– Martin popped up to Campanella.
– Mize PH for Gorman, slugged a solo shot into the lower left
  field seats.
– Rizzuto flied out to Snider.
– Sain PH for Collins, flied out to Snider.

1 Runs **1** Hits **0** Errors **0** LOB

DODGERS – 5   **YANKEES – 3**

HIGHLIGHTS

- Eddie Lopat, gave up 10 base hits, pitched with
  Dodgers on base in all but one frame
- Yankee hurler Johnny Sain as a PH made the last out
- Gil Hodges and Preacher Roe are the only Brooklynites
  without a hit
- Berra was a triple shy of a cycle, totaling seven total
  bases, but scoring and driving in only one
- Yankee hurlers did not record a strikeout
- 17 total base hits, of which 13 were singles
- Roe hurled the third straight complete game win in
  front of a sellout crowd

DIAMOND DUST

- Berra (1947) and Mize are the first two players to hit pinch-hit home runs in World Series history
- Mize tied the record with his third career pinch hit
- Dodger starter Preacher Roe allowed the 79th and 80th franchise home run as well as the 230th all time

Game 3 BOX SCORE SUMMARY

BROOKLYN DODGERS	AB	R	H	RBI	BB	K	1B	2B	3B	HR	TB	SB
CARL FURILLO, RF	5	1	1	0	0	0	0	1	0	0	2	0
PEE WEE REESE, SS	5	1	3	1	0	0	3	0	0	0	3	1
JACKIE ROBINSON, 2B	4	2	2	1	1	0	2	0	0	0	2	1
ANDY PAFKO, LF	5	0	2	1	0	0	2	0	0	0	2	0
NEW YORK YANKEES	AB	R	H	RBI	BB	K	1B	2B	3B	HR	TB	SB
YOGI BERRA, C	4	1	3	1	0	0	1	1	0	1	7	0
HANK BAUER, RF	2	1	0	0	1	0	0	0	0	0	0	0
EDDIE LOPAT, P	2	0	1	1	1	1	1	0	0	0	1	0
JOHNNY MIZE, PH	1	1	1	1	0	0	0	0	0	1	4	0

BROOKLYN DODGERS	IP	H	R	ER	HR	K	BB	HBP	ERA
PREACHER ROE W (1-0)	9	6	3	3	2	5	5	1	3.00
NEW YORK YANKEES	IP	H	R	ER	HR	K	BB	HBP	ERA
EDDIE LOPAT L (0-1)	8.1	10	5	5	0	0	4	0	5.40

GAME TIME:	**2:56**
ATTENDANCE:	**66,698**
BEST OF 7:	**DODGERS - 2 YANKEES - 1**

Game 4

BROOKLYN DODGERS vs. NEW YORK YANKEES

October 4

LINE SCORE	1	2	3	4	5	6	7	8	9	R	H	E
BROOKLYN DODGERS	0	0	0	0	0	0	0	0	0	0	4	1
NEW YORK YANKEES	0	0	0	1	0	0	0	1	X	2	4	1

--- **RECAP** ---

Over 70,000 fans sold out the stadium. Brooklyn starter Joe Black spun a seven inning three-hitter. One hit was a fourth inning solo home run by Johnny Mize. Reliever Johnny Rutherford gave up the second run on a triple torqued by Mickey Mantle who scored on an error. Bomber starter Vic Raschi spun a complete game, four-hit shutout. Along the way he struck out 10 Dodgers. Jackie Robinson was victimized three times. Andy Pafko and Roy Campanella went down twice each. The rematch between Raschi and Black resulted in a different outcome but in identical records of 1-1, leveling the Series at two apiece.

--- **SCORING SUMMARY** ---

Fourth Inning - New York Yankees
- Black starting.
- Mize slugged a solo shot into the lower left field seats.
- Berra flied out to Snider (leaping, one-handed catch).
- Woodling fouled out to Cox.
- Bauer flied out to Pafko.

① Runs ① Hits ⓪ Errors ⓪ LOB

DODGERS – 0   **YANKEES – 1**

Eighth Inning - New York Yankees
- Rutherford pitching. Morgan to 3B.
- Mantle torqued a triple to center field; scored on Reese's throwing error.
- Mize got a walk.
- Collins PR
- Berra flied out to Furillo.
- Woodling pushed Collins up on a ground out, Morgan to Hodges.
- Bauer was a strikeout.

① Runs ① Hits ① Errors ⓪ LOB

DODGERS – 0   **YANKEES – 2**

--- **HIGHLIGHTS** ---

- SRO crowd of over 70,000 in Yankee Stadium for the fifth time - all versus the Dodgers
- A total of 138,485 fans in the stands for the two games
- Allie Reynolds, in eighth career start, collects fifth win, second career shutout
- Johnny Mize, playing 1B, homered in consecutive games
- Each team stroked four base hits - all singles for the Dodgers, all extra-base hits for the Yankees
- 1B Gil Hodges is in the throes of an 0-for-11 slump

Game 4

Game 4 BOX SCORE SUMMARY

NEW YORK YANKEES	AB	R	H	RBI	BB	K	1B	2B	3B	HR	TB	SB
MICKEY MANTLE, CF	3	1	1	0	1	0	0	0	1	0	3	0
JOHNNY MIZE, 1B	3	1	2	1	1	0	0	1	0	1	6	0

BROOKLYN DODGERS	IP	H	R	ER	HR	K	BB	HBP	ERA
JOE BLACK L (1-1)	7	3	1	1	1	2	5	0	1.69
JOHNNY RUTHERFORD	1	1	1	1	0	1	1	0	9.00
NEW YORK YANKEES	IP	H	R	ER	HR	K	BB	HBP	ERA
ALLIE REYNOLDS W (1-1)	9	4	0	0	0	10	3	0	0.00

(National Baseball Hall of Fame and Museum)

Allie Reynolds capped off his greatest season (20-8, 2.06 ERA, second in league in MVP) with 2 wins in the 1952 WS (G4, G7). His 4-hit, 10 K shutout in Game 4 was one of the finest of Reynolds' Fall Classic career, in which he went 7-2 overall in 15 games (9 starts and 77.2 IP). Reynolds' Game 4 performance was to that point only the sixth CG shutout with 10 or more strikeouts in World Series history.

GAME TIME:	2:33	
ATTENDANCE:	71,787	
BEST OF 7:	DODGERS - 2	YANKEES - 2

173

Game 5

BROOKLYN DODGERS vs. NEW YORK YANKEES

October 5

LINE SCORE	1	2	3	4	5	6	7	8	9	10	11	R	H	E
BROOKLYN DODGERS	0	1	0	0	3	0	1	0	0	0	1	6	10	0
NEW YORK YANKEES	0	0	0	0	5	0	0	0	0	0	0	5	5	1

───────────────────── **RECAP** ─────────────────────

In the 100th World Series game of the New York Yankee franchise, Brooklyn starter Carl Erskine pitched all 11 innings. The Yankees' bats were shackled for 10 of those frames. In the fifth, he weathered a four-hit, five-run rally that put the New Yorkers in the lead. Erskine then set down the next 18 Pinstripers.

Dodger CF Duke Snider had a great day at the plate. In the fifth, Snider extended the team lead with a two-run home run. In his next at-bat, he singled home 3B Billy Cox with the tying run. In the top of the 11th, Cox was again in scoring position when Snider doubled to break the 5-5 tie and put the Dodgers up 3-2.

───────────────────── **SCORING SUMMARY** ─────────────────────

Second Inning - Brooklyn Dodgers
– Blackwell starting.
– J. Robinson got to first on a walk.
– Shuba singled J. Robinson to second base; J. Robinson swiped third.
– Campanella was a strikeout.
– Pafko singled into right field, driving in J. Robinson; Shuba slid into second.
– Hodges walked the bases full.
– Erskine squeezed Shuba out at home plate, Blackwell to Berra.
– Cox forced Erskine at second base, Rizzuto to Martin.

① Runs **②** Hits **⓪** Errors **③** LOB

DODGERS – 1　　　**YANKEES – 0**

Fifth Inning - Brooklyn Dodgers
– Hodges drew a walk.
– Erskine safe at first base on a sacrifice/FC; Hodges slid into second base.
– Cox sacrificed both runners into scoring position, Mize to Martin.
– Reese lofted a sacrifice fly to Woodling plating Hodges.

– Snider clobbered a home run into left-center field, driving Erskine home.
– J. Robinson struck out.

③ Runs **①** Hits **⓪** Errors **⓪** LOB

DODGERS – 4　　　**YANKEES – 0**

Fifth Inning - New York Yankees
– Bauer worked a free pass.
– Martin singled Bauer to second base.
– Noren PH for Blackwell, singled into center field, driving in Bauer; Martin steamed into third.
– McDougald scored Martin on a forced of Noren at second, Reese to J.Robinson.
– Rizzuto singled McDougald to second base.
– Mantle fouled out to Cox.
– Mize powered a home run over the right field fence, driving home Rizzuto and McDougald.
– Berra flied out to Snider.

⑤ Runs **④** Hits **⓪** Errors **⓪** LOB

DODGERS – 4　　　**YANKEES – 5**

174

Seventh Inning - Brooklyn Dodgers

- Erskine flied out to Mantle.
- Cox raced across first base on a bang-bang play.
- Reese sacrificed Cox to second base, Sain to Mize.
- Snider singled up the middle, driving in Cox; Snider slid into second base on the throw home.
- J. Robinson intentionally walked.
- Furillo skied a warning track out to Woodling.

1 Runs **2** Hits **0** Errors **2** LOB

DODGERS – 5   **YANKEES – 5**

Eleventh Inning - Brooklyn Dodgers

- Erskine went down on strikes.
- Cox cuffed a single off of McDougald's glove.
- Reese smoked a hit-and-run single; Cox flew into third base.
- Snider doubled into right field, driving in Cox; Reese slid into third.

- J. Robinson walked; runners on the corners.
- Furillo grounded into a double play, McDougald to Berra to Mize.

1 Runs **3** Hits **0** Errors **2** LOB

DODGERS – 6   **YANKEES – 5**

HIGHLIGHTS

- Ewell Blackwell, acquired by the Yankees in late August, lost in the only WS appearance of his career
- Snider, a triple shy of the cycle, collected seven total bases
- Dodger 1B Gil Hodges' slump extended to 14 at-bats
- Carl Erskine authored the fifth straight complete-game victory of the series

DIAMOND DUST

- Twenty-fifth extra-inning game in World Series history
- Snider became the third player to hit four home runs in a Series (Ruth, 1926; Gehrig, 1928)
- Johnny Mize became the eighth player to hit three home runs in a Series
- Mize is the first player to homer in three consecutive games
- Johnny Sain is the second pitcher to lose in both leagues (1948 Boston Braves)
- 2B Jackie Robinson, in the 11th inning, is the second player to draw a walk in extra innings (1924)

Game 5 BOX SCORE SUMMARY

BROOKLYN DODGERS	AB	R	H	RBI	BB	K	1B	2B	3B	HR	TB	SB
BILLY COX, 3B	5	2	3	0	0	0	3	0	0	0	3	0
PEE WEE REESE, SS	5	0	1	1	0	0	1	0	0	0	1	0
DUKE SNIDER, CF	5	1	3	4	0	0	1	1	0	1	7	0
JACKIE ROBINSON, 2B	2	1	0	0	0	1	0	0	0	0	0	2
GIL HODGES, 1B	3	1	0	0	2	1	0	0	0	0	0	0
CARL ERSKINE, P	4	1	0	0	0	1	0	0	0	0	0	0
NEW YORK YANKEES	AB	R	H	RBI	BB	K	1B	2B	3B	HR	TB	SB
GIL MCDOUGALD, 3B	4	1	0	1	1	0	0	0	0	0	0	0
PHIL RIZZUTO, SS	5	1	1	0	0	0	1	0	0	0	1	0
JOHNNY MIZE, 1B	5	1	1	0	3	1	0	0	0	1	4	0
HANK BAUER, RF	3	1	0	0	1	0	0	0	0	0	0	0
BILLY MARTIN, 2B	4	1	1	0	0	0	1	0	0	0	1	0
IRV NOREN, PH	1	0	1	1	0	0	1	0	0	0	1	0

BROOKLYN DODGERS	IP	H	R	ER	HR	K	BB	HBP	ERA
CARL ERSKINE W (1-1)	11	5	5	5	1	6	3	0	5.06
NEW YORK YANKEES	IP	H	R	ER	HR	K	BB	HBP	ERA
EWELL BLACKWELL	5	4	4	4	1	4	3	0	7.20
JOHNNY SAIN L (0-1)	6	6	2	2	0	3	3	1	3.00

GAME TIME:	**3:00**
ATTENDANCE:	**70,536**
BEST OF 7:	**DODGERS - 3 YANKEES - 2**

Game 6

NEW YORK YANKEES vs. BROOKLYN DODGERS

October 6

LINE SCORE	1	2	3	4	5	6	7	8	9	R	H	E
NEW YORK YANKEES	0	0	0	0	0	0	2	1	0	3	9	0
BROOKLYN DODGERS	0	0	0	0	0	1	0	1	0	2	8	1

RECAP

For the first five frames, Brooklyn's Billy Loes and the Bombers' Vic Raschi pitched matching shutouts. Both worked their way out of potential rallies and both allowed only one hit. In the sixth, Duke Snider slugged a solo shot to break the scorelessness. In the seventh, Yogi Berra's solo was the knotter and Raschi's RBI single the tie-breaker. The fourth solo shot by Mickey Mantle, his first, added the last run to the scoreboard, ensuring the Yankees their 100th World Series victory.

SCORING SUMMARY

Sixth Inning - Brooklyn Dodgers
– Snider slugged a solo shot over the right field fence.
– J. Robinson flied out to Woodling.
– Shuba struck out.
– Campanella bounced a beebee back to the box, Raschi to Mize.

1 Runs **1** Hits **0** Errors **0** LOB

YANKEES – 0　　　　**DODGERS – 1**

Seventh Inning - New York Yankees
– Berra slugged a solo shot over the right field screen.
– Woodling stroked a single into center field; balked to second base
– Noren was a strikeout.
– Mantle popped up to Cox.
– Raschi cleaved a single off of Loes' leg, driving Woodling home.
– McDougald walked Raschi to second base.
– Rizzuto nubbed out, Cox to Hodges.

2 Runs **3** Hits **0** Errors **2** LOB

YANKEES – 2　　　　**DODGERS – 1**

Eighth Inning - New York Yankees
– Mantle slugged a solo shot into the left-center field seats.
– Mize popped up to Hodges.
– Berra flied out to Snider.
– Woodling jogged to first on a walk.
– Noren singled Woodling to second base.
– Martin rolled out, Cox to Hodges.

1 Runs **2** Hits **0** Errors **2** LOB

YANKEES – 3　　　　**DODGERS – 1**

Eighth Inning - Brooklyn Dodgers
– Collins to 1B.
– Reese dribbled out, Rizzuto to Collins.
– Snider slugged a solo shot over the right field fence
– J. Robinson flied out to Woodling.
– Shuba rattled a double into the left field corner.
– Amoros PR.
– Reynolds relieved Raschi.
– Campanella was a strikeout.

1 Runs **2** Hits **0** Errors **1** LOB

YANKEES – 3　　　　**DODGERS – 2**

HIGHLIGHTS

- Duke Snider (6), Yogi Berra (7) and Mickey Mantle (8) led off consecutive frames slugging solo shots
- Dodger 1B Gil Hodges slump extended to 0-17
- Vic Raschi posted second win
- The teams traded wins for the third time

DIAMOND DUST

- Snider's homer in the eighth inning made him the 11th player to homer twice in the same game (first for a losing team)
- Billy Loes became the second pitcher in WS history to steal a base ("Wild Bill" Donovan, Det 1908).

Game 6 BOX SCORE SUMMARY

NEW YORK YANKEES	AB	R	H	RBI	BB	K	1B	2B	3B	HR	TB	SB
MICKEY MANTLE, CF	3	1	1	1	2	0	0	0	0	1	4	0
YOGI BERRA, C	5	1	1	1	0	0	0	0	0	1	4	0
GENE WOODLING, LF	3	1	2	0	1	0	2	0	0	0	2	0
VIC RASCHI, P	3	0	1	1	0	0	1	0	0	0	1	0
BROOKLYN DODGERS	AB	R	H	RBI	BB	K	1B	2B	3B	HR	TB	SB
DUKE SNIDER, CF	3	2	2	2	1	0	0	0	0	2	8	0

NEW YORK YANKEES	IP	H	R	ER	HR	K	BB	HBP	ERA
VIC RASCHI W (2-0)	7.2	8	2	2	2	9	1	0	1.62
ALLIE REYNOLDS SV (1)	1.1	0	0	0	0	2	1	0	1.56
BROOKLYN DODGERS	IP	H	R	ER	HR	K	BB	HBP	ERA
BILLY LOES L (0-1)	8.1	9	3	3	2	3	5	0	4.35

The Dodgers failed to put away the Yankees in Game 6 through no fault of Duke Snider, who belted 2 home runs to account for Brooklyn's only runs. Snider went deep 4 times in the Series, while collecting 10 hits and 8 RBI overall. The Duke of Flatbush also went deep 4 times in the 1955 Series. For a complete list of 4-homer World Series players, see page 180.

(National Baseball Hall of Fame and Museum)

GAME TIME:	2:56
ATTENDANCE:	30,037
BEST OF 7:	DODGERS - 3 YANKEES - 3

Game 7

NEW YORK YANKEES vs. BROOKLYN DODGERS

October 7

LINE SCORE	1	2	3	4	5	6	7	8	9	R	H	E
NEW YORK YANKEES	0	0	0	1	1	1	1	0	0	4	10	4
BROOKLYN DODGERS	0	0	0	1	1	0	0	0	0	2	8	1

RECAP

Offensively, CF Mickey Mantle, and defensively, 2B Billy Martin, were the standouts. In consecutive innings, Mantle's bat changed the game. In the sixth he broke a 2-2 tie with a long, bases empty home run. In the top of the seventh he drove in Gil McDougald with the fourth and final run. In the bottom of the seventh, Martin's glove snuffed a Dodger rally. With the bases loaded 2B Jackie Robinson popped up. As the ball spiraled down beyond the reach of 1B Joe Collins and pitcher Bob Kuzava, Martin dashed in, making a spectacular, knee-high catch for the third out. Two innings later, the Yankee celebrated their fourth straight world championship.

SCORING SUMMARY

Fourth Inning - New York Yankees

– Black starting.
– Rizzuto lashed a double into left field.
– Mantle advanced Rizzuto on a ground out to Hodges.
– Mize singled into left field, driving Rizzuto home.
– Berra grounded into a double play, J. Robinson to Reese to Hodges.

1 Runs **2** Hits **0** Errors **0** LOB

YANKEES – 1   **DODGERS – 0**

Fourth Inning - Brooklyn Dodgers

– Lopat starting.
– Snider waffled a single into right field.
– J. Robinson bunted Snider to second base.
– Campanella bunted to load the bases.
– Reynolds relieved Lopat.
– Hodges hoisted a sacrifice fly to Woodling plating Snider; on Reynolds' fumble, J. Robinson slid into third; Campanella held.
– Shuba was a strikeout.
– Furillo grounded out, McDougald to Mize.

1 Runs **3** Hits **1** Errors **2** LOB

YANKEES – 1   **DODGERS – 1**

Fifth Inning - New York Yankees

– Woodling slugged a solo shot over the right field screen.
– Noren popped up to Cox.
– Martin chipped a single into center field.
– Reynolds bounded out, J. Robinson to Hodges; Martin raced to second.
– McDougald nubbed out, J. Robinson to Hodges.

1 Runs **2** Hits **0** Errors **1** LOB

YANKEES – 2   **DODGERS – 1**

Fifth Inning - Brooklyn Dodgers

– Black went down on strikes.
– Cox rammed a rocket double off of the right-center field wall.
– Reese singled into left field, driving in Cox; Reese took third base on Woodling's wild throw.
– Snider grounded out, Martin to Reynolds.
– J. Robinson zapped out to McDougald.

1 Runs **2** Hits **1** Errors **1** LOB

YANKEES – 2   **DODGERS – 2**

Sixth Inning - New York Yankees

– Rizzuto zapped out to Reese.
– Mantle slugged a solo shot over the right field scoreboard.
– Mize crackled a single into right field.

Roe relieved Black.

Berra struck out.

Woodling singled Mize to second base.

Bauer PH for Noren, got to first base on Cox's miscue; bases loaded.

Martin flied out to Snider.

① Runs ③ Hits ① Errors ③ LOB

YANKEES – 3   DODGERS – 2

Seventh Inning - New York Yankees

Houk PH for Reynolds, rolled out, Cox to Hodges.

McDougald stroked a single into center field.

Rizzuto sacrificed McDougald to second base, Cox to Hodges.

Mantle single into left field, driving McDougald home.

Mize fouled out to Furillo.

① Runs ② Hits ⓪ Errors ① LOB

YANKEES – 4   DODGERS – 2

HIGHLIGHTS

- Dodger starter Ralph Branca, arguing balls and strikes from the bench, was ejected
- Gil Hodges' slump reached 21 at-bats
- Bob Kuzava, in the seventh inning, escaped a one-out, bases loaded jam, helped by a Billy Martin spectacular running catch of a Jackie Robinson pop-up
- Kuzava retired eight of the last nine Dodgers; the only baserunner reached on an error
- Allie Reynolds posted sixth career win
- All scoring drives, in consecutive frames, netted one run - the Yankees had four versus the Dodgers two
- New York homered in every game
- A double play was turned in every game

DIAMOND DUST

- 12th seven-game set
- Brooklyn starter Joe Black is the fourth rookie to start three games as well as a Game 7
- Joe Black is the fourth pitcher to allow four homers in a Series
- Black is the 13th rookie to lose two games
- Kuzava is first pitcher to save consecutive clinching games, and the fourth to save a Game 7
- Bombers are the ninth team to rebound from a 2-3 deficit
- The Yankees are the third team, first American League franchise, to win Games 6 & 7 on the road (1926/34)
- Game Seven team stats: the Yankees are 2-1 while the Brooklynites are 0-2
- Game Seven wins: National League (7) vs American League (5)

Game 7 BOX SCORE SUMMARY

NEW YORK YANKEES	AB	R	H	RBI	BB	K	1B	2B	3B	HR	TB	SB
GI, McDOUGALD, 3B	5	1	2	0	0	0	2	0	0	0	2	0
PHIL RIZZUTO, SS	4	1	1	0	0	0	0	1	0	0	2	0
MICKEY MANTLE, CF	5	1	2	2	0	1	1	0	0	1	5	0
JOHNNY MIZE, 1B	3	0	2	1	1	0	2	0	0	0	2	0
GENE WOODLING, LF	4	1	2	1	0	0	1	0	0	1	5	0
BROOKLYN DODGERS	AB	R	H	RBI	BB	K	1B	2B	3B	HR	TB	SB
BILLY COX, 3B	5	1	2	0	0	1	1	1	0	0	3	0
PEE WEE REESE, SS	4	0	1	1	1	0	1	0	0	0	1	0
DUKE SNIDER, CF	4	1	1	0	0	1	1	0	0	0	1	0
GIL HODGES	4	0	0	1	0	0	0	0	0	0	0	0

NEW YORK YANKEES	IP	H	R	ER	HR	K	BB	HBP	ERA
EDDIE LOPAT	3	4	1	1	0	3	0	0	4.76
ALLIE REYNOLDS W (2-1)	3	3	1	1	0	2	0	0	1.77
BOB KUZAVA S (1)	2.2	0	0	0	0	2	0	0	0.00
BROOKLYN DODGERS	IP	H	R	ER	HR	K	BB	HBP	ERA
JOE BLACK L (1-2)	5.1	6	3	3	2	1	1	0	2.53
PREACHER ROE	1.2	3	1	1	0	1	0	0	3.18

GAME TIME:	**2:54**
ATTENDANCE:	**33,195**
BEST OF 7:	**DODGERS - 3 YANKEES - 4**

PLAYERS WITH 4 OR MORE HOME RUNS IN A WORLD SERIES

Player	HR	Tm	Year	Opponent	Gm	Series Result
Reggie Jackson	5	NYY	1977	LA Dodgers	6	Yankees win 4 - 2
Chase Utley	5	Phi NL	2009	NY Yankees	6	Yankees win 4 - 2
George Springer	5	Hou	2017	LA Dodgers	7	Astros win 4 - 3
Lou Gehrig	4	NYY	1928	St.Louis NL	4	Yankees win 4 - 0
Willie Aikens	4	KC Roy	1980	Phi NL	6	Phillies win 4 - 2
Len Dykstra	4	Phi NL	1993	Toronto	6	Blue Jays win 4 - 2
Babe Ruth	4	NYY	1926	St. Louis NL	7	Cardinals win 4 - 3
Duke Snider	4	Bkln	1952	NY Yankees	7	Yankees win 4 - 3
Duke Snider	4	Bkln	1955	NY Yankees	7	Dodgers win 4 - 3
Hank Bauer	4	NYY	1958	Milwaukee	7	Yankees win 4 - 3
Gene Tenace	4	Oak	1972	Cincinnati	7	Athletics win 4 - 3
Barry Bonds	4	SFG	2002	Anaheim	7	Angels win 4 - 3

Additional World Series Home Run Feats

- Duke Snider is the only player to hit 4 HR in a series twice. He had a 2-HR game in each series.
- George Springer's last 4 home runs in 2017 came in consecutive games, Games 4-7.
- Lou Gehrig's 4 HRs in 1928 were in a 4-game sweep in which Gehrig was 6-for-11 with 6 BB. Babe Ruth went 10-for-16 in the Series, with 3 2B and 3 HR.
- Gehrig hit 3 HRs in the Yankees' next trip to the WS, a 4-game sweep over the Cubs, giving him 7 in 8 games.
- Gene Tenace hit only 5 HR during the regular season in 1972 (227 AB) and his 4 in the Series were the only post-season HRs in his career in 114 ABs.
- Reggie Jackson homered in 4 consecutive at-bats in 1977, his last of Game 5 (off Don Sutton) and first 3 of Game 6.

1952

BROOKLYN DODGERS vs. NEW YORK YANKEES

--- **BROOKLYN DODGERS** ---

Overall World Series Record: 0 WINS 6 LOSSES. 36 Games Played (11 - 25 .306)
- Joe Black, rookie starter, won one, lost two and struck out in six straight at-bats
- Black is the fourth pitcher to allow four home runs and the fourth to win Game 1 and lose Game 7
- Duke Snider is the third player to hammer four home runs in a Series
- Snider's eight ribbies led both clubs
- Reese and Snider rapped 10 base hits each, nine singles for Reese, third set of teammates to bang out double digit base hits (1923/1940)
- Dressen is the fifth manager to debut in the Subway Series (1921/1941/1947/1949); only Casey Stengel won his debut
- Dodgers only team with six World Series losses

--- **NEW YORK YANKEES** ---

Overall World Series record: 15 WINS 4 LOSSES. 101 Games Played [67-33 (1 tie) .670]
- Vic Raschi (2) and Allie Reynolds (2) are the 17th set of pitchers to win all four games
- Reynolds has posted a victory in five consecutive World Series appearances (1947/49/50/51)
- Reynolds had a hand in four decisons - one loss (Game 1), two wins (Games 4/7) and one save (Game 6), and became the first pitcher to save a Game 6 and win Game 7 in the same series
- Johnny Mize, hammered three home runs (most on the team), drove in six and scored three
- McCarthy (1936/37/38/39) and Stengel are the only managers to win four titles in a row (1949/50/51/52)

--- **FUNGOES** ---

- Mickey Mantle and Duke Snider, centerfielders, hammered first career Series home runs.
- 50 base hits for each team.
- 16 combined home runs, a new record, were hammered by eight hitters.
- The American League's lead in the overall standings is now 32-17.

--- **SIX-GAME DATA** ---

TIME	19:27	PLAYERS POOL
ATTENDANCE	340,706	SHARES

$500,003
BROOKLYN DODGERS - $4,201
NEW YORK YANKEES - $5,983

181

1952

BROOKLYN DODGERS vs. NEW YORK YANKEES

Brooklyn Dodgers Composite Stats

BATTING	G	AB	R	H	RBI	2B	3B	HR	BB	SO	BA	OBP	SLG	OPS
Pee Wee Reese	7	29	4	10	4	0	0	1	2	2	.345	.387	.448	.835
Duke Snider	7	29	5	10	8	2	0	4	1	5	.345	.387	.828	1.215
Roy Campanella	7	28	0	6	1	0	0	0	1	6	.214	.241	.214	.456
Billy Cox	7	27	4	8	0	2	0	0	3	4	.296	.367	.370	.737
Jackie Robinson	7	23	4	4	2	0	0	1	7	5	.174	.367	.304	.671
Carl Furillo	7	23	1	4	0	2	0	0	3	3	.174	.269	.261	.530
Gil Hodges	7	21	1	0	1	0	0	0	5	6	.000	.192	.000	.192
Andy Pafko	7	21	0	4	2	0	0	0	0	4	.190	.190	.190	.381
George Shuba	4	10	0	3	0	1	0	0	0	4	.300	.300	.400	.700
Joe Black	3	6	0	0	0	0	0	0	1	6	.000	.143	.000	.143
Carl Erskine	3	6	1	0	0	0	0	0	0	1	.000	.000	.000	.000
Rocky Nelson	4	3	0	0	0	0	0	0	1	2	.000	.250	.000	.250
Billy Loes	2	3	0	1	0	0	0	0	0	1	.333	.333	.333	.667
Preacher Roe	3	2	0	0	0	0	0	0	0	0	.000	.000	.000	.000
Tommy Holmes	3	1	0	0	0	0	0	0	0	0	.000	.000	.000	.000
Bobby Morgan	2	1	0	0	0	0	0	0	0	0	.000	.000	.000	.000
Sandy Amoros	1	0	0	0	0	0	0	0	0	0				
Ken Lehman	1	0	0	0	0	0	0	0	0	0				
Johnny Rutherford	1	0	0	0	0	0	0	0	0	0				
Totals	7	233	20	50	18	7	0	6	24	49	.215	.291	.322	.613

PITCHING	G	GS	ERA	W	L	SV	CG	IP	H	R	ER	BB	SO	WHIP
Joe Black	3	3	2.53	1	2	0	1	21.1	15	6	6	8	9	1.078
Carl Erskine	3	2	4.50	1	1	0	1	18.0	12	10	9	10	10	1.222
Preacher Roe	3	1	3.18	1	0	0	1	11.1	9	4	4	6	7	1.324
Billy Loes	2	1	4.35	0	1	0	0	10.1	11	5	5	5	5	1.548
Ken Lehman	1	0	0.00	0	0	0	0	2.0	2	0	0	1	0	1.500
J. Rutherford	1	0	9.00	0	0	0	0	1.0	1	1	1	1	1	2.000
Totals	7	7	3.52	3	4	0	3	64.0	50	26	25	31	32	1.266

1952

BROOKLYN DODGERS vs. NEW YORK YANKEES

New York Yankees Composite Stats

BATTING	G	AB	R	H	RBI	2B	3B	HR	BB	SO	BA	OBP	SLG	OPS
Mickey Mantle	7	29	5	10	3	1	1	2	3	4	.345	.406	.655	1.061
Yogi Berra	7	28	2	6	3	1	0	2	2	4	.214	.267	.464	.731
Phil Rizzuto	7	27	2	4	0	1	0	0	5	2	.148	.281	.185	.466
Gil McDougald	7	25	5	5	3	0	0	1	5	2	.200	.333	.320	.653
Gene Woodling	7	23	4	8	1	1	1	1	3	3	.348	.423	.609	1.032
Billy Martin	7	23	2	5	4	0	0	1	2	2	.217	.308	.348	.656
Hank Bauer	7	18	2	1	1	0	0	0	4	3	.056	.227	.056	.283
Johnny Mize	5	15	3	6	6	1	0	3	3	1	.400	.500	1.067	1.567
Joe Collins	6	12	1	0	0	0	0	0	1	3	.000	.077	.000	.077
Irv Noren	4	10	0	3	1	0	0	0	1	3	.300	.364	.300	.664
Allie Reynolds	4	7	0	0	0	0	0	0	0	2	.000	.000	.000	.000
Vic Raschi	3	6	0	1	1	0	0	0	1	2	.167	.286	.167	.452
Eddie Lopat	2	3	0	1	1	0	0	0	1	1	.333	.500	.333	.833
Johnny Sain	2	3	0	0	0	0	0	0	0	0	.000	.000	.000	.000
Ewell Blackwell	1	1	0	0	0	0	0	0	0	0	.000	.000	.000	.000
Ralph Houk	1	1	0	0	0	0	0	0	0	0	.000	.000	.000	.000
Bob Kuzava	1	1	0	0	0	0	0	0	0	0	.000	.000	.000	.000
Tom Gorman	1	0	0	0	0	0	0	0	0	0				
Ray Scarborough	1	0	0	0	0	0	0	0	0	0				
Totals	**7**	**232**	**26**	**50**	**24**	**5**	**2**	**10**	**31**	**32**	**.216**	**.311**	**.384**	**.694**

PITCHING	G	GS	ERA	W	L	SV	CG	IP	H	R	ER	BB	SO	WHIP
Allie Reynolds	4	2	1.77	2	1	1	1	20.1	12	4	4	6	18	0.885
Vic Raschi	3	2	1.59	2	0	0	1	17.0	12	3	3	8	18	1.176
Eddie Lopat	2	2	4.76	0	1	0	0	11.1	14	6	6	4	3	1.588
Johnny Sain	1	0	3.00	0	1	0	0	6.0	6	2	2	3	3	1.500
Ewell Blackwell	1	1	7.20	0	0	0	0	5.0	4	4	4	3	4	1.400
Bob Kuzava	1	0	0.00	0	0	1	0	2.2	0	0	0	0	2	0.000
Ray Scarborough	1	0	9.00	0	0	0	0	1.0	1	1	1	0	1	1.000
Tom Gorman	1	0	0.00	0	0	0	0	0.2	1	0	0	0	0	1.500
Totals	**7**	**7**	**2.81**	**4**	**3**	**2**	**2**	**64.0**	**50**	**20**	**20**	**24**	**49**	**1.156**

BROOKLYN DODGERS vs. NEW YORK YANKEES

FUNGOES

- Yankees: Subway Series #11, 20th overall appearance.
- Dodgers: Subway Series #5, 7th overall appearance.
- Both teams in first place at the All-Star break.
- No travel days.
- Umpire info: Artie Gore was a minor league shortstop; Bill Stewart was a four-sport athlete, a WWI Navy veteran, and as the head coach of the Chicago Blackhawks, who won the 1938 Stanley Cup; Hank Soar was a running back for the New York Giants football team.

SERIES SUMMARY

In the 50 years of the World Series, all 16 teams have appeared at least once. Of the 100 total franchise appearances, 40 have been teams from New York, of which 20 were winners (Yankees 16-4, Giants 4-8).

Game 1 of the 1953 Series went the Yankees' way, as usual, as they jumped to a 4-0 lead in the first inning on the strength of two triples. Brooklyn fought back into a 5-5 tie in the seventh, but the Yankees put up four more runs for a 9-5 win.

The Dodgers led Game 2 by a run in the seventh, but the Yankees tied it up on Billy Martin home run and then went ahead when Mantle went deep with a two-out, two-run blast of starter Preacher Roe. Eddie Lopat threw a complete-game 9-hitter for the win.

More good pitching was the theme of Game 3, as Vic Raschi held Brooklyn to three runs in eight innings and Carl Erskine, KO'ed in the second inning of Game 1, bounced back for a record-setting 14-strikeout complete game for a 3-2 win.

In Game 4, the Dodgers jumped all over Whitey Ford with three runs in the first, after which Stengel pulled him. The Dodgers tacked on another four runs against a variety of relievers, eclipsing the Yankees' comeback efforts for a 7-3 win. Duke Snider and Junior Gilliam combined for five hits and six RBI

The Yankees brought their big bats for Game 5, belting four home runs, including Mickey Mantle's grand slam. By the time the Dodgers rallied with four runs in the eighth, they were down 10-2. Brooklyn outhit the Yankees 14-11, but they also walked six batters and hit one, three of which scored, while Yankees hurlers issued zero free passes.

Game 6 was another tight one, and an even greater heartbreak than usual for the Dodgers, as they scored two runs in the top of the ninth to tie the game at three, only to have Billy Martin single home the game and series winner in the bottom half. It was Martin's twelfth hit and eighth RBI of the series, both by far the most of anyone in the Series.

THE TEAMS

BROOKLYN DODGERS
105 – 49 .682 +13 G

The Team
- Consecutive appearances for the first time; third 100-win season.

The Players
- 13 players returning from the 1952 Subway Series.
- Reese played on the 1941/47/49/52/53 pennant-winning teams—all five Dodgers' Subway Series.
- Furillo, Hodges, and Robinson played on the 1947/49/52 pennant-winning teams.
- Campanella, Cox, Erskine, Roe and Snider played on the 1949/52 pennant-winning team.
- Carl Erskine is the only 20-game winner on the staff.
- 2B Junior Gilliam won the Rookie of the Year award.
- Gilliam, the seventh ROY to appear, is the fourth Dodger.
- Gilliam tatooed 17 triples, to lead the league, while scoring 125 runs.
- C Roy Campanella won the Most Valuable Player award, leading the National League with 142 RBI.
- RF Carl Furillo led the majors with a .344 batting average.
- Snider led the National League with 132 runs scored and 370 total bases.
- The Dodgers hammered 208 homers to lead the major leagues.

Top Batters

Pos	Name	AB	R	H	HR	RBI	BA	OPS
C	Roy Campanella	519	103	162	41	142	.312	1.006
1B	Gil Hodges	520	101	157	31	122	.302	.943
2B	Jim Gilliam	605	125	168	6	63	.278	.798
OF	Duke Snider	590	132	198	42	126	.336	1.046

Top Pitchers

Pos	Name	W	L	ERA	G	SV	IP	SO
St	Carl Erskine	20	6	3.54	39	3	246.2	187
St	Russ Meyer	15	5	4.56	34	0	191.1	106
St	Billy Loes	14	8	4.54	32	0	162.2	75
St	Preacher Roe	11	3	4.36	25	0	157.0	85
Rel	Clem Labine	11	6	2.77	37	7	110.1	44

NEW YORK YANKEES
99 – 52 .656 +8.5 G

The Team
- First team to make five consecutive appearances. The only other is the Yankees of 1960-1964.

The Players
- 16 returning players from the 1952 Subway Series.
- Rizzuto played on the 1941/42/47/49/50/51/52 pennant-winning teams, winning six titles.
- Berra, Raschi, Reynolds played on the 1947/49/50/51/52/53 title winning teams.
- Bauer, Lopat, Mize, Woodling played on the 1949/50/51/52/53 title winning teams.
- Joe Collins played on the 1950/51/52/53 title winning teams.
- Lopat, Raschi and Reynolds anchored a pitching staff making fifth straight and last appearances.
- Johnny Sain is making fourth appearance with second team (1948 Boston Braves and the 1951/52 New York Yankees).
- Casey Stengel is the first and only manager to appear in five straight Fall Classics.

Top Batters

Pos	Name	AB	R	H	HR	RBI	BA	OPS
C	Yogi Berra	503	80	149	27	108	.296	.886
2B	Billy Martin	587	72	151	15	75	.257	.710
3B	Gil McDougald	541	82	154	10	83	.285	.777
OF	Mickey Mantle	461	105	136	21	92	.295	.895

Top Pitchers

Pos	Name	W	L	ERA	G	SV	IP	SO
St	Whitey Ford	18	6	3.00	32	0	207.0	110
St	Vic Raschi	13	6	3.33	28	1	181.0	76
St	Eddie Lopat	16	4	2.42	25	0	178.1	50
R-St	Allie Reynolds	13	7	3.41	41	13	145.0	86

BROOKLYN DODGERS vs. NEW YORK YANKEES

September 30

LINE SCORE	1	2	3	4	5	6	7	8	9	R	H	E
BROOKLYN DODGERS	0	0	0	0	1	3	1	0	0	5	12	2
NEW YORK YANKEES	4	0	0	0	1	0	1	3	X	9	12	0

RECAP

Six hurlers gave up a grand total of 24 base hits and 14 runs. None of the six pitchers escaped the battering. Ten of the hits were nailed for extra bases netting 12 runs. From the fifth inning on the score changed every inning. Hank Bauer and Billy Martin tripled in the first inning for four Bomber runs. The Dodgers did tie the score in the top of the seventh, but the Yankees took back the lead in the bottom of the inning and never looked back. Brooklyn started from that deficit and never recovered, despite hammering three of the five home runs. The final double, which plated two runs, was drilled by the winning pitcher, Yankees reliever Johnny Sain.

SCORING SUMMARY

First Inning - New York Yankees
– Erskine starting.
– McDougald popped up to Gilliam.
– Collins drew a walk.
– Bauer tripled into deep right-center field, driving Collins home.
– Berra was a strikeout.
– Mantle managed a walk; runners on the corners.
– Woodling walked; bases loaded.
– Martin tripled into deep left-center field, driving home Bauer, Mantle and Woodling.
– Rizzuto grounded out, Cox to Hodges.

4 Runs **2** Hits **0** Errors **1** LOB

DODGERS – 0   **YANKEES – 4**

Fifth Inning - Brooklyn Dodgers
– Hughes went down on strikes.
– Gilliam slugged a solo shot deep into the right field seats.
– Reese flied out to Bauer.
– Snider drilled a 'tweener double into right-center field.
– J. Robinson coaxed a walk.
– Campanella flied out to Woodling.

1 Runs **2** Hits **0** Errors **2** LOB

DODGERS – 1   **YANKEES – 4**

Fifth Inning - New York Yankees
– Collins flied out to Snider (great leaping catch).
– Bauer flied out to Furillo.
– Berra slugged a solo shot deep into the right field crowd.
– Martin squibbed out, Gilliam to Hodges.

1 Runs **1** Hits **0** Errors **0** LOB

DODGERS – 1   **YANKEES – 5**

Sixth Inning - Brooklyn Dodgers
– Hodges slugged a solo shot deep into the left field seats.
– Furillo flied out to Bauer.
– Cox singled past the left side of the mound.
– Shuba PH for Hughes, skyrocketed a home run into the lower right field seats, driving Cox home.
– Sain relieved Reynolds.
– Gilliam grounded out, Martin to Collins.
– Reese trotted to first on a free pass.
– Snider smashed a hit-and-run single; Reese loped over to third base.
– J. Robinson bounded out, McDougald to Collins.

3 Runs **4** Hits **0** Errors **2** LOB

DODGERS – 4   **YANKEES – 5**

Seventh Inning - Brooklyn Dodgers

- Campanella pinged a single into left field.
- Hodges dinked a single off of Rizzuto's glove; Campanella took third.
- Furillo singled up the middle, driving in Campanella; Hodges slid into second.
- Cox forced Hodges at third base, Berra to McDougald; Furillo moved up.
- Labine forced Furillo at third base, Berra to McDougald.
- Gilliam fouled out to Berra.

1 Runs **3** Hits **0** Errors **2** LOB

DODGERS – 5   **YANKEES – 5**

Seventh Inning - New York Yankees

- Sain went down on strikes.
- McDougald flied out to Snider.
- Collins slugged a solo shot into the right field seats.
- Bauer rippled a single into left field.
- Berra singled Bauer to second base.
- Wade relieved Labine.
- Mantle was a strikeout.

1 Runs **3** Hits **0** Errors **2** LOB

DODGERS – 5   **YANKEES – 6**

Eighth Inning - New York Yankees

- Woodling out on a grounder, Gilliam to Hodges.
- Martin singled through the right side of the mound; swiped second base.

- Rizzuto got a walk.
- Sain doubled into right-center field, driving home Martin and Rizzuto.
- McDougald flied out to Furillo.
- Collins singled into right field, driving Sain home.
- Bauer struck out.

3 Runs **3** Hits **0** Errors **1** LOB

DODGERS – 5   **YANKEES – 9**

HIGHLIGHTS

- Dodger starter Carl Erskine, in the first inning, issued three walks and gave up two RBI triples
- Brooklyn committed two errors on the same play in the fourth inning
- Jim Gilliam (5), Yogi Berra (5), Gil Hodges (6) and George Shuba (6) homered in consecutive frames
- Hodges' bases empty four-bagger broke an 0-23 slump (0-21 in 1952), and is the 15th for the franchise
- Labine got the loss, but Ben Wade gave up three runs on three hits in the next frame
- Only three Yanks went hitless and two did not score
- All six pitchers gave up at least one hit and one run
- New York is 15-5 in openers while the Brooklynites are 1-6
- Game One winners have won it all 31 times

DIAMOND DUST

- Shuba powered the third pinch-hit home run, first by a National Leaguer, and the first in an opening game
- Allie Reynolds is the third pitcher to allow three homers in a game
- Johnny Sain, in relief, is the third pitcher to win in both leagues (Boston Braves, 1948) Jack Coombs (PHA 1910/11, BRK, 1916) and Hank Bowory (NYY 1942/43, CHC, 1945) were the first two.

Johnny Sain, who divided the 1953 season between starting and relieving, collected a save in Game 1 with 3.2 innings of 1-run relief. Sain also doubled and walked and scored a run. Sain was an excellent hitting pitcher, finishing his career with a batting average of .245 in 774 at bats. Even more impressive was Sain's bat control. In 856 major league plate appearances, he fanned only 20 times.

Game 1 BOX SCORE SUMMARY

BROOKLYN DODGERS	AB	R	H	RBI	BB	K	1B	2B	3B	HR	TB	SB
JUNIOR GILLIAM, 2B	5	1	2	1	0	1	1	0	0	1	5	0
ROY CAMPANELLA, C	4	1	1	0	0	0	1	0	0	0	1	0
GIL HODGES, 1B	5	1	3	1	0	0	2	0	0	1	6	0
CARL FURILLO, RF	4	0	1	1	1	0	1	0	0	0	1	0
BILLY COX, 3B	5	1	2	0	0	0	1	1	0	0	3	0
GEORGE SHUBA, PH	1	1	1	2	0	0	0	0	0	1	4	0

NEW YORK YANKEES	AB	R	H	RBI	BB	K	1B	2B	3B	HR	TB	SB
JOE COLLINS, 1B	4	2	2	2	1	0	1	0	0	1	5	0
HANK BAUER, RF	5	1	2	1	0	2	1	0	1	0	4	0
YOGI BERRA, C	4	1	2	1	0	2	1	0	0	1	5	0
MICKEY MANTLE, CF	3	1	1	0	1	1	1	0	0	0	1	0
BILLY MARTIN, 2B	4	1	3	3	0	0	2	0	1	0	5	0
PHIL RIZZUTO, SS	3	1	0	0	1	0	0	0	0	0	0	1
JOHNNY SAIN, P	2	1	1	2	1	0	0	1	0	0	2	0

BROOKLYN DODGERS	IP	H	R	ER	HR	BB	SO	HBP	ERA
CARL ERSKINE	1	2	4	4	0	3	1	0	36.00
JIM HUGHES	4	3	1	1	1	1	3	0	2.25
CLEM LABINE L (0-1)	1.2	4	1	1	1	0	1	0	5.40
BEN WADE	1.1	3	3	3	0	1	2	0	20.2

NEW YORK YANKEES	IP	H	R	ER	HR	BB	SO	HBP	ERA
ALLIE REYNOLDS	5.1	7	4	4	3	3	6	1	6.75
JOHNNY SAIN W (1-0)	3.2	5	1	1	0	1	0	0	2.45

GAME TIME: **3:10**
ATTENDANCE: **69,374**
BEST OF 7: **YANKEES - 1   DODGERS - 0**

Game 2

BROOKLYN DODGERS vs. NEW YORK YANKEES

October 1

LINE SCORE	1	2	3	4	5	6	7	8	9	R	H	E
BROOKLYN DODGERS	0	0	0	2	0	0	0	0	0	2	9	1
NEW YORK YANKEES	1	0	0	0	0	0	1	2	X	4	5	0

RECAP

For the first six innings, the starters, Eddie Lopat for the Pinstripers and Preacher Roe for Brooklyn, kept the score at a difference of one in favor of the National Leaguers. In the next two frames Roe gave up a Billy Martin solo shot for the tie and a two-run four-bagger to Mickey Mantle for the lead. Lopat maintained his form for the win and a two-game edge to the Yankees.

SCORING SUMMARY

First Inning - New York Yankees

– Roe starting.
– Woodling worked a walk.
– Collins walked Woodling to second base.
– Bauer flied out to Furillo; Woodling slid into third base.

– Berra lifted a sacrifice fly to Furillo plating Woodling; Collins took second.
– Mantle finagled a walk.
– McDougald hit by a pitch; bases loaded.
– Martin flied out to Furillo.

0 Runs **0** Hits **0** Errors **3** LOB

DODGERS – 0   **YANKEES – 1**

Fourth Inning - Brooklyn Dodgers

– J. Robinson flied out to Woodling.
– Campanella grounded out, Martin to Collins.
– Hodges stroked a single into center field.
– Furillo zinged a hit-and-run single; Hodges moseyed into third base.
– Cox doubled into the left field corner, driving home Hodges and Furillo.
– Roe was a strikeout.

2 Runs **3** Hits **0** Errors **1** LOB

DODGERS – 2   **YANKEES – 1**

Seventh Inning - New York Yankees

– Martin slugged a solo shot into the lower left field seats.
– Rizzuto flied out to J. Robinson.
– Lopat went down on strikes.
– Woodling rolled out, Reese to Hodges.

1 Runs **1** Hits **0** Errors **0** LOB

DODGERS – 2   **YANKEES – 2**

Eighth Inning - New York Yankees

– Collins flied out to Furillo.
– Bauer stroked a single into left field.
– Berra flied out to Snider.
– Mantle belted a home run into the left field seats, driving Bauer home.
– McDougald flied out to J. Robinson.

2 Runs **2** Hits **0** Errors **0** LOB

DODGERS – 2   **YANKEES – 4**

HIGHLIGHTS

- Dodgers starter Preacher Roe, in the first inning, faced seven Yankees but allowed only one run on zero hits (3 BB, HBP)
- Yankee starter Eddie Lopat gave up the Dodgers' two runs in the fourth, and thereafter put up all zeros, despite allowing runners in scoring position in four out of the next five frames
- Both starters went the distance
- SRO for the second consecutive game

DIAMOND DUST

- Roe is the second pitcher in WS history to allow a home run in consecutive innings. The first was also in a Subway series, Cliff Melton in Game 5 of the 1937 Series, in the second and third.

Game 2 BOX SCORE SUMMARY

BROOKLYN DODGERS	AB	R	H	RBI	BB	K	1B	2B	3B	HR	TB	SB
GIL HODGES, 1B	3	1	2	0	1	0	2	0	0	0	2	1
CARL FURILLO, RF	4	1	2	0	0	0	1	1	0	0	3	0
BILLY COX, 3B	3	0	1	2	1	0	0	1	0	0	2	0

NEW YORK YANKEES	AB	R	H	RBI	BB	K	1B	2B	3B	HR	TB	SB
GENE WOODLING, LF	3	1	0	0	1	1	0	0	0	0	0	0
HANK BAUER, RF	4	1	1	0	0	1	1	0	0	0	1	0
YOGI BERRA, C	3	0	0	1	1	0	0	0	0	0	0	0
MICKEY MANTLE, CF	3	1	1	2	1	0	0	0	0	1	4	0
BILLY MARTIN, 2B	3	1	2	1	0	0	1	0	0	1	5	0

BROOKLYN DODGERS	IP	H	R	ER	HR	K	BB	HBP	ERA
PREACHER ROE L (0-1)	8	5	4	4	2	4	4	1	4.50

NEW YORK YANKEES	IP	H	R	ER	HR	K	BB	HBP	ERA
EDDIE LOPAT W (1-0)	9	9	2	2	0	3	4	0	2.00

GAME TIME: **2:42**
ATTENDANCE: **66,786**
BEST OF 7:   **DODGERS - 0   YANKEES - 2**

Game 3

NEW YORK YANKEES vs. BROOKLYN DODGERS

October 2

LINE SCORE	1	2	3	4	5	6	7	8	9	R	H	E
NEW YORK YANKEES	0	0	0	0	1	0	0	1	0	2	6	0
BROOKLYN DODGERS	0	0	0	0	1	1	0	1	X	3	9	0

RECAP

Brooklyn moundsman Carl Erskine jump started his record-setting 14 strikeout performance by fanning the first two Yankees. 1B Joe Collins and CF Mickey Mantle went down four times each. In the early innings Pinstripe starter Vic Raschi matched zeroes with his mound opponent. Both gave up a run in the fifth and eighth innings. The difference was the Dodger run in the sixth frame. Erskine, in pitching the entire nine for the victory, stopped his team's two-game losing streak. Securing this awesome accomplishment, Brooklyn C Roy Campanella broke the 2-2 tie in the eighth inning on a solo home run.

SCORING SUMMARY

Fifth Inning - New York Yankees

– Martin singled to shortstop.
– Rizzuto singled to second base, Martin to second.
– Raschi advanced the runners on a sac hit, Erskine to Gilliam covering.
– McDougald collected another IF hit to third to drive in Martin, Rizzuto to third.
– Collins took a third strike.
– Bauer grounded out Gilliam to J. Robinson

1 Runs **3** Hits **0** Errors **2** LOB

YANKEES – 1   **DODGERS – 0**

Fifth Inning - Brooklyn Dodgers

– Furillo flied out to Mantle.
– J. Robinson ricochet a double off of the right field screen; balked to third.
– Cox squeezed J. Robinson home and was safe on a fielder's choice.
– Erskine singled Cox to second base.
– Gilliam fouled out to Berra.
– Reese bounded out, Martin to Collins.

1 Runs **2** Hits **0** Errors **2** LOB

YANKEES – 1   **DODGERS – 1**

Sixth Inning - Brooklyn Dodgers

– Snider spiked a single into right field.
– Hodges walked Snider to second base.
– Campanella popped up to Raschi.
– Furillo struck out.
– J. Robinson singled into left field, driving in Snider; Hodges slid into second.
– Cox was a strikeout.

1 Runs **2** Hits **0** Errors **2** LOB

YANKEES – 1   **DODGERS – 2**

Eighth Inning - New York Yankees

– Collins strikeout.
– Bauer hot-shotted a single over the second base bag.
– Berra hit by a pitch. Bauer moved up.
– Mantle strikeout.
– Woodling singled up the middle, driving in Bauer; Berra braked at third.
– Martin grounded out, Gilliam to Hodges.

1 Runs **2** Hits **0** Errors **2** LOB

YANKEES – 2   **DODGERS – 2**

Eighth Inning - Brooklyn Dodgers

– Hodges dribbled out, Rizzuto to Collins.
– Campanella slugged a solo shot into the lower left field seats.
– Furillo out on a ground ball, McDougald to Collins.
– J. Robinson arched a single into center field.
– Cox fouled out to Martin.

1 Runs **2** Hits **0** Errors **1** LOB

YANKEES – 2　　　　**DODGERS – 3**

HIGHLIGHTS

- Vic Raschi balked following a Jackie Robinson double to set up the Dodgers first run
- Bomber hits were all singles
- Yankees Joe Collins (4) and Mickey Mantle (4) combined for eight of Carl Erskine's 14 strikeouts
- Erskine fanned two batters in five different frames
- Unusual game in which a hit batsmen, a wild pitch, and a balk occurred
- Both starters went the distance

DIAMOND DUST

- Bomber C Yogi Berra is the second player and first American Leaguer hit by a pitch twice in the same game (1925)
- Erskine is the first pitcher to hit two batters and fling a wild pitch in the same game
- Carl Erskine, in the ninth inning, struck out the 13th and 14th Yankee, and got the 27th out on an assist
- Erskine's 14 K's set a new World Series record

Game 3 BOX SCORE SUMMARY

NEW YORK YANKEES	AB	R	H	RBI	BB	K	1B	2B	3B	HR	TB	SB
GIL MCDOUGALD, 3B	4	0	1	1	0	1	1	0	0	0	1	0
HANK BAUER, RF	4	1	1	0	0	0	1	0	0	0	1	0
YOGI BERRA, C	1	0	1	0	1	0	1	0	0	0	1	0
GENE WOODLING, LF	4	0	1	1	0	1	1	0	0	0	1	0
BILLY MARTIN, 2B	3	1	1	1	0	1	1	0	0	0	1	0
BROOKLYN DODGERS	AB	R	H	RBI	BB	K	1B	2B	3B	HR	TB	SB
DUKE SNIDER, CF	3	1	1	0	1	0	1	0	0	0	1	0
ROY CAMPANELLA, C	4	1	1	1	0	1	0	0	0	1	4	0
JACKIE ROBINSON, LF	4	1	3	1	0	0	2	1	0	0	4	0
BILLY COX, 3B	3	0	0	1	0	1	0	0	0	0	0	0

NEW YORK YANKEES	IP	H	R	ER	HR	K	BB	HBP	ERA
VIC RASCHI L (0-1)	8	9	3	3	1	4	3	0	3.38
BROOKLYN DODGERS	IP	H	R	ER	HR	K	BB	HBP	ERA
CARL ERSKINE W (1-0)	9	6	2	2	0	14	3	0	5.40

(National Baseball Hall of Fame and Museum)

Billy Martin tumbles past Roy Campanella in an unsuccesful attempt to score in Game 4. Martin collected 12 hits and drove in 8 runs in the series.

GAME TIME:	**3:00**
ATTENDANCE:	**35,270**
BEST OF 7:	**DODGERS - 1　YANKEES - 2**

NEW YORK YANKEES vs. BROOKLYN DODGERS

October 3

LINE SCORE	1	2	3	4	5	6	7	8	9	R	H	E
NEW YORK YANKEES	0	0	0	0	2	0	0	0	1	3	9	0
BROOKLYN DODGERS	3	0	0	1	0	2	1	0	X	7	12	0

RECAP

Neither starting pitcher went the distance but each earned a decision. For the Yankees, Whitey Ford lasted for just one frame, posting the loss. For the Dodgers Billy Loes lasted eight, posting the win. Brooklyn took the lead in the first with double threes - hits and runs. They added more runs in the fourth, sixth and seventh frames. CF Duke Snider drove in four runs with the long ball, two doubles and a home run. 2B Jim Gilliam stroked three hits, all doubles. The victory gave Brooklyn a two-game winning streak to even the Series.

SCORING SUMMARY

First Inning - Brooklyn Dodgers
– Ford starting.
– Gilliam bounced a ground-rule double into the right field seats.
– Reese advanced Gilliam on a ground out to Collins.
– J. Robinson singled over second, driving Gilliam home.
– Hodges forced J. Robinson at second base, McDougald to Martin; wild pitched to second base.
– Campanella intentionally walked.
– Snider doubled off the right field wall, driving home Hodges and Campanella.
– Furillo flied out to Bauer.

3 Runs **3** Hits **0** Errors **1** LOB

YANKEES – 0   **DODGERS – 3**

Fourth Inning - Brooklyn Dodgers
– Snider tapped out, Martin to Collins.
– Furillo jabbed a single into center field.
– Cox flied out to Woodling.
– Loes smashed a hit-and-run single; Furillo barreled into third base.
– Gilliam doubled off of the right field screen, driving in Furillo; Loes took third.
– Reese popped up to Martin.

1 Runs **3** Hits **0** Errors **2** LOB

YANKEES – 0   **DODGERS – 4**

Fifth Inning - New York Yankees
– Martin thumped a triple to straight away center field.
– McDougald orbited a home run into the left field seats, driving Martin home.
– Rizzuto flied out to Snider.
– Bollweg PH for Gorman, whiffed; tagged out by Campanella.
– Mantle struck out.

2 Runs **2** Hits **0** Errors **0** LOB

YANKEES – 2   **DODGERS – 4**

Sixth Inning - Brooklyn Dodgers
– Snider slugged a solo shot over the right field screen.
– Furillo struck out.
– Cox chucked a double into left field.
– Loes singled Cox to third base.
– Gilliam lofted a sacrifice fly to Bauer plating Cox; Loes slid into second base on the throw to the plate.
– Reese rolled out, McDougald to Collins.

2 Runs **3** Hits **0** Errors **1** LOB

YANKEES – 2   **DODGERS – 6**

Seventh Inning - Brooklyn Dodgers

– Schallock pitching.
– J. Robinson flied out to Bauer.
– Hodges struck out.
– Campanella drew a free pass.
– Snider doubled into left field, driving Campanella home.
– Furillo dribbled out, Martin to Collins.

1 Runs **1** Hits **0** Errors **1** LOB

YANKEES – 2 **DODGERS – 7**

Ninth Inning - New York Yankees

– Thompson to LF.
– Woodling singled through the right side of the infield.
– Martin singled Woodling to second base.
– McDougald walked; bases loaded.
– Labine relieved Loes.
– Rizzuto was a strikeout.
– Mize PH for Schallock, popped up to Snider.

– Mantle singled into right field, driving in Woodling; Martin tagged out at the plate on a laser throw from Thompson to Campanella.

1 Runs **3** Hits **0** Errors **2** LOB

YANKEES – 3 **DODGERS – 7**

HIGHLIGHTS

- Yankee starter Whitey Ford was knocked out in the first inning with a three-hit, three-run rally
- Dodger C Roy Campanella got two free passes and was driven in each time by CF Duke Snider
- Snider's three hits all went for extra bases
- Snider has had a four RBI day in consecutive Classics
- Snider amassed eight and Junior Gilliam six total bases
- Dodgers totaled six doubles, three by Gilliam
- Yankee 2B Billy Martin was thrown out at home on Mantle's single by backup outfielder Don Thompson (who had replaced Jackie Robinson for defensive purposes) to end the game
- The teams have traded two-game winning streaks

DIAMOND DUST

- Gilliam is the fourth player to drill three doubles in a game and the third to do so in consecutive at-bats
- Billy Loes tallied two singles and a sac hit after collecting only seven hits and 2 sacs all season long

Game 4 BOX SCORE SUMMARY

NEW YORK YANKEES	AB	R	H	RBI	BB	K	1B	2B	3B	HR	TB	SB
MICKEY MANTLE, CF	5	0	1	1	0	2	1	0	0	0	1	0
GENE WOODLING, LF	3	1	1	0	1	0	0	0	0	0	0	0
BILLY MARTIN, 2B	4	1	2	0	0	1	1	0	1	0	4	0
GIL MCDOUGALD, 3B	3	1	1	2	1	0	0	0	0	1	4	0
BROOKLYN DODGERS	AB	R	H	RBI	BB	K	1B	2B	3B	HR	TB	SB
JUNIOR GILLIAM, 2B	5	1	3	2	0	0	0	3	0	0	6	0
JACKIE ROBINSON, LF	4	0	1	1	0	0	1	0	0	0	1	0
GIL HODGES, 1B	4	1	0	0	0	1	0	0	0	0	0	0
ROY CAMPANELLA, C	2	2	0	0	2	1	0	0	0	0	0	0
DUKE SNIDER, CF	4	1	3	4	0	0	0	2	0	1	8	0
CARL FURILLO, RF	4	1	1	0	0	1	1	0	0	0	1	0
BILLY COX, 3B	4	1	2	0	0	1	1	1	0	0	3	0

NEW YORK YANKEES	IP	H	R	ER	HR	K	BB	HBP	ERA
WHITEY FORD L (0-1)	1	3	3	3	0	0	1	0	27.00
TOM GORMAN	3	4	1	1	0	1	0	0	3.00
JOHNNY SAIN	2	3	2	2	1	1	0	0	4.76
ART SHALLOCK	2	2	1	1	0	1	1	0	4.50
BROOKLYN DODGERS	IP	H	R	ER	HR	K	BB	HBP	ERA
BILLY LOES W (1-0)	8	8	3	3	1	8	2	0	3.38
CLEM LABINE S (1)	1	1	0	0	0	1	0	0	0.00

GAME TIME:	2:46
ATTENDANCE:	36,775
BEST OF 7:	DODGERS - 2 YANKEES - 2

Game 5

NEW YORK YANKEES vs. BROOKLYN DODGERS

October 4

LINE SCORE	1	2	3	4	5	6	7	8	9	R	H	E
NEW YORK YANKEES	1	0	5	0	0	0	3	1	1	11	11	1
BROOKLYN DODGERS	0	1	0	0	1	0	0	4	1	7	14	1

RECAP

Brooklyn outhit the Bombers 14-11; the Bombers out-homered Brooklyn 4-2; and the Bombers outscored Brooklyn 11-7. The six home runs parlayed 12 of the combined 18 runs.

The Dodger home runs came late in the game producing four tallies. They were down by seven in the eighth inning before Billy Cox's three-run blast. Jim Gilliam's solo shot in the ninth changed the deficit from five to four. The Yankee home runs produced eight tallies. Gene Woodling led off the game with a four-bagger. The big blow was the grand slam in the third, by Mickey Mantle. Billy Martin drove in two with a four-bagger in the seventh and Gil McDougald's solo in the ninth rounded out the long balls.

SCORING SUMMARY

First Inning - New York Yankees
– Podres starting.
– Woodling slugged a solo shot into the left field seats.
– Collins skyed out to Snider.
– Bauer bounced out, Reese to Hodges.
– Berra flied out to Snider.

1 Runs **1** Hits **0** Errors **0** LOB

YANKEES – 1 **DODGERS – 0**

Second Inning - Brooklyn Dodgers
– Campanella singled up the middle.
– Hodges singled Campanella to second base.
– Furillo flashed across first, Campanella rumbled home and Hodges pulled up at third base on Rizzuto's off-target throw.
– Cox flied out to Woodling who uncorked a straight arrow to Berra who tagged Hodges out at the plate.
– Podres singled Furillo to second base.
– Gilliam grounded out, Martin to Collins.

1 Runs **3** Hits **0** Errors **2** LOB

YANKEES – 1 **DODGERS – 1**

Third Inning - New York Yankees
– Rizzuto got to first on a free pass.
– McDonald sacrificed Rizzuto to second base, Campanella to Gilliam.
– Woodling moved Rizzuto up on a comebacker, Podres to Hodges.
– Collins safe at first as Rizzuto scored on Hodges' fielding error.
– Bauer plunked by a pitch; Collins moved to second base.
– Berra walked; bases loaded.
– Meyer relieved Podres.
– Mantle slammed the 4th grand slam in WS history into the left field deck, driving home Collins, Bauer and Berra.
– Martin singled through the box; thrown out trying to steal second base, Campanella to Gilliam.

5 Runs **2** Hits **1** Errors **0** LOB

YANKEES – 6 **DODGERS – 1**

Fifth Inning - Brooklyn Dodgers
– Meyers went down on strikes.
– Gilliam grazed by a pitch.
– Reese singled Gilliam to second base.

Snider singled up the middle, driving in Gilliam; Reese slid into second.

J. Robinson fouled out to Berra.

Campanella forced Snider at second base, Rizzuto to Martin.

1 Runs **2** Hits **0** Errors **2** LOB

YANKEES – 6   **DODGERS – 2**

Seventh Inning - New York Yankees

- Berra muscled a single into left field.
- Mantle advanced Berra on a ground out to Hodges.
- Martin boomed a home run into the left field deck, driving Berra home.
- McDougald nubbed out, Cox to Hodges.
- Rizzuto threaded a single into left field.
- McDonald doubled into left field, driving Rizzuto home.
- Woodling out on a grounder, Gilliam to Hodges.

3 Runs **4** Hits **0** Errors **1** LOB

YANKEES – 9   **DODGERS – 2**

Eighth Inning - New York Yankees

- Wade pitching.
- Collins rammed a rocket double off of the left field wall.
- Bauer sacrificed Collins to third base, Hodges to Gilliam.
- Berra lifted a sacrifice fly to Snider plating Collins.
- Mantle out on a ground ball, Gilliam to Hodges.

1 Runs **1** Hits **0** Errors **0** LOB

YANKEES – 10   **DODGERS – 2**

Eighth Inning - Brooklyn Dodgers

- Snider bounced out, Collins to McDonald (great stop).
- J. Robinson bashed a single into center field.
- Campanella singled J. Robinson to second base.
- Hodges was a strikeout.
- Furillo singled up the middle, driving in J. Robinson; Campanella slid into second base.

- Cox hammered a home run into the lower left field deck, driving home Campanella and Furillo.
- Shuba announced as a PH for Wade.
- Kuzava relieved McDonald.
- Williams PH for Shuba, struck out.

4 Runs **4** Hits **0** Errors **0** LOB

YANKEES – 10   **DODGERS – 6**

Ninth Inning - New York Yankees

- Black pitching.
- Mantle struck out.
- McDougald slugged a solo shot over the left field fence.
- Rizzuto popped up to Gilliam.
- Kuzava went down on strikes.

1 Runs **1** Hits **0** Errors **0** LOB

YANKEES – 11   **DODGERS – 6**

Ninth Inning - Brooklyn Dodgers

- Gilliam slugged a solo shot into the left field crowd.
- Reese flied out to Woodling.
- Snider singled past the right side of the mound.
- Reynolds relieved Kuzava.
- J. Robinson hit into a double play, Martin to Rizzuto to Collins.

1 Runs **2** Hits **0** Errors **0** LOB

YANKEES – 11   **DODGERS – 7**

HIGHLIGHTS

- Mantle drove in four runs
- Billy Martin (5) and Gil McDougald (6) combined to collect 11 total bases
- Every Dodgers hitter stroked at least one base hit
- Pinstripers mound staff did not issue a walk
- Brooklyn hit into three double plays, and the third ended the game

DIAMOND DUST

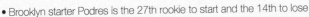

- Brooklyn starter Podres is the 27th rookie to start and the 14th to lose
- The teams set a record with a combined 46 total bases (Yankees 26/Dodgers 20)
- The game's six home runs (Bombers 4, Brooks 2) set a new record for most in one game
- New York Gene Woodling launched the fifth lead-off home run, the 250th in history
- Mantle's grand slam in the third was the fourth in World Series history
- Yankee Gil McDougald slugged a solo shot off of Joe Black, the second African American to appear in relief (Satchel Paige, 1948)

Game 5 BOX SCORE SUMMARY

NEW YORK YANKEES	AB	R	H	RBI	BB	K	1B	2B	3B	HR	TB	SB
GENE WOODLING, LF	3	1	1	1	2	0	0	0	0	1	4	0
JOE COLLINS, 1B	5	2	1	0	0	1	0	1	0	0	2	0
HANK BAUER, RF	3	1	0	0	0	1	0	0	0	0	0	0
YOGI BERRA, C	4	2	2	1	1	0	2	0	0	0	2	0
MICKEY MANTLE, CF	5	1	1	4	0	1	0	0	0	1	4	0
BILLY MARTIN, 2B	5	1	2	2	0	1	1	0	0	1	5	0
GIL MCDOUGALD, 3B	5	1	2	1	0	1	0	1	0	1	6	0
PHIL RIZZUTO, SS	3	2	1	0	2	0	1	0	0	0	1	1
JIM MCDONALD, P	2	1	1	0	1	1	0	1	0	0	2	0
BROOKLYN DODGERS	AB	R	H	RBI	BB	K	1B	2B	3B	HR	TB	SB
JUNIOR GILLIAM, 2B	4	2	2	1	0	0	1	0	0	1	5	0
DUKE SNIDER, CF	5	0	2	1	0	1	2	0	0	0	2	0
JACKIE ROBINSON, 2B	5	1	1	0	0	0	1	0	0	0	1	0
ROY CAMPANELLA, C	4	2	3	0	0	0	1	0	0	0	1	0
BILLY COX, 3B	4	1	1	3	0	0	0	0	0	1	4	0

NEW YORK YANKEES	IP	H	R	ER	HR	K	BB	HBP	ERA
JIM MCDONALD W (1-0)	7.2	12	6	5	1	3	0	1	5.87
BOB KUZAVA	0.1	2	1	1	1	1	0	0	13.50
ALLIE REYNOLDS S (1)	0.2	0	0	0	0	0	0	0	6.00
BROOKLYN DODGERS	IP	H	R	ER	HR	K	BB	HBP	ERA
JOHNNY PODRES L (0-1)	2.2	1	5	1	1	0	2	1	3.38
RUSS MEYER	4.1	8	4	3	2	5	4	0	6.23
BEN WADE	1	1	1	1	0	0	0	0	15.43
JOE BLACK	1	1	1	1	1	2	0	0	9.00

GAME TIME:	**3:02**
ATTENDANCE:	**36,775**
BEST OF 7:	**YANKEES - 3 DODGERS - 2**

Game 6

BROOKLYN DODGERS vs. NEW YORK YANKEES

October 6

LINE SCORE	1	2	3	4	5	6	7	8	9	R	H	E
BROOKLYN DODGERS	0	0	0	0	0	1	0	0	2	3	8	3
NEW YORK YANKEES	2	1	0	0	0	0	0	0	1	4	13	0

RECAP

Until the bottom of the ninth inning both teams had put together scoring drives producing three runs apiece. The Yankees scored their runs on a Yogi Berra RBI double, a Dodger fielding error and Gene Woodling sac fly. The Dodgers got on the board via a Roy Campanella RBI and a Carl Furillo two-run home run. In their last at-bat, the Pinstripers broke the 3-3 tie on a Hank Bauer walk, a Mickey Mantle single and a Billy Martin RBI, the 19th walk-off in World Series History. That final hit was Martin's twelfth of the Series, a record, as the Yankees wrapped up their fifth consecutive championship, another record.

SCORING SUMMARY

First Inning - New York Yankees
– Erskine starting.
– Woodling legged it to first on a walk
– Collins struck out.
– Bauer singled Woodling to second base.
– Berra bounced a ground rule double into the right field stands, driving in Woodling; Bauer awarded third base.
– Mantle walked; bases loaded.
– Martin sprinted to first base, Bauer scored, Berra and Mantle moved up on Gilliam's fielding error; bases loaded.
– McDougald banged into a double play, Cox to Gilliam to Hodges.

2 Runs **2** Hits **1** Errors **2** LOB
DODGERS – 0   **YANKEES – 2**

Second Inning - New York Yankees
– Rizzuto singled through the left side of the diamond.
– Ford smacked a hit-and-run single; Rizzuto landed at third base.
– Woodling hoisted a sacrifice fly to J. Robinson plating Rizzuto.
– Collins got to first base as Ford slid into second base on an infield single; both advanced on Erskine's throwing error.
– Bauer walked; bases loaded.
– Berra flied out to the warning track to Snider; Ford thrown out at the plate, Snider to Gilliam to Campanella

1 Runs **2** Hits **1** Errors **2** LOB
DODGERS – 0   **YANKEES – 3**

Sixth Inning - Brooklyn Dodgers
– Ford starting.
– Reese flied out to Mantle.
– J. Robinson doubled against the left field wall; swiped third base.
– Campanella scored J. Robinson on a grounder, Rizzuto to Collins.
– Hodges grounded out to Collins.

1 Runs **1** Hits **0** Errors **0** LOB
DODGERS – 1   **YANKEES – 3**

Ninth Inning - Brooklyn Dodgers
– Bollweg to 1B.
– Hodges flied out to Mantle.
– Snider trotted to first on a walk.
– Furillo clouted a home run into the right field seats, driving Snider home.
– Cox struck out.
– Labine went down in strikes.

2 Runs **1** Hits **0** Errors **0** LOB
DODGERS – 3   **YANKEES – 3**

Ninth Inning - New York Yankees
– Bauer got a free pass.
– Berra flied out to Furillo.
– Mantle singled Bauer to second base.
– Martin singled (12th hit, tied a record) Bauer home with the winning run.

1 Runs **2** Hits **0** Errors **2** LOB
DODGERS – 3   **YANKEES – 4**

HIGHLIGHTS
- Twelfth six-game set
- SRO, including the 11th millionth fan, watched five pitchers give up a combined 21 base hits
- Carl Erskine, in third start, faced 15 Yankees over the first two innings
- Erskine, after walking the bases full in the first and second innings, was bailed out by the double play, limiting the damage
- Pinstripers hit into three double plays and had two runners thrown out at the plate

---

DIAMOND DUST

- Billy Martin is the sixth player to end a Fall Classic with a walk-off RBI
- Martin's game-winning single was his 12th hit of the Series, setting a new record
- Reynolds is the first pitcher to win two series-ending walk-offs (1949), both versus the Dodgers
- Brooklyn reliever Clem Labine is the second hurler (1906) to lose the first and the last games in a six-game set
- Labine is the third pitcher to lose a Series ending walk-off (1929/35)
- The Yankees are 5-1 while the Dodgers are 1-2 in walk-offs
- Allie Reynolds is the eighth pitcher to post consecutive decisions, is the second starter to win seven games, is the fifth pitcher to win consecutive clinchers, is the fifth pitcher to give up four home runs
- New York has defeated Brooklyn in five straight meetings

Game 6 BOX SCORE SUMMARY

BROOKLYN DODGERS	AB	R	H	RBI	BB	K	1B	2B	3B	HR	TB	SB
JACKIE ROBINSON, LF	4	1	2	0	0	0	1	1	0	0	3	1
ROY CAMPANELLA, C	4	0	1	1	0	0	1	0	0	0	1	0
DUKE SNIDER, CF	3	1	0	0	1	3	0	0	0	0	0	O
CARL FURILLO, RF	4	1	3	2	0	0	1	1	0	1	7	0
NEW YORK YANKEES	AB	R	H	RBI	BB	K	1B	2B	3B	HR	TB	SB
GENE WOODLING, LF	4	1	2	1	1	0	2	0	0	0	2	0
HANK BAUER, RF	3	2	1	0	2	0	1	0	0	0	1	0
YOGI BERRA, C	5	0	2	1	0	0	1	1	0	0	3	0
BILLY MARTIN, 2B	5	0	2	2	0	0	1	1	0	0	3	0
PHIL RIZZUTO, SS	4	1	2	0	0	0	2	0	0	0	2	0

BROOKLYN DODGERS	IP	H	R	ER	HR	K	BB	HBP	ERA
CARL ERSKINE	4	6	3	3	0	1	3	0	5.79
BOB MILLIKEN	2	2	0	0	0	0	1	0	0.00
CLEM LABINE L (0-2)	2.1	5	1	1	0	1	1	0	3.60
NEW YORK YANKEES	IP	H	R	ER	HR	K	BB	HBP	ERA
WHITEY FORD	7	6	1	1	0	7	1	0	4.50
ALLIE REYNOLDS W (1-0)	2	2	2	2	1	3	1	0	6.76

Billy Martin, Hank Bauer, and Mickey Mantle collected 20 World Series rings between them, 18 as Yankees players, along with one each for Martin and Bauer as managers.

(National Baseball Hall of Fame and Museum)

Eight players were on all five Yankees' consecutive championship teams, 1949-1953: Hank Bauer, Yogi Berra, Eddie Lopat, Johnny Mize, Vic Raschi, Allie Reynolds, Phil Rizzuto, and Gene Woodling. Woodling led the AL in OBA in 1953 with a .429 mark. That year, he drew 82 bases on balls and struck out just 29 times. Woodling played for several teams after leaving the Yankees in 1955, and was one of the few productive batters on the infamous 1962 Mets team, where he closed out his career at age 39 playing part-time for Casey Stengel, batting .274 in 190 at-bats.

GAME TIME:	**2:55**
ATTENDANCE:	**62,370**
BEST OF 7:	**YANKEES - 4 DODGERS - 2**

1953

BROOKLYN DODGERS vs. NEW YORK YANKEES

BROOKLYN DODGERS

Overall World Series Record: 0 WINS 7 LOSSES. 42 Games Played (13 - 29 .310)

- Roy Campanella scored six runs to lead the team.
- PH George Shuba in first and only at-bat slugged a solo home run.
- Robinson did not strikeout.
- Pee Wee Reese did not score nor drive in a run.
- Chuck Dressen is the fourth manager to lose consecutive appearances.
- Fourth team to lose in consecutive Series appearances, (all from New York).
- The Dodgers are the fourth team to lose 2 consecutive Subway Series matchups (Yankees 1921-1922, Giants 1923-1924, Giants 1936-1937).

NEW YORK YANKEES

Overall World Series Record: 16 WINS 4 LOSSES. TOTAL GAMES PLAYED: 107 [71 - 35 (1 tie) .670].

- Reynolds is the first pitcher to win at least one game in six different World Series (1947/49/50/51/52/53).
- Reynolds career record is seven wins, two losses and four saves.
- Vic Raschi lost the final game of his Yankees career, one that produced five wins versus three losses in the World Series.
- Eddie Lopat won the fourth and final game of his World Series career, against only one loss.
- Billy Martin, batted .500, stroked 12 base hits and smacked a hit in all six games.
- Martin hit for the cycle while compiling 23 total bases.
- Martin drove in eight runs to lead the team.
- Hank Bauer scored six runs to lead the team.
- First time any franchise in any sport won five titles under the same manager or coach, let alone consecutively.

FUNGOES

- 13 players hammered 17 home runs (Yankees 9 - Dodgers 8) to set the record.
- The AL now leads the overall World Series standings 33-17.

SIX-GAME DATA

TIME	**17:35**	PLAYERS POOL	**$691,342**
ATTENDANCE	**307,350**	SHARES	**BROOKLYN DODGERS - $6,178**
			NEW YORK YANKEES - $8,281

1953

BROOKLYN DODGERS vs. NEW YORK YANKEES

Brooklyn Dodgers Composite Stats

BATTING	G	AB	R	H	RBI	2B	3B	HR	BB	SO	BA	OBP	SLG	OPS
Jim Gilliam	6	27	4	8	4	3	0	2	0	2	.296	.321	.630	.951
Duke Snider	6	25	3	8	5	3	0	1	2	6	.320	.370	.560	.930
Jackie Robinson	6	25	3	8	2	2	0	0	1	0	.320	.346	.400	.746
Pee Wee Reese	6	24	0	5	0	0	1	0	4	1	.208	.321	.292	.613
Carl Furillo	6	24	4	8	4	2	0	1	1	3	.333	.360	.542	.902
Billy Cox	6	23	3	7	6	3	0	1	1	4	.304	.333	.565	.899
Gil Hodges	6	22	3	8	1	0	0	1	3	3	.364	.440	.500	.940
Roy Campanella	6	22	6	6	2	0	0	1	2	3	.273	.360	.409	.769
Carl Erskine	3	4	0	1	0	0	0	0	0	1	.250	.250	.250	.500
Billy Loes	1	3	0	2	0	0	0	0	0	0	.667	.667	.667	1.333
Preacher Roe	1	3	0	0	0	0	0	0	0	2	.000	.000	.000	.000
Dick Williams	3	2	0	1	0	0	0	0	1	1	.500	.667	.500	1.167
Wayne Belardi	2	2	0	0	0	0	0	0	0	1	.000	.000	.000	.000
Clem Labine	3	2	0	0	0	0	0	0	0	1	.000	.000	.000	.000
Jim Hughes	1	1	0	0	0	0	0	0	0	1	.000	.000	.000	.000
Russ Meyer	1	1	0	0	0	0	0	0	0	1	.000	.000	.000	.000
Bobby Morgan	1	1	0	0	0	0	0	0	0	0	.000	.000	.000	.000
Johnny Podres	1	1	0	1	0	0	0	0	0	0	1.000	1.000	1.000	2.000
George Shuba	2	1	1	1	2	0	0	1	0	0	1.000	1.000	4.000	5.000
Joe Black	1	0	0	0	0	0	0	0	0	0				
Bob Milliken	1	0	0	0	0	0	0	0	0	0				
Don Thompson	2	0	0	0	0	0	0	0	0	0				
Ben Wade	2	0	0	0	0	0	0	0	0	0				
Totals	6	213	27	64	26	13	1	8	15	30	.300	.352	.484	.836

PITCHING	G	GS	ERA	W	L	SV	CG	IP	H	R	ER	BB	SO	WHIP
Carl Erskine	3	3	5.79	1	0	0	1	14.0	14	9	9	9	16	1.643
Billy Loes	1	1	3.38	1	0	0	0	8.0	8	3	3	2	8	1.250
Preacher Roe	1	1	4.50	0	1	0	1	8.0	5	4	4	4	4	1.125
Clem Labine	3	0	3.60	0	2	1	0	5.0	10	2	2	1	3	2.200
Russ Meyer	1	0	6.23	0	0	0	0	4.1	8	4	3	4	5	2.769
Jim Hughes	1	0	2.25	0	0	0	0	4.0	3	1	1	1	3	1.000
Johnny Podres	1	1	3.38	0	1	0	0	2.2	1	5	1	2	0	1.125
Ben Wade	2	0	15.43	0	0	0	0	2.1	4	4	4	1	2	2.143
Bob Milliken	1	0	0.00	0	0	0	0	2.0	2	0	0	1	0	1.500
Joe Black	1	0	9.00	0	0	0	0	1.0	1	1	1	0	2	1.000
Totals	6	6	4.91	2	4	1	2	51.1	56	33	28	25	43	1.578

1953

BROOKLYN DODGERS vs. NEW YORK YANKEES

New York Yankees Composite Stats

BATTING	G	AB	R	H	RBI	2B	3B	HR	BB	SO	BA	OBP	SLG	OPS
Joe Collins	6	24	4	4	2	1	0	1	3	8	.167	.259	.333	.593
Mickey Mantle	6	24	3	5	7	0	0	2	3	8	.208	.296	.458	.755
Billy Martin	6	24	5	12	8	1	2	2	1	2	.500	.520	.958	1.478
Gil McDougald	6	24	2	4	4	0	1	2	1	3	.167	.231	.500	.731
Hank Bauer	6	23	6	6	1	0	1	0	2	4	.261	.346	.348	.694
Yogi Berra	6	21	3	9	4	1	0	1	3	3	.429	.538	.619	1.158
Gene Woodling	6	20	5	6	3	0	0	1	6	2	.300	.462	.450	.912
Phil Rizzuto	6	19	4	6	0	1	0	0	3	2	.316	.409	.368	.778
Whitey Ford	2	3	0	1	0	0	0	0	0	0	.333	.333	.333	.667
Eddie Lopat	1	3	0	0	0	0	0	0	0	2	.000	.000	.000	.000
Johnny Mize	3	3	0	0	0	0	0	0	0	1	.000	.000	.000	.000
Jim McDonald	1	2	0	1	1	1	0	0	1	1	.500	.667	1.000	1.667
Allie Reynolds	3	2	0	1	0	0	0	0	1	1	.500	.667	.500	1.167
Don Bollweg	3	2	0	0	0	0	0	0	0	2	.000	.000	.000	.000
Vic Raschi	1	2	0	0	0	0	0	0	0	1	.000	.000	.000	.000
Johnny Sain	2	2	1	1	2	1	0	0	0	1	.500	.500	1.000	1.500
Irv Noren	2	1	0	0	0	0	0	0	1	0	.000	.500	.000	.500
Tom Gorman	1	1	0	0	0	0	0	0	0	1	.000	.000	.000	.000
Bob Kuzava	1	1	0	0	0	0	0	0	0	1	.000	.000	.000	.000
Art Schallock	1	0	0	0	0	0	0	0	0	0				
Totals	**6**	**201**	**33**	**56**	**32**	**6**	**4**	**9**	**25**	**43**	**.279**	**.370**	**.483**	**.852**

PITCHING	G	GS	ERA	W	L	SV	CG	IP	H	R	ER	BB	SO	WHIP
Eddie Lopat	1	1	2.00	1	0	0	1	9.0	9	2	2	4	3	1.444
Allie Reynolds	3	1	6.75	1	0	1	0	8.0	9	6	6	4	9	1.625
Whitey Ford	2	2	4.50	0	1	0	0	8.0	9	4	4	2	7	1.375
Vic Raschi	1	1	3.38	0	1	0	1	8.0	9	3	3	3	4	1.500
Jim McDonald	1	1	5.87	1	0	0	0	7.2	12	6	5	0	3	1.565
Johnny Sain	2	0	4.76	1	0	0	0	5.2	8	3	3	1	1	1.588
Tom Gorman	1	0	3.00	0	0	0	0	3.0	4	1	1	0	1	1.333
Art Schallock	1	0	4.50	0	0	0	0	2.0	2	1	1	1	1	1.500
Bob Kuzava	1	0	13.50	0	0	0	0	0.2	2	1	1	0	1	3.000
Totals	**6**	**6**	**4.50**	**4**	**2**	**1**	**2**	**52.0**	**64**	**27**	**26**	**15**	**30**	**1.519**

BROOKLYN DODGERS vs. NEW YORK YANKEES

FUNGOES

- Subway Series is the sixth meeting between the two clubs. Pee Wee Reese and Phil Rizzuto have played in all of them.
- Both teams are in first place at the All-Star break.
- No travel days.
- NBC televised the Series in color for the first time.
- Umpire data: Lee Ballanfant is a WWI US Army veteran who taught marksmanship, a former minor league infielder and play-ing manager; became a major league scout; inducted into both the Texas Baseball Hall of Fame (1980) and posthumously into both the Texas Sports Hall of Fame and the Texas League Hall of Fame. Augie Donatelli played SS for 14 years in the minor leagues; served in the US Army during WWII; as a tail-gunner was shot down during a mission and spent 15 months as a POW. Jim Honochick served in the US Navy during WWII. Bill Summers is a former boxer, mill worker and road worker; umpired in high school, semi-pro and industrial league games.

SERIES SUMMARY

1955 marked the seventh consecutive season in which a New York team reached the Fall Classic, and it proved to be the first and only time the Brooklyn franchise claimed victory. It was far from easy, though, requiring the full seven games to vanquish the mighty Yankees.

Game 1 was a nail-biter that saw the Yankees build a 6-3 lead only to have the Dodgers cut the lead to one in the eighth, their final run coming on a steal of home by Jackie Robinson. Joe Collins was the Yankees' offensive hero, belting two home runs that accounted for three of the runs.

Tommy Byrne led the way for the Yankees in Game 2, hurling a complete-game five-hitter and driving in runs three and four with a two-out single in the fifth. Brooklyn was grateful to be heading home, but must have been concerned about their chances to take the series.

Johnny Podres, who had been a mediocre 9-10 on the season, and a strong offense, allowed the Dodgers to relax a bit as they cruised to an 8-3 victory in Game 3. Three two-run innings of the first four gave them a solid lead they would not relinquish. Roy Campanella collected three hits and three RBI.

Campanella came back with three more hits and another home run in Game 5 as the Dodgers put up another eight-spot and an

8-5 victory in Game 4. Gil Hodges also had three hits, and he and Duke Snider each had three RBI. Suddenly, momentum was on Brooklyn's side.

That momentum carried through to the next day when the Dodgers won their third in a row, a tight 5-3 contest. Roger Craig got the win and Clem Labine had a three-inning save. Snider had three hits, including a homer, while Yogi Berra's home run in the eighth inning brought the Yankees to within one run.

The Yankees made it clear right off the bat that there was no quit in them as they jumped all over sometimes-starter Carl Spooner for five runs in the first and New York coasted to a 5-1 victory behind Whitey Ford. Bill Skowron's 3-run blast was the big blow of the game, while the Dodgers managed on four hits in the entire game off Ford. Yet another Game 7 was on tap for the crosstown rivals.

Twenty-two-year-old Johnny Podres made his second start and earned his second complete-game victory, a 2-0 shutout of the Yankees, in the most important win in the history of the Brooklyn franchise. Gil Hodges drove in both runs, on a single and a sac fly, and Sandy Amoros, who had just entered the game, robbed Yogi Berra of extra bases and doubled a runner off first to end the Yankees' rally in the sixth

---

THE TEAMS

BROOKLYN DODGERS
98 – 55 .641 +13.5 G

The Team
- Subway Series #6, 8th overall appearance.
- Third wire-to-wire team to appear (1923 Giants/1927 Yankees).
- Clinched pennant on September 8 and won by 13.5 games, .5 better than 1953.

The Players
- 1953 Subway Series returning players (13) - Roy Campanella, Carl Erskine, Carl Furillo, Jim Gilliam, Gil Hodges, Clem Labine, Billy Loes, Russ Meyer, Johnny Podres, Pee Wee Reese, Jackie Robinson, George Shuba and Duke Snider.
- Reese played on the 1941/47/49//52/53 pennant-winning teams.
- Furillo, Hodges and Robinson played on the 1947/49/52/53 pennant-winning teams.
- Newcombe is the first African-American pitcher to win 20 games.
- Roy Campanella won the MVP award for the third time (1951/53).
- Campanella batted .318 and drove in 107 runs.
- Snider is the ninth 40-home run hitter (42) to appear. He also led the National League in runs scored (126) and RBI (136).

The Manager
- Walt Alston is the 44th manager to debut.
- Alston is the sixth skipper to debut in the Subway Series (1921/1941/1947/1949/1952).
- Alston, as a 1936 St. Louis Cardinals, struck out in his only at-bat in the only game of his playing career.

Top Batters

Pos	Name	AB	R	H	HR	RBI	BA	OPS
C	Roy Campanella	446	81	142	32	107	.318	.978
SS	Pee Wee Reese	553	99	156	10	61	.282	.774
CF	Duke Snider	538	126	166	42	136	.309	1.046
RF	Carl Furillo	523	83	164	26	95	.314	.891

Top Pitchers

Pos	Name	W	L	ERA	G	SV	IP	SO
St	Don Newcombe	20	5	3.20	34	0	233.2	143
St	Carl Erskine	11	8	3.79	31	1	194.2	84
St	Johnny Podres	9	10	3.95	27	0	159.1	114
St	Billy Loes	10	4	3.59	22	0	128.0	85
Rel	Clem Labine	13	5	3.24	60	11	144.1	67

NEW YORK YANKEES
94 – 60 .610 +1.0 G

The Team
- Subway Series #12, 21st overall appearance.

The Players
- 1953 Subway Series returning players (9): Hank Bauer, Yogi Berra, Joe Collins, Whitey Ford, Mickey Mantle, Billy Martin, Gil McDougald, Irv Noren, and Phil Rizzuto.
- Rizzuto played on the 1941/42/47/49/50/51/52/53 pennant-winning teams, winning seven titles.
- Berra played on the 1947/49/50/51/52/53 six title-winning teams.
- Bauer played on the 1949/50/51/52/53 five straight title-winning teams.
- Collins played on the 1950/51/52/53 title-winning teams.
- Mantle, Martin and McDougald played on the 1951/52/53 title-winning team.
- Yogi Berra won the MVP award for the third time (1951/54).
- Mantle led the American League in home runs (37).

The Manager
- Stengel tied Miller Huggins with the most pennants won by a Yankee manager (6).

Top Batters

Pos	Name	AB	R	H	HR	RBI	BA	OPS
C	Yogi Berra	541	84	147	27	108	.272	.819
2B	Gil McDougald	533	79	152	13	53	.285	.768
CF	Mickey Mantle	517	121	158	37	99	.306	1.042
RF	Hank Bauer	492	97	137	20	53	.278	.821

Top Pitchers

Pos	Name	W	L	ERA	G	SV	IP	SO
St	Whitey Ford	18	7	2.63	39	2	253.2	137
St	Bob Turley	17	13	3.06	36	1	246.2	210
St	Tommy Byrne	16	5	3.15	27	2	160.0	76
Rel	Jim Konstanty	7	2	2.32	45	12	73.2	19

Game 1

BROOKLYN DODGERS vs. NEW YORK YANKEES

September 28

LINE SCORE	1	2	3	4	5	6	7	8	9	R	H	E
BROOKLYN DODGERS	0	2	1	0	0	0	0	2	0	5	10	0
NEW YORK YANKEES	0	2	1	1	0	2	0	0	X	6	9	1

RECAP

Nineteen base hits in the game, with only a one-run differential. Five home runs accounted for seven of the 11 tallies. In between, CF Irv Noren grounded into two double plays and 2B Billy Martin was caught stealing twice, diffusing four Yankee rallies. The Yankees still won.

The first four-bagger, slugged by RF Carl Furillo, gave the Dodgers the lead. The second, a two-run clout off of the bat of Elston Howard, tied the score. The third, a Duke Snider solo shot, gave the Dodgers the lead again. The fourth and fifth, hammered by Joe Collins, put the Bombers in the lead for good.

SCORING SUMMARY

Second Inning - Brooklyn Dodgers

– Ford starting.
– Furillo slugged a solo shot into the right field seats.
– Hodges out on a grounder, Martin to Collins.
– J. Robinson torched a triple to the left-center field wall.
– Zimmer singled up the middle, driving J. Robinson home.
– Newcombe bounced out to the box, Ford to Collins.
– Gilliam walked Zimmer to second base.
– Reese forced Gilliam at second base, McDougald to Martin.

2 Runs **3** Hits **0** Errors **2** LOB

DODGERS – 2   **YANKEES – 0**

Second Inning - New York Yankees

– Newcombe starting.
– Berra rolled out, Zimmer to Hodges.
– Collins drew a free pass.
– Howard clocked a home run into the left field seats, driving Collins home.
– Martin flied out to Furillo.
– Rizzuto dribbled out, J. Robinson to Hodges.

2 Runs **1** Hits **0** Errors **0** LOB

DODGERS – 2   **YANKEES – 2**

Third Inning - Brooklyn Dodgers

– Snider slugged a solo shot into the upper right field deck.
– Campanella popped up to McDougald.
– Furillo finagled a walk.
– Hodges flied out to Noren.
– J. Robinson struck out.

1 Runs **1** Hits **0** Errors **1** LOB

DODGERS – 3   **YANKEES – 2**

Third Inning - New York Yankees

– Ford jogged to first on a free pass.
– Bauer singled Ford to second base.
– McDougald advanced both runners on a ground out, Reese to Hodges.
– Noren scored Ford on a grounder, Zimmer to Hodges; Bauer took third.
– Berra thrown out on a comebacker, Ford to Collins.

1 Runs **1** Hits **0** Errors **1** LOB

DODGERS – 3   **YANKEES – 3**

Fourth Inning - New York Yankees

– Collins slugged a solo shot into the right field seats.
– Howard struck out.

– Martin hummed a single into left field; caught trying to steal second base, Campanella to Reese.
– Rizzuto struck out.

1 Runs **2** Hits **0** Errors **0** LOB

DODGERS – 3　　　**YANKEES – 4**

Sixth Inning - New York Yankees

– Noren out on a ground ball to Collins.
– Berra mustered a single into right field.
– Collins clobbered a home run into right field, driving Berra home.
– Howard tapped out, Reese to Hodges.
– Martin torqued a triple into deepest left field.
– Bessent relieved Newcombe.
– E. Robinson PH for Rizzuto; Martin nabbed trying to steal home plate, Bessent to Campanella.

2 Runs **3** Hits **0** Errors **0** LOB

DODGERS – 3　　　**YANKEES – 6**

Eighth Inning - Brooklyn Dodgers

– Furillo ripped a single into center field.
– Hodges flied out to Howard.

– J. Robinson sprinted into second base as Furillo braked at third base on McDougald's fielding error.
– Zimmer lifted a sacrifice fly to Noren plating Furillo; J. Robinson slid into third base.
– Robinson swiped home plate.
– Kellert PH for Bessent, singled through the right side of the diamond.
– Gilliam popped up to McDougald.

2 Runs **3** Hits **1** Errors **1** LOB

DODGERS – 5　　　**YANKEES – 6**

HIGHLIGHTS

- Collins knocked in three and scored three
- RF Carl Furillo stroked a hit in first three at-bats, collecting six total bases
- Billy Martin caught stealing twice - in the fourth inning at second base and in the sixth inning at home plate
- Dodger 3B Jackie Robinson, in the eighth inning, steals home on a controversial call

DIAMOND DUST

- C Elston Howard is the seventh player to homer in first at-bat, the fifth in a Game One
- 1B Joe Collins is the 12th player to homer twice in the same game (1953), the first in a Game One, and the second time he did it.
- Don Newcombe is the fourth starter to allow three home runs in a game and the second to do so in an opener (1953)
- Robinson is the fourth player to steal home plate in an opener, the 12th overall
- New York is 16-5 in openers while the Dodgers are 1-7

Game 1 BOX SCORE SUMMARY

BROOKLYN DODGERS	AB	R	H	RBI	BB	K	1B	2B	3B	HR	TB	SB
DUKE SNIDER, CF	5	1	2	1	0	1	1	0	0	1	5	0
CARL FURILLO, RF	4	2	3	1	1	1	2	0	0	1	6	0
JACKIE ROBINSON, 3B	4	2	1	0	0	1	0	0	1	0	3	1
DON ZIMMER, 2B	2	0	1	2	1	0	1	0	0	0	1	0
NEW YORK YANKEES	AB	R	H	RBI	BB	K	1B	2B	3B	HR	TB	SB
IRV NOREN, CF	4	0	0	1	0	0	0	0	0	0	0	0
YOGI BERRA, C	3	1	1	0	1	0	1	0	0	0	1	0
JOE COLLINS, 1B	3	3	2	3	1	0	0	0	0	2	8	0
ELSTON HOWARD, LF	3	1	1	2	0	1	0	0	0	1	4	0
WHITEY FORD, P	2	1	0	0	1	1	0	0	0	0	0	0

BROOKLYN DODGERS	IP	H	R	ER	HR	K	BB	HBP	ERA
DON NEWCOMBE L (0-1)	5.2	8	6	6	3	4	2	0	9.53
DON BESSENT	1.1	0	0	0	0	0	0	0	0.00
NEW YORK YANKEES	IP	H	R	ER	HR	K	BB	HBP	ERA
WHITEY FORD W (1-0)	8	9	5	3	2	2	4	0	3.38
BOB GRIM S (1)	1	1	0	0	0	2	0	0	0.00

GAME TIME:	2:31
ATTENDANCE:	63,869
BEST OF 7:	**DODGERS - 0 YANKEES - 1**

BROOKLYN DODGERS vs. NEW YORK YANKEES

September 29

LINE SCORE	1	2	3	4	5	6	7	8	9	R	H	E
BROOKLYN DODGERS	0	0	0	1	1	0	0	0	0	2	5	2
NEW YORK YANKEES	0	0	0	4	0	0	0	0	X	4	8	0

RECAP

Zero home runs but more double plays. Six this time, three for each team, took the punch out of scoring drives in the first, third, fourth, fifth, seventh and eighth innings. Also, keeping the score low were the 11 Bombers who struck out, five as the last out. On the strength of five singles, a walk and a hit batter the Yankees scored the four runs they needed. Driving in two of those tallies, New York starter Tommy Byrne, also held the Dodgers to five hits and two runs. The American League champs were up by two.

SCORING SUMMARY

Fourth Inning - Brooklyn Dodgers
– Byrne starting.
– Reese laced a double into left field.
– Snider singled into right field, driving in Reese; thrown out at second base, Howard to Rizzuto.
– Campanella reached on a walk.
– Furillo flied out to Noren.
– Hodges flied out to Noren.

1 Runs **2** Hits **0** Errors **1** LOB

DODGERS – 1   **YANKEES – 0**

Fourth Inning - New York Yankees
– ·Loes starting
– McDougald scalded a single into right field.
– Noren knocked into a double play, Hodges to Reese.
– Berra spun a single into left field.
– Collins walked Berra to second base.
– Howard singled into left field, driving in Berra; Collins advanced.
– Martin singled into left field, driving in Collins; Howard slid into second.
– E. Robinson PH for Rizzuto, hit by a pitch; bases loaded.
– J. Coleman PR for E. Robinson.
– Byrne singled up the middle, driving in Howard and Martin; Coleman slid into second base.
– Bessent relieved Loes.
– Cerv out on a grounder, Zimmer to Hodges.

4 Runs **5** Hits **0** Errors **2** LOB

DODGERS – 1   **YANKEES – 4**

Fifth Inning - Brooklyn Dodgers
– J. Coleman to SS.
– J. Robinson managed a walk.
– Zimmer singled J. Robinson to second base.
– Kellert PH for Bessent, hit into a double play, J. Coleman to Martin to Collins.
– J. Robinson took third base.
– Gilliam singled into left field, driving home J. Robinson.
– Reese struck out.

1 Runs **1** Hits **0** Errors **1** LOB

DODGERS – 2   **YANKEES – 4**

HIGHLIGHTS

- Yogi Berra, in the second inning, was hit by a pitch for the third time in his World Series career
- CF Irv Noren has hit into three double plays over the two games
- Teams hit into a total of six double plays (3 each), tying the combined record (Philadelphia A's vs. Boston Braves, 1914)
- 3B Gil McDougald fanned three times
- Yankee starter Tommy Byrne drove in two runs

DIAMOND DUST

Game 2 BOX SCORE SUMMARY

BROOKLYN DODGERS	AB	R	H	RBI	BB	K	1B	2B	3B	HR	TB	SB
JUNIOR GILLIAM, LF	4	0	1	1	0	1	1	0	0	0	1	0
PEE WEE REESE, SS	4	1	2	0	0	1	1	1	0	0	3	0
DUKE SNIDER, CF	4	0	1	1	0	1	1	0	0	0	1	0
JACKIE ROBINSON, 3B	2	1	0	0	1	0	0	0	0	0	0	0
NEW YORK YANKEES	AB	R	H	RBI	BB	K	1B	2B	3B	HR	TB	SB
YOGI BERRA, C	3	1	2	0	0	1	2	0	0	0	2	0
JOE COLLINS, 1B	3	1	0	0	1	2	0	0	0	0	0	0
ELSTON HOWARD, LF/RF	4	1	1	1	0	1	1	0	0	0	1	0
BILLY MARTIN, 2B	3	1	1	1	0	2	1	0	0	0	1	0
TOMMY BYRNE, P	3	0	1	2	0	0	1	0	0	0	1	0

BROOKLYN DODGERS	IP	H	R	ER	HR	K	BB	HBP	ERA
BILLY LOES L (0-1)	3.2	7	4	4	0	5	1	0	9.82
NEW YORK YANKEES	IP	H	R	ER	HR	K	BB	HBP	ERA
TOMMY BYRNE W (1-0)	9	5	2	2	0	6	5	0	2.00

(National Baseball Hall of Fame and Museum)

Tommy Byrne's CG victory was the only win of his World Series career, which included a total of 6 games and 3 starts. Byrne benefited greatly from playing for the Yankees, finishing his career at 72-40 for New York and a combined 13-29 for 3 other teams. Poor control plagued Byrne, as he exceeded 100 BB in a season 6 times, leading the league 3 straight years with incredible totals of 179/160/150 in only 196.0/203.1/143.2 innings per season, respectively.

GAME TIME:	**2:28**
ATTENDANCE:	**64,707**
BEST OF 7:	**DODGERS - 0 YANKEES - 2**

NEW YORK YANKEES vs. BROOKLYN DODGERS

September 30

LINE SCORE	1	2	3	4	5	6	7	8	9	R	H	E
NEW YORK YANKEES	0	2	0	0	0	0	1	0	0	3	7	0
BROOKLYN DODGERS	2	2	0	2	0	0	2	0	X	8	11	1

RECAP

On his 23rd birthday, Dodger starter Johnny Podres crafted a seven-hit, three-run complete game. As a birthday gift, Brooklyn batters peppered four Yankee pitchers for 11 hits and eight runs. Two of those runs came home on bases loaded walks, allowed by Bob Turley and Tom Morgan to consecutive batters.

Every Brooklynite in the line-up except Gil Hodges spiked a hit. Only Hodges and Carl Furillo did not cross the plate. C Roy Campanella had a particularly good day with the bat, driving in three teammates. 3B Jackie Robinson had a two-hit day. Robinson and SS Pee Wee Reese drove in two. The Dodgers' losing streak was stopped at two.

SCORING SUMMARY

First Inning - Brooklyn Dodgers
– Turley starting.
– Gilliam flied out to Mantle.
– Reese reached first on a free pass.
– Snider struck out.
– Campanella powered a home run into the left field seats, driving Reese home.
– Furillo flied out to Mantle.

2 Runs **1** Hits **0** Errors **0** LOB

YANKEES – 0   **DODGERS - 2**

Second Inning - New York Yankees
– Podres starting.
– Mantle slugged a solo shot into the center field seats.
– Skowron pounded a double into left field.
– Howard grounded out, J. Robinson to Hodges.
– Martin was a strikeout.
– Rizzuto singled home Skowron who collided with Campanella; Rizzuto took third base.
– Turley bounced out, J. Robinson to Hodges.

2 Runs **3** Hits **0** Errors **1** LOB

YANKEES – 2   **DODGERS - 2**

Second Inning - Brooklyn Dodgers
– Mantle to RF. Cerv to CF. Howard to LF.
– Hodges flied out to Cerv.
– J. Robinson scratched a single into center field.
– Amoros grazed by a pitch; J. Robinson trotted to second base.
– Podres hustled across first base on a very close play; bases loaded.
– Gilliam walked; J. Robinson scored; bases loaded.
– Morgan relieved Turley.
– Reese walked; Amoros scored; bases loaded.
– Snider forced Podres at the plate, Skowron to Berra; bases loaded.
– Campanella zapped out to Martin.

2 Runs **2** Hits **0** Errors **3** LOB

YANKEES – 2   **DODGERS - 4**

Fourth Inning - Brooklyn Dodgers
– Gilliam stroked a single into left field.
– Reese flied out to Cerv.
– Snider walked Gilliam to second base.
– Campanella singled into left field, driving in Gilliam; Snider raced to third.

– Furillo lifted a sacrifice foul fly to Howard plating Snider; Campanella slid into second base on the throw to the plate.
– Hodges tapped out, Rizzuto to Skowron.

2 Runs **2** Hits **0** Errors **1** LOB

YANKEES – 2 **DODGERS - 6**

Seventh Inning - New York Yankees

– Howard hoisted a high warning track out to Amoros.
– Martin nubbed out, J. Robinson to Hodges.
– Rizzuto legged it to first base on a walk.
– Carey PH for Kucks, tripled to the left field wall, driving Rizzuto home.
– Cerv was a strikeout.

1 Runs **1** Hits **0** Errors **1** LOB

YANKEES – 3 **DODGERS - 6**

Seventh Inning - Brooklyn Dodgers

– Sturdivant pitching.
– Hodges lost a home run on a stretching catch by Howard.

– J. Robinson looped a double into left field; slid into third base on the throw to second.
– Amoros singled into left field, driving J. Robinson home.
– Podres forced Amoros at second base, Sturdivant to Rizzuto.
– Gilliam walked Podres to second base.
– Reese singled up the middle, driving in Podres; Gilliam sprinted into third.
– Snider flied out to Howard.

2 Runs **3** Hits **0** Errors **2** LOB

YANKEES – 3 **DODGERS - 8**

HIGHLIGHTS

- Brooklyn's Johnny Podres is the 13th pitcher with a losing regular season record (9-10) to start and the sixth to win
- Yankee hurlers Bob Turley and Tom Morgan are the second set of pitchers to issue bases loaded walks in the same inning
- Yankee LF/CF Bob Cerv struck out in three straight at-bats, twice to end an inning

DIAMOND DUST

- Mickey Mantle is the fifth player to homer in the Mid-Summer Classic and the Fall Classic in the same season
- Mantle's second inning blast is the 100th for the franchise in World Series History
- This is the last Fall Classic game ever played in September

Game 3 BOX SCORE SUMMARY

NEW YORK YANKEES	AB	R	H	RBI	BB	K	1B	2B	3B	HR	TB	SB
MICKEY MANTLE, CF/RF	4	1	1	1	0	0	0	0	0	1	4	0
BILL SKOWRON, 1B	4	1	2	0	0	1	1	1	0	0	3	0
PHIL RIZZUTO, SS	2	1	1	0	2	0	1	0	0	0	1	0
ANDY CAREY, PH	1	0	1	1	0	0	0	0	1	0	3	0
BROOKLYN DODGERS	AB	R	H	RBI	BB	K	1B	2B	3B	HR	TB	SB
JUNIOR GILLIAM, 2B	3	1	1	1	2	0	1	0	0	0	1	0
PEE WEE REESE, SS	3	1	1	2	2	0	1	0	0	0	1	0
DUKE SNIDER, CF	4	1	1	0	1	1	1	0	0	0	1	0
ROY CAMPANELLA, C	5	1	3	3	0	0	1	1	0	1	7	0
CARL FURILLO, RF	5	0	1	1	0	0	0	1	0	0	2	0
JACKIE ROBINSON, 3B	5	2	2	0	0	0	1	1	0	0	3	0
SANDY AMOROS, LF	1	1	1	1	2	0	1	0	0	0	1	0
JOHNNY PODRES, P	3	1	1	0	0	1	1	0	0	0	1	0

NEW YORK YANKEES	IP	H	R	ER	HR	K	BB	HBP	ERA
BOB TURLEY L (0-1)	1.1	3	4	4	1	1	2	1	27.00
TOM MORGAN	2.2	3	2	2	0	1	3	0	6.75
TOM STURDIVANT	2	4	2	2	0	0	1	0	9.00
BROOKLYN DODGERS	IP	H	R	ER	HR	K	BB	HBP	ERA
JOHNNY PODRES W (1-0)	9	7	3	2	1	6	2	0	2.25

GAME TIME: **2:20**
ATTENDANCE: **34,209**
BEST OF 7: **DODGERS - 1 YANKEES - 2**

NEW YORK YANKEES vs. BROOKLYN DODGERS

October 1

LINE SCORE	1	2	3	4	5	6	7	8	9	R	H	E
NEW YORK YANKEES	1	1	0	1	0	2	0	0	0	5	9	0
BROOKLYN DODGERS	0	0	1	3	3	0	1	0	X	8	14	0

--- **RECAP** ---

Of the 14 Dodgers' hits, both Roy Campanella and Gil Hodges stroked three each. Of the eight Dodgers' runs, Duke Snider and Hodges drove in three each. Of the four home runs, the one by the Bombers produced one run, while the three Brooklyn dingers produced six runs. Both mound staffs got knocked around. Runners crossed the plate in every inning except the final two. Clem Labine's four frames of relief sealed Brooklyn's victory and evened the Series at two apiece.

--- **SCORING SUMMARY** ---

First Inning - New York Yankees
– Erskine starting.
– Noren struck out.
– McDougald slugged a solo shot into the left field seats.
– Mantle struck out.
– Berra flied out to Snider.

1 Runs **1** Hits **0** Errors **0** LOB

YANKEES – 1   **DODGERS - 0**

Second Inning - New York Yankees
– Collins coaxed a free pass.
– Howard sacrificed Collins to second base, Erskine to Hodges.
– Martin moved Collins up on a grounder, Gilliam to Hodges.
– Rizzuto singled into left field, driving in Collins; swiped second base.
– Larsen flied out to Snider.

1 Runs **1** Hits **0** Errors **1** LOB

YANKEES – 2   **DODGERS - 0**

Third Inning - Brooklyn Dodgers
– Larsen starting.
– Amoros trotted to first on a walk.
– Erskine fouled out to Rizzuto.
– Gilliam doubled into left field, driving Amoros home.
– Reese flied out to Mantle.
– Snider out on a ground ball, Martin to Collins.

1 Runs **1** Hits **0** Errors **1** LOB

YANKEES – 2   **DODGERS - 1**

Fourth Inning - New York Yankees
– Berra whipped a single into center field.
– Collins walked Berra to second base.
– Bessent relieved Erskine.
– Howard forced Berra at third, Bessent to J. Robinson; Collins swiped third.
– Martin singled into right field, driving in Collins; Howard hustled to third.
– Rizzuto grounded into a double play, J. Robinson to Gilliam to Hodges.

1 Runs **2** Hits **0** Errors **1** LOB

YANKEES – 3   **DODGERS - 1**

Fourth Inning - Brooklyn Dodgers
– Campanella slugged a solo shot into the left field stands.
– Furillo hustled out a high-hopper past the mound.
– Hodges yanked a home run over the right-center field fence, driving Furillo home.
– J. Robinson tapped out, McDougald to Collins.
– Amoros rolled out to the box, Larsen to Collins.
– Bessent went down on strikes.

3 Runs **3** Hits **0** Errors **0** LOB

YANKEES – 3   **DODGERS - 4**

Fifth Inning - Brooklyn Dodgers

Gilliam hurried to first on a free pass; swiped second base.
Reese got to a 2-0 count; Kucks relieved Larsen; flew across first on a very close play; Gilliam stood at third.
Snider boomed a home run over the right field screen, driving home Gilliam and Reese.
Campanella clubbed a double into right field.
Furillo was a strikeout.
Hodges thrown out on a come-backer, Kucks to Collins; Campanella hustled into third base.
J. Robinson zapped out to McDougald.

3 Runs **3** Hits **0** Errors **1** LOB

YANKEES – 3 **DODGERS - 7**

Sixth Inning - New York Yankees

- Howard stroked a single into left field.
- Martin doubled into center field, driving Howard home.
- Rizzuto flied out to Hodges.
- E. Robinson PH for Kucks, singled into right field, driving Martin home.
- Carroll PR.
- Noren flied out to Snider.
- McDougald flied out to Snider.

2 Runs **3** Hits **0** Errors **1** LOB

YANKEES – 5 **DODGERS - 7**

Seventh Inning - Brooklyn Dodgers

– Campanella hacked a single into center field.
– Furillo smacked a hit-and-run single; Campanella charged into third.
– Hodges singled up the middle, driving in Campanella; Furillo slid into second.
– Morgan relieved R. Coleman.
– J. Robinson flied out to Noren.
– Amoros advanced both runners on a sacrifice, Martin to Collins.
– Labine bounded out, Rizzuto to Collins.

1 Runs **3** Hits **0** Errors **2** LOB

YANKEES – 5 **DODGERS - 8**

HIGHLIGHTS

- Roy Campanella was a triple shy of a cycle, racking up seven total bases
- Campanella has homered in consecutive games
- Gil Hodges chipped in with two singles and a home run for six total bases
- The three Brooklyn flingers gave up three hits each

DIAMOND DUST

- Campanella's homer is the 270th in history as well as the 25th for the franchise
- Campanella has two consecutive games with a single, double, and home run, good for 14 total bases in 10 at bats
- Yankees' reliever Rip Coleman faces eight batters and gives up five hits, but allows only one run in one official IP

Game 4 BOX SCORE SUMMARY

NEW YORK YANKEES	AB	R	H	RBI	BB	K	1B	2B	3B	HR	TB	SB
GIL MCDOUGALD, 3B	5	1	1	1	0	1	0	0	0	1	4	0
JOE COLLINS, 1B	2	2	0	0	2	0	0	0	0	0	0	1
ELSTON HOWARD, LF	3	1	1	0	0	0	1	0	0	0	1	0
BILLY MARTIN, 2B	4	1	2	2	0	0	1	1	0	0	3	0
PHIL RIZZUTO, SS	3	0	1	1	1	0	1	0	0	0	1	1
EDDIE ROBINSON, PH	1	0	1	1	0	0	1	0	0	0	1	0

BROOKLYN DODGERS	AB	R	H	RBI	BB	K	1B	2B	3B	HR	TB	SB
JUNIOR GILLIAM, 2B	4	1	2	1	1	0	1	1	0	0	3	1
PEE WEE REESE, SS	4	1	2	0	0	0	2	0	0	0	2	0
DUKE SNIDER, CF	4	1	1	3	1	0	0	0	0	1	4	0
ROY CAMPANELLA, C	5	2	3	1	0	0	1	1	0	1	7	0
CARL FURILLO, RF	5	1	3	0	0	0	2	0	0	0	2	0
GIL HODGES, 1B	4	1	3	3	0	0	2	0	0	1	6	0
SANDY AMOROS, LF	3	1	1	0	1	0	1	0	0	0	1	0

NEW YORK YANKEES	IP	H	R	ER	HR	K	BB	HBP	ERA
DON LARSEN L (0-1)	4	5	5	5	2	2	2	0	11.25
JOHNNY KUCKS	1	3	2	2	1	1	0	0	6.00
RIP COLEMAN	1	5	1	1	0	1	0	0	9.00

BROOKLYN DODGERS	IP	H	R	ER	HR	K	BB	HBP	ERA
CARL ERSKINE	3	3	3	3	1	3	2	0	9.00
CLEM LABINE W (1-0)	4.1	3	2	2	0	0	1	0	2.84

GAME TIME:	2:57	
ATTENDANCE:	36,242	
BEST OF 7:	DODGERS - 2	YANKEES - 2

NEW YORK YANKEES vs. BROOKLYN DODGERS

October 2

LINE SCORE	1	2	3	4	5	6	7	8	9	R	H	E
NEW YORK YANKEES	0	0	0	1	0	0	1	1	0	3	6	0
BROOKLYN DODGERS	0	2	1	0	1	0	0	1	X	5	9	2

RECAP

Power hitting, defense and pitching were how the Dodgers dominated this contest. Home runs, hammered by LF Sandy Amoros, plated the first two runs in the second inning, followed by CF Duke Snider's solos slugged in consecutive at-bats put the Dodgers ahead to stay. Double plays squashed three Yankee rallies; two grounded into by CF Irv Noren, giving him a total of five for the Series. Brooklyn mounders, rookie Roger Craig and reliever Clem Labine, held the Yankees to six hits and three runs. The National League champs had rebounded from two down to one up.

SCORING SUMMARY

Second Inning - Brooklyn Dodgers
– Grim starting.
– Furillo zapped out to McDougald.
– Hodges jammed a single into left field.
– J. Robinson lined out to Rizzuto.
– Amoros clouted a home run over the right field screen, driving Hodges home.
– Craig wangled a free pass.
– Gilliam smoked a hit-and-run single; Craig chugged into third base.
– Reese out on a ground ball, McDougald to E. Robinson.

2 Runs **3** Hits **0** Errors **2** LOB

YANKEES – 0　　　**DODGERS - 2**

Third Inning - Brooklyn Dodgers
– Snider slugged a solo shot over the right field screen.
– Campanella flied out to Noren.
– Furillo fanned.
– Hodges struck out.

1 Runs **1** Hits **0** Errors **0** LOB

YANKEES – 0　　　**DODGERS - 3**

Fourth Inning - New York Yankees
– Craig starting.

– Berra bounced a single off of the right field scoreboard.
– Collins struck out.
– E. Robinson walked Berra to second base.
– Martin singled into left field, driving in Berra; E. Robinson moved up.
– Skowron PH for Rizzuto, fouled out to Campanella.
– Grim zapped out to Reese.

1 Runs **2** Hits **0** Errors **2** LOB

YANKEES – 1　　　**DODGERS - 3**

Fifth Inning - Brooklyn Dodgers
– Reese flied out to Noren.
– Snider slugged a solo shot over the right-center field screen.
– Campanella looked at four wide pitches.
– Furillo grounded into a double play, Martin to E. Robinson.

1 Runs **1** Hits **0** Errors **0** LOB

YANKEES – 1　　　**DODGERS - 4**

Seventh Inning - New York Yankees
– Cerv PH for Grim, slugged a solo shot into the left field stands.
– Howard hurried to first base on a walk.
– Labine relieved Craig.
– Noren grounded into a double play, Hodges to Reese to Hodges.

– McDougald batted back to the box, Labine to Hodges.

1 Runs **1** Hits **0** Errors **0** LOB

YANKEES – 2   **DODGERS - 4**

Eighth Inning - New York Yankees

– Berra slugged a solo shot over the right field screen.
– Collins fanned; tagged out by Campanella.
– E. Robinson stroked a single into right field.
– Carroll PR.
– Martin rolled into a double play, J. Robinson to Gilliam to Hodges.

1 Runs **2** Hits **0** Errors **0** LOB

YANKEES – 3   **DODGERS - 4**

Eighth Inning - Brooklyn Dodgers

– Collins to 1B. Bauer to RF.
– Furillo nicked a single off of Martin's glove.
– Hodges sacrificed Furillo to second base, Turley to Martin.

– J. Robinson singled into left-center field, driving Furillo home.
– Amoros struck out.
– Labine went down on strikes.

1 Runs **2** Hits **0** Errors **1** LOB

YANKEES – 3   **DODGERS - 5**

HIGHLIGHTS

- Dodger LF Sandy Amoros hammered the first home run then struck out in three straight at-bats
- Snider collected 10 total bases on two homers and a double
- Snider joined teammate Roy Campanella (Games 3 & 4) with home runs in consecutive games
- Yankee Bob Cerv powered the sixth pinch-hit home run
- CF Irv Noren has twice hit into two double plays (Game 1);
- New York starter Bob Grim allowed three home runs as Don Newcombe had done in Game 1
- Clem Labine, in consecutive games, earned a win and notched a save
- Five home runs were blasted and five double plays were turned

---

DIAMOND DUST

- Brooklyn starter Roger Craig is the 29th rookie to start and the 12th to win
- Dodger CF Duke Snider is the 13th player to homer twice in the same game
- The second time in Snider's career to do so (1952)
- Snider hit the Dodgers ninth home run to tie the Yankees 1953 record versus the Dodgers
- Brooklyn, in winning the 300th game in World Series history, is on a three-game winning streak

---

Game 5 BOX SCORE SUMMARY

NEW YORK YANKEES	AB	R	H	RBI	BB	K	1B	2B	3B	HR	TB	SB
YOGI BERRA, C	4	2	2	1	0	0	1	0	0	1	5	0
BILLY MARTIN, 2B	4	0	1	1	0	0	1	0	0	0	1	0
BOB CERV, PH	1	1	1	1	0	0	0	0	0	1	4	0
BROOKLYN DODGERS	AB	R	H	RBI	BB	K	1B	2B	3B	HR	TB	SB
DUKE SNIDER, CF	4	2	3	2	0	0	0	1	0	2	10	0
CARL FURILLO, RF	4	1	1	0	0	1	1	0	0	0	0	0
GIL HODGES, 1B	3	1	2	0	0	1	2	0	0	0	2	0
JACKIE ROBINSON, 3B	3	0	1	1	1	0	1	0	0	0	1	0
SANDY AMOROS, LF	4	1	1	2	0	3	0	0	0	1	4	0

NEW YORK YANKEES	IP	H	R	ER	HR	K	BB	HBP	ERA
BOB GRIM L (0-1)	6	6	4	4	3	5	4	0	5.14
BOB TURLEY	2	3	1	1	0	5	1	0	13.50
BROOKLYN DODGERS	IP	H	R	ER	HR	K	BB	HBP	ERA
ROGER CRAIG W (1-0)	6	4	2	2	1	4	5	0	3.00
CLEM LABINE S (1)	3	2	1	1	1	1	0	0	2.89

GAME TIME:	**2:40**
ATTENDANCE:	**36,796**
BEST OF 7:	**DODGERS - 3 YANKEES - 2**

Game 6

BROOKLYN DODGERS vs. NEW YORK YANKEES

October 3

LINE SCORE	1	2	3	4	5	6	7	8	9	R	H	E
BROOKLYN DODGERS	0	0	0	1	0	0	0	0	0	1	4	1
NEW YORK YANKEES	5	0	0	0	0	0	0	0	X	5	8	0

RECAP

The Yankees came out swinging after having been beaten three times in three days. Brooklyn's starting pitcher, a rookie, Karl Spooner, did not survive the first inning as the entire Yankee line-up stepped to the plate. Facing six of the nine, Spooner got one out, issued two walks, gave up two singles and a three-run home run for five runs. The Yankees made that score stand. Whitey Ford, posting his second win, pitched a complete game, one run, four-hitter, setting up the showdown game.

SCORING SUMMARY

First Inning - New York Yankees

- Spooner starting.
- Rizzuto drew a walk.
- Martin struck out; Rizzuto swiped second base.
- McDougald walked; Rizzuto held.
- Berra singled up the middle, driving in Rizzuto; McDougald made third.
- Bauer singled into left field, driving in McDougald; Berra slid into second.
- Skowron clouted a home run into the right field seats, driving home Berra and Bauer.
- Meyer relieved Spooner.
- Cerv sped across first base on a bang-bang play.
- Howard struck out.
- Ford flied out to Amoros.

5 Runs **4** Hits **0** Errors **1** LOB

DODGERS - 0   **YANKEES – 5**

Fourth Inning - Brooklyn Dodgers

- Ford starting.
- Reese one-hopped a single over the second base bag.
- Zimmer PH for Snider (injured knee), whiffed.
- Campanella walked Reese to second base.
- Furillo singled into left field, driving in Reese; Campanella slid into second.
- Hodges forced Furillo at second, Rizzuto to Martin; Campanella made third.
- J. Robinson forced Hodges at second, Rizzuto to Martin.

1 Runs **2** Hits **0** Errors **2** LOB

DODGERS - 1   **YANKEES – 5**

HIGHLIGHTS

- Bill Skowron hit the Yankees eighth home run to tie the Dodgers 1953 record
- Brooklyn stranded base runners in five frames
- Ford set down the last seven batters of the game

DIAMOND DUST

- Karl Spooner is the second straight Dodger rookie to start (30th all time) and is the 15th to lose
- Phil Rizzuto, in the second inning, swiped career base #10 to tie the all-time record
- Whitey Ford is the seventh pitcher to hit a batter and throw a wild pitch in the same game

Game 6 BOX SCORE SUMMARY

BROOKLYN DODGERS	AB	R	H	RBI	BB	K	1B	2B	3B	HR	TB
PEE WEE REESE, SS	4	1	1	0	1	0	1	0	0	0	1
CARL FURILLO, RF	3	0	1	1	0	1	1	0	0	0	1

NEW YORK YANKEES	AB	R	H	RBI	BB	K	1B	2B	3B	HR	TB
PHIL RIZZUTO, SS	3	1	0	0	1	0	0	0	0	0	0
GIL MCDOUGALD, 3B	3	1	0	0	1	0	0	0	0	0	0
YOGI BERRA, C	3	1	2	1	1	0	2	0	0	0	2
HANK BAUER, RF	4	1	3	1	0	0	3	0	0	0	3
BILL SKOWRON, 1B	2	1	1	3	0	0	0	0	0	1	4

BROOKLYN DODGERS	IP	H	R	ER	HR	K	BB	HBP	ERA
KARL SPOONER L (0-1)	0.1	3	5	5	1	1	2	0	13.50
RUSS MEYER	5.2	4	0	0	0	4	2	0	0.00
ED ROEBUCK	2	1	0	0	0	0	0	0	0.00

NEW YORK YANKEES	IP	H	R	ER	HR	K	BB	HBP	ERA
WHITEY FORD W (2-0)	9	4	1	1	0	8	4	1	2.12

Home Run in First WS AB (Subway Series)		Year	Opponent
Chick Fewster	NYY	1921	NY Giants
George Selkirk	NYY	1936	NY Giants
Elston Howard	NYY	1955	Brooklyn
Home Run in First 2 WS AB	Team	Year	Opponent
Gene Tenace	OAK	1972	Cincinnati
Andruw Jones	ATL	1996	NY Yankees
Home Run in First 3 WS AB	Team	Year	Opponent
Pablo Sandoval	SFG	2012	Detroit

Elston Howard made the most of being the first African American to bat for the Yankees in the World Series by belting a homer off another African-American pioneer, Don Newcombe.

Howard hit a solid .290 in his rookie season in 1955, which also included 43 RBI in 279 AB. He was the first African American to play for the Yankees, and after a long and productive career, he became their first African American coach, in 1969.

Howard made the AL All Star team for 9 consecutive seasons; he won the MVP award in 1963 and the next year came in third in the balloting. As an aging veteran in 1967, Howard was traded to the "Impossible Dream" Red Sox, and his veteran presence and experience helped Boston win the pennant on the last day of the season and allowed Howard to play in the 10th World Series of his 14-year career.

GAME TIME:	**2:34**	
ATTENDANCE:	**64,022**	
BEST OF 7:	**DODGERS - 3**	**YANKEES - 3**

Game 7

BROOKLYN DODGERS vs. NEW YORK YANKEES

October 4

LINE SCORE	1	2	3	4	5	6	7	8	9	R	H	E
BROOKLYN DODGERS	0	0	0	1	0	1	0	0	0	2	5	0
NEW YORK YANKEES	0	0	0	0	0	0	0	0	0	0	8	1

RECAP

From frames one through three, the starters, the Yankees Tommy Byrne and the Dodgers Johnny Podres, gave up zero runs. Byrne yielded the first run in the fourth on a Roy Campanella double and a Gil Hodges single. He gave up the second run in the sixth on a Hodges sac fly, which plated Pee Wee Reese. Podres almost gave up a run in the sixth if not for an outstanding catch by LF Sandy Amoros. Amoros turned a potential game-tying double into a rally killing double play. In the end, Podres pitched a complete game shutout, nailing down the first Brooklyn Dodgers World Series title.

SCORING SUMMARY

Fourth Inning - Brooklyn Dodgers

- Byrne starting.
- Snider struck out.
- Campanella ricocheted a double into the left field corner.
- Furillo advanced Campanella on a ground out, Rizzuto to Skowron.
- Hodges singled into left field, driving Campanella home.
- Hoak grounded out, McDougald to Skowron.

1 Runs **2** Hits **0** Errors **1** LOB

DODGERS - 1   **YANKEES - 0**

Sixth Inning - Brooklyn Dodgers

- Reese rapped a single into center field.
- Snider sacrificed Reese to second; sped across first on Skowron's fumble.
- Campanella sacrificed up both runners, Byrne to Martin.
- Furillo walked intentionally to load the bases.
- Grim relieved Byrne.
- Hodges lofted a sacrifice fly to Cerv plating Reese; Snider moved up; Furillo wild-pitched to second base.
- Hoak walked; bases loaded.
- Shuba PH for Zimmer, bounded out, Skowron to Grim.

1 Runs **1** Hits **1** Errors **3** LOB

DODGERS - 2   **YANKEES - 0**

THE FIRST SUBWAY SERIES WIN FOR THE DODGERS

(National Baseball Hall of Fame and Museum)

Hall of Fame manager Walt Alston, seeing embracing warm and fuzzy Dodgers' owner Walter O'Malley. Alston managed the Dodgers 23 years, winning seven pennants, four World Series, and finishing second in the National League 8 times. He won 2040 games in his career, against 1613 losses, good for .558 winning percentage.

Through all that success over all those years, it is difficult to imagine that any of his accomplishments matched the thrill of the first one, also the first for the long-suffering Brooklyn Dodgers.

HIGHLIGHTS

- Thirteenth seven-game set
- Brooklyn 1B Gil Hodges drove in all of the runs of the day
- Dodger LF Sandy Amoros' fantastic catch in the sixth inning is rated as one of the most memorable, and he then doubled off Berra from first base
- The home team won every game of the series except the last

DIAMOND DUST

- Johnny Podres is the second (1936) pitcher with a losing regular season record (9-10) to start twice and first to win twice
- Podres is the second pitcher with a regular-season losing record to start a Game Seven and the first to win
- Podres pitched the 10th clincher shutout and the fourth Game Seven shutout
- Yogi Berra hit into the 12th Yankees double play, setting a new team record
- Game Seven team stats: Brooklyn is 1-2 while New York is 2-2
- Brooklyn recorded a trifecta in winning their first ever Fall Classic title, their first Subway Series, and capturing the first World Series MVP

Game 7 BOX SCORE SUMMARY

BROOKLYN DODGERS	AB	R	H	RBI	BB	K	1B	2B	3B	HR	TB	SB
PEE WEE REESE, SS	4	1	1	0	0	1	1	0	0	0	1	0
ROY CAMPANELLA, C	3	1	1	0	0	0	0	1	0	0	2	0
GIL HODGES, 1B	2	0	1	2	1	0	1	0	0	0	1	0

BROOKLYN DODGERS	IP	H	R	ER	HR	K	BB	HBP	ERA
JOHNNY PODRES W (2-0)	9	8	0	0	0	4	2	0	1.00
NEW YORK YANKEES	IP	H	R	ER	HR	K	BB	HBP	ERA
TOMMY BYRNE L (1-1)	5.1	3	2	1	0	2	3	0	1.88
BOB GRIM	1.2	1	0	0	0	1	1	0	4.15
BOB TURLEY	2	1	0	0	0	1	1	1	8.44

GAME TIME:	**2:44**	
ATTENDANCE:	**62,465**	
BEST OF 7:	**DODGERS - 4**	**YANKEES - 3**

1955

BROOKLYN DODGERS vs. NEW YORK YANKEES

Jackie Robinson stealing home during Game 1. Yogi Berra argued the safe call vehemently, as captured famously on film. Robinson was 6 for 6 in stolen bases in his World Series career—with fewer attempts than would be expected—a testament to the station-to-station style of baseball employed by the slugging Dodgers and all of baseball in the 1950's, and to Yogi Berra.

Johnny Podres won the first-ever World Series MVP award, with his 2 complete-game wins. Podres' win in Game 3 was extremely clutch, too, as Brooklyn had lost the first 2 games. Podres had gone 9-10 for the Dodgers as a 22-year-old. He then missed the entire 1956 season due to military service, but came back in 1957 to lead the NL in ERA.

Podres had a solid big league career in the 1950s and 1960s, winning 148 games (all but 12 for the Dodgers), along with wins in the 1959 and 1963 World Series. After his retirement, Podres was a major league pitching coach for 23 years.

(All three photos on this page property of National Baseball Hall of Fame and Museum)

Carl Furillo diving under the tag of Billy Martin. Martin started all 7 games of the 1955 series at 2B, after having played in only 20 games during the regular season due to military service. Martin was a solid 8-for-25 in the Series, after having collected a record-tying 12 hits (in 24 ABs) in 1953. For his career, Martin went 33-for-99 in 28 games of World Series play, belting 5 home runs, driving in 19, with a slugging average of .566. The only area Martin's aggressive style of play did not pay off was base stealing, as he was thrown out in 5 of his 6 attempts. Of course, Roy Campanella, who threw out 57% of would-be base stealers in his career, had something to do with that.

1955

BROOKLYN DODGERS vs. NEW YORK YANKEES

——— BROOKLYN DODGERS ———

Overall World Series Record 1 WIN 7 LOSSES. 49 Games Played (17-32 .347)
- Fall Classic losing streak stopped at seven straight, the longest in history.
- MVP winner Johnny Podres - the first player to win that award - won two games while posting a 1.00 ERA over 18 innings.
- Clem Labine notched the only save.
- CF Duke Snider is the fourth player to hit four home runs in a Series - first to do so twice (1952).
- Snider collected 21 total bases and is the only Dodger to hit .300 (.320).
- Second wire-to-wire pennant-winner to win the World Series.
- Second team to rebound from a 0-2 deficit.
- Walt Alston is the 20th manager to win debut appearance.

——— NEW YORK YANKEES ———

Overall World Series Record: 16 WINS 5 LOSSES. 114 Games Played [74 - 39 (1 tie) .649]
- Subway Series winning streak stopped at nine.
- Fall Classic winning streak stopped at five.
- Yogi Berra rapped 10 hits in 24 at-bats, with a least one in all seven games.
- Berra hit .417 (10/24), the second straight World Series in which he surpassed the .400 mark (.429 in 1953).
- Hank Bauer, playing in six games, batted .429.
- Collins is the first player whose only hits were home runs (2), both hammered in Game 1.
- CF Irv Noren hit into five double plays to set an all-time World Series record.
- Phil Rizzuto's final game in a career spanning nine Fall Classics and seven titles.
- Rizzuto is sixth on the all-time list with with 52 games played and seventh in at bats with 183.

——— FUNGOES ———

- MVP match-up: the Dodgers Roy Campanella batted .259 and the Yankees Yogi Berra batted .417.
- The two teams tied the record for most home runs, with 17 (Dodgers 9/Yankees 8).
- They tied the record they set in 1953 when the home run totals were reversed.
- 19 double plays were turned, setting a new combined record (Dodgers 12/Yankees 7).
- Six managers have debuted in the Subway Series, with only Casey Stengel and Walt Alston winning.
- The National League now leads in Game 7 wins, 8-5.
- Overall World Series totals are now 33-19 in favor of the American League.

——— SEVEN-GAME DATA ———

TIME	18:14	PLAYERS POOL	$737,854
ATTENDANCE	362,310	SHARES	BROOKLYN DODGERS - $9,768
			NEW YORK YANKEES - $5,559

1955

BROOKLYN DODGERS vs. NEW YORK YANKEES

Brooklyn Dodgers Composite Stats

BATTING	G	AB	R	H	RBI	2B	3B	HR	BB	SO	BA	OBP	SLG	OPS
Roy Campanella	7	27	4	7	4	3	0	2	3	3	.259	.333	.593	.926
Carl Furillo	7	27	4	8	3	1	0	1	3	5	.296	.387	.444	.832
Pee Wee Reese	7	27	5	8	2	1	0	0	3	5	.296	.367	.333	.700
Duke Snider	7	25	5	8	7	1	0	4	2	6	.320	.370	.840	1.210
Jim Gilliam	7	24	2	7	3	1	0	0	8	1	.292	.469	.333	.802
Gil Hodges	7	24	2	7	5	0	0	1	3	2	.292	.357	.417	.774
Jackie Robinson	6	22	5	4	1	1	1	0	2	1	.182	.250	.318	.568
Sandy Amoros	5	12	3	4	3	0	0	1	4	4	.333	.529	.583	1.113
Don Zimmer	4	9	0	2	2	0	0	0	2	5	.222	.333	.222	.556
Johnny Podres	2	7	1	1	0	0	0	0	0	1	.143	.143	.143	.286
Clem Labine	4	4	0	0	0	0	0	0	0	3	.000	.000	.000	.000
Don Hoak	3	3	0	1	0	0	0	0	2	0	.333	.600	.333	.933
Frank Kellert	3	3	0	1	0	0	0	0	0	0	.333	.333	.333	.667
Don Newcombe	1	3	0	0	0	0	0	0	0	0	.000	.000	.000	.000
Russ Meyer	1	2	0	0	0	0	0	0	0	1	.000	.000	.000	.000
Don Bessent	3	1	0	0	0	0	0	0	0	1	.000	.000	.000	.000
Carl Erskine	1	1	0	0	0	0	0	0	0	0	.000	.000	.000	.000
Billy Loes	1	1	0	0	0	0	0	0	0	0	.000	.000	.000	.000
George Shuba	1	1	0	0	0	0	0	0	0	0	.000	.000	.000	.000
Roger Craig	1	0	0	0	0	0	0	0	1	0		1.000		
Ed Roebuck	1	0	0	0	0	0	0	0	0	0				
Karl Spooner	2	0	0	0	0	0	0	0	0	0				
Totals	**7**	**223**	**31**	**58**	**30**	**8**	**1**	**9**	**33**	**38**	**.260**	**.358**	**.426**	**.784**

PITCHING	G	GS	ERA	W	L	SV	CG	IP	H	R	ER	BB	SO	WHIP
Johnny Podres	2	2	1.00	2	0	0	2	18.0	15	3	2	4	10	1.056
Clem Labine	4	0	2.89	1	0	1	0	9.1	6	3	3	2	2	0.857
Roger Craig	1	1	3.00	1	0	0	0	6.0	4	2	2	5	4	1.500
Russ Meyer	1	0	0.00	0	0	0	0	5.2	4	0	0	2	4	1.059
Don Newcombe	1	1	9.53	0	1	0	0	5.2	8	6	6	2	4	1.765
Billy Loes	1	1	9.82	0	1	0	0	3.2	7	4	4	1	5	2.182
Don Bessent	3	0	0.00	0	0	0	0	3.1	3	0	0	1	1	1.200
Karl Spooner	2	1	13.50	0	1	0	0	3.1	4	5	5	3	6	2.100
Carl Erskine	1	1	9.00	0	0	0	0	3.0	3	3	3	2	3	1.667
Ed Roebuck	1	0	0.00	0	0	0	0	2.0	1	0	0	0	0	0.500
Totals	**7**	**7**	**3.75**	**4**	**3**	**1**	**2**	**60.0**	**55**	**26**	**25**	**22**	**39**	**1.283**

1955

BROOKLYN DODGERS vs. NEW YORK YANKEES

New York Yankees Composite Stats

BATTING	G	AB	R	H	RBI	2B	3B	HR	BB	SO	BA	OBP	SLG	OPS
Gil McDougald	7	27	2	7	1	0	0	1	2	6	.259	.310	.370	.681
Elston Howard	7	26	3	5	3	0	0	1	1	8	.192	.222	.308	.530
Billy Martin	7	25	2	8	4	1	1	1	1	5	.320	.346	.440	.786
Yogi Berra	7	24	5	10	2	1	0	1	3	1	.417	.500	.583	1.083
Irv Noren	5	16	0	1	1	0	0	0	1	1	.063	.118	.063	.180
Bob Cerv	5	16	1	2	1	0	0	1	0	4	.125	.125	.313	.438
Phil Rizzuto	7	15	2	4	1	0	0	0	5	1	.267	.450	.267	.717
Hank Bauer	6	14	1	6	1	0	0	0	0	1	.429	.429	.429	.857
Joe Collins	5	12	6	2	3	0	0	2	6	4	.167	.444	.667	1.111
Bill Skowron	5	12	2	4	3	2	0	1	0	1	.333	.333	.750	1.083
Mickey Mantle	3	10	1	2	1	0	0	1	0	2	.200	.200	.500	.700
Whitey Ford	2	6	1	0	0	0	0	0	1	1	.000	.143	.000	.143
Tommy Byrne	3	6	0	1	2	0	0	0	0	2	.167	.167	.167	.333
Eddie Robinson	4	3	0	2	1	0	0	0	2	1	.667	.833	.667	1.500
Jerry Coleman	3	3	0	0	0	0	0	0	0	1	.000	.000	.000	.000
Andy Carey	2	2	0	1	1	0	1	0	0	0	.500	.500	1.500	2.000
Bob Grim	3	2	0	0	0	0	0	0	0	0	.000	.000	.000	.000
Don Larsen	1	2	0	0	0	0	0	0	0	0	.000	.000	.000	.000
Bob Turley	3	1	0	0	0	0	0	0	0	0	.000	.000	.000	.000
Tom Carroll	2	0	0	0	0	0	0	0	0	0				
Rip Coleman	1	0	0	0	0	0	0	0	0	0				
Johnny Kucks	2	0	0	0	0	0	0	0	0	0				
Tom Morgan	2	0	0	0	0	0	0	0	0	0				
Tom Sturdivant	2	0	0	0	0	0	0	0	0	0				
Totals	**7**	**222**	**26**	**55**	**25**	**4**	**2**	**8**	**22**	**39**	**.248**	**.321**	**.329**	**.713**

PITCHING	G	GS	ERA	W	L	SV	CG	IP	H	R	ER	BB	SO	WHIP
Whitey Ford	2	2	2.12	2	0	0	1	17.0	13	6	4	8	10	1.235
Tommy Byrne	2	2	1.88	1	1	0	1	14.1	8	4	3	8	8	1.116
Bob Grim	3	1	4.15	0	1	1	0	8.2	8	4	4	5	8	1.500
Bob Turley	3	1	8.44	0	1	0	0	5.1	7	5	5	4	7	2.063
Don Larsen	1	1	11.25	0	1	0	0	4.0	5	5	5	2	2	1.750
Tom Morgan	2	0	4.91	0	0	0	0	3.2	3	2	2	3	1	1.636
Johnny Kucks	2	0	6.00	0	0	0	0	3.0	4	2	2	1	1	1.667
Tom Sturdivant	2	0	6.00	0	0	0	0	3.0	5	2	2	2	0	2.333
Rip Coleman	1	0	9.00	0	0	0	0	1.0	5	1	1	0	1	5.000
Totals	**7**	**7**	**4.20**	**3**	**4**	**1**	**2**	**60.0**	**58**	**31**	**28**	**33**	**38**	**1.517**

BROOKLYN DODGERS vs. NEW YORK YANKEES

FUNGOES

- ⚾ MVP winners on both teams.
- ⚾ No travel days, though there was a rain out after game 1.
- ⚾ Umpire data: Dusty Boggess played in the minor leagues for the St. Louis Cardinals, where he appeared at every position; was a minor league manager and owner. Tom Gorman pitched four games for the New York Giants during the 1939 season. Larry Napp is a former catcher, a former boxer, a judo expert and was a fitness instructor in the US Navy; Babe Pinelli is a former 3B with various teams, wrote magazine articles, and was elected to the Italian American Sports Hall of Fame (2000). Hank Soar played for the New York Giants football team, catching the game-winning touchdown in the 1938 NFL Championship Game vs. the Green Bay Packers.

SERIES SUMMARY

The Bombers and the Bums matched in the World Series for the fifth time in eight years, and although Brooklyn rode the momentum from their first-ever championship to start strong in the 1956 Classic, the Yankees turned things around in their direction behind tremendous pitching.

The Dodgers took Game 1 behind a complete game from Sal Maglie, who had faced the Yankees in the 1951 Subway Series as a member of the New York Giants. Gil Hodges' 3-run homer off Whitey Ford in the third inning was the big blow.

Twelve hits, 10 bases on balls, and four more RBI from Gil Hodges resulted in a Dodgers' slugfest victory in Game 2, as Brooklyn bounced back from a 6-0 deficit in the second inning with a six runs of their own in the second frame. They piled on five more over the next three and coasted to a 13-8 win.

Needing a win, the Yankees came back with Whitey Ford in Game 3, and the Chairman of the Board did not disappoint, posting a complete-game 5-3 win. Forty-year-old Enos Slaughter collected his third straight multi-hit game and drove in three to lead the Bombers.

In Game 4 it was Tom Sturdivant's turn to stifle the Dodgers, as he turned in another complete-game victory, allowing just four

singles and two doubles. The Yankees had a balanced attack, with Hank Bauer and Mickey Mantle each providing insurance runs with a late-inning home run.

Sal Maglie was back on the mound for the Dodgers in Game 5 and he pitched another complete game. But he was bested by Don Larsen's perfect game. A solo home run by Mantle in the fourth was all Larsen needed. Just like that, the Yankees were in the driver's seat once more.

Brooklyn's offensive ineptitude continued for nine innings in Game 6, but with two outs in the top of the 10th, Jackie Robinson singled in the game's only run. Clem Labine closed out the Yankees in the bottom half with his 10th inning of shutout ball, completing one of the great clutch pitching performances in World Series history.

There was no drama in Game 7 as the Yankees scored early and often, and 18-game winner Johnny Kucks ensured Brooklyn's bats remain silent, with a 3-hit shutout. After scoring 19 runs in the first two games, the Dodgers plated only six more in the final five, including only one run over the final three.

THE TEAMS

BROOKLYN DODGERS
93 – 61 .604 +1.0 G

The Team
- 7th Subway Series appearance (ninth overall).
- The Dodgers' nickname first appeared on their uniforms in 1933.
- In third place at the All-Star break.
- 10th team to make consecutive appearances.

The Players
- 1955 Subway Series returning players (14): Sandy Amoros, Don Bessent, Roy Campanella, Roger Craig, Carl Erskine, Carl Furillo, Jim Gilliam, Gil Hodges, Clem Labine, Don Newcombe, Pee Wee Reese, Jackie Robinson, Ed Roebuck and Duke Snider.
- Reese played on the 1941/47/49/51/52/53/55 pennant-winning teams, winning title in '55.
- Reese is the only player appear in all seven Brooklyn Subway Series.
- Furillo, Hodges and Robinson played on the 1947/49/52/53/55 pennant-winning teams, winning one title in (1955).
- Campanella, Erskine and Snider played on the 1949/52/53/55 pennant-winning teams, winning the title in '55.
- Sal Maglie, as a New York Giant, pitched on the 1951 pennant-winning and the 1954 title-winning clubs.
- Don Newcombe is the first pitcher to win the league MVP and the Cy Young in the same season and the first African-American Cy Young winner.
- Carl Erskine and Sal Maglie both authored no-hitters during the season.
- On May 12 Erskine mesmerized crosstown rival New York Giants; six weeks later, on June 19th, Erskine threw a no-hitter at the Chicago Cubs.
- Maglie, a mid-season trade from Cleveland, did the same to the Philadelphia Phillies on September 25.
- Clem Labine led the majors with 19 saves.

The Manager
- Walt Alston is the 21st manager to make consecutive appearances.
- Alston is the only Brooklyn Dodgers manager to win a Fall Classic.

Top Batters

Pos	Name	AB	R	H	HR	RBI	BA	OPS
C	Roy Campanella	388	39	85	20	73	.219	.727
1B	Gil Hodges	550	86	146	32	87	.265	.861
CF	Duke Snider	542	112	158	43	101	.292	.997
RF	Carl Furillo	523	66	151	21	83	.289	.824

Top Pitchers

Pos	Name	W	L	ERA	G	SV	IP	SO
St	Don Newcombe	27	7	3.06	38	0	268.0	139
St	Sal Maglie	13	5	2.87	28	0	191.0	108
St	Carl Erskine	13	11	4.25	31	0	186.1	95
Rel	Clem Labine	10	6	3.35	62	19	115.2	75

NEW YORK YANKEES
97 – 57 .630 +9.0 G

The Team
- Subway Series #13; 22nd overall appearance.
- In first place at the All-Star break.

The Players
- 1955 Subway Series returning players (17) - Hank Bauer, Yogi Berra, Tommy Byrne, Andy Carey, Bob Cerv, Jerry Coleman, Joe Collins, Whitey Ford, Elston Howard, Johnny Kucks, Don Larsen, Mickey Mantle, Billy Martin, Gil McDougald, Phil Rizzuto, Bill Skowron, Tom Sturdivant and Bob Turley.
- Rizzuto played on the 1941/42/47/49/50/51/52/53/55 pennant-winning teams, capturing seven titles.
- Berra played on the 1947/49/50/51/52/53/55 pennant-winning teams, capturing six straight titles.
- Bauer played on the 1949/50/51/52/53/55 pennant-winning teams, capturing five titles in a row.
- Coleman played on the 1949/50/51/55 pennant-winning teams, capturing three titles.
- Ford pitched on the 1950/53/55 pennant-winning teams, capturing two titles.
- Collins played on the 1950/51/52/53/55 pennant-winning teams, capturing four titles.
- Mantle, Martin and McDougald played on the 1951/52/53/55 pennant-winning teams, capturing three titles.
- Enos Slaughter played on the 1942/46 pennant-winning St. Louis Cardinals, winning two titles ('42 against the Yankees).
- Enos Slaughter was acquired in a mid-season trade with the Kansas City Athletics.
- Ford led the majors with a 2.47 era.
- Mickey Mantle is the second Triple Crown (.353/52/130) winner to appear.

The Manager
- Stengel tied Miller Huggins with the most pennants won by a Yankee manager (6).

Top Batters

Pos	Name	AB	R	H	HR	RBI	BA	OPS
C	Yogi Berra	521	93	155	30	105	.298	.911
1B	Bill Skowron	464	78	143	23	90	.308	.910
CF	Mickey Mantle	533	132	188	52	130	.353	1.169
RF	Hank Bauer	539	96	130	26	84	.241	.761

Top Pitchers

Pos	Name	W	L	ERA	G	SV	IP	SO
St	Whitey Ford	19	6	2.47	31	1	225.2	141
St	Johnny Kucks	18	9	3.85	34	0	224.1	67
St	Tom Sturdivant	16	8	3.30	32	5	158.1	110
Rel	Tom Morgan	6	7	4.16	41	11	71.1	20

NEW YORK YANKEES vs. BROOKLYN DODGERS

October 3

LINE SCORE	1	2	3	4	5	6	7	8	9	R	H	E
NEW YORK YANKEES	2	0	0	1	0	0	0	0	0	3	9	1
BROOKLYN DODGERS	0	2	3	1	0	0	0	0	X	6	9	0

RECAP

Both starting pitchers gave up two home runs. Mickey Mantle and Billy Martin homered off of Brooklyn's Sal Maglie, plating a total of three runs, which was the sum of their entire offense. Jackie Robinson and Gil Hodges homered off of New York's Whitey Ford for a total of four runs, which added to their total offense of six runs. Four Pinstripers toed the rubber and Ford was tagged with the loss. On the way to pitching a complete game, Maglie fanned 10 Bombers.

SCORING SUMMARY

First Inning - New York Yankees
– Maglie starting.
– Bauer dribbled out, J. Robinson to Hodges.
– Slaughter grazed a single off of Hodges' glove.
– Mantle blasted a home run over the right field screen, driving Slaughter home.
– Berra jogged to first on a free pass.
– Skowron strikeout.
– McDougald strikeout.

2 Runs **2** Hits **0** Errors **1** LOB

YANKEES – 2   **DODGERS – 0**

Second Inning - Brooklyn Dodgers
– Ford starting.
– J. Robinson slugged a solo shot into the left field stands.
– Hodges hopped a single into center field.
– Furillo doubled into left-center field, driving Hodges home.
– Campanella flied out to Bauer; Furillo crossed over to third base.
– Amoros flied out to Mantle.
– Maglie went down on strikes.

2 Runs **3** Hits **0** Errors **1** LOB

YANKEES – 2   **DODGERS – 2**

Third Inning - Brooklyn Dodgers
– Gilliam popped up to Carey.
– Reese seared a single to the shortstop spot.
– Snider singled Reese to second base.
– J. Robinson flied out to Mantle.
– Hodges hammered a home run into the left field seats, driving home Reese and Snider.
– Furillo flied out to Bauer.

3 Runs **3** Hits **0** Errors **0** LOB

YANKEES – 2   **DODGERS – 5**

Fourth Inning - New York Yankees
– McDougald flied out to Amoros.
– Martin slugged a solo shot into the left field stands.
– Carey flied out to Furillo.
– Wilson PH for Ford, strikeout; thrown out at first base, Campanella to Hodges.

1 Runs **1** Hits **0** Errors **0** LOB

YANKEES – 3   **DODGERS – 5**

Fourth Inning - Brooklyn Dodgers

– Kucks pitching.
– Campanella rattled a double off of the center field gate.
– Amoros singled up the middle, driving Campanella home.
– Maglie bunted into a double play, Skowron to McDougald to Martin.
– Gilliam got to first on Skowron's fielding error; swiped second base.
– Reese was a strikeout.

1 Runs **2** Hits **1** Errors **1** LOB

YANKEES – 3   **DODGERS – 6**

- Dwight Eisenhower, the 34th President of the United States, threw out the first pitch
- Eisenhower is the seventh sitting president to throw out the first pitch
- SS Gil McDougald struck out three times
- Maglie is the 11th starter to record double digit strikeouts in an opener
- Brooklyn is 2-7 while the Yankees are 16-6 in openers

DIAMOND DUST

- Mickey Mantle is the sixth player to homer in both the Mid-Summer Classic and the Fall Classic in the same season
- Lou Gehrig (1936/37) and Mantle (1955/56) are the only players to do so twice, consecutively
- 3B Jackie Robinson starts in fourth position (1B/2B/LF)
- Gil Hodges is the first player to score in consecutive frames in an opener

Game 1 BOX SCORE SUMMARY

NEW YORK YANKEES	AB	R	H	RBI	BB	K	1B	2B	3B	HR	TB	SB
ENOS SLAUGHTER, LF	5	1	3	0	0	0	3	0	0	0	3	0
MICKEY MANTLE, CF	3	1	1	2	2	1	0	0	0	1	4	0
BILLY MARTIN, 2B/3B	3	1	1	1	1	0	0	0	0	1	4	0
BROOKLYN DODGERS	AB	R	H	RBI	BB	K	1B	2B	3B	HR	TB	SB
PEE WEE REESE, SS	4	1	2	0	0	1	2	0	0	0	2	0
DUKE SNIDER, CF	3	1	1	0	1	0	0	0	0	0	1	0
JACKIE ROBINSON, 3B	4	1	1	1	0	0	0	0	0	1	4	0
GIL HODGES, 1B	4	2	2	3	0	1	1	0	0	1	5	0
CARL FURILLO, RF	4	0	1	1	0	0	0	1	0	0	2	0
ROY CAMPANELLA, C	4	1	1	0	0	1	0	1	0	0	2	0

NEW YORK YANKEES	IP	H	R	ER	HR	K	BB	HBP	ERA
WHITEY FORD L (0-1)	3	6	5	5	2	0	1	0	15.00
BROOKLYN DODGERS	IP	H	R	ER	HR	K	BB	HBP	ERA
SAL MAGLIE W (1-0)	9	9	3	3	2	10	4	0	3.00

39-year-old Sal Maglie was acquired by the Dodgers on May 15th from Cleveland for $100. Maglie went on to win 13 games for Brooklyn, including several big ones down the stretch of a tight pennant race. Writers were enamored, and incredibly, Maglie came in second in both the Cy Young Award and the NL MVP despite making only 26 starts and pitching 191 innings. Teammate Duke Snider belted 43 HR with 101 RBI, 112 RS, had a slash line of .292/.399/.598, and finished a distant 10th in the voting.

GAME TIME:	2:32
ATTENDANCE:	34,479
BEST OF 7:	**DODGERS – 1 YANKEES – 0**

Game 2

NEW YORK YANKEES vs. BROOKLYN DODGERS

September 29

LINE SCORE	1	2	3	4	5	6	7	8	9	R	H	E
NEW YORK YANKEES	1	5	0	1	0	0	0	0	1	8	12	2
BROOKLYN DODGERS	0	6	1	2	2	0	0	2	X	13	12	0

--- **RECAP** ---

The one-day rain delay, while a boost for the hitters, was a bust for the pitchers. Ten hurlers, seven for the Yankees (a record), took the mound issuing a total of 24 hits and 21 runs. The 20 singles were even at 10 apiece. By the end of the second inning the score was tied at 6-6 and knotted again at 7-7 in the fourth. The Dodgers surged ahead in their half of the fourth, added two in the fifth and two more in the eighth. The Yankees did score again, but their ninth-inning rally fell five runs short.

--- **SCORING SUMMARY** ---

First Inning - New York Yankees
– Newcombe starting.
– McDougald grounded out, Reese to Hodges.
– Slaughter lasered a single into right field.
– Mantle flied out to Snider.
– Berra walked Slaughter to second base.
– Collins singled up the middle, driving in Slaughter; Bauer slid into second.
– Bauer popped up to Gilliam.

1 Runs **2** Hits **0** Errors **2** LOB

YANKEES – 1   **DODGERS – 0**

Second Inning - New York Yankees
– Martin hustled across first base on a bang-bang play.
– Coleman sacrificed Martin to second base, Newcombe to Hodges.
– Larsen singled into left field, driving Martin home.
– McDougald singled Larsen to second base.
– Slaughter forced McDougald at second base, Reese to Gilliam; Larsen slid into third base.
– Mantle loaded the bases on a walk.
– Berra slammed the 5th WS grand slam home run over the right field fence, driving home Larsen, Slaughter and Mantle.

– Roebuck relieved Newcombe.
– Collins grounded out, Gilliam to Hodges.

5 Runs **4** Hits **0** Errors **0** LOB

YANKEES – 6   **DODGERS – 0**

Second Inning - Brooklyn Dodgers
– Hodges flogged a single into right field.
– Amoros flashed across first as Hodges slid into second on Collins' fumble.
– Furillo walked to stack the sacks.
– Campanella lifted a sacrifice fly to Slaughter plating Hodges.
– Mitchell PH for Roebuck, fouled out to Martin.
– Gilliam walked; bases loaded.
– Kucks relieved Larsen.
– Reese singled into left field, driving in Amoros and Furillo; Gilliam slid into second base.
– Byrne relieved Kucks.
– Snider belted a home run over the right-center field screen, driving home Gilliam and Reese.
– J. Robinson struck out.

6 Runs **3** Hits **1** Errors **0** LOB

YANKEES – 6   **DODGERS – 6**

Third Inning - Brooklyn Dodgers
Sturdivant pitching.
Hodges got on a walk.
Amoros struck out.
Furillo singled Hodges to second base.
Campanella was a strikeout.
Bessent singled into left field, driving in Hodges; Furillo advanced.
Gilliam again walked to load the bases.
Morgan relieved Sturdivant.
Reese popped up to Coleman.

1 Runs **2** Hits **0** Errors **3** LOB

YANKEES – 6   **DODGERS – 7**

Fourth Inning - New York Yankees
- Morgan singled past the left side of the mound.
- McDougald sacrificed Morgan to second base, J. Robinson to Gilliam; Bessent wild-pitched Morgan to third base.
- Slaughter lifted a sacrifice fly to Snider plating Morgan.
- Mantle struck out.

1 Runs **1** Hits **0** Errors **0** LOB

YANKEES – 7   **DODGERS – 7**

Fourth Inning - Brooklyn Dodgers
- Snider stroked a single into right field.
- J. Robinson smashed a hit-and-run single; Snider charged into third.
- Hodges doubled off of the left field wall, driving home Snider and J. Robinson.
- Amoros was a strikeout.
- Furillo moved Hodges to third on a grounder, Coleman to Collins.
- Campanella walked intentionally; runners on the corners.
- Bessent was a strikeout.

2 Runs **3** Hits **0** Errors **2** LOB

YANKEES – 7   **DODGERS – 9**

Fifth Inning - Brooklyn Dodgers
- Gilliam struck out.
- Reese flied out to Bauer.
- Snider got to first on a walk.
- J. Robinson singled Snider to second base.
- Hodges doubled into left-center field, driving home Snider and J. Robinson.

- Turley relieved Morgan.
- Amoros was a strikeout.

2 Runs **2** Hits **0** Errors **1** LOB

YANKEES – 7   **DODGERS – 11**

Eighth Inning - Brooklyn Dodgers
- Martin to 2B. Carey to 3B.
- Furillo hump-backed a single into left field.
- Campanella safe at first base as Furillo slid into second base after Bauer dropped the high pop.
- Bessent advanced both runners on a bouncer, Carey to Martin.
- Gilliam singled up the middle, driving home Furillo and Campanella.
- Reese flied out to Mantle.
- Snider struck out.

2 Runs **2** Hits **1** Errors **1** LOB

YANKEES – 7   **DODGERS – 13**

Ninth Inning - New York Yankees
- Slaughter rifled a single into center field.
- Mantle flied out to Snider.
- Berra zinged a hit-and-run single; Slaughter scrambled into third base.
- Collins scored Slaughter on a force of Berra at second, Reese to Gilliam.
- Bauer flied out to Furillo.

1 Runs **2** Hits **0** Errors **1** LOB

YANKEES – 8   **DODGERS – 13**

HIGHLIGHTS

- In the bottom of the third, Dodger reliever Don Bessent singled home the go-ahead run; then on the mound in the next frame Bessent gave back the run
- Bessent pitched seven innings of relief for the W
- 1B Gil Hodges reached base five times, scoring twice, driving in four
- Berra and Hodges each drove home four
- The two teams have matched hit totals in the first two games
- 21 combined run scored tied the record
- 21 combined runs batted in tied the record

DIAMOND DUST

- Yogi Berra is the first player in history to hit a pinch-hit home run (1947) and a grand slam
- Berra's grand slam is the first for the losing team
- Duke Snider's 10th career home run in the second inning is the 33rd and last for the Brooklyn franchise
- Yankee pitchers set a record by reaching double figures in 4 main categories—13 runs, 12 hits, 11 walks and 10 strikeouts
- The Yankees' 11 walks allowed tied a World Series record
- 3:26 game time is the longest ever

Game 2 BOX SCORE SUMMARY

NEW YORK YANKEES	AB	R	H	RBI	BB	K	1B	2B	3B	HR	TB	SB
ENOS SLAUGHTER, LF	4	3	2	1	1	0	2	0	0	0	2	0
MICKEY MANTLE, CF	4	1	1	0	1	1	1	0	0	0	1	0
YOGI BERRA, C	4	1	2	4	0	1	1	0	0	1	5	0
JOE COLLINS, 1B	4	0	1	2	1	0	1	0	0	0	1	0
BILLY MARTIN, 2B/3B	4	1	1	0	0	2	1	0	0	0	1	0
DON LARSEN, P	1	1	1	1	0	0	1	0	0	0	1	0
TOM MORGAN, P	1	1	1	0	0	0	0	0	0	0	1	0
BROOKLYN DODGERS	AB	R	H	RBI	BB	K	1B	2B	3B	HR	TB	SB
JUNIOR GILLIAM, 2B	3	1	1	2	3	1	1	0	0	0	1	0
PEE WEE REESE, SS	6	1	1	2	0	0	1	0	0	0	1	0
DUKE SNIDER, CF	4	3	2	3	2	2	1	0	0	1	5	0
JACKIE ROBINSON, 3B	4	2	2	0	1	1	2	0	0	0	2	0
GIL HODGES, 1B	3	2	3	4	2	0	1	2	0	0	5	0
SANDY AMOROS, LF	4	1	0	0	0	3	0	0	0	0	0	0
CARL FURILLO, RF	4	2	2	0	1	0	2	0	0	0	2	0
ROY CAMPANELLA, C	3	1	0	1	1	1	0	0	0	0	0	0
DON BESSENT, P	2	0	1	1	1	1	1	0	0	0	1	0

NEW YORK YANKEES	IP	H	R	ER	HR	K	BB	HBP	ERA
DON LARSEN	1.2	1	4	0	0	0	4	0	0.00
JOHNNY KUCKS	0	1	1	0	0	0	0	0	4.50
TOMMY BYRNE	0.1	1	1	0	1	1	0	0	0.00
TOM STURDIVANT	0.2	2	1	1	0	2	2	0	13.50
TOM MORGAN L (0-1)	2	5	4	4	0	3	2	0	9.00
MIKE MCDERMOTT	3	2	2	1	0	3	3	0	3.00
BROOKLYN DODGERS	IP	H	R	ER	HR	K	BB	HBP	ERA
DON NEWCOMBE	1.2	6	6	6	1	0	2	0	32.40
DON BESSENT W (1-0)	7	6	2	2	0	4	2	0	2.57

Casey Knows Old Pros

Johnny Mize was one of many veteran players picked by Casey Stengel who helpd the Yankees win 10 pennants and seven World Series during Stengel's 12-year tenure. In August of 1949, the Yankees purchased 36-year-old Johnny Mize from the Giants. Mize played sparingly down the stretch but then was 2-for-2 in the World Series, with 2 clutch pinch-hit singles. In 1950, Mize belted 25 home runs and drove in 72 in only 274 at-bats, and in 1952 he played a critical role in the hard-fought World Series, batting .400, belting 3 home runs, and driving in six.

Johnny Sain was rescued from an abysmal Boston Braves team in the summer of 1951, and he went on to win a total of 25 games as a starter-reliever in 1952-1953, and then save a league-leading 26 games in 1954. In Game 5 of the 1952 World Series, Sain pitched 5 shutout innings in relief before allowing two runs in the 11th inning to take the loss, and then was the winner in Game 1 of the 1953 Series, with 3.2 innings in relief of Allie Reynolds, along with hitting a 2-run double.

Jim Konstanty, who faced the Yankees in the 1950 World Series, the year he won the NL MVP with 16 wins and 22 saves in relief, was claimed on waivers by the Yankees in August 1954 and went on to post an ERA of 0.98 in nine appearances over the rest of the season. In 1955, at the age of 38, Konstanty was perhaps the Yankees top reliever, going 7-2 with 12 saves and an ERA of 2.32. He did not appear in that year's (losing) World Series.

Enos Slaughter, at age 40, was picked off waivers from the Kansas City Athletics in August of 1956, two years after KC traded for him from the Cardinals. Slaughter played in 24 games down the stretch in 1956 and then in 6 of the 7 games of the World Series, batting 7-for-20 with 4 RBI.

Tom Ferrick (1950), **Ewell Blackwell** (1952), **Sal Maglie** (1957), and **Virgil Trucks** (1958) are other players scooped up at the end of their careers by Stengel and the Yankees who contributed to the team's success.

GAME TIME:	3:26
ATTENDANCE:	36,217
BEST OF 7:	DODGERS - 2 YANKEES - 0

Game 3

BROOKLYN DODGERS vs. NEW YORK YANKEES

October 6

LINE SCORE	1	2	3	4	5	6	7	8	9	R	H	E
BROOKLYN DODGERS	0	1	0	0	0	1	1	0	0	3	8	1
NEW YORK YANKEES	0	1	0	0	0	3	0	1	X	5	8	1

RECAP

The Dodgers' offense consisted of two sacrifice flies and a Yankee fielding error. In the second and sixth innings, Roy Campanella and Duke Snider lifted RBI outs. In the seventh inning Gil Hodges raced across home plate with the final run.

The Yankee offense consisted of just the opposite, extra base hits. Billy Martin slugged a solo home run in the second inning. Enos Slaughter crushed a three-run home run in the sixth and Yogi Berra doubled home the fifth Bomber run in the eighth. The Dodger two-game winning streak was stopped.

SCORING SUMMARY

Second Inning - Brooklyn Dodgers

– Ford starting.
– J. Robinson worked a walk.
– Hodges got to first as J. Robinson slid into second on an infield hit.
– Furillo flied out to Bauer; J. Robinson crossed over to third base.
– Campanella lifted a sacrifice fly to Bauer plating J. Robinson.
– Neal fouled out to Berra.

1 Runs **1** Hits **0** Errors **1** LOB

DODGERS - 1   **YANKEES – 0**

Second Inning - New York Yankees

– Craig starting.
– Slaughter flied out to Gilliam.
– Martin slugged a solo shot into the left field seats.
– McDougald reached first on a free pass.
– Carey struck out.
– Ford went down on a strikes.

1 Hits **1** Runs **0** Errors **1** LOB

DODGERS - 1   **YANKEES – 1**

Sixth Inning - Brooklyn Dodgers

– Gilliam popped up to Martin.
– Reese tomahawked a triple into the right-center field alley.
– Snider lofted a sacrifice fly to Mantle plating Reese.
– J. Robinson tapped out, Carey to Collins.

1 Runs **1** Hits **0** Errors **0** LOB

DODGERS - 2   **YANKEES – 1**

Sixth Inning - New York Yankees

– Bauer poked a single into left field.
– Collins flied out to Snider.
– Mantle popped up high to Hodges.
– Berra smoked a hit-and-run single; Bauer wound up at third base.
– Slaughter crushed a home run into the left field seats, driving home Bauer and Berra.
– Martin flied out to Snider.

3 Runs **3** Hits **0** Errors **0** LOB

DODGERS - 2   **YANKEES – 4**

Seventh Inning - Brooklyn Dodgers

—Hodges legged it to first base on a walk.
—Furillo smashed a hit-and-run single; Hodges flashed to third base.
—Campanella fouled out to McDougald.
—Neal sprinted to first base, Hodges hustled across the plate and Furillo slid into second base on Carey's juggle.
—Jackson PH for Craig, flied out to Slaughter.
—Gilliam forced Neal at second base, McDougald unassisted.

1 Runs **1** Hits **1** Errors **2** LOB

DODGERS - 3   **YANKEES – 4**

Eighth Inning - New York Yankees

—Bauer flied out to Snider (great running catch).
—Collins reached first base on Neal's throwing error.
—Mantle popped up to Neal.
—Berra doubled into right-center field, driving Collins home.
—Slaughter received an intentional walk; Berra held.
—Martin flied out to Gilliam.

1 Runs **1** Hits **1** Errors **2** LOB

DODGERS - 3   **YANKEES – 5**

HIGHLIGHTS

- New York 3B Andy Carey, batting eighth, and Yankee starter Whitey Ford, batting ninth, struck out five times between them in six at bats
- 70,000 in Yankee Stadium for the seventh time - all versus the Dodgers

DIAMOND DUST

- Billy Martin's second inning solo shot is the 285th in history
- Enos Slaughter, at 40 years of age, became the oldest player to hammer a Fall Classic home run. This one was the difference in the game
- In 83 at bats for the Yankees during the regular season, Slaughter drove in only four runs and had no home runs

Game 3 BOX SCORE SUMMARY

BROOKLYN DODGERS	AB	R	H	RBI	BB	K	1B	2B	3B	HR	TB	SB
PEE WEE REESE, SS	4	1	2	0	0	0	1	0	1	0	4	0
DUKE SNIDER, CF	3	0	0	1	0	2	0	0	0	0	0	0
JACKIE ROBINSON, 3B	3	1	1	0	1	0	1	0	0	0	1	0
GIL HODGES, 1B	3	1	1	0	1	0	1	0	0	0	1	0
ROY CAMPANELLA, C	3	0	1	1	0	2	1	0	0	0	1	0
NEW YORK YANKEES	AB	R	H	RBI	BB	K	1B	2B	3B	HR	TB	SB
HANK BAUER, RF	4	1	1	0	0	0	1	0	0	0	1	0
JOE COLLINS, 1B	4	1	1	0	0	0	0	0	0	0	0	0
YOGI BERRA, C	4	1	2	1	0	0	1	1	0	0	3	0
ENOS SLAUGHTER, LF	3	1	2	3	1	0	1	0	0	1	5	0
BILLY MARTIN, 2B	4	1	1	1	0	0	0	0	0	1	4	0

BROOKLYN DODGERS	IP	H	R	ER	HR	K	BB	HBP	ERA
ROGER CRAIG L (0-1)	6	7	4	4	2	4	1	0	6.00
CLEM LABINE	2	1	1	0	0	2	1	0	0.00
NEW YORK YANKEES	IP	H	R	ER	HR	K	BB	HBP	ERA
WHITEY FORD W (1-1)	9	8	3	2	0	7	2	0	5.25

GAME TIME:	2:17
ATTENDANCE:	73,977
BEST OF 7:	**DODGERS - 2 YANKEES - 1**

Game 4

BROOKLYN DODGERS vs. NEW YORK YANKEES

October 7

LINE SCORE	1	2	3	4	5	6	7	8	9	R	H	E
BROOKLYN DODGERS	0	0	0	1	0	0	0	0	1	2	6	0
NEW YORK YANKEES	1	0	0	2	0	1	2	0	X	6	7	2

RECAP

Close to 70,000 fans watched four pitchers take the mound. Each yielded at least one run. Brooklyn starter Carl Erskine gave up RBI's to Yogi Berra, Billy Martin and Gil McDougald. Middle reliever Ed Roebuck was slugged by a Mickey Mantle solo shot and the third hurler, Don Drysdale, was clocked by a Hank Bauer two-run blast for the fifth and sixth runs. Yankee starter Tom Sturdivant pitched a solid, six-hit, two-run complete game to even the Series.

SCORING SUMMARY

First Inning - New York Yankees
– Erskine starting.
– Bauer flied out to Snider.
– Collins rattled a double into the right field corner.
– Mantle moved Collins to third on a ground out, Hodges to Erskine.
– Berra singled up the middle, driving Collins home.
– Slaughter bounced out to the box, Erskine to Hodges.

1 Runs **2** Hits **0** Errors **1** LOB

DODGERS - 0 **YANKEES – 1**

Fourth Inning - Brooklyn Dodgers
– Sturdivant starting.
– Snider doubled high off of the right field wall.
– J. Robinson fouled out to Berra.
– Hodges singled over the second base bag, driving Snider home.
– Amoros whomped into a double play, Collins unassisted.

1 Runs **2** Hits **0** Errors **1** LOB

DODGERS - 1 **YANKEES –1**

Fourth Inning - New York Yankees
– Mantle got a free pass.
– Berra struck out; Mantle swiped second base.

– Slaughter drew an intentional walk.
– Martin singled into left field, driving in Mantle; Slaughter flew into third.
– McDougald hoisted a sacrifice fly to Snider plating Slaughter.
– Carey bunted out to the mound, Erskine to Hodges.

2 Runs **1** Hits **0** Errors **1** LOB

DODGERS - 1 **YANKEES – 3**

Sixth Inning - New York Yankees
– Mantle slugged a solo shot into the right field stands.
– Berra flied out to Snider.
– Slaughter out on a ground ball, J. Robinson to Hodges.
– Martin struck out.

1 Runs **1** Hits **0** Errors **0** LOB

DODGERS - 1 **YANKEES – 4**

Seventh Inning - New York Yankees
– Drysdale pitching.
– McDougald grounded out, Reese to Hodges.
– Carey plugged a single into left field.
– Sturdivant went down on strikes.
– Bauer clocked a home run into the lower left field seats, driving Carey home.

– Collins finagled a free pass.

– Mantle out on a ground ball, Gilliam to Hodges.

2 Runs **2** Hits **0** Errors **1** LOB

DODGERS - 1   **YANKEES – 6**

Ninth Inning - Brooklyn Dodgers

– J. Robinson whacked a right-center field gapper for a double.

– Hodges struck out.

– Amoros jogged to first on a walk.

– Furillo loaded the bases on a walk.

– Campanella singled into left field, driving in J. Robinson; bases loaded.

– Jackson PH for Drysdale, was a strikeout.

– Gilliam flied out to Mantle.

1 Runs **2** Hits **0** Errors **3** LOB

DODGERS - 2   **YANKEES – 6**

HIGHLIGHTS

• Gil McDougald and Enos Slaughter are the only Yankees to not get a hit

DIAMOND DUST

• Mickey Mantle's sixth inning solo shot is the 110th in franchise World Series history

• Consecutive complete games for Yankees' staff

Game 4 BOX SCORE SUMMARY

BROOKLYN DODGERS	AB	R	H	RBI	BB	K	1B	2B	3B	HR	TB	SB
DUKE SNIDER, CF	4	1	1	0	0	1	0	1	0	0	2	0
JACKIE ROBINSON, 3B	3	1	1	0	1	0	0	1	0	0	2	0
GIL HODGES, 1B	4	0	1	1	0	2	1	0	0	0	1	0
ROY CAMPANELLA, C	2	0	2	1	2	0	2	0	0	0	2	0
NEW YORK YANKEES	AB	R	H	RBI	BB	K	1B	2B	3B	HR	TB	SB
HANK BAUER, RF	4	1	1	2	0	1	0	0	0	1	4	0
JOE COLLINS, 1B	3	1	1	0	1	0	0	1	0	0	2	0
MICKEY MANTLE, CF	3	2	1	1	1	0	0	0	0	1	4	1
YOGI BERRA, C	4	0	1	1	0	1	1	0	0	0	1	0
ENOS SLAUGHTER, LF	3	1	0	0	1	0	0	0	0	0	0	0
BILLY MARTIN, 2B	4	0	1	1	0	1	1	0	0	0	1	0
GIL MCDOUGALD, SS	2	0	0	1	0	0	0	0	0	0	0	0
ANDY CAREY, 3B	3	1	1	0	0	1	1	0	0	0	1	0

BROOKLYN DODGERS	IP	H	R	ER	HR	K	BB	HBP	ERA
CARL ERSKINE L (0-1)	4	4	3	3	0	2	2	0	6.75
ED ROEBUCK	2	1	1	1	1	2	0	0	3.86
DON DRYSDALE	2	2	2	2	1	1	1	0	9.00
NEW YORK YANKEES	IP	H	R	ER	HR	K	BB	HBP	ERA
TOM STURDIVANT W (1-0)	9	6	2	2	0	7	6	0	2.79

GAME TIME:	**2:43**
ATTENDANCE:	**69,705**
BEST OF 7:	**DODGERS - 2 YANKEES - 2**

Game 5

BROOKLYN DODGERS vs. NEW YORK YANKEES

October 8

LINE SCORE	1	2	3	4	5	6	7	8	9	R	H	E
BROOKLYN DODGERS	0	0	0	0	0	0	0	0	0	0	0	0
NEW YORK YANKEES	0	0	0	1	0	1	0	0	X	2	5	0

RECAP

As this game reached the late innings, the 64,519 fans in the stands and the thousands listened and watched and realized that a never-before event was unfolding. None of this was evident in the beginning, when Don Larsen retired the first three Dodgers and then got a lucky break for the fourth out. The next nine outs were fairly routine, but a great running catch was needed to put away the 14th straight batter. As each scoreless inning ended, the tension mounted. The audience was transfixed in anticipation, while the scoreboard spoke the words - no-hitter - that would not part their lips until Larsen recorded the last out of his mastery. An analysis of the 27 outs reveals eight fly balls, seven strikeouts, six grounders, three pop-ups and three line drives. Larsen did the job on just 97 pitches.

SCORING SUMMARY

First Inning - Brooklyn Dodgers
– Larsen starting.
– Gilliam struck out.
– Reese struck out.
– Snider skied out to Bauer.
– Larsen threw 15 pitches.

0 Runs **0** Hits **0** Errors **0** LOB

DODGERS – 0   **YANKEES – 0**

First Inning - New York Yankees
– Maglie starting.
– Bauer popped up to Reese.
– Collins bunted out, J. Robinson to Hodges.
– Mantle flied out to Amoros.

0 Runs **0** Hits **0** Errors **0** LOB

DODGERS – 0   **YANKEES – 0**

Second Inning - Brooklyn Dodgers
– J. Robinson lined out off of Carey's glove to McDougald to Collins.
– Hodges struck out.
– Amoros popped up to Martin.
– Larsen threw 11 pitches for a total of 26.

0 Runs **0** Hits **0** Errors **0** LOB

DODGERS – 0   **YANKEES – 0**

Second Inning - New York Yankees
– Berra popped up to Reese.
– Slaughter skied out to Amoros.
– Martin fanned; tagged out by Campanella.

0 Runs **0** Hits **0** Errors **0** LOB

DODGERS – 0   **YANKEES – 0**

Third Inning - Brooklyn Dodgers
– Furillo flied out to Bauer.
– Campanella struck out.
– Maglie lined out to Mantle.
– Larsen threw 7 pitches for a total of 33.

0 Runs **0** Hits **0** Errors **0** LOB

DODGERS – 0   **YANKEES – 0**

Third Inning - New York Yankees
– McDougald bounded out, J. Robinson to Hodges.
– Carey fouled out to Campanella.
– Larsen fouled out to Campanella.

0 Runs **0** Hits **0** Errors **0** LOB

DODGERS – 0   **YANKEES – 0**

Fourth Inning - Brooklyn Dodgers
– Gilliam nubbed out, Martin to Collins.
– Reese out on a grounder, Martin to Collins.
– Snider struck out.
– Larsen threw 8 pitches for a total of 41.

0 Runs **0** Hits **0** Errors **0** LOB

DODGERS – 0   **YANKEES – 0**

Fourth Inning - New York Yankees
– Bauer rolled out, J. Robinson to Hodges.
– Collins struck out.
– Mantle slugged a solo shot into the left field stands.
– Berra flied out to Snider (great shoestring catch).

1 Runs **1** Hits **0** Errors **1** LOB

DODGERS – 0   **YANKEES – 1**

Fifth Inning - Brooklyn Dodgers
– J. Robinson hoisted a warning track out to Bauer.
– Hodges lifted a warning track out to Mantle (great catch).
– Amoros dribbled out, Martin to Collins.
– Larsen threw 15 pitches for a total of 56.

0 Runs **0** Hits **0** Errors **0** LOB

DODGERS – 0   **YANKEES – 1**

Fifth Inning - New York Yankees
– Slaughter wangled a free pass.
– Martin forced Slaughter at second base, Maglie to Reese.
– McDougald grounded into a double play, Reese to Hodges.

0 Runs **0** Hits **0** Errors **0** LOB

DODGERS – 0   **YANKEES – 1**

Sixth Inning - Brooklyn Dodgers
– Furillo popped up to Martin.
– Campanella popped up to Martin.
– Maglie went down on strikes.
– Larsen threw 10 pitches for a total of 66.

0 Runs **0** Hits **0** Errors **0** LOB

DODGERS – 0   **YANKEES – 1**

Sixth Inning - New York Yankees
– Carey busted a single into center field.
– Larsen sacrificed Carey to second base, Campanella to Gilliam.
– Bauer singled into right field, driving Carey home.
– Collins blistered a hit-and-run single; Bauer barreled into third base.
– Mantle hit into a double play as Hodges stepped on first base and then fired a perfect peg to Campanella trapping Bauer in a run-down, J. Robinson to Campanella to J. Robinson.

1 Runs **3** Hits **0** Errors **1** LOB

DODGERS – 0   **YANKEES – 2**

Seventh Inning - Brooklyn Dodgers
– Gilliam out on a ground ball, McDougald to Collins.
– Reese flied out to Mantle.
– Snider flied out to Slaughter.
– Larsen threw 8 pitches for a total of 74.

0 Runs **0** Hits **0** Errors **0** LOB

DODGERS – 0   **YANKEES – 2**

Seventh Inning - New York Yankees
– Berra fouled out to J. Robinson.
– Slaughter flied out to Amoros.
– Martin one-hopped a single into left field.
– McDougald walked Martin to second base.
– Carey forced McDougald at second base, Reese to Gilliam.

0 Runs **1** Hits **0** Errors **2** LOB

DODGERS – 0   **YANKEES – 2**

Eighth Inning - Brooklyn Dodgers
– J. Robinson thrown out on a comebacker, Larsen to Collins.
– Hodges lined out to Carey.
– Amoros lifted a warning track out to Mantle.
– Larsen threw 10 pitches for a total of 84.

0 Runs **0** Hits **0** Errors **0** LOB

DODGERS – 0   **YANKEES – 2**

Eighth Inning - New York Yankees
– Larsen struck out.
– Bauer struck out.
– Collins struck out.

0 Runs **0** Hits **0** Errors **0** LOB

DODGERS – 0   **YANKEES – 2**

Ninth Inning - Brooklyn Dodgers

Furillo flied out to Bauer.
Campanella bounced out, Martin to Collins.
Mitchell PH for Maglie, looked at a called third strike.
Larsen threw 13 pitches for a total of 97 and a perfect game.

0 Runs **0** Hits **0** Errors **0** LOB

DODGERS – 0   **YANKEES – 2**

HIGHLIGHTS

- Larsen never shook off any of Berra's pitches, throwing 70 strikes and 27 balls
- Sal Maglie also pitched a complete game, giving up five hits
- Larsen & Maglie, through two batters in the fourth inning, combined to retire 23 batters in a row
- Snider and Mantle made spectacular catches in the 4th and 5th frames, respectively, to preserve their pitcher's shutout
- Yankee mounders pitched three straight complete games in the three-game winning streak
- Attendance for the three games in Yankee Stadium totaled 208,201

DIAMOND DUST

- Don Larsen set these records:
  1) most consecutive hitless innings in a Series (11)
  2) most consecutive hitless innings in a game (9)
  3) most consecutive perfect innings in a Series (11)
  4) most consecutive perfect innings in a game (9)
- Mickey Mantle is the 10th player to homer in consecutive games

Game 5 BOX SCORE SUMMARY

NEW YORK YANKEES	AB	R	H	RBI	BB	K	1B	2B	3B	HR	TB	SB
HANK BAUER, RF	4	0	1	1	0	1	1	0	0	0	1	0
MICKEY MANTLE, CF	3	1	1	1	0	0	0	0	0	1	4	0
ANDY CAREY, 3B	3	1	1	0	0	0	1	0	0	0	1	0

BROOKLYN DODGERS	IP	H	R	ER	HR	K	BB	HBP	ERA
SAL MAGLIE L (1-1)	8	5	2	2	1	5	2	0	2.65

NEW YORK YANKEES	IP	H	R	ER	HR	K	BB	HBP	ERA
DON LARSEN W (1-0)	9	0	0	0	0	7	0	0	0.00

Dale Mitchell, who famously took a called third strike to end Larson's perfect game, grounded out to short as a pinch hitter in the Dodgers' Game 7 loss, and never appeared in another big-league game.

Mitchell was a strong hitter who spent his entire career as an outfielder for the Cleveland Indians until the Dodgers acquired him at the end of July, 1956. Mitchell led the AL in hits and triples in 1949, and in 1952 batted .323, with only 9 strikeouts in 571 plate appearances. He retired with a career batting average of .312 in just under 4000 at bats.

GAME TIME:	**2:06**	
ATTENDANCE:	**64,519**	
BEST OF 7:	**DODGERS - 2**	**YANKEES - 3**

Game 6

NEW YORK YANKEES vs. BROOKLYN DODGERS

October 9

LINE SCORE	1	2	3	4	5	6	7	8	9	10	R	H	E
NEW YORK YANKEES	0	0	0	0	0	0	0	0	0	0	0	7	0
BROOKLYN DODGERS	0	0	0	0	0	0	0	0	0	1	1	4	0

RECAP

A perfect game is impossible to outdo from a pitching perspective, but dual shutouts comes close. Both starters, Clem Labine for the Dodgers and Bob Turley for the Yankees, blanked the opposition for nine full frames. In the top of the 10th, Labine faced three batters, recorded the 30th Bomber out, sustaining his shutout. In the bottom of the 10th, Turley, with 11 strikeouts under his belt, walked Jim Gilliam and Duke Snider and then gave up the game-winning, walk-off single to Jackie Robinson to set up the showdown game.

SCORING SUMMARY

Tenth Inning - Brooklyn Dodgers
– Labine popped up to Martin.
– Gilliam drew a walk.
– Reese sacrificed Gilliam to second base, Turley to Collins.
– Snider again intentionally walked; Gilliam held.
– J. Robinson singled into left field, driving Gilliam home with the winning run.

1 Runs **1** Hits **0** Errors **2** LOB

YANKEES – 0   **DODGERS - 1**

21st WALK-OFF, 10th SINGLE, 15th GAME WINNER

Robinson's walk-off single to stave off elimination for the Dodgers, proved to be the last hit of his career.

HIGHLIGHTS

- 27th extra-inning game
- Only Jackie Robinson and Gil Hodges were not victims in starter Bob Turley's 11-strikeout performance
- Turley struck out the side in order twice
- Yankee SS Gil McDougald and Dodger C Roy Campanella struck out three times
- Brooklyn CF Duke Snider walked three times but never scored
- First game of the series without a home run
- Yankees pitchers shutout the Dodgers for 18 consecutive innings until Robinson's walk-off single
- Brooklyn's pitchers held the Yankees scoreless for 12 consecutive innings - from the seventh inning of Game 5 through Game 6
- Labine in walk-offs is .500, losing in 1953 to the Yankees

DIAMOND DUST

- Clem Labine became the second hurler in Series history to pitch an extra-inning shutout, joining the mighty Christy Mathewson (1913). Jack Morris also did it to close out the 1991 World Series
- Brooklyn is 2-2 while the Yanks are 5-2 in walk-offs

Game 6 BOX SCORE SUMMARY

BROOKLYN DODGERS	AB	R	H	RBI	BB	K	1B	2B	3B	HR	TB	SB
JUNIOR GILLIAM, 2B	3	1	1	0	2	1	1	0	0	0	1	0
JACKIE ROBINSON, 3B	4	0	1	1	1	0	1	0	0	0	1	0

NEW YORK YANKEES	IP	H	R	ER	HR	K	BB	HBP	ERA
BOB TURLEY L (0-1)	9.2	4	1	1	0	11	8	0	0.82
BROOKLYN DODGERS	IP	H	R	ER	HR	K	BB	HBP	ERA
CLEM LABINE W (1-0)	10	7	0	0	0	5	2	0	0.00

Yogi Berra lines up a pop up off the bat of Pee Wee Reese. Berra enhanced his reputation as a big-game player in the following game, belting two two-run homers in his first two at-bats, which allowed the Yankees to cruise to a game-seven victory.

(National Baseball Hall of Fame and Museum)

GAME TIME:	**2:37**	
ATTENDANCE:	**33,224**	
BEST OF 7:	**DODGERS - 3**	**YANKEES - 3**

Game 7

NEW YORK YANKEES vs. BROOKLYN DODGERS

October 10

LINE SCORE	1	2	3	4	5	6	7	8	9	R	H	E
NEW YORK YANKEES	2	0	2	1	0	0	4	0	0	9	10	0
BROOKLYN DODGERS	0	0	0	0	0	0	0	0	0	0	3	1

RECAP

 Of the five Dodgers to pitch, three gave up the 10 hits and two the nine runs. Bomber power took charge in the very first inning when Yogi Berra belted a two-run home run and carried over into the third inning when Berra did it again. In the fourth, Elston Howard slugged a solo and in the seventh Bill Skowron belted a grand slam. All of the Bombers' nine runs came via the home run. Complementing the hitters, Johnny Kucks pitched the 11th final game shutout, earning the Yankees their 17th World Championship.

SCORING SUMMARY

First Inning - New York Yankees
– Newcombe starting.
– Bauer stroked a single into left field; swiped second base.
– Martin was a strikeout.
– Mantle was a strikeout.
– Berra belted a right field home run, driving Bauer home.
– Skowron struck out.

2 Runs **2** Hits **0** Errors **0** LOB

YANKEES – 2   **DODGERS – 0**

Third Inning - New York Yankees
– Bauer bunted out, Newcombe to Hodges.
– Martin notched a single into center field.
– Mantle struck out.
– Berra, who got a second chance after Campanella dropped a third strike foul, powered a home run over the right field scoreboard, driving Martin home.
– Skowron popped up to Gilliam.

2 Runs **2** Hits **0** Errors **0** LOB

YANKEES – 4   **DODGERS – 0**

Fourth Inning - New York Yankees
– Howard slugged a solo shot over the right field scoreboard.
– Bessent relieved Newcombe.
– McDougald popped up to Gilliam.

– Carey sped across first on Reese's fielding error.
– Kucks sacrificed Carey to second base, Hodges to Gilliam.
– Bauer grounded out, Gilliam to Hodges.

1 Runs **1** Hits **1** Errors **1** LOB

YANKEES – 5   **DODGERS – 0**

Seventh Inning - New York Yankees
– Craig pitching.
– Martin stroked a single into left field.
– Mantle walked Martin to second; both runners advanced on a wild pitch.
– Berra loaded the bases on an intentional pass.
– Skowron slammed the 6th grand slam home run into the lower left field seats, driving home Martin, Mantle and Berra.
– Howard walloped a double off of the right field wall.
– Roebuck relieved Craig.
– McDougald popped up to Hodges.
– Carey whiffed; thrown out at first, Campanella to Hodges.
– Kucks out on a ground ball, Reese to Hodges.

4 Runs **3** Hits **0** Errors **0** LOB

YANKEES – 9   **DODGERS – 0**

The Yankees Win 10th Subway Series

238

HIGHLIGHTS

- Fourteenth Game Seven, second consecutive
- Newcombe is the sixth pitcher to allow three home runs in a game (two to Berra) and is the first to do so twice (1955) and the first to do so in a Game Seven
- Berra is the 14th player to homer twice in the same game, a first in a Game 7
- Berra has twice stroked a game-ending hit (1950)
- Third straight complete-game shutout, second for the Pinstripers

Bill Skowron's 7th inning grand slam was his only hit of the series (1/10) and the first ever hit in a Game 7. 35 players in WS history homered for their only hit, with Brooklyn's George Shuba (1953) being the only other one to do it in a Subway Series.

DIAMOND DUST

- Game 7 firsts -
  1) Dodger starter Don Newcombe is the first allow three home runs
  2) Yogi Berra is the first player to homer twice;
  3) Brooklyn reliever Roger Craig is the first to allow a grand slam - Bill Skowron is the first to hit a grand slam
  4) Berra and Skowron, teammates, drove in four runs
  5) Yankees are the first team to hammer four home runs
- Bill Skowron's grand slam, his only hit, was the twelfth homer by a Yankee, to set a new team record
- Game Seven shutouts in consecutive Classics for the first time
- Game Seven team stats: New York is 3-2 while the Dodgers are 1-3
- Game Seven league stats: National League (8) - American League (6).

Game 7 BOX SCORE SUMMARY

NEW YORK YANKEES	AB	R	H	RBI	BB	K	1B	2B	3B	HR	TB	SB
HANK BAUER, RF	5	1	1	0	0	0	1	0	0	0	1	1
BILLY MARTIN, 2B	5	2	2	0	0	2	2	0	0	0	2	0
MICKEY MANTLE, CF	4	1	1	0	1	3	0	1	0	0	2	0
YOGI BERRA, C	3	3	2	4	2	0	0	0	0	2	8	0
BILL SKOWRON, 1B	5	1	1	4	0	1	0	0	0	1	4	0
ELSTON HOWARD, LF	5	1	2	1	0	0	0	1	0	1	6	0
GIL MCDOUGALD, SS	4	0	1	0	0	0	1	0	0	0	1	0

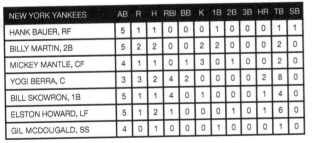

NEW YORK YANKEES	IP	H	R	ER	HR	K	BB	HBP	ERA
JOHNNY KUCKS W (1-0)	9	3	0	0	0	1	3	0	0.00
BROOKLYN DODGERS	IP	H	R	ER	HR	K	BB	HBP	ERA
DON NEWCOMBE L (0-1)	3	5	5	5	3	4	1	0	21.21
ROGER CRAIG	0	3	4	4	1	0	2	0	12.00

GAME TIME:	2:19	
ATTENDANCE:	33,782	
BEST OF 7:	**DODGERS - 3**	**YANKEES - 4**

FIFTEEN GREAT MOMENTS IN SUBWAY SERIES HISTORY

1956 - Game 5: Don Larsen's perfect game Larsen faced only one 3-2 count—Pee Wee Reese as the second batter of the game. Larsen was the recipient of the second World Series MVP award.

1955 - Game 7: Johnny Podres pitches Brooklyn to first and only title Podres overcame incredible pressure and the weight of history in shutting down the Yankees. Sandy Amoros squashes New York's best chance with a miracle catch that turns into a double play.

1947 – Game 1: Jackie Robinson's World Series debut As a 28-year-old rookie, Robinson became the first African American to play in a major league baseball game. Five plus months later, he broke the same barrier in the World Series. Robinson walked twice and scored a run in the game.

1923 - Game 1: Casey Stengel's inside-the-park game winner The first World Series home run at Yankee Stadium in the top of the 9th inning was the game's only run.

1923 - Game 2: Babe Ruth goes deep twice Babe Ruth not only hit the Yankees' first Yankee Stadium World Series home run, he hit two. The Bombers' 4-2 win broke the Giants' 8-game win streak against them.

1947 - Game 4: Bill Bevens pitches 8.2 no-hit innings—and loses Bevens tempted fate with 8 walks in 8 innings. The 9th and 10th free passes in the bottom of the ninth were followed by a Cookie Lavagetto 2-run pinch-hit double to give the Dodgers a 3-2 win.

1941 - Game 4: Mickey Owen's passed ball opens gate to comeback win Instead of strike 3, end of game, Henrich reaches, the Yankees rally, and take a 3-1 game lead in the Series.

1949 - Game 1: Tommy Henrich and Don Newcombe Henrich's walk-off home run off Don Newcombe is the first in World Series history and breaks a scoreless tie.

1953 - Game 3: Carl Erskine sets strikeout record Not only did Erskine set a new World Series record with a 14-strikeout performance, he kept the Yankees from going up 3-0 in the Series.

1951 - Game 2: Mickey Mantle's devastating injury Mantle steps in a drain pipe and rips up his knee chasing after a Willie Mays fly ball. The injury plagues him the rest of his career.

1955 - Game 1: Robinson steals home; Berra disagrees In the eight inning of the opener Robinson was called safe; Berra argues vigorously and remains unhappy about the call for years to come.

1953 - Game 6 - Billy Martin caps incredible Series Martin singles in the game- and series-winning run in walk-off fashion, capping a 12-for-24 Series.

1956 - Game 6: Jackie Robinson's walk-off hit A 10th inning single kept the Dodgers alive in the Series and turned out to be the last hit of Jackie Robinson's Hall Of Fame career.

2000 – Game 4: Derek Jeter's single-handed victory Jeter led off the first with a homer and the third with a triple in the Yankees' 3-2 win to give them a 3 games to 1 lead in the Series.

2000 – Game 3: The Clemens-Piazza confrontation After a beanball followed by a home run in the summer, Roger Clemens flings Piazza's broken bat at him, claiming he thought it was the ball.

1956

NEW YORK YANKEES vs. BROOKLYN DODGERS

NEW YORK YANKEES

Overall World Series Record: 17 WINS 5 LOSSES. 121 Games Played [78 WINS 42 LOSSES (1 tie) .650]
- The staff hurled five consecutive complete games, posting four wins.
- The staff, over the last three games (28 innings), allowed seven hits and only 1 run.
- Yogi Berra is the first player to drive in 10 runs and was one of two Yankee regulars to hit .300 (Slaughter .350, 7/20).
- Berra twice drove in four in a game (2/7).
- Mantle and Berra are the second set of teammates to each hammer three home runs (1925).
- Berra's three home runs all off of starter Don Newcombe.
- Berra (Game 2) and Bill Skowron (Game 7) the first set of teammates to hit grand slams.
- Don Larsen is named the second MVP of the World Series.
- The third team to rebound from a 0-2 deficit.
- Stengel has defeated the Dodgers four times against three different Dodger skippers.
- 17 Fall Classic championships are the most in MLB, 11 more than the St. Louis Cardinals.

BROOKLYN DODGERS

Overall World Series Record: 1 WIN 8 LOSSES. 56 Games Played (20-36, .357)
- SS Pee Wee Reese is the only player to play in all seven Brooklyn Dodgers Subway Series, a total of 44 games.
- Jackie Robinson and Gil Hodges played in six straight Subway match-ups, a total of 39 games.
- MVP/Cy Young winner Don Newcombe, in four career Series starts, won none while allowing eight home runs.
- Gil Hodges and Snider had identical number of at-bats (23), batting averages of .304, base hits (7) and runs scored (5).
- First franchise in a seven-game contest to have a composite batting average below the Mendoza line (.195).

FUNGOES

- Final Fall Classic in which there were no scheduled off days.
- New York teams have won the last eight Series.
- American League overall record is now 34-19.

SEVEN-GAME DATA

TIME	**18:00**	PLAYERS POOL	**$758,562**
ATTENDANCE	**345,903**	SHARES	**BROOKLYN DODGERS - $6,934**
			NEW YORK YANKEES - $8,715

241

1956

NEW YORK YANKEES vs. BROOKLYN DODGERS

Brooklyn Dodgers Composite Stats

BATTING	G	AB	R	H	RBI	2B	3B	HR	BB	SO	BA	OBP	SLG	OPS
Pee Wee Reese	7	27	3	6	2	0	1	0	2	6	.222	.276	.296	.572
Carl Furillo	7	25	2	6	1	2	0	0	2	3	.240	.296	.320	.616
Jim Gilliam	7	24	2	2	2	0	0	0	7	3	.083	.290	.083	.374
Jackie Robinson	7	24	5	6	2	1	0	1	5	2	.250	.379	.417	.796
Duke Snider	7	23	5	7	4	1	0	1	6	8	.304	.433	.478	.912
Gil Hodges	7	23	5	7	8	2	0	1	4	4	.304	.407	.522	.929
Roy Campanella	7	22	2	4	3	1	0	0	3	7	.182	.259	.227	.487
Sandy Amoros	6	19	1	1	1	0	0	0	2	4	.053	.143	.053	.195
Sal Maglie	2	5	0	0	0	0	0	0	0	2	.000	.000	.000	.000
Clem Labine	2	4	0	1	0	1	0	0	0	2	.250	.250	.500	.750
Dale Mitchell	4	4	0	0	0	0	0	0	0	1	.000	.000	.000	.000
Charlie Neal	1	4	0	0	0	0	0	0	0	1	.000	.000	.000	.000
Randy Jackson	3	3	0	0	0	0	0	0	0	2	.000	.000	.000	.000
Don Bessent	2	2	0	1	1	0	0	0	1	1	.500	.667	.500	1.167
Roger Craig	2	2	0	1	0	0	0	0	0	0	.500	.500	.500	1.000
Rube Walker	2	2	0	0	0	0	0	0	0	0	.000	.000	.000	.000
Carl Erskine	2	1	0	0	0	0	0	0	0	1	.000	.000	.000	.000
Don Newcombe	2	1	0	0	0	0	0	0	0	0	.000	.000	.000	.000
Gino Cimoli	1	0	0	0	0	0	0	0	0	0				
Don Drysdale	1	0	0	0	0	0	0	0	0	0				
Ed Roebuck	3	0	0	0	0	0	0	0	0	0				
Totals	82	215	25	42	24	8	1	3	32	47	.195	.296	.284	.580

PITCHING	G	GS	ERA	W	L	SV	CG	IP	H	R	ER	BB	SO	WHIP
Sal Maglie	2	2	2.65	1	1	0	2	17.0	14	5	5	6	15	1.176
Clem Labine	2	1	0.00	1	0	0	1	12.0	8	1	0	3	7	0.917
Don Bessent	2	0	1.80	1	0	0	0	10.0	8	2	2	3	5	1.100
Roger Craig	2	1	12.00	0	1	0	0	6.0	10	8	8	3	4	2.167
Carl Erskine	2	1	5.40	0	1	0	0	5.0	4	3	3	2	2	1.200
Don Newcombe	2	2	21.21	0	1	0	0	4.2	11	11	11	3	4	3.000
Ed Roebuck	3	0	2.08	0	0	0	0	4.1	1	1	1	0	5	0.231
Don Drysdale	1	0	9.00	0	0	0	0	2.0	2	2	2	1	1	1.500
Totals	7	7	4.72	3	4	0	3	61.0	58	33	32	21	43	1.295

1956

NEW YORK YANKEES vs. BROOKLYN DODGERS

New York Yankees Composite Stats

BATTING	G	AB	R	H	RBI	2B	3B	HR	BB	SO	BA	OBP	SLG	OPS
Hank Bauer	7	32	3	9	3	0	0	1	0	5	.281	.281	.375	.656
Billy Martin	7	27	5	8	3	0	0	2	1	6	.296	.321	.519	.840
Yogi Berra	7	25	5	9	10	2	0	3	4	1	.360	.448	.800	1.248
Mickey Mantle	7	24	6	6	4	1	0	3	6	5	.250	.400	.667	1.067
Gil McDougald	7	21	0	3	1	0	0	0	3	6	.143	.240	.143	.383
Joe Collins	6	21	2	5	2	2	0	0	2	3	.238	.304	.333	.638
Enos Slaughter	6	20	6	7	4	0	0	1	4	0	.350	.440	.500	.940
Andy Carey	7	19	2	3	0	0	0	0	1	6	.158	.200	.158	.358
Bill Skowron	3	10	1	1	4	0	0	1	0	3	.100	.100	.400	.500
Elston Howard	1	5	1	2	1	1	0	1	0	0	.400	.400	1.200	1.600
Whitey Ford	2	4	0	0	0	0	0	0	0	3	.000	.000	.000	.000
Bob Turley	3	4	0	0	0	0	0	0	0	1	.000	.000	.000	.000
Johnny Kucks	3	3	0	0	0	0	0	0	0	1	.000	.000	.000	.000
Don Larsen	2	3	1	1	1	0	0	0	0	1	.333	.333	.333	.667
Tom Sturdivant	2	3	0	1	0	0	0	0	0	1	.333	.333	.333	.667
Jerry Coleman	2	2	0	0	0	0	0	0	0	0	.000	.000	.000	.000
Tommy Byrne	2	1	0	0	0	0	0	0	0	0	.000	.000	.000	.000
Bob Cerv	1	1	0	1	0	0	0	0	0	0	1.000	1.000	1.000	2.000
Mickey McDermott	1	1	0	1	0	0	0	0	0	0	1.000	1.000	1.000	2.000
Tom Morgan	2	1	1	1	0	0	0	0	0	0	1.000	1.000	1.000	2.000
Norm Siebern	1	1	0	0	0	0	0	0	0	0	.000	.000	.000	.000
George Wilson	1	1	0	0	0	0	0	0	0	1	.000	.000	.000	.000
Totals	80	229	33	58	33	6	0	12	21	43	.253	.313	.437	.750

PITCHING	G	GS	ERA	W	L	SV	CG	IP	H	R	ER	BB	SO	WHIP
Whitey Ford	2	2	5.25	1	1	0	1	12.0	14	8	7	2	8	1.333
Johnny Kucks	3	1	0.82	1	0	0	1	11.0	6	2	1	3	2	0.818
Bob Turley	3	1	0.82	0	1	0	1	11.0	4	1	1	8	14	1.091
Don Larsen	2	2	0.00	1	0	0	1	10.2	1	4	0	4	7	0.469
Tom Sturdivant	2	1	2.79	1	0	0	1	9.2	8	3	3	8	9	1.655
Tom Morgan	2	0	9.00	0	1	0	0	4.0	6	4	4	4	3	2.500
M. McDermott	1	0	3.00	0	0	0	0	3.0	2	2	1	3	3	1.667
Tommy Byrne	1	0	0.00	0	0	0	0	0.1	1	1	0	0	1	3.000
Totals	7	7	2.48	4	3	0	5	61.2	42	25	17	32	47	1.200

NEW YORK METS   vs.   NEW YORK YANKEES

FUNGOES

- Subway Series meeting between the two clubs for the first time.
- 44 years since last Subway Series (1956).
- In the first Subway Series of 1921, a subway ride cost 15 cents; in 2000, $2.00; box seats sold for $5.00; in 2000, $160.00, or much more.
- Shea Stadium is the fourth New York ballpark to host a Fall Classic.
- First Subway Series without the league designations for umpires or league presidents, and more importantly, with six divisions.
- Umpire data: Jerry Crawford is the son of retired umpire Shag Crawford; Jeff Kellogg earned a BS in criminal justice; Tim Welke's brother Bill is also an umpire.

SERIES SUMMARY

After a 44-year break, due mainly to the departure from New York in the 1950's of the Giants and Dodgers, the Subway Series resumed in 2000. It was a low-scoring, hard-fought series, with a couple of breaks, Mets mistakes, and Derek Jeter leading to a Yankees' Series win in five games.

A blown save by Armando Benitez in the ninth inning of Game 1 gave the Bombers a chance to push across a run in the bottom of the 12th inning. Jeff Nelson, Mariano Rivera, and Mike Stanton pitched 5.1 innings of shutout relief to lock in the win.

The Yankees coasted in Game 2 for eight innings, scoring in five separate frames for a 6-0 lead. But a big Mets rally in the ninth, featuring a 3-run home run off Mariano Rivera by Jay Payton, pulled the Amazins within one run, but that was as close as they got.

The Mets pulled into the win column in Game 3 with a 4-2 victory behind Rick Reed and four relievers. Benny Agbayani delivered the big blow, an RBI single in the bottom of the 8th to break a 2-2 tie. Todd Zeile and Robin Ventura each chipped in two hits, an RBI, and a RS.

All the scoring in Game 4 took place in the first three innings, as Derek Jeter homered and tripled and scored two runs. Thanks to the same relief trio of Nelson, Stanton, and Rivera, the Yankees made their 3-2 lead hold up.

Game 5 was another tight one, with the Yankees drawing even with the Mets 2-2 with a run in the sixth. The scored remained tied until the ninth when a 2-out walk, two singles, and a throwing error led to two runs. Stanton again pitched the eighth and picked up the win, and of course Rivera recorded the final three outs.

244

THE TEAMS

NEW YORK METS
94 – 68 .580 WC

The Team
- Subway Series debut; 4th overall appearance (14-year hiatus).
- Most appearances of any expansion team.
- Second Wild Card pennant winner (Florida, 1997).
- In the Wild Card spot at the All-Star break.

The Players
- Four players with Fall Classic appearances with other teams: Mike Bordick, 1990, Oakland Athletics; Al Leiter, 1993 Toronto Blue Jays and 1997 Florida Marlins; Leiter's teammates on that team included Kurt Abbott and Dennis Cook, also on the Mets.
- Mike Hampton won the National League Championship MVP, pitching 16 shutout innings and winning two games.

The Manager
- Bobby Valentine is the 86th manager to debut.
- Valentine is the seventh manager to debut in the Subway Series (Huggins, Durocher, Shotton, Stengel, Dressen, Alston). Only Stengel and Alston were victorious.

Top Batters

Pos	Name	AB	R	H	HR	RBI	BA	OPS
C	Mike Piazza	482	90	156	38	113	.324	1.012
2B	Edgardo Alfonzo	544	109	176	25	94	.324	.967
3B	Robin Ventura	469	61	109	24	84	.232	.777
RF	Derek Bell	546	87	145	18	69	.266	.773

Top Pitchers

Pos	Name	W	L	ERA	G	SV	IP	SO
St	Mike Hampton	15	10	3.14	33	0	217.2	151
St	Al Leiter	16	8	3.20	31	0	208.0	200
St	Rick Reed	11	5	4.11	30	0	184.0	121
Rel	Armando Benitez	4	4	2.61	76	41	76.0	106

NEW YORK YANKEES
87 – 74 .540 +2.5

The Team
- 37th overall appearance, third consecutive.
- Tied for first place with the Toronto Blue Jays at the All-Star break.
- Fall Classic appearance in ninth straight decade, only team.
- 13th team to appear with less than 90 regular season wins.
- First time to reach the WS with less than 90 wins since strike-shortened 1981.
- Three straight American League pennants for the fourth time.
- Facing 13th different opponent and third New York National League franchise.

The Players
- 1996/98/99 returning players (8) from the championship clubs - David Cone, Derek Jeter, Tino Martinez, Jeff Nelson, Paul O'Neill, Andy Pettitte, Mariano Rivera, and Bernie Williams.
- 1998/99 returning players (4) from the championship clubs - Scott Brosius, Orlando Hernandez, Chuck Knoblauch, and Jorge Posada.
- David Justice, acquired in a mid-season trade, hammered 41 homers (Cleveland 21/Yankees 20).
- 19 players with prior World Series experience on the roster.
- Justice won the American League Championship MVP, powering 2 HR and 8 RBI in the six games.

The Manager
- Joe Torre is making fourth managerial appearance, third consecutive.
- Torre, as a 1971 St. Louis Cardinal 3B, won the National League batting title (.363) and RBI title (137), as well as the MVP.
- Torre is the fourth manager to win the regular season MVP as a player.
- Torre played for (1975-1977) and managed (1977-1981) the Mets.

Top Batters

Pos	Name	AB	R	H	HR	RBI	BA	OPS
C	Jorge Posada	505	92	145	28	86	.287	.943
SS	Derek Jeter	593	119	201	15	73	.339	.896
CF	Bernie Williams	537	108	165	30	121	.307	.957
RF	Paul O'Neill	566	79	160	18	100	.283	.760

Top Pitchers

Pos	Name	W	L	ERA	G	SV	IP	SO
St	Andy Pettitte	19	9	4.35	32	0	204.2	125
St	Roger Clemens	13	8	3.70	32	0	204.1	188
St	Orlando Hernandez	12	13	4.51	29	0	195.2	141
Rel	Mariano Rivera	7	4	2.85	66	36	75.2	58

NEW YORK METS vs. NEW YORK YANKEES

October 21

LINE SCORE	1	2	3	4	5	6	7	8	9	10	11	12	R	H	E
NEW YORK METS	0	0	0	0	0	0	3	0	0	0	0	0	3	10	0
NEW YORK YANKEES	0	0	0	0	0	2	0	0	1	0	0	1	4	12	1

RECAP

A record-setting, 4-hour, 50-minute, 12-inning opening game that produced 22 base hits but only seven runs. Through the first five frames, the starters gave up hits but zero runs. Al Leiter was broken first, allowing a two-run double to David Justice in the bottom of the sixth. In the top of the seventh, the Mets responded by knocking Andy Pettitte out with four hits in a three-run rally. The Pinstripers scored the tying run in the bottom of the ninth inning on a sacrifice fly. In the bottom of the 12th inning, Jose Vizcaino singled home Tino Martinez with the walk-off win, the Yankees 13th straight World Series victory.

SCORING SUMMARY

Sixth Inning - New York Yankees

– Leiter starting.
– Vizcaino sizzled a single to deep short.
– Knoblauch reached first base on a fielder's choice; Vizcaino tagged out at the second base, Leiter to Bordick.
– Jeter walked Knoblauch to second base.
– Justice doubled into left field, driving home Knoblauch and Jeter.
– Williams walked intentionally.
– Martinez advanced the runners on a grounder to Zeile.
– Posada flied out to Payton.

2 Runs **2** Hits **0** Errors **2** LOB

METS – 0　　　　**YANKEES – 2**

Seventh Inning - New York Mets

– Ventura popped up to Vizcaino.
– Agbayani scalded a single into right field.
– Payton singled Agbayani to second base.
– Pratt walked the bases full.
– Trammell PH for Bordick, singled into left field, driving in Agbayani and Payton.
– Pratt slid into second base.
– Perez advanced the runners on a ground out, Pettitte to Martinez.
– Nelson relieved Pettitte.

– Alfonzo scored Pratt on hot single to the hot corner; Trammell slid into third.
– Piazza flied out to Williams.

3 Runs **4** Hits **0** Errors **2** LOB

METS – 3　　　　**YANKEES – 2**

Ninth Inning - New York Yankees

– Benitez pitching.
– Posada flied out to Payton.
– O'Neill hurried to first base on a walk.
– Polonia PH for Brosius, singled O'Neill to second base.
– Vizcaino loaded the bases on a single to left field.
– Knoblauch lofted a sacrifice fly to McEwing, plating O'Neill.
– Jeter was a strikeout.

1 Runs **2** Hits **0** Errors **2** LOB

METS – 3　　　　**YANKEES – 3**

Twelfth Inning - New York Yankees

– Wendell on the mound.
– Williams rolled out, Alfonzo to Zeile.
– Martinez stroked a single into right field.
– Posada doubled Martinez to third base.
– O'Neill intentionally walked; bases loaded.
– Sojo fouled out to Pratt.

Vizcaino singled into left field, driving Martinez home with the winning run.

1 Runs **3** Hits **0** Errors **3** LOB

METS – 3   **YANKEES – 4**

HIGHLIGHTS

- Mets reliever Glendon Rusch threw a wild pitch in the 10th and 11th innings; neither runner scored
- 22 singles and doubles bounced around the ballpark.
- Yankees' 2B Jose Vizcaino collected 4 hits in the game, including the walk-off game winner. Vizcaino went 0-for-11 in the remainder of the Series.
- The Metropolitans' lone walk scored in the seventh inning
- Pinstriper reliever Mike Stanton pitched one-two-three frames in the 11th and 12th, striking out three, earning the win
- Stanton made 1178 appearances in his career, second all time to Jesse Orosco

DIAMOND DUST

- 51st extra-inning game, the 7th opener
- Mets starter Al Leiter is the 16th hurler to start for both leagues
- Leiter is the fourth pitcher to start for three teams (1993 Toronto Blue Jays/1997 Florida Marlins)
- Mets C Todd Pratt is the fourth player hit by a pitch twice in same game; stranded on second base both times
- 13th straight wins for the Bronx Bombers, stretching over four Classics (1996/1998/1999)
- The Yankees are 10-6 in walk-offs while the Mets are 2-1
- The Yankees are 24-13 in openers while the Mets are 0-4
- Game One winners have won it all 58 times

Game 1 BOX SCORE SUMMARY

NEW YORK METS	AB	R	H	RBI	BB	K	1B	2B	3B	HR	TB	SB
EDGARDO ALFONZO, 2B	6	0	1	1	0	2	1	0	0	0	1	0
BENNY AGBAYANI, LF	4	1	2	0	0	1	1	1	0	0	3	0
JAY PAYTON, CF	5	1	1	0	0	0	1	0	0	0	1	0
TODD PRATT, C	2	1	0	0	1	2	0	0	0	0	0	0
BUBBA TRAMMELL	1	0	1	2	0	0	1	0	0	0	1	0

NEW YORK YANKEES	AB	R	H	RBI	BB	K	1B	2B	3B	HR	TB	SB
CHUCK KNOBLAUCH, DH	4	1	0	1	1	1	0	0	0	0	0	0
DEREK JETER, SS	4	1	1	0	2	2	1	0	0	0	1	0
DAVID JUSTICE, LF	4	0	1	2	1	0	0	1	0	0	2	0
TINO MARTINEZ, 1B	6	1	2	0	0	1	2	0	0	0	2	0
PAUL O'NEILL, RF	4	1	1	0	2	1	1	0	0	0	1	0
JOSE VISCAINO, 2B	6	0	4	1	0	1	4	0	0	0	4	0

NEW YORK METS	IP	H	R	ER	HR	K	BB	HBP	ERA
AL LEITER	7	5	2	2	0	7	3	0	2.86
ARMANDO BENITEZ	1	2	1	1	0	1	1	0	3.86
TURK WENDELL L (0-1)	1	3	1	1	0	0	1	0	2.08

NEW YORK YANKEES	IP	H	R	ER	HR	K	BB	HBP	ERA
ANDY PETTITTE	6.2	8	3	3	0	4	1	0	3.65
MIKE STANTON W (1-0)	2	0	0	0	0	3	0	0	1.42

GAME TIME: **4:51**
ATTENDANCE: **55,913**
BEST OF 7:   **METS - 0   YANKEES - 1**

THE LONGEST GAMES IN WORLD SERIES HISTORY (12 INNINGS OR MORE)

Year	Game	No Inn	Away	Sc	Home	Sc	Note
1907	G1	12	Detroit	3	Chicago Cub	3	Evers caught stealing home to end bottom 9th
1914	G3	12	Philadelphia A's	4	Boston Brv	5	Hank Gowdy's heroics help Miracle Braves to shocking sweep
1916	G2	14	Brooklyn Rob	1	Boston RS	2	Babe Ruth goes distance and drives in first run
1924	G1	12	NY Giants	4	Washington	3	Big Train labors through 12-inning loss (14 H, 6 BB)
1924	G7	12	NY Giants	3	Washington	4	Johnson's 4 IP of relief gives Washington their only championship
1934	G2	12	St. Louis Cards	2	Detroit	3	Tigers tie in 9th and win in 12th
1945	G6	12	Detroit	7	Chicago Cub	8	Stan Hack's fourth hit (plus 2 BB) staves off elimination for Cubs
1973	G2	12	NY Mets	10	Oakland	7	Mets score 4 in 12th off Fingers; A's make 5 errors in all
1975	G6	12	Cincinnati	6	Boston RS	7	"The Game" ends with Fisk's blast and Red Sox stay alive
1977	G1	12	Los Angeles	3	NY Yankees	4	Blair drives home Randolph after Dodgers tie in 9th
1991	G3	12	Minnesota	4	Atlanta	5	One of 3 extra-inning games of series, including G6 and G7
2000	G1	12	NY Mets	3	NY Yankees	4	Jose Vizcaino's fourth hit of game drives in winner
2001	G5	12	Arizona	2	NY Yankees	3	Yankees score 2 in 9th to tie then win in 12th
2003	G4	12	NY Yankees	3	Florida	4	Yankees score 2 in 9th to tie, but Alex Gonzalez homers for win
2015	G1	14	NY Mets	4	KC Royals	5	Royals tie in 9th then win in 14th on error, single, sac fly
2015	G5	12	KC Royals	7	NY Mets	2	Royals tie in 9th and error in 12th contributes to winning rally
2018	G3	18	Boston RS	2	Los Angeles	3	Muncy HR ends longest WS gm ever; Dodgers' only win in Series

Although Game 1 of the 2000 World Series is the only Subway Series game to last at least 12 innings, New York teams have appeared in 10 of the 17 marathon games (Giants 2, Dodgers 1, Mets 4, Yankees 4).

For the Mets, the percentage of super-long games is remarkably high (4 of 29, or 13.8%). Unfortunately for them, they lost 3 of the 4 games, including 2 against the Kansas City Royals. The Mets lost that series and the Subway Series in five games, but both were tighter than the 4-1 margins suggest; they just couldn't win enough of the close ones.

Utility man Jose Vizcaino batted only 3 times in the 2000 ALCS, but he collected 2 hits and a sac fly. Vizcaino continued his clutch play in Game 1 of the World Series, collecting 4 hits, including the game-winner. He was hitless in 11 at bats for the remainder of the series.

NEW YORK METS vs. NEW YORK YANKEES

October 22

LINE SCORE	1	2	3	4	5	6	7	8	9	R	H	E
NEW YORK METS	0	0	0	0	0	0	0	0	5	5	7	3
NEW YORK YANKEES	2	1	0	0	1	0	1	1	X	6	12	1

RECAP

In the first inning, Roger Clemens and Mike Piazza became embroiled in a bizarre incident, the origins of which came during the regular season. On July 8th, Clemens beaned Piazza. Piazza suffered a concussion and spent time on the disabled list, causing him to miss the All-Star Game. Tonight, also in the first inning, Piazza shattered his bat on a Clemens pitch. The barrel of the bat landed near the mound as Pizza headed toward first. Clemens picked up the barrel and heaved it toward Piazza who stopped and moved toward Clemens. Both benches emptied. The umpires and personnel on both sides diffused a potential brawl.

With the aid of three Met errors, the Yankees had a 3-0 edge at the end of the second inning, which was expanded to six by the eighth. Yankee starter Roger Clemens, over those eight, gave up two Met singles, both to Todd Zeile. The Mets offense was dormant until their last at bat. They were three up and three down in four innings. Only once did a runner reach second base. In the top of the ninth, however, needing six to tie, the Mets scored five, on home runs by Mike Piazza and Jay Payton. But it was not enough, as Rivera fanned Alfonzo for the final out. The Yankees extended their World Series winning streak to 14.

SCORING SUMMARY

First Inning - New York Yankees

– Hampton starting.
– Knoblauch flied out to Payton (good play).
– Jeter struck out.
– Justice jogged to first on a walk.
– Williams walked Justice to second base.
– Martinez singled into left field, driving Justice home.
– Posada singled into center field, driving in Williams; on Payton's fielding error both runners moved up.
– O'Neill was a strikeout.

2 Runs **2** Hits **1** Errors **2** LOB

METS – 0   **YANKEES – 2**

Second Inning - New York Yankees

– Brosius slugged a solo shot into the left field seats.
– Vizcaino safe at first base on Bordick's fielding error; caught stealing, Piazza to Bordick.
– Knoblauch worked a walk.
– Jeter hitched a hit-and-run single; Knoblauch steamed into third base.
– Jeter slid into second base on Perez's fielding error. Knoblauch thrown out at the plate, Perez to Piazza.

– Justice tapped out, Alfonzo to Zeile.

1 Runs **2** Hits **2** Errors **2** LOB

METS – 0   **YANKEES – 3**

Fifth Inning - New York Yankees

– Justice struck out.
– Williams bounced out, Bordick to Zeile.
– Martinez doubled into the right-center field alley.
– Posada intentionally walked; Martinez held.
– O'Neill singled into right field, driving in Martinez; Posada pulled up at third.
– Brosius flied out to Payton.

1 Runs **2** Hits **0** Errors **2** LOB

METS – 0   **YANKEES – 4**

Seventh Inning - New York Yankees

– Rusch pitching.
– Martinez topped out, Bordick to Zeile.
– Posada fisted a single into right field.
– O'Neill doubled Posada to third base.
– White relieved Rusch.

– Brosius lifted a sacrifice fly to Perez plating Posada; O'Neill moved up.

– Vizcaino was a strikeout.

❶ Runs ❸ Hits ❾ Errors ❸ LOB

METS – 0   **YANKEES – 5**

Eighth Inning - New York Yankees

– Abbott to SS.

– Knoblauch grounded out, Alfonzo to Zeile.

– Jeter doubled along the first base line.

– Justice bounced out, Abbott to Zeile.

– Williams intentionally walked.

– Cook relieved White.

– Martinez singled into left-center field, driving in Jeter; Williams took second.

– Posada reached first base on a fielder's choice; Martinez out at second base, Alfonzo to Abbott.

❶ Runs ❷ Hits ❾ Errors ❷ LOB

METS – 0   **YANKEES – 6**

Ninth Inning - New York Mets

– Nelson pitching. Bellinger to LF

– Alfonzo singled through the left side of the infield.

– Piazza blasted a home run off of the left field foul pole, driving Alfonzo home.

– Ventura whipped a single into center field.

– Rivera relieved Nelson.

– Zeile flied out to Bellinger.

– Agbayani singled Ventura to second base; both runners advanced on a passed ball.

– Harris safe at first base on a fielder's choice; Ventura thrown out at the plate, Jeter to Posada; Agbayani slid into third base; Harris advanced to second uncontested.

– Payton hammered a home run into the right field seats, driving home Agbayani and Harris.

– Alfonzo struck out.

❺ Runs ❺ Hits ❾ Errors ❾ LOB

METS – 5   **YANKEES – 6**

HIGHLIGHTS

- Roger Clemens, as a 1986 Boston Red Sox, also started Game 2 versus the Mets
- Clemens was relieved after the eighth inning with a six-run lead, having pitched a two-hit shutout
- Both teams had runners thrown out at the plate; both starters hit a batter
- Payton's 9th inning homer is the 20th in franchise history
- Three Bronx Bombers stroked three hits
- Yankees drilled all four doubles
- The three Yankee pitchers did not issue a free pass and struck out 10

DIAMOND DUST

- Clemens is one of a few pitchers in World Series history to throw a wild pitch, hit a batter, and commit an error in the same game
- Yankee reliever Mariano Rivera's 14-game scoreless streak was stopped

Game 2 BOX SCORE SUMMARY

NEW YORK METS	AB	R	H	RBI	BB	K	1B	2B	3B	HR	TB	SB
EDGARDO ALFONZO, 2B	3	1	1	0	0	1	1	0	0	0	1	0
MIKE PIAZZA, C	4	1	1	2	0	0	0	0	0	1	4	0
BENNY AGBAYANI, LF	4	1	1	0	0	2	1	0	0	0	1	0
LENNY HARRIS, DH	4	1	0	0	0	0	0	0	0	0	0	0
JAY PAYTON, CF	4	1	1	3	0	1	0	0	0	1	4	0
NEW YORK YANKEES	AB	R	H	RBI	BB	K	1B	2B	3B	HR	TB	SB
DEREK JETER, SS	5	1	3	0	0	1	1	2	0	0	5	0
DAVID JUSTICE	3	1	0	0	1	1	0	0	0	0	0	0
BERNIE WILLIAMS, CF	3	1	0	0	2	0	0	0	0	0	0	0
TINO MARTINEZ, 1B	5	1	3	2	0	0	2	1	0	0	4	0
JORGE POSADA, C	3	1	2	1	2	0	2	0	0	0	2	0
PAUL O'NEILL, RF	4	0	3	1	0	1	2	1	0	0	4	0
SCOTT BROSIUS, 3B	3	1	1	2	0	1	0	0	0	1	4	0

NEW YORK METS	IP	H	R	ER	HR	K	BB	HBP	ERA
MIKE HAMPTON L (0-1)	6	8	4	4	1	4	5	1	2.96
GLENDON RUSCH	0.1	2	1	1	0	0	0	0	1.42
RICK WHITE	1.1	1	1	1	0	1	1	0	5.14
NEW YORK YANKEES	IP	H	R	ER	HR	K	BB	HBP	ERA
ROGER CLEMENS W (1-0)	8	2	0	0	0	9	0	1	3.21
JEFF NELSON	0	3	2	2	1	0	0	0	8.53
MARIANO RIVERA	1	2	3	3	1	1	0	0	2.13

GAME TIME:	**3:30**
ATTENDANCE:	**56,059**
BEST OF 7:	**METS - 0 YANKEES - 2**

NEW YORK YANKEES vs. NEW YORK METS

October 24

LINE SCORE	1	2	3	4	5	6	7	8	9	R	H	E
NEW YORK YANKEES	0	0	1	1	0	0	0	0	0	2	8	0
NEW YORK METS	0	1	0	0	0	1	0	2	X	4	9	0

--- RECAP ---

Seven pitchers for the two teams combined to strikeout 25 batters. The Amazin's starter Rick Reed in six innings fanned eight. Bombers starter Orlando Hernandez fanned 12 in seven innings. David Justice and Paul O'Neill tagged Reed for extra-base hits, driving in two. Robin Ventura, Mike Piazza, Todd Zeile and Joe McEwing scored the four runs off of Hernandez. The home team's victory stopped three streaks: 14 wins in a row for the Yankees, two straight wins for starter Orlando Hernandez and two straight losses for the Mets.

--- SCORING SUMMARY ---

Second Inning - New York Mets
– Hernandez starting.
– Ventura slugged a solo shot into the right field seats.
– Zeile strikeout.
– Agbayani strikeout.
– Payton strikeout.

1 Runs **1** Hits **0** Errors **0** LOB

YANKEES – 0   **METS – 1**

Third Inning - New York Yankees
– Hernandez went down on strikes.
– Vizcaino nubbed out, Bordick to Zeile.
– Jeter stroked a single into left field.
– Justice doubled down the right field line, driving in Jeter; Justice took third on the throw to the plate.
– Williams grounded out, Alfonzo to Zeile.

1 Runs **2** Hits **0** Errors **1** LOB

YANKEES – 1   **METS – 1**

Fourth Inning - New York Yankees
– Martinez hacked a single into right field.
– Posada struck out.
– O'Neill tripled into right-center field, driving Martinez home.
– Brosius hit by a pitch.

– Hernandez sacrificed Brosius to second base, Reed to Alfonzo.
– Vizcaino was a strikeout.

1 Runs **1** Hits **0** Errors **1** LOB

YANKEES – 2   **METS – 1**

Sixth Inning - New York Mets
– Pizza doubled inside the left field line.
– Ventura walked; Pizza held.
– Zeile doubled into left field, driving in Piazza; Ventura chugged into third base.
– Agbayani filled up the bases on a walk.
– Payton strikeout.
– Bordick strikeout.
– Hamilton PH for Reed, forced Agbayani at second base, Jeter to Vizcaino.

1 Runs **2** Hits **0** Errors **3** LOB

YANKEES – 2   **METS – 2**

Eighth Inning - New York Mets
– Sojo to 3B.
– Ventura strikeout.
– Zeile lobbed a single into left field.
– Agbayani doubled off of the left-center field wall, driving Zeile home.
– McEwing PR.

Game 3

- Payton singled McEwing to third base.
- Harris PH for Bordick.
- Stanton relieved Hernandez.
- Trammell PH for Harris, lofted a sacrifice fly to Williams plating McEwing.
- Abbott PH for J. Franco, struck out.

2 Runs **3** Hits **0** Errors **1** LOB

YANKEES – 2   **METS – 4**

HIGHLIGHTS

- Ventura is the fifth Met to homer in the third game of a Fall Classic (1969 Agee & Kranepool/1973 Wayne Garrett/1986 Lenny Dykstra)
- Hernandez struck out the side for third time in career (twice also in 1999)
- Yankee RF Paul O'Neill was a home run shy of the cycle
- Mets 3B Robin Ventura collected six total bases

DIAMOND DUST

- Yankee starter Orlando Hernandez is the 36th pitcher with a losing regular season record (12-13) to start and the 21st to lose
- Six combined strikeouts in the second inning tie a record
- Hernandez is the sixth pitcher to fan 12 in a game
- 25 strikeouts (Yankees 13/Mets 12) tied a record
- Second Series (1973) in which the Mets were part of a team record 25 strikeouts in a game
- Pinstriper Luis Polonia extends his World Series record for pinch-hit appearances to 12 in the ninth with a fly out to center for Vizcaino
- Franco is the second 40-year-old pitcher to win a World Series game. Cuban-born Dolph Luque was the first, winning the clinching Game 5 for the NY Giants in 1933 at the age of 43

Game 3 BOX SCORE SUMMARY

NEW YORK YANKEES	AB	R	H	RBI	BB	K	1B	2B	3B	HR	TB	SB
DEREK JETER, SS	4	1	2	0	1	2	2	0	0	0	2	0
DAVID JUSTICE, LF	3	0	1	1	1	0	0	1	0	0	2	0
TINO MARTINEZ, 1B	3	1	1	0	1	1	1	0	0	0	1	0
PAUL O'NEILL, RF	4	0	3	1	0	0	1	1	1	0	6	0
NEW YORK METS	AB	R	H	RBI	BB	K	1B	2B	3B	HR	TB	SB
MIKE PIAZZA, C	4	1	1	0	0	2	0	1	0	0	2	0
ROBIN VENTURA, 3B	3	1	2	1	1	1	1	0	1	0	1	6	0
TODD ZEILE, 1B	4	1	2	1	0	2	1	1	0	0	3	0
BENNY AGBAYANI, LF	3	0	1	1	1	1	0	1	0	0	2	0
JOE McEWING, PR/LF	0	1	0	0	0	0	0	0	0	0	0	0
BUBBA TRAMMELL, PH	0	0	0	1	0	0	0	0	0	0	0	0

Longest World Series Team Winning Streaks

Team	Wins	Years	Opponents
NY Yankees	14	1996-2000	1996 Atl (4), '98 Atl (4), '99 SDP (4), '00 Mets (2)
NY Yankees	12	1927-1932	1927 PIT (4), '28 StL (4), '32 ChC (4)
NY Yankees	11	1937-1941	1937 NYG (2), '38 ChC (4), '39 Cin (4), '41 (1)
Cincinnati Reds	9	1975-1980	1975 Bos (1), '76 NYY (4), '90 (4)
Boston Red Sox	9	2004-2013	2004 StL (4), '07 Col (4), '13 StL (1)

NEW YORK YANKEES	IP	H	R	ER	HR	K	BB	HBP	ERA
ORLANDO HERNANDEZ L (0-1)	7.1	9	4	4	1	12	3	0	3.94
NEW YORK METS	IP	H	R	ER	HR	K	BB	HBP	ERA
RICK REED	6	6	2	2	0	8	1	1	4.70
JOHN FRANCO W (1-0)	1	1	0	0	0	0	0	0	2.70
ARMANDO BENITEZ S (1)	1	1	0	0	0	1	0	0	3.38

GAME TIME:	**3:39**	
ATTENDANCE:	**55,299**	
BEST OF 7:	**METS - 1**	**YANKEES - 2**

The Jeter Postseason Juggernaut

The 2000 baseball season was historic in that Derek Jeter became the first player ever to win the All-Star Game and the World Series MVP Award in the same season. 2000 marked Jeter's third All-Star Game appearance, his first as the starting shortstop, Derek Jeter had a great day in the Summer Classic. He doubled off Randy Johnson in the first inning, singled and scored his next time up, and then in the fourth inning he broke a 1-1 tie with a 2-run single. The American League went on to win 6-3, with Jeter, amazingly, becoming the first Yankees player to win the game's MVP.

Derek Jeter's 2000 World Series appearance was the best of his career. He hit safely in all five games and scored at least one run in every game. He ripped two home runs and overall put up a slash line of .409/.480/.864/1.344.

Jeter was fortunate to play on a strong Yankees team throughout his career. Of course, he was one of the main reasons the team was so strong. The Hall of Fame shortstop played in the postseason in 16 of his 20 years, including 16 of the 18 in which he was a full-time player. In terms of overall statistics, this amazing October stretch worked out neatly to 158 games, and his totals align very closely with his regular-season 162-game averages.

In 650 postseason at bats, Jeter collected exactly 200 hits, hit 20 HR, and scored 111 runs. His career postseason slash line of .308/.374/.465 is remarkably close to his regular season's of .310/.377/.440—a tribute to his excellence under pressure, facing far tougher pitching than he did in the regular season.

Game 4

NEW YORK YANKEES vs. NEW YORK METS

October 25

LINE SCORE	1	2	3	4	5	6	7	8	9	R	H	E
NEW YORK YANKEES	1	1	1	0	0	0	0	0	0	3	8	0
NEW YORK METS	0	0	2	0	0	0	0	0	0	2	6	1

RECAP

Over the first three innings a Derek Jeter solo home run, a Scott Brosius sacrifice fly and a Luis Sojo grounder gave the Yankees an early and lasting three-run lead. Mike Piazza's two-run homer with Timo Perez on first was the Mets offense. The final six innings saw good pitching backed by good fielding hold tight the slim difference. The starters were charged with all of the runs, as neither bullpen gave up a tally. The 3-1 edge in the Series was as formidable for the Yankees as it was daunting for the Mets.

SCORING SUMMARY

First Inning - New York Yankees
– Jones starting.
– Jeter slugged a first-pitch solo shot into the left field seats.
– Sojo nipped at first base, Ventura to Zeile.
– Justice flied out to Perez.
– Williams flied out to Payton.

1 Runs **1** Hits **0** Errors **0** LOB

YANKEES – 1   **METS – 0**

Second Inning - New York Yankees
– Martinez struck out.
– O'Neill tomahawked a triple into the left field corner.
– Posada purposely walked; O'Neill held; runners on the corners.
– Brosius lifted a sacrifice fly to Payton plating O'Neill; Posada held.
– Neagle went down on strikes.

1 Runs **1** Hits **0** Errors **1** LOB

YANKEES – 2   **METS – 0**

Third Inning - New York Yankees
– Jeter triggered a triple into right-center field.
– Sojo scored Jeter on a grounder, Alfonzo to Zeile.

– Justice grounded out to Zeile.
– Williams flied out to Payton.

1 Runs **1** Hits **0** Errors **0** LOB

YANKEES – 3   **METS – 0**

Third Inning - New York Mets
– Perez singled wide of second base.
– Alfonzo advanced Perez on a ground out, Brosius to Martinez.
– Piazza clouted a home run into the left field seats, driving Perez home.
– Zeile popped up to Sojo.
– Ventura grounded out to Martinez.

2 Runs **2** Hits **0** Errors **0** LOB

YANKEES – 3   **METS – 2**

HIGHLIGHTS

• Paul O'Neill and Jeter torched run-producing triples in consecutive innings
• After the third inning, all scoring stopped
• Mike Stanton, in relief, struck out the two pinch hitters

DIAMOND DUST

- Derek Jeter launched the 16th lead-off home run
- Tying a record, the Mets used four pinch hitters in the seventh inning (one walk, two strikeouts, one no plate appearance)
- Mariano Rivera's game-ending strikeout was the third of his World Series career

Game 4 BOX SCORE SUMMARY

NEW YORK YANKEES	AB	R	H	RBI	BB	K	1B	2B	3B	HR	TB	SB
DEREK JETER, SS	5	2	2	1	0	1	0	0	1	1	7	0
LUIS SOJO, 2B	4	0	1	1	1	0	1	0	0	0	1	0
PAUL O'NEILL, RF	4	1	2	0	0	0	1	0	1	0	4	0
SCOTT BROSIUS, 3B	1	0	1	1	2	0	1	0	0	0	1	0
NEW YORK METS	AB	R	H	RBI	BB	K	1B	2B	3B	HR	TB	SB
TIMO PEREZ, RF	3	1	1	0	0	1	1	0	0	0	1	0
MIKE PIAZZA, C	4	1	1	2	0	1	0	0	0	1	4	0

NEW YORK YANKEES	IP	H	R	ER	HR	K	BB	HBP	ERA
DENNY NEAGLE	4.2	4	2	2	1	3	2	0	4.30
JEFF NELSON W (1-0)	1.1	1	0	0	0	1	1	0	7.04
MIKE STANTON	0.2	0	0	0	0	2	0	0	0.00
MARIANO RIVERA S (1)	2	1	0	0	0	2	0	0	1.84
NEW YORK METS	IP	H	R	ER	HR	K	BB	HBP	ERA
BOBBY JONES L (0-1)	5	4	3	3	1	3	3	0	4.50
GLENDON RUSCH	2	3	0	0	0	2	0	0	2.25

Mike Piazza reached the postseason five times (3 LAD, 1 NYM, 1 SDP. He had his best performance with the Mets in 2000, when he followed up a 3-2BH, 2-HR, .412 BA NLCS against the Cardinals with a 2-2B, 2-HR performance against the Yankees, giving Piazza 9 extra-base hits in 10 games.

GAME TIME:	**3:20**	
ATTENDANCE:	**55,290**	
BEST OF 7:	**METS - 1**	**YANKEES - 3**

Game 5

NEW YORK YANKEES vs. NEW YORK METS

October 26

LINE SCORE	1	2	3	4	5	6	7	8	9	R	H	E
NEW YORK YANKEES	0	1	0	0	0	1	0	0	2	4	7	1
NEW YORK METS	0	2	0	0	0	0	0	0	0	2	8	1

--- **RECAP** ---

At 2-2 in the top of the ninth inning, the tension rippled through the 55,000 fans. Amazins' starter Al Leiter's 140th pitch was a free pass to Jorge Posada. Back-to-back singles by Scott Brosius and Luis Sojo snapped the tie. On Soj's single, Brosius scored the insurance run on a throwing error. At 4-2 in the bottom of the ninth, Yankee fans were anticipating a victory while Mets fans were hoping for a miracle. With two outs, the Mets threatened with Benny Agbayani on third and Mike Piazza in the batter's box but were thwarted by reliever Mariano Rivera's record-setting seventh save. The Yankees were champions of the baseball world for the 26th time.

--- **SCORING SUMMARY** ---

Second Inning - New York Yankees
– Leiter starting.
– Williams slugged a solo shot into the left field seats.
– Martinez flied out to Agbayani.
– O'Neill struck out.
– Posada skittered out, Alfonzo to Zeile.

1 Runs **1** Hits **0** Errors **0** LOB

YANKEES – 1   **METS – 0**

Second Inning - New York Mets
– Pettitte starting.
– Ventura struck out.
– Trammell coaxed a walk.
– Payton singled Trammell to second base.
– Abbott advanced the runners on a ground out, Jeter to Martinez.
– Leiter safe at first base on Pettitte's fielding error; Trammell scored; Payton darted into third base.
– Agbayani scored Payton on an infield single; Leiter moved up.
– Alfonzo popped up to Vizcaino.

2 Runs **2** Hits **1** Errors **2** LOB

YANKEES – 1   **METS – 2**

Sixth Inning - New York Yankees
– Vizcaino grounded out, Leiter to Zeile.
– Jeter slugged a solo shot into the left field stands.
– Justice struck out.
– Williams trotted to first on a walk.
– Martinez tapped out, Abbott to Zeile.

1 Runs **1** Hits **0** Errors **1** LOB

YANKEES – 2   **METS – 2**

Ninth Inning - New York Yankees
– Perez to RF.
– Martinez struck out.
– O'Neill struck out.
– Posada wangled a walk.
– Brosius singled Posada to second base.
– Sojo singled into center field, driving in Posada; Brosius scored and Sojo slid into third on Payton's throwing error.
– J. Franco relieved Leiter.
– Hill PH for Stanton, flied out to Agbayani.

2 Runs **2** Hits **1** Errors **1** LOB

YANKEES – 4   **METS – 2**

Yankees Win Their 11th Subway Series
Most Valuable Player
Derek Jeter
The 47th Player
The Third Shortstop
The 11th New York Yankee

HIGHLIGHTS

- Twenty-third five-game set
- Yankees reliever Mariano Rivera got the final three outs to notch his second straight save

DIAMOND DUST

- Derek Jeter is the first same-season MVP winner of both the All-Star Game and the Fall Classic
- Jeter hit and scored in all five games, extending his Fall Classic hitting streak to 14 games, the final game of 1996 and then all 13 games of 1998-2000
- Jeter is the 18th player to slug solo shots in consecutive games
- Andy Pettitte second game-clinching start (1998)
- Pettitte, in the fourth inning, tied the record for most pick-offs with 2
- Jeter's fourth inning solo shot is the 200th in franchise World Series history
- Yankees reliever Mike Stanton, in the bottom of the eighth inning, got three quick outs for the win, becoming the seventh reliever to win two games as well as the 10th to win in both leagues (Atlanta Braves, 1991)
- Rivera is the second reliever to post wins and/or saves in three straight Classics
- The Mets are the first Wild Card team to lose a World Series

Game 5 BOX SCORE SUMMARY

NEW YORK YANKEES	AB	R	H	RBI	BB	K	1B	2B	3B	HR	TB	SB
DEREK JETER, SS	4	1	1	1	0	2	0	0	0	1	4	0
BERNIE WILLIAMS, CF	3	1	2	1	1	1	1	1	0	0	1	5	0
JORGE POSADA, C	3	1	1	0	0	0	1	0	0	0	1	0
SCOTT BROSIUS, 3B	4	1	1	0	0	0	0	0	0	0	1	0
LUIS SOJO, 2B	1	0	1	1	0	0	1	0	0	0	1	0
NEW YORK METS	AB	R	H	RBI	BB	K	1B	2B	3B	HR	TB	SB
BENNY AGBAYANI, LF	4	0	1	1	1	1	1	0	0	0	1	0
BUBBA TRAMMELL, RF	3	1	1	0	1	0	1	0	0	0	1	0
JAY PAYTON, CF	4	1	2	0	0	1	2	0	0	0	2	0

In notching his second win of the Series, Mike Stanton capped another fantastic postseason of pitching. To this point in his career, Stanton had pitched in 40 postseason games, compiling a record of 5-1 in 41.2 IP, with an ERA of 1.20, much of which was accomplished with the Atlanta Braves.

NEW YORK YANKEES	IP	H	R	ER	HR	K	BB	HBP	ERA
ANDY PETTITTE	7	8	2	0	0	5	3	0	2.84
MIKE STANTON W (2-0)	1	0	0	0	0	1	0	0	1.04
MARIANO RIVERA S (2)	1	0	0	0	0	1	1	0	1.72
NEW YORK METS	IP	H	R	ER	HR	K	BB	HBP	ERA
AL LEITER L (0-1)	8.2	7	4	3	2	9	3	0	2.93

GAME TIME:	**3:32**	
ATTENDANCE:	**55,292**	
BEST OF 7:	**METS - 1**	**YANKEES - 4**

SUMMARY OF THE 14 SUBWAY SERIES

Year	Lg	Team	Wins	Losses	RS/Gm	ERA	Highlights
1921	NL	NY Giants	5	3	3.62	2.54	Giants used only 4 pitchers in 8-game series
	AL	NY Yankees	3	5	2.75	3.09	Yankees scored 1 run in last 25 inn of Series
1922	NL	NY Giants	4	0 (1 tie)	3.60	1.76	Heinie Groh got 9 hits in 5 games
	AL	NY Yankees	0 (1 tie)	4	2.20	3.35	Babe Ruth was held to a 2-for-17
1923	NL	NY Giants	2	4	2.83	4.75	SS Bancroft hit .145 for the 1921-23 Series
	AL	NY Yankees	4	2	5.00	2.83	Herb Pennock won 2 in 1923, 5-0 in WS career
1936	NL	NY Giants	2	4	3.83	6.79	Ott had 2X more RBI than next best Giants' player
	AL	NY Yankees	4	2	7.17	3.50	Infamous Jake Powell led Yanks with .455 (10/22)
1937	NL	NY Giants	1	4	2.40	4.81	Hubbell held DiMaggio to 3-for-16 in '36, '37 Series
	AL	NY Yankees	4	1	5.60	2.45	Outscored Giants 28-12 during Series
1941	NL	Brooklyn Dodgers	1	4	2.20	2.66	Casey lost G3, G4 in 1941 and won G3, G4 in 1947
	AL	NY Yankees	4	1	3.40	1.80	Joe Gordon 7-for-14 with 7 BB and 0 K's in Series
1947	NL	Brooklyn Dodgers	3	4	4.14	5.55	Gionfriddo's catch came in his last big league game
	AL	NY Yankees	4	3	5.43	4.09	Johnny Lindell went 9-for-18 with 7 RBI
1949	NL	Brooklyn Dodgers	1	4	2.80	4.30	Brooklyn batted .210 as a team
	AL	NY Yankees	4	1	4.20	2.80	Allie Reynolds allowed 0 R in 12.1 IP, with a W and SV
1951	NL	NY Giants	2	4	3.00	4.67	Maglie & Jansen won 23 in '51, but went 0-3 in WS
	AL	NY Yankees	4	2	4.83	1.87	Lopat allowed 1 ER total in 2 CG victories
1952	NL	Brooklyn Dodgers	3	4	2.86	3.52	Hodges 0-for-21 and Robinson 4-for-23
	AL	NY Yankees	4	3	3.71	2.81	Kuzava got final 8 outs in G7 in his only Series game
1953	NL	Brooklyn Dodgers	2	4	4.50	4.91	The Dodgers used the same starting 8 in all 6 games
	AL	NY Yankees	4	2	5.50	4.50	Martin's .500 BA and 8 RBI led all players
1955	NL	Brooklyn Dodgers	4	3	4.43	3.75	Dodgers' G7 victory was only road win of Series
	AL	NY Yankees	3	4	3.71	4.20	Yankees team ERA without Ford was 5.02
1956	NL	Brooklyn Dodgers	3	4	3.57	4.72	Dodgers totaled 3 RS in final 4 games of Series
	AL	NY Yankees	4	3	4.71	2.48	Berra batted .400 (28/70) over 1953, '55, '56 Series
2000	NL	NY Mets	1	4	3.20	3.47	Alfonzo (.143), Ventura (.150) totaled 2 RBI in Series
	AL	NY Yankees	4	1	3.80	2.68	O'Neill hit .474 with 4 extra-base hits in Series

	Team	Ser W	Ser L	Gm W	Gm L	Pct
	NY Yankees	11	3	50	34	.595
OVERALL	NY Giants	2	4	16	19	.457
RECORDS	Bklyn Dodgers	1	6	17	27	.386
	NY Mets	0	1	1	4	.200

2000

NEW YORK METS vs. NEW YORK YANKEES

NEW YORK METS

Overall World Series Record: 2 WINS 2 LOSSES. 24 Games Played (12-12, .500)
- 25 players (10 pitchers) took the field.
- Bobby Valentine, in only appearance, is the 44th manager to lose debut appearance

NEW YORK YANKEES

Overall World Series Record: 26 WINS 11 LOSSES. 206 Games Played [125-80 WINS (1 tie) .610]
- MVP Derek Jeter's six runs scored is twice more than any other player.
- Jeter hit for the cycle, as five of the nine hits went for extra bases (two homers, two doubles, and a triple).
- Roger Clemens has won and lost (1986) versus the Mets.
- Stanton won Games 1 and 5; Stanton allowed only 5 ER in his first 41.2 IP of post-season play.
- Orlando Hernandez, in only appearance, struck out 12 but lost the only game for the Yankees.
- Jose Canseco, David Cone, David Justice, Chuck Knoblauch, Paul O'Neill and Luis Polonia all won championships with other teams.
- Joe Torre's managerial record is 4-0.
- Torre joins Joe McCarthy and Casey Stengel as the only managers to win three straight Classics.
- The 1998-2000 club became the first team since the 1972-74 Oakland Athletics to win three consecutive titles.
- Seventh team with fewer than 90 regular season wins to capture the title.

FUNGOES

564 games have been played since 1903
- Derek Jeter, along with Mets CF Jay Payton and C Mike Piazza, are the only players to smack a hit in all five games.
- Joe Torre joins Casey Stengel and Walter Alston as the only managers to win Subway Series debut appearance.
- Last World Series in both ballparks.

FIVE-GAME DATA

TIME	19:10	PLAYERS POOL	$43,010,412
ATTENDANCE	277,853	SHARES	NEW YORK METS - $238,654
			NEW YORK YANKEES - $294,783

LEAGUE TALLY

57 - AMERICAN LEAGUE	96	NATIONAL LEAGUE - 39

2000

NEW YORK METS vs. NEW YORK YANKEES

New York Mets Composite Stats

BATTING	G	AB	R	H	RBI	2B	3B	HR	BB	SO	BA	OBP	SLG	OPS
Mike Piazza	5	22	3	6	4	2	0	2	0	4	.273	.273	.636	.909
Edgardo Alfonzo	5	21	1	3	1	0	0	0	1	5	.143	.217	.143	.360
Jay Payton	5	21	3	7	3	0	0	1	0	5	.333	.333	.476	.810
Robin Ventura	5	20	1	3	1	1	0	1	1	5	.150	.190	.350	.540
Todd Zeile	5	20	1	8	1	2	0	0	1	5	.400	.429	.500	.929
Benny Agbayani	5	18	2	5	2	2	0	0	3	6	.278	.381	.389	.770
Timo Perez	5	16	1	2	0	0	0	0	1	4	.125	.176	.125	.301
Kurt Abbott	5	8	0	2	0	1	0	0	1	3	.250	.333	.375	.708
Mike Bordick	4	8	0	1	0	0	0	0	0	3	.125	.125	.125	.250
Bubba Trammell	4	5	1	2	3	0	0	0	1	1	.400	.429	.400	.829
Lenny Harris	3	4	1	0	0	0	0	0	1	1	.000	.200	.000	.200
Darryl Hamilton	4	3	0	0	0	0	0	0	0	2	.000	.000	.000	.000
Todd Pratt	1	2	1	0	0	0	0	0	1	2	.000	.600	.000	.600
Bobby Jones	1	2	0	0	0	0	0	0	0	1	.000	.000	.000	.000
Al Leiter	2	2	0	0	0	0	0	0	0	0	.000	.000	.000	.000
Matt Franco	1	1	0	0	0	0	0	0	0	1	.000	.000	.000	.000
Joe McEwing	3	1	1	0	0	0	0	0	0	0	.000	.000	.000	.000
Rick Reed	1	1	0	1	0	0	0	0	0	0	1.000	1.000	1.000	2.000
Armando Benitez	3	0	0	0	0	0	0	0	0	0				
Dennis Cook	3	0	0	0	0	0	0	0	0	0				
John Franco	4	0	0	0	0	0	0	0	0	0				
Mike Hampton	1	0	0	0	0	0	0	0	0	0				
Glendon Rusch	3	0	0	0	0	0	0	0	0	0				
Turk Wendell	2	0	0	0	0	0	0	0	0	0				
Rick White	1	0	0	0	0	0	0	0	0	0				
Totals	**5**	**175**	**16**	**40**	**15**	**8**	**0**	**4**	**11**	**48**	**.229**	**.284**	**.343**	**.627**

PITCHING	G	GS	ERA	W	L	SV	CG	IP	H	R	ER	BB	SO	WHIP
Al Leiter	2	2	2.87	0	1	0	0	15.2	12	6	5	6	16	1.149
Mike Hampton	1	1	6.00	0	1	0	0	6.0	8	4	4	5	4	2.167
Rick Reed	1	1	3.00	0	0	0	0	6.0	6	2	2	1	8	1.167
Bobby Jones	1	1	5.40	0	1	0	0	5.0	4	3	3	3	3	1.400
Glendon Rusch	3	0	2.25	0	0	0	0	4.0	6	1	1	2	2	2.000
John Franco	4	0	0.00	1	0	0	0	3.1	3	0	0	0	1	0.900
Armando Benitez	3	0	3.00	0	0	0	1	3.0	3	1	1	2	2	1.667
Turk Wendell	2	0	5.40	0	1	0	0	1.2	3	1	1	2	2	3.000
Rick White	1	0	6.75	0	0	0	0	1.1	1	1	1	1	1	1.500
Dennis Cook	3	0	0.00	0	0	0	0	0.2	1	0	0	3	1	6.000
Totals	**5**	**5**	**3.47**	**1**	**4**	**1**	**0**	**46.2**	**47**	**19**	**18**	**25**	**40**	**1.543**

2000

NEW YORK METS vs. NEW YORK YANKEES

New York Yankees Composite Stats

BATTING	G	AB	R	H	RBI	2B	3B	HR	BB	SO	BA	OBP	SLG	OPS
Derek Jeter	5	22	6	9	2	2	1	2	3	8	.409	.480	.864	1.344
Tino Martinez	5	22	3	8	2	1	0	0	1	4	.364	.391	.409	.800
David Justice	5	19	1	3	3	2	0	0	3	2	.158	.333	.263	.596
Paul O'Neill	5	19	2	9	2	2	2	0	3	4	.474	.545	.789	1.335
Jorge Posada	5	18	2	4	1	1	0	0	5	4	.222	.391	.278	.669
Bernie Williams	5	18	2	2	1	0	0	1	5	5	.111	.304	.278	.582
Jose Vizcaino	4	17	0	4	1	0	0	0	0	5	.235	.235	.235	.471
Scott Brosius	5	13	2	4	3	0	0	1	2	2	.308	.389	.538	.927
Chuck Knoblauch	4	10	1	1	1	0	0	0	2	1	.100	.231	.100	.331
Luis Sojo	4	7	0	2	2	0	0	0	1	0	.286	.375	.286	.661
Glenallen Hill	3	3	0	0	0	0	0	0	0	0	.000	.000	.000	.000
Andy Pettitte	2	3	0	0	0	0	0	0	0	1	.000	.000	.000	.000
Orlando Hernandez	1	2	0	0	0	0	0	0	0	2	.000	.000	.000	.000
Denny Neagle	1	2	0	0	0	0	0	0	0	1	.000	.000	.000	.000
Luis Polonia	2	2	0	1	0	0	0	0	0	0	.500	.500	.500	1.000
Jose Canseco	1	1	0	0	0	0	0	0	0	1	.000	.000	.000	.000
Mariano Rivera	4	1	0	0	0	0	0	0	0	0	.000	.000	.000	.000
Clay Bellinger	4	0	0	0	0	0	0	0	0	0				
Roger Clemens	1	0	0	0	0	0	0	0	0	0				
David Cone	1	0	0	0	0	0	0	0	0	0				
Jeff Nelson	3	0	0	0	0	0	0	0	0	0				
Mike Stanton	4	0	0	0	0	0	0	0	0	0				
Totals	**5**	**179**	**19**	**47**	**18**	**8**	**3**	**4**	**25**	**40**	**.263**	**.357**	**.408**	**.765**

PITCHING	G	GS	ERA	W	L	SV	CG	IP	H	R	ER	BB	SO	WHIP
Andy Pettitte	2	2	1.98	0	0	0	0	13.2	16	5	3	4	9	1.463
Roger Clemens	1	1	0.00	1	0	0	0	8.0	2	0	0	0	9	0.250
O. Hernandez	1	1	4.91	0	1	0	0	7.1	9	4	4	3	12	1.636
Mariano Rivera	4	0	3.00	0	0	2	0	6.0	4	2	2	1	7	0.833
Denny Neagle	1	1	3.86	0	0	0	0	4.2	4	2	2	2	3	1.286
Mike Stanton	4	0	0.00	2	0	0	0	4.1	0	0	0	0	7	0.000
Jeff Nelson	3	0	10.13	1	0	0	0	2.2	5	3	3	1	1	2.250
David Cone	1	0	0.00	0	0	0	0	0.1	0	0	0	0	0	0.000
Totals	**5**	**5**	**2.68**	**4**	**1**	**2**	**0**	**47.0**	**40**	**16**	**14**	**11**	**48**	**1.085**

Appendix

SUBWAY SERIES
—————— CAREER BATTING LEADERS ——————

Batting Average - All Players With 40 or More At Bats

Tm	Player	G	AB	R	H	RBI	2	3	HR	EBH	BB	SO	BA	SA
NYG	Frankie Frisch	19	72	10	27	4	1	2	0	3	5	3	.375	.444
NYY	Red Rolfe	16	65	10	22	5	2	1	0	3	8	4	.338	.400
NYY	Billy Martin	28	99	14	33	19	2	3	5	10	5	15	.333	.566
NYG	Ross Youngs	19	64	7	21	9	1	1	1	3	12	3	.328	.422
NYG	Heinie Groh	11	41	7	13	2	0	2	0	2	5	2	.317	.415
NYY	George Selkirk	13	45	11	14	9	1	1	2	4	6	4	.311	.511
NYG	Dick Bartell	11	42	8	13	4	4	0	1	5	4	7	.310	.476
BRK	Billy Cox	15	53	7	16	6	5	0	1	6	4	9	.302	.453
NYG	Irish Meusel	19	74	10	22	16	3	2	3	8	2	6	.297	.514
NYY	Gene Woodling	22	71	19	21	5	5	2	3	10	17	8	.296	.549
NYG	Jo-Jo Moore	11	51	5	15	2	3	0	1	4	1	5	.294	.412
BRK	Duke Snider	32	123	20	36	24	8	0	10	18	11	33	.293	.602
NYY	Lou Gehrig	11	41	9	12	10	2	1	3	6	8	6	.293	.610
NYY	Aaron Ward	19	63	8	18	9	0	0	3	3	6	12	.286	.429
NYY	Yogi Berra	43	156	23	44	22	6	0	8	14	16	15	.282	.474
NYG	Frank Snyder	16	54	6	15	5	1	0	2	3	0	5	.278	.407
BRK	Pee Wee Reese	44	169	20	46	16	3	2	2	7	18	17	.272	.349
NYY	Wally Schang	19	59	4	16	1	3	1	0	4	6	9	.271	.356
NYY	Babe Ruth	17	52	12	14	8	2	1	4	7	15	17	.269	.577
NYY	Joe Dugan	11	45	9	12	5	3	1	1	5	3	1	.267	.444

Players With 40 or More At Bats (cont'd)

Tm	Player	G	AB	R	H	RBI	2	3	HR	EBH	BB	SO	BA	SA
BRK	Carl Furillo	36	124	13	33	11	9	0	2	11	13	14	.266	.387
NYY	Mickey Mantle	25	92	16	24	15	2	1	8	11	14	21	.261	.565
BRK	Tommy Holmes	20	69	10	18	7	3	0	3	6	8	6	.261	.435
NYG	Mel Ott	11	43	5	11	6	2	0	2	4	4	5	.256	.442
NYY	Joe DiMaggio	34	134	15	34	20	5	0	5	10	14	19	.254	.403
NYY	Bob Meusel	19	76	6	19	13	4	2	0	6	3	11	.250	.355
BRK	Gil Hodges	30	108	13	26	19	2	0	4	6	16	20	.241	.370
BRK	Roy Campanella	32	114	14	27	12	5	0	4	9	12	20	.237	.386
NYY	Phil Rizzuto	43	148	18	35	7	3	0	1	4	25	10	.236	.277
NYY	Hank Bauer	35	111	12	26	9	0	2	1	3	7	14	.234	.297
BRK	Jackie Robinson	38	137	22	32	12	7	1	2	10	21	14	.234	.343
NYG	High Pockets Kelly	19	70	4	16	7	1	0	0	1	4	15	.229	.243
BRK	Jim Gilliam	20	75	8	17	9	4	0	2	6	15	6	.227	.360
NYY	Wally Pipp	19	67	3	15	6	2	0	0	2	6	6	.224	.254
BRK	Dixie Walker	12	45	4	10	4	3	0	1	4	5	2	.222	.356
NYY	Gil McDougald	33	120	11	25	16	1	1	5	7	13	19	.208	.358
NYG	Eddie Stanky	13	47	7	9	3	1	0	0	1	6	4	.191	.213
NYY	Joe Collins	29	87	15	15	10	3	0	4	7	14	19	.172	.345
NYY	Frankie Crosetti	11	47	7	8	3	2	0	0	2	6	7	.170	.213
NYY	Bill Dickey	16	62	11	10	9	1	1	1	3	8	7	.161	.258
NYG	Dave Bancroft	19	76	8	11	6	1	0	0	1	4	8	.145	.158

	HONORABLE MENTIONS Player	G	AB	R	H	RBI	2	3	HR	EBH	BB	SO	BA	SA
NYY	Bobby Brown	13	29	7	14	8	4	2	0	6	5	3	.483	.759
NYY	Paul O'Neill	5	19	2	9	2	2	2	0	4	3	4	.474	.545
NYG	Monte Irvin	6	24	3	11	2	0	1	0	1	2	1	.458	.542
NYY	Casey Stengel	8	17	3	7	4	0	0	2	2	4	0	.412	.765
NYY	Derek Jeter	5	22	6	9	2	2	1	2	5	3	8	.409	.480
NYY	Johnny Lindell	8	25	3	10	7	3	1	0	4	5	4	.400	.600
NYM	Todd Zeile	5	20	1	8	1	2	0	0	2	1	5	.400	.500
NYY	Tino Martinez	5	22	3	8	2	1	0	0	1	1	4	.364	.391
NYY	Enos Slaughter	6	20	6	7	4	0	0	1	1	4	0	.350	.500
NYG	George Burns	8	33	2	11	2	4	1	0	5	3	5	.333	.515
NYG	Johnny Rawlings	8	30	2	10	3	3	0	0	3	0	3	.333	.433
NYY	Johnny Mize	14	25	5	8	7	2	0	3	5	5	2	.320	.760
NYY	Tony Lazzeri	11	35	7	11	9	0	1	2	3	7	7	.314	.543

Home Runs

Tm	Player	G	AB	R	H	RBI	2	3	HR	EBH	BB	K	BA	SA
BRK	Duke Snider	32	123	20	36	24	8	0	10	18	11	33	.293	.602
NYY	Mickey Mantle	25	92	16	24	15	2	1	8	11	14	21	.261	.565
NYY	Yogi Berra	43	156	23	44	22	6	0	8	14	16	15	.282	.474
NYY	Billy Martin	28	99	14	33	19	2	3	5	10	5	15	.333	.566
NYY	Gil McDougald	33	120	11	25	16	1	1	5	7	13	19	.208	.358
NYY	Joe DiMaggio	34	134	15	34	20	5	0	5	10	14	19	.254	.403
NYY	Babe Ruth	17	52	12	14	8	2	1	4	7	15	17	.269	.577
NYY	Joe Collins	29	87	15	15	10	3	0	4	7	14	19	.172	.345
BRK	Gil Hodges	30	108	13	26	19	2	0	4	6	16	20	.241	.370
BRK	Roy Campanella	32	114	14	27	12	5	0	4	9	12	20	.237	.386

Runs Batted In

Tm	Player	G	AB	R	H	RBI	2	3	HR	EBH	BB	K	BA	SA
BRK	Duke Snider	32	123	20	36	24	8	0	10	18	11	33	.293	.602
NYY	Yogi Berra	43	156	23	44	22	6	0	8	14	16	15	.282	.474
NYY	Joe DiMaggio	34	134	15	34	20	5	0	5	10	14	19	.254	.403
NYY	Billy Martin	28	99	14	33	19	2	3	5	10	5	15	.333	.566
BRK	Gil Hodges	30	108	13	26	19	2	0	4	6	16	20	.241	.370
NYG	Irish Meusel	19	74	10	22	16	3	2	3	8	2	6	.297	.514
NYY	Gil McDougald	33	120	11	25	16	1	1	5	7	13	19	.208	.358
BRK	Pee Wee Reese	44	169	20	46	16	3	2	2	7	18	17	.272	.349
NYY	Mickey Mantle	25	92	16	24	15	2	1	8	11	14	21	.261	.565
NYY	Bob Meusel	19	76	6	19	13	4	2	0	6	3	11	.250	.355

Runs Scored

Tm	Player	G	AB	R	H	RBI	2	3	HR	EBH	BB	K	BA	SA
NYY	Yogi Berra	43	156	23	44	22	6	0	8	14	16	15	.282	.474
BRK	Jackie Robinson	38	137	22	32	12	7	1	2	10	21	14	.234	.343
BRK	Duke Snider	32	123	20	36	24	8	0	10	18	11	33	.293	.602
BRK	Pee Wee Reese	44	169	20	46	16	3	2	2	7	18	17	.272	.349
NYY	Gene Woodling	22	71	19	21	5	5	2	3	10	17	8	.296	.549
NYY	Phil Rizzuto	43	148	18	35	7	3	0	1	4	25	10	.236	.277
NYY	Mickey Mantle	25	92	16	24	15	2	1	8	11	14	21	.261	.565
NYY	Joe Collins	29	87	15	15	10	3	0	4	7	14	19	.172	.345
NYY	Joe DiMaggio	34	134	15	34	20	5	0	5	10	14	19	.254	.403

Base Hits

Tm	Player	G	AB	R	H	RBI	2	3	HR	EBH	BB	K	BA	SA
BRK	Pee Wee Reese	44	169	20	46	16	3	2	2	7	18	17	.272	.349
NYY	Yogi Berra	43	156	23	44	22	6	0	8	14	16	15	.282	.474
BRK	Duke Snider	32	123	20	36	24	8	0	10	18	11	33	.293	.602
NYY	Phil Rizzuto	43	148	18	35	7	3	0	1	4	25	10	.236	.277
NYY	Joe DiMaggio	34	134	15	34	20	5	0	5	10	14	19	.254	.403
NYY	Billy Martin	28	99	14	33	19	2	3	5	10	5	15	.333	.566
BRK	Carl Furillo	36	124	13	33	11	9	0	2	11	13	14	.266	.387
BRK	Jackie Robinson	38	137	22	32	12	7	1	2	10	21	14	.234	.343
NYG	Frankie Frisch	19	72	10	27	4	1	2	0	3	5	3	.375	.444
BRK	Roy Campanella	32	114	14	27	12	5	0	4	9	12	20	.237	.386
BRK	Gil Hodges	30	108	13	26	19	2	0	4	6	16	20	.241	.370
NYY	Hank Bauer	35	111	12	26	9	0	2	1	3	7	14	.234	.297
NYY	Gil McDougald	33	120	11	25	16	1	1	5	7	13	19	.208	.358
NYY	Mickey Mantle	25	92	16	24	15	2	1	8	11	14	21	.261	.565

Bases on Balls (Batters)

Tm	Player	G	AB	R	H	RBI	2	3	HR	EBH	BB	K	BA	SA
NYY	Phil Rizzuto	43	148	18	35	7	3	0	1	4	25	10	.236	.277
BRK	Jackie Robinson	38	137	22	32	12	7	1	2	10	21	14	.234	.343
BRK	Pee Wee Reese	44	169	20	46	16	3	2	2	7	18	17	.272	.349
NYY	Gene Woodling	22	71	19	21	5	5	2	3	10	17	8	.296	.549
BRK	Gil Hodges	30	108	13	26	19	2	0	4	6	16	20	.241	.370
NYY	Yogi Berra	43	156	23	44	22	6	0	8	14	16	15	.282	.474
NYY	Babe Ruth	17	52	12	14	8	2	1	4	7	15	17	.269	.577
BRK	Jim Gilliam	20	75	8	17	9	4	0	2	6	15	6	.227	.360

SINGLE-SERIES BATTING LEADERS

Batting Average Above .350 (min 10 AB)

Year	Team	Player	G	AB	R	H	RBI	HR	BB	SO	BA	OBP
1953	NYY	Billy Martin	6	24	5	12	8	2	1	2	.500	.520
1947	NYY	Johnny Lindell	6	18	3	9	7	0	5	2	.500	.625
1941	NYY	Joe Gordon	5	14	2	7	5	1	7	0	.500	.667
1949	NYY	Bobby Brown	4	12	4	6	5	0	2	2	.500	.571
2000	NYY	Paul O'Neill	5	19	2	9	2	0	3	4	.474	.545
1922	NYG	Heinie Groh	5	19	4	9	0	0	2	1	.474	.524
1922	NYG	Frankie Frisch	5	17	3	8	2	0	1	0	.471	.500
1951	NYG	Monte Irvin	6	24	3	11	2	0	2	1	.458	.500
1936	NYY	Jake Powell	6	22	8	10	5	1	4	4	.455	.538
1953	NYY	Yogi Berra	6	21	3	9	4	1	3	3	.429	.538
1955	NYY	Hank Bauer	6	14	1	6	1	0	0	1	.429	.429
1955	NYY	Yogi Berra	7	24	5	10	2	1	3	1	.417	.500
1951	NYG	Al Dark	6	24	5	10	4	1	2	3	.417	.462
1923	NYY	Aaron Ward	6	24	4	10	2	1	1	3	.417	.440
1923	NYG	Casey Stengel	6	12	3	5	4	2	4	0	.417	.563
2000	NYY	Derek Jeter	5	22	6	9	2	2	3	8	.409	.480

Top Batting Averages (cont'd)

Year	Team	Player	G	AB	R	H	RBI	HR	BB	SO	BA	OBP
1936	NYY	Red Rolfe	6	25	5	10	4	0	3	1	.400	.464
1923	NYG	Frankie Frisch	6	25	2	10	1	0	0	0	.400	.400
2000	NYM	Todd Zeile	5	20	1	8	1	0	1	5	.400	.429
1952	NYY	Johnny Mize	5	15	3	6	6	3	3	1	.400	.500
1937	NYY	Tony Lazzeri	5	15	3	6	2	1	3	3	.400	.526
1949	NYY	Gene Woodling	3	10	4	4	0	0	3	0	.400	.538
1937	NYG	Jo-Jo Moore	5	23	1	9	1	0	0	1	.391	.391
1941	NYY	Charlie Keller	5	18	5	7	5	0	3	1	.389	.476
1936	NYG	Dick Bartell	6	21	5	8	3	1	4	4	.381	.480
1922	NYG	Ross Youngs	5	16	2	6	2	0	3	1	.375	.474
1923	NYY	Babe Ruth	6	19	8	7	3	3	8	6	.368	.556
1953	BRK	Gil Hodges	6	22	3	8	1	1	3	3	.364	.440
1921	NYG	Frank Snyder	7	22	4	8	3	1	0	2	.364	.364
2000	NYY	Tino Martinez	5	22	3	8	2	0	1	4	.364	.391
1937	NYG	Hank Leiber	3	11	2	4	2	0	1	1	.364	.417
1956	NYY	Yogi Berra	7	25	5	9	10	3	4	1	.360	.448
1951	NYY	Bobby Brown	5	14	1	5	0	0	2	1	.357	.438
1947	BRK	Carl Furillo	6	17	2	6	3	0	3	0	.353	.450

More Than 2 Home Runs

Year	Team	Player	G	AB	R	H	RBI	HR	BB	SO
1952	BRK	Duke Snider	7	29	5	10	8	4	1	5
1955	BRK	Duke Snider	7	25	5	8	7	4	2	6
1956	NYY	Mickey Mantle	7	24	6	6	4	3	6	5
1956	NYY	Yogi Berra	7	25	5	9	10	3	4	1
1923	NYY	Babe Ruth	6	19	8	7	3	3	8	6
1952	NYY	Johnny Mize	5	15	3	6	6	3	3	1

More Than 5 RBI

Year	Team	Player	G	AB	R	H	RBI	HR
1956	NYY	Yogi Berra	7	25	5	9	10	3
1952	BRK	Duke Snider	7	29	5	10	8	4
1956	BRK	Gil Hodges	7	23	5	7	8	1
1923	NYY	Bob Meusel	6	26	1	7	8	0
1953	NYY	Billy Martin	6	24	5	12	8	2
1921	NYG	Irish Meusel	8	29	4	10	7	1
1936	NYY	Lou Gehrig	6	24	5	7	7	2
1955	BRK	Duke Snider	7	25	5	8	7	4
1953	NYY	Mickey Mantle	6	24	3	5	7	2
1951	NYY	Gil McDougald	6	23	2	6	7	1
1936	NYY	Tony Lazzeri	6	20	4	5	7	1
1947	NYY	Johnny Lindell	6	18	3	9	7	0
1922	NYG	Irish Meusel	5	20	3	5	7	1
1953	BRK	Billy Cox	6	23	3	7	6	1
1937	NYY	George Selkirk	5	19	5	5	6	0
1952	NYY	Johnny Mize	5	15	3	6	6	3

More Than 5 RS

Year	Team	Player	G	AB	R	H	RBI	HR
1923	NYY	Babe Ruth	6	19	8	7	3	3
1936	NYY	Jake Powell	6	22	8	10	5	1
1947	NYY	Billy Johnson	7	26	8	7	2	0
1955	NYY	Joe Collins	5	12	6	2	3	2
2000	NYY	Derek Jeter	5	22	6	9	2	2
1951	NYY	Gene Woodling	6	18	6	3	1	1
1956	NYY	Enos Slaughter	6	20	6	7	4	1
1953	BRK	Roy Campanella	6	22	6	6	2	1
1953	NYY	Hank Bauer	6	23	6	6	1	0
1936	NYY	George Selkirk	6	24	6	8	3	2
1956	NYY	Mickey Mantle	7	24	6	6	4	3

More Than 5 BB

Year	Team	Player	G	PA	AB	R	H	RBI	BB	HR
1923	NYY	Babe Ruth	6	27	19	8	7	3	8	3
1955	BRK	Jim Gilliam	7	32	24	2	7	3	8	0
1947	NYY	Snuffy Stirnweiss	7	35	27	3	7	3	8	0
1941	NYY	Joe Gordon	5	21	14	2	7	5	7	1
1952	BRK	Jackie Robinson	7	30	23	4	4	2	7	1
1956	BRK	Jim Gilliam	7	31	24	2	2	2	7	0
1921	NYG	Ross Youngs	8	32	25	3	7	4	7	0
1955	NYY	Joe Collins	5	18	12	6	2	3	6	2
1953	NYY	Gene Woodling	6	26	20	5	6	3	6	1
1956	BRK	Duke Snider	7	29	23	5	7	4	6	1
1947	BRK	Pee Wee Reese	7	29	23	5	7	4	6	0
1956	NYY	Mickey Mantle	7	30	24	6	6	4	6	3
1947	NYY	Joe DiMaggio	7	32	26	4	6	5	6	2

0 Strikeouts With 20 or More Plate Appearances

Year	Team	Player	G	AB	R	H	RBI	HR	BB	SO
1947	NYY	Phil Rizzuto	7	26	3	8	2	0	4	0
1923	NYY	Joe Dugan	6	25	5	7	5	1	3	0
1951	NYG	Bobby Thomson	6	21	1	5	2	0	5	0
1953	BRK	Jackie Robinson	6	25	3	8	2	0	1	0
1923	NYG	Ross Youngs	6	23	2	8	3	1	2	0
1923	NYG	Frankie Frisch	6	25	2	10	1	0	0	0
1956	NYY	Enos Slaughter	6	20	6	7	4	1	4	0
1949	NYY	Tommy Henrich	5	19	4	5	1	1	3	0
1941	NYY	Joe Gordon	5	14	2	7	5	1	7	0
1937	NYY	George Selkirk	5	19	5	5	6	0	2	0
1947	BRK	Carl Furillo	6	17	2	6	3	0	3	0
1949	BRK	Pee Wee Reese	5	19	2	6	2	1	1	0
1941	BRK	Pee Wee Reese	5	20	1	4	2	0	0	0

On Base Percentage >.500

Year	Team	Player	G	PA	AB	R	H	RBI	2B	3B	HR	BB	SO	BA	OBP	SLG	OPS
1941	NYY	Joe Gordon	5	21	14	2	7	5	1	1	1	7	0	.500	.667	.929	1.595
1947	NYY	Johnny Lindell	6	23	18	3	9	7	3	1	0	5	2	.500	.625	.778	1.403
1949	NYY	Bobby Brown	4	14	12	4	6	5	1	2	0	2	2	.500	.571	.917	1.488
1923	NYG	Casey Stengel	6	16	12	3	5	4	0	0	2	4	0	.417	.563	.917	1.479
1923	NYY	Babe Ruth	6	27	19	8	7	3	1	1	3	8	6	.368	.556	1.000	1.556
2000	NYY	Paul O'Neill	5	22	19	2	9	2	2	2	0	3	4	.474	.545	.789	1.335
1936	NYY	Jake Powell	6	26	22	8	10	5	1	0	1	4	4	.455	.538	.636	1.175
1953	NYY	Yogi Berra	6	24	21	3	9	4	1	0	1	3	3	.429	.538	.619	1.158
1949	NYY	Gene Woodling	3	13	10	4	4	0	3	0	0	3	0	.400	.538	.700	1.238
1955	BRK	Sandy Amoros	5	16	12	3	4	3	0	0	1	4	4	.333	.529	.583	1.113
1937	NYY	Tony Lazzeri	5	18	15	3	6	2	0	1	1	3	3	.400	.526	.733	1.260
1922	NYG	Heinie Groh	5	21	19	4	9	0	0	1	0	2	1	.474	.524	.579	1.103
1953	NYY	Billy Martin	6	25	24	5	12	8	1	2	2	1	2	.500	.520	.958	1.478

On Base + Slugging (OPS) >1.200

Year	Team	Player	G	PA	AB	R	H	RBI	2B	3B	HR	BB	SO	BA	OBP	SLG	OPS
1941	NYY	Joe Gordon	5	21	14	2	7	5	1	1	1	7	0	.500	.667	.929	1.595
1952	NYY	Johnny Mize	5	18	15	3	6	6	1	0	3	3	1	.400	.500	1.067	1.567
1923	NYY	Babe Ruth	6	27	19	8	7	3	1	1	3	8	6	.368	.556	1.000	1.556
1949	NYY	Bobby Brown	4	14	12	4	6	5	1	2	0	2	2	.500	.571	.917	1.488
1923	NYG	Casey Stengel	6	16	12	3	5	4	0	0	2	4	0	.417	.563	.917	1.479
1953	NYY	Billy Martin	6	25	24	5	12	8	1	2	2	1	2	.500	.520	.958	1.478
1947	NYY	Johnny Lindell	6	23	18	3	9	7	3	1	0	5	2	.500	.625	.778	1.403
2000	NYY	Derek Jeter	5	25	22	6	9	2	2	1	2	3	8	.409	.480	.864	1.344
2000	NYY	Paul O'Neill	5	22	19	2	9	2	2	2	0	3	4	.474	.545	.789	1.335
1937	NYY	Tony Lazzeri	5	18	15	3	6	2	0	1	1	3	3	.400	.526	.733	1.260
1956	NYY	Yogi Berra	7	29	25	5	9	10	2	0	3	4	1	.360	.448	.800	1.248
1952	BRK	Duke Snider	7	30	29	5	10	8	2	0	4	1	5	.345	.387	.828	1.215
1955	BRK	Duke Snider	7	27	25	5	8	7	1	0	4	2	6	.320	.370	.840	1.210

SINGLE-GAME BATTING RECORDS

Most Runs Batted One Game

Year	Gm	Tm	Batter	RBI	AB	Opponent
1936	2	NYY	Tony Lazzeri	5	4	Dodgers
1936	2	NYY	Bill Dickey	5	5	Dodgers

Most Runs Scored One Game

Year	Gm	Tm	Batter	RS	AB	Opponent
1936	2	NYY	Frank Crosetti	4	5	Giants

Most Hits One Game

Year	Gm	Tm	Batter	Hits	AB	Opponent
1921	1	NYG	Frankie Frisch	4	4	Yankees
1951	1	NYG	Monte Irvin	4	4	Yankees
1923	4	NYG	Ross Youngs	4	5	Yankees
1923	5	NYY	Joe Dugan	4	5	Giants
1941	4	NYY	Charlie Keller	4	5	Dodgers
1921	3	NYG	George Burns	4	6	Yankees

Two Home Runs in One Game

Year	Gm	Tm	Batter	HR	AB	Opponent
1923	2	NYY	Babe Ruth	2	3	Giants
1952	6	BRK	Duke Snider	2	3	Yankees
1955	1	NYY	Joe Collins	2	3	Dodgers
1955	5	BRK	Duke Snider	2	4	Yankees
1956	7	NYY	Yogi Berra	2	3	Dodgers

Run Scored Every Game of a Series

Year	Gm	Tm	Batter	RS	AB	Opponent
2000	5	NYY	Derek Jeter	6		Mets

Double-Digit Hits in One Series

Year	Gm	Tm	Batter	Hits	AB	Opponent
1953	6	NYY	Billy Martin	12	24	Dodgers
1951	6	NYG	Monte Irvin	11	24	Yankees
1921	8	NYG	George Burns	11	32	Yankees
1923	6	NYY	Aaron Ward	10	24	Giants
1951	6	NYG	Al Dark	10	24	Yankees
1955	7	NYY	Yogi Berra	10	24	Dodgers
1923	6	NYG	Frankie Frisch	10	25	Yankees
1936	6	NYY	Red Rolfe	10	25	Giants
1936	6	NYY	Jake Powell	10	27	Giants
1952	7	NYY	Mickey Mantle	10	29	Dodgers
1952	7	BRK	Pee Wee Reese	10	29	Yankees
1952	7	BRK	Duke Snider	10	29	Yankees
1921	8	NYG	Irish Meusel	10	29	Yankees
1921	8	NYG	Johnny Rawlings	10	30	Yankees
1947	7	NYG	Tommy Henrich	10	31	Giants

Hits in All Games of a Series

Year	Gm	Tm	Batter	Hits	AB	Opponent
1955	7	NYY	Yogi Berra	10	24	Dodgers
1947	7	NYY	Tommy Henrich	10	31	Dodgers
1956	7	NYY	Hank Bauer	9	32	Dodgers
1956	7	NYY	Billy Martin	8	24	Dodgers
1953	6	NYY	Billy Martin	12	24	Dodgers
1923	6	NYY	Aaron Ward	10	24	Giants
1951	6	NYG	Al Dark	10	24	Yankees
1936	6	NYG	Dick Bartell	8	21	Yankees
1936	6	NYY	George Selkirk	8	24	Giants
1951	6	NYY	Phil Rizzuto	8	25	Dodgers
1923	6	NYY	Babe Ruth	7	19	Giants
1923	6	NYY	Wally Schang	7	22	Giants
1922	5	NYG	Heine Groh	9	19	Yankees
2000	5	NYY	Derek Jeter	9	22	Mets
1937	5	NYG	Jo-Jo Moore	9	23	Yankees
1941	5	NYY	Joe Gordon	7	14	Dodgers
2000	5	NYM	Jay Payton	7	21	Yankees
1937	5	NYY	Tony Lazzeri	6	15	Giants
1922	5	NYY	Bob Meusel	6	20	Giants
1922	5	NYY	Wally Pipp	6	21	Giants
1941	5	NYY	Johnny Sturm	6	21	Giants
2000	5	NYM	Mike Piazza	6	22	Yankees
1922	5	NYG	Irish Meusel	5	21	Yankees

SINGLE-GAME PITCHING RECORDS

Complete Game Shutouts

Year	Gm	Tm	Pitcher	Hits	K	Opponent
1921	1	NYY	Carl Mays	5	1	Giants
1921	2	NYY	Waite Hoyt	2	5	Giants
1921	6	NYG	Art Nehf	4	3	Yankees
1922	3	NYG	Jack Scott	4	2	Yankees
1923	3	NYG	Art Nehf	6	4	Yankees
1949	1	NYY	Allie Reynolds	2	9	Dodgers
1949	2	BKN	Preacher Roe	6	5	Yankees
1952	4	NYY	Allie Reynolds	3	10	Dodgers
1955	7	BKN	Johnny Podres	8	4	Yankees
1956	5	NYY	Don Larsen	0	7	Dodgers
1956	6	BKN	Clem Labine	7	5	Yankees
1956	7	NYY	Johnny Kucks	3	1	Dodgers

Double-Digit Strikeouts in a Game

Year	Gm	Tm	Pitcher	K	IP	Opponent
1953	2	BRK	Carl Eskine	14	9.0	Yankees
2000	3	NYY	Orlando Hernandez	12	7.1	Mets
1949	1	BRK	Don Newcombe	11	8.0	Yankees
1956	6	NYY	Bob Turley	11	9.2	Dodgers
1921	6	NYG	Jesse Barnes	10	8.1	Yankees
1952	4	NYY	Allie Reynolds	10	9.0	Dodgers
1956	1	BRK	Sal Maglie	10	9.0	Yankees
1936	5	NYG	Hal Schumacher	10	10.0	Yankees

CAREER PITCHING LEADERS

All Pitchers, 20 or More IP, Ranked by ERA

Tm	Name	G	GS	W	L	SV	ERA	IP	H	R	ER	BB	K
NYY	Waite Hoyt	6	5	2	2	0	1.21	37.3	33	9	5	14	22
BRK	Johnny Podres	3	3	2	1	0	1.31	20.7	16	8	3	6	10
BRK	Clem Labine	9	1	2	2	2	1.71	26.3	24	6	5	3	7
NYG	Jesse Barnes	4	1	2	0	0	1.71	26.3	18	6	5	8	24
NYG	Art Nehf	7	7	3	3	0	2.01	58.3	34	16	13	22	21
NYG	Phil Douglas	3	3	2	1	0	2.08	26.0	20	6	6	5	17
NYG	Carl Mays	4	4	1	3	0	2.38	34.0	29	10	9	2	10
BRK	Preacher Roe	5	3	2	1	0	2.54	28.3	20	8	8	10	11
NYY	Vic Raschi	10	7	4	3	0	2.63	51.3	50	21	15	24	38
NYY	Eddie Lopat	6	6	4	1	0	2.66	44.0	42	14	13	12	14
NYY	Red Ruffing	4	4	2	1	0	2.81	32.0	29	13	10	11	25
BRK	Joe Black	4	3	1	2	0	2.82	22.3	16	7	7	8	11
NYY	Bullet Joe Bush	5	3	1	3	0	2.84	31.7	28	10	10	9	11
NYG	Carl Hubbell	4	4	2	2	0	2.97	30.3	27	15	10	6	17
NYY	Lefty Gomez	4	4	4	0	0	2.97	33.3	30	11	11	13	17
NYY	Allie Reynolds	13	8	6	2	3	3.09	67.0	54	24	23	28	55
NYY	Joe Page	7	0	2	1	2	3.27	22.0	18	8	8	5	15
NYY	Whitey Ford	6	6	3	2	0	3.65	37.0	36	18	15	12	25
GI/BK	Sal Maglie	3	3	1	2	0	3.68	22.0	22	9	9	8	18
NYY	Bob Shawkey	4	3	1	1	0	4.05	26.7	33	13	12	12	11
BRK	Billy Loes	4	3	0	1	2	4.91	22.0	26	12	12	8	18
BRK	Carl Erskine	11	7	2	2	0	5.83	41.7	36	28	27	24	31
HONORABLE MENTION													
NYY	Tommy Byrne	4	3	1	1	0	2.00	18.0	11	6	4	10	11
NYY	Monte Pearson	2	2	2	0	0	1.53	17.7	12	3	3	4	11
NYY	Andy Pettitte	2	2	0	0	0	1.98	13.7	16	5	3	4	9

Career Wins

Tm	Name	G	GS	W	L	SV	IP	ER	BB	K	ERA
NYY	Allie Reynolds	13	8	6	2	3	67.0	23	28	55	3.09
NYG	Lefty Gomez	4	4	4	0	0	33.3	11	13	17	2.97
BRK	Eddie Lopat	6	6	4	1	0	44.0	13	12	14	2.66
BRK	Vic Raschi	10	7	4	3	0	51.3	15	24	38	2.63
NYG	Whitey Ford	6	6	3	2	0	37.0	15	12	25	3.65
NYG	Art Nehf	7	7	3	3	0	58.3	13	22	21	2.01

Career Strikeouts

Tm	Name	G	GS	W	L	SV	ERA	IP	K	BB
NYY	Allie Reynolds	13	8	6	2	3	3.09	67.0	55	28
NYY	Vic Raschi	10	7	4	3	0	2.63	51.3	38	24
BRK	Carl Erskine	11	7	2	2	0	5.83	41.7	31	24
NYY	Red Ruffing	4	4	2	1	0	2.81	32.0	25	11
NYY	Whitey Ford	6	6	3	2	0	3.65	37.0	25	12
NYG	Jesse Barnes	4	1	2	0	0	1.71	26.3	24	8
NYY	Waite Hoyt	6	5	2	2	0	1.21	37.3	22	14
NYG	Art Nehf	7	7	3	3	0	2.01	58.3	21	22
GI/BK	Sal Maglie	3	3	1	2	0	3.68	22.0	18	8
BRK	Billy Loes	4	3	0	1	2	4.91	22.0	18	8

Manager Win-Loss Records

Team	Manager	Series W	Series L	Games W	Games L	Pct
NYY	Casey Stengel	5	1	23	15	.605
NYY	Joe McCarthy	3	0	12	4	.750
NYG	John McGraw	2	1	11	7	.611
NYY	Joe Torre	1	0	4	1	.800
NYY	Bucky Harris	1	0	4	3	.571
BRK	Walt Alston	1	1	7	7	.500
NYY	Miller Huggins	1	2	7	11	.389
NYM	Bobby Valentine	0	1	1	4	.200
BRK	Charlie Dressen	0	2	5	8	.385
BRK	Burt Shotten	0	2	4	8	.333
NYG	Bill Terry	0	2	3	8	.273
BRK/NYG	Leo Durocher	0	2	3	8	.273

Lightning Source UK Ltd.
Milton Keynes UK
UKHW030628060121
376458UK00007B/577

9 781938 545757